THE MENU

DEVELOPMENT, STRATEGY, AND APPLICATION

THE MENU

DEVELOPMENT, STRATEGY, AND APPLICATION

David J. Barrish, M.P.A., CHA

Interim Dean

School of Business and Engineering

J. Sargeant Reynolds Community College

Boston   Columbus   Indianapolis   New York   San Francisco   Upper Saddle River
Amsterdam   Cape Town   Dubai   London   Madrid   Milan   Munich   Paris   Montreal   Toronto
Delhi   Mexico City   São Paulo   Sydney   Hong Kong   Seoul   Singapore   Taipei   Tokyo

Editorial Director: Vernon Anthony
Senior Acquisitions Editor: William Lawrensen
Editorial Assistant: Lara Dimmick
Director of Marketing: David Gesell
Campaign Marketing Manager: Leigh Ann Sims
Curriculum Marketing Manager: Thomas Hayward
Senior Marketing Coordinator: Alicia Wozniak
Marketing Assistant: Les Roberts
Associate Managing Editor: Alex Wolf
Production & Development Editor: Alexis Biasell
Production Manager: Meghan DeMaio

Art Director: Diane Ernsberger
Creative Director: Jayne Conte
Cover Designer: Mary Siener
Cover Art: © Erika Cespedes Photography & Design
Media Director: Tim Peyton
Lead Media Project Manager: Karen Bretz
Full-Service Project Management & Composition:
   Munesh Kumar/Aptara®, Inc.
Printer/Binder: Edwards Brothers
Cover Printer: Lehigh-Phoenix
Text Font: Adobe Garamond

Credits and acknowledgments borrowed from other sources and reproduced, with permission, in this textbook appear on appropriate page within text.

Many of the designations by manufacturers and seller to distinguish their products are claimed as trademarks. Where those designations appear in this book, and the publisher was aware of a trademark claim, the designations have been printed in initial caps or all caps.

Library of Congress Cataloging-in-Publication Data

Barrish, David.
  The menu : development, strategy, and application/David Barrish.
    p. cm.
  ISBN-13: 978-0-13-507866-2
  ISBN-10: 0-13-507866-0
  1. Menus. I. Title.
  TX911.3.M45B37 2013
  642—dc23

2011038643

10 9 8 7 6 5 4 3 2 1

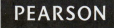

ISBN 10: 0-13-507866-0
ISBN 13: 978-0-13-507866-2

This work is dedicated to my family.
To my wife, Sydney; my daughters, Sarah and Rachel; my father Howard;
and the loving memory of my mother Helene.

I thank you for your patience, encouragement, and support.

Brief Contents

Contents

Preface

This textbook is the result of my devotion to student success. For more than 20 years, I sought a textbook to anchor my menu management classes, and despite the availability of several good books, I always believed the ideal book had yet to be written. So often, students are treated as vessels that must be filled with facts, and a core textbook is selected to serve as a font of incontrovertible truths. That paradigm has proved to be of limited value, and I hope to have authored a work that bridges understanding and action. Today's learner seeks to transform learning actively into relevant, career-based skill sets. Knowledge is meant to be used, and the contextual exercises throughout this book are intended to serve that purpose. A conscious effort was made to avoid quizzes, end-of-chapter drills, and other ephemera that might mean something on campus but bear little relevance in the real world. This is a business book for the creative culinarian and hospitality manager. This textbook is meant to be used, revisited, and serve as a managerial resource for transitioning into careers.

Too often, students are told what to do and what they must refrain from; however, the creative nature of hospitality actually embraces the iconoclast and welcomes the maverick. Accordingly, a conscious effort has been made to avoid prescriptions. Any generalities throughout the text were intentional. Rules often run counter to the creative process, so they have been replaced with recommendations or examples of best practices.

- The textbook follows a logical sequence, beginning in Chapter 1 with a holistic view of how various food services satisfy the needs and lifestyles of customers. This chapter acknowledges the dynamic nature of consumer behavior, and the concomitant menu lifecycle from conception to retirement.
- Chapter 2 examines where menus are used and the characteristics that distinguish menus within the broad spectrum of food services.
- Chapter 3 begins with a discussion of how cuisine and menus have changed over time. The remainder of this chapter discusses the various types of food and beverage menus and principles for creating them.
- Chapter 4's focus is on the strategic value of knowledge. Menus are only as effective as the menu planner's understanding of the market and its behavior. The chapter concludes with a study of information technology that supports menu planning, management, and analysis.
- Chapter 5 studies opportunities to maximize dayparts so that resource investments are used to their fullest extent. This chapter also focuses on positioning your business for profit generation. The discussion evolves with a study of forecasting, calculating costs, and estimating profitability.
- Chapter 6 discusses operational considerations beginning with risk management. As is discussed within the chapter, hard-earned successes can be erased if food and beverage items injure your guests, and subsequent legal actions decimate your business. Developing safe menu items is central to this chapter. The chapter continues with a study of operational considerations, including the physical space, workstations, equipment, and supplies that must support your

---

[1]See www.brainyquote.com/quotes/quotes/j/johnciardi402193.html; retrieved May 1, 1011.

menus, as well as staff considerations for delivering quality food and beverage. The chapter synthesizes the preceding chapters and lessons into a comprehensive deployment model.

- Chapter 7 examines the contemporary landscape, including sustainability, regional cuisine, the public's desire for healthy food, strategies for success in challenging economic times, and research-based predictions of the future.
- Chapter 8 discusses the psychological factors related to menu pricing, and objective approaches for pricing your menus.
- Chapter 9 examines best practices in menu communications, including effective menu copy, organization, layout and design, and contemporary communications media.
- Chapter 10 expands the menu creation model introduced in previous chapters by illustrating several menu analysis models. As such, the planning development and deployment cycle is punctuated with tools to entrench market acceptance, profit enhancement, and risk containment.

Each chapter is accompanied with an Action Toolkit that directs readers to additional resources. These textbooks and Web links weave a rich fabric that merges the classroom and the outside world.

Whereas this book was written for a broad audience, special attention was paid to covering *American Culinary Federation Required Knowledge and Competencies* for the *Menu Planning Knowledge Area*. As the coordinator for an *American Culinary Federation Education Foundation Accrediting Commission*-accredited program, I can attest to the importance of supporting lessons with a comprehensive resource such as this text. Students and educators will also find that several other competencies have been addressed, specifically in the areas of *Beverage Management, Business and Math Skills, Food Preparation, Nutrition, Purchasing and Receiving*, and *Sanitation*.

So many of today's students are efficient, deductive, and action-oriented, and to them, textbooks need not be read cover to cover. With this book, that would be a mistaken strategy. As few words as necessary have been used to illustrate as many concepts as possible, and a conscious attempt to avoid "knowledge overload" is in evidence. Some topics are addressed with deceptive brevity, yet the essential concepts are there to be understood. Consequently, every paragraph, exhibit, exercise, and reference can make a difference in the reader's career.

Proprietary software has not been prescribed, nor it is used for learning this material; rather, the student is provided with Microsoft Excel workbooks that do not require extraordinary investment in technology. Students should possess introductory spreadsheet skills with the ability to 1) navigate among worksheets within a workbook, 2) enter data into cells, and 3) link cells by pasting links.

The various exercises throughout these chapters are intended to reinforce the lessons therein. An integrated menu development term project is also provided so that the various concepts can be progressively built into a realistic menu management model.

To access supplementary materials online, instructors must request an instructor access code. Go to www.pearsonhighered.com/irc, where you can register. Within 48 hours after registering, you will receive a confirming e-mail, including an instructor access code. Once you have received your code, go to the site and log on for full instructions on downloading the materials you wish to use.

As a final note, this textbook and accompanying digital files may be used for synchronous instruction in the classroom or asynchronous distance learning on the Web. Learning styles vary, yet the subject lends itself to a variety of learning environments. This textbook and the associated digital files are intended to serve as tools for a wide variety of experiences soon to unfold. Although not a perfect metaphor, the content may be thought of as a management toolkit for building a successful enterprise. It is my sincere hope that this book helps transform students into skilled menu developers who can provide customers with satisfying meals and deliver above-average profits to owners and investors.

David J. Barrish, M.P.A., CHA
Richmond, Virginia
May 2011

Acknowledgments

My thanks go out to the editorial staff at Pearson Higher Education for the support they provided on this, my first publication. The welcome task of transferring my thoughts to paper could not have been done without the help of William Lawrensen, Alexis Biasell, and the creative staff who gave life to my words.

For years, I have wanted to recognize my professors properly at The Ohio State University for directing me onto a path that has shaped my professional life. In particular, Drs. Marion Cremer and Virginia Vivian deserve my profound thanks. Little did they know that their teaching would still have an impact on my view of hospitality 30 years later. Go Buckeyes!

I also extend my thanks to Lisa Benson-Aherin, Lane Community College; Earl R. Arrowood, Jr., Bucks County Community College; Charles A. Becker, Pueblo Community College; Dirk Boon, Oxnard College; Dr. Anne Bridges, University of Alaska, Anchorage; Timothy Gilmore, Northeast Mississippi Community College; Brent Kelley, SUNY Alfred; Charles W. King, Amarillo College; Charles J. Martin, Spokane Community College; Chay Runnels, Stephen F. Austin State University; and Donald A. Sprinkle, University of Hawaii–Maui College. These other voices reminded me of the larger universe that learning takes place within. The scholarly discussions regarding academic rigor and student achievement still resonate with me. I am convinced that this book is intellectually balanced and has been enriched from their input. I hope I have convinced my peers that today's students are bright, capable, and efficient, and when provided with compelling course materials, they will rise to the occasion.

Last and certainly not least, my profound thanks to my wife Sydney, who graciously tolerated my incessant requests for feedback and input as if it was a marital duty, welcomed or otherwise. This book is a testament to her patience and good humor. On more than one occasion, I would emerge from a marathon writing session, doubtlessly in a zone that only I could explain, yet never was I made to feel self-conscious or the least bit obsessive (authoring can do that to the best of us). I will always love you, Sydney, for allowing me the time and space to share my words and experience through this project.

1

A Holistic Context for Menu Development

(*Source:* Monkey Business/Fotolia)

Key Terms

À la carte menu
Check average
Consumer behavior
Degustation menu
Demographics
Incidental market
Intended market
Market
Prix fixe
Value decisions
Vision statement

Objectives

Upon completion of this chapter, you should be able to:

1.1 Explain how menu selections are driven by your business vision.

1.2 Explain how customer motivations define your business.

1.3 Explain how your menus influence staffing, facility design, tableware, and profit potential.

1.4 Recognize the time-limited and cyclical nature of menus.

1.5 Identify paradigm shifts that affect restaurants and food services.

ENLIVENING YOUR BUSINESS VISION THROUGH MENUS

> "The best vision is insight."
>
> —MALCOLM S. FORBES[1]

Your business vision represents where you would like to see your restaurant in the future. Does your vision involve receiving awards from rating organizations such as Zagat or *Le Guide Michelin*? Do you seek to become a **market** leader in neighborhood dining? Does your vision involve sustainable food supplies and a social consciousness? Your answer to these and other questions should drive your overall business concept and the food and beverage selections that you sell. You must create a **vision statement**

EXERCISE 1-1
CREATING A VISION STATEMENT

1. Select three successful foodservice or hospitality businesses and by studying their menus, graphic imagery, and business practices, deduce what their vision is.

2. Create your own business vision by completing the following sentence: "Within two years, people will talk about my restaurant in the following terms: _____."

3. Author a sample restaurant vision statement that provides specificity and long-term flexibility.

(*Source:* Rachael Santillan/Fotolia)

specific enough to energize your strategic planning, yet general enough to allow for market developments over time. For example, consider the following statement:

"Our vision is to serve the tastiest sandwiches and largest selection of microbrews within our market."

This statement, although appealing, fails to address customer behavior. It is unduly focused on food and beverage, which may or may not be the reason customers would choose to patronize your business. More so, it is focused on two particular categories of goods and may restrain future business success if trends emerge that you never may have imagined. A better statement might read,

"Our vision is to be the preferred evening restaurant for college students attending Colorado State University."

Notice how this revised statement identifies your intended market and guides your operating hours. Sandwiches and beer can still be the primary menu focus of the business, but the revised statement allows for future changes that may occur with this target market population. With this approach, if coffee beverages emerge as a viable new option or a different food category becomes popular, your vision will not necessarily hinder these opportunities. Regardless of prevailing culinary preferences, you should target your proposed client base, thus possessing a guidepost with which to periodically assess your plans versus your outcomes. Once you have authored your vision statement you can develop a business model, including menu offerings.

HOW CUSTOMERS USE YOUR BUSINESS

The moment you assume that customers seek your business for food and beverage is the moment you limit your success. Certainly, a significant percentage of the market regards restaurants primarily as places to eat; however, you must understand **consumer behavior** if you are to align your product and service offerings with the greatest number of potential customers.

Lesson: Food services, restaurants, and catering operations have the potential to satisfy multiple consumer needs.

As foodservice professionals, we inevitably bring our experiences and biases with us when we go to work. Whereas this is a typical, if not necessary, tendency, it also blinds us to varying degrees and causes us to act in a less than objective manner. Your menu selections must parallel your target market's needs and motivations. In fact, the concept

AUTHOR'S INSIGHT

During my years in college classrooms, students repeatedly asked me, "What is your most memorable dining experience?" Invariably, they expected me to tell of an elaborate gourmet meal in an exotic resort, or perhaps a coveted dinner at a celebrity chef's exclusive restaurant. Undoubtedly, I have enjoyed special moments in dining rooms such as these; however, my fondest experiences share a common thread—*I knew what I wanted, the businesses I selected understood their capabilities and their customers, and each experience delivered more than what was promised.* When further pressed by my students, I shared the *ne plus ultra* of my dining reminiscences. I fondly recalled a late lunch in a village pub in the English countryside. It seemed like only yesterday. I was seated at a sturdy table with corners well worn by hands belonging to scores of satisfied guests. The regulation dartboard invited friendly competition and was flanked by an honor jar where tips and bets could be deposited. The natty gents in the adjacent booth relaxed and chatted as if in their own homes. I asked the server, "What are the house specialties?" He recommended the rainbow trout and a pint of scrumpy, to which I gamely agreed. He excused himself and said, "Let me go out back and find you a nice fat one." I was soon made aware of the trout farm behind the pub, and the fact that my dinner was still swimming. Meanwhile, the bartender deftly poured a slow stream of farmhouse cider ("scrumpy"), the apples having been grown across the street in a neighboring farm, into a squat goblet crested with the Queen's seal. As the sun began to set, and the brown bread, cider, and flavorsome fish were but a memory, I scanned the cozy bar and the lively scene. The music alternated between local folk ballads and sing-along pop tunes. The friendly room, genuine hospitality, and simple ingredients, redolent of the local water and earth, created an indelible memory. Nothing was fancy, nor was there pretense of gastronomic exploits. This was world-class dining bared naked to its essence. For a handful of coins, I received a priceless reward of spirit, heart, and soul.

of a target market is in itself a somewhat fabricated construct. The majority of operators develop menus and business models based on whom they wish to attract, the **intended market**, also referred to as the **target market**. Yet marketing of restaurants is an imprecise science, and we often find ourselves hosting potentially lucrative guests that we hadn't planned on, the **incidental market**. To understand your markets, you must also be aware of your customers' **value decisions**, how they decide which goods and services they find important enough to spend their money on.

The prescient menu planner understands that their actual customer base will likely be represented as is illustrated in Figure 1-1.

The questions that must be answered from the onset are as follows:

Figure 1-1
Your Customer Base

- What mix of intended market and incidental market shall I plan for?
- What is the profit potential of each of these two market segments?
- What products, services, and resources will I commit to these markets?
- What types of value decisions do the members of these market segments make?

Your answers to these questions must precede your initial menu planning. For example, if you intend to offer **degustation menus**, whereby a procession of courses is sold *prix fixe*, then what will you provide to the (incidental) customers who prefer to choose from an *à la carte* menu? Each of these segments has a different profit potential and merits short- and long-term sales forecasting. (Concepts and tools for forecasting profit potential are discussed in Chapter 5.)

Our discussion started with a caution that food and beverages are not the only motivation for customers to patronize your business. The question that begs asking is, "How will customers use my business?" Some, but certainly not all of the reasons are as follows:

- to save time or reduce travel
- to obtain nourishment

- to avoid cooking for themselves due to limited culinary ability
- to avoid the work of preparing a meal and cleaning up afterward

More specifically, you can classify dining behaviors based on where customers live or how they spend their time. Consider the following scenarios.

Dining Based on Living Arrangements

Many dining decisions are based on the reality stemming from where one lives. The value calculation that a customer makes in these instances is often moderated by institutional factors and dimensions that are part of a larger decision (e.g., dining while at school, dining as part of a medical or healing regimen, dining provided as part of the senior living routine). Examples of this include the following:

- campus dining
- hospital and healthcare food service
- assisted living and continuing care retirement dining

Dining Based on Activities

Some dining decisions are based on how customers spend repetitive or prolonged periods of time. With few exceptions, this foodservice concept is subjugated to a primary agenda. For example:

- employee dining
- conducting business or business-related entertainment
- travelers and tourists away from their homes

Dining for Pleasure

Dining for pleasure is a purpose-oriented motivation where food and beverage represent varying degrees of importance, and are sometimes eclipsed by social or attitudinal factors. Some examples include

- social networking and dining as a recreational act
- status/ego ("Show off their riches")
- food art as culture
- escape, particularly in the case of ethnic dining

Motivations such as status and ego, food art as culture, and escape are the motivations least governed by customer-value decisions. Customers dining out for those reasons are less likely to evaluate the prices you charge for the goods and services that satisfy these motivations. The experience of dining to embellish one's lifestyle complicates a value decision, where the worth of the recipe ingredients is joined by the perceived value of the entire experience. Savvy operators understand that some customers will pay elevated sums of money for rare wines, artistic food presentations, and memorable dining occasions.

Astute operators augment their intuition with historical performance data and industry trend research. An example of industry data available for operators is illustrated in Figure 1-2.

Regularly scanning industry research from a variety of sources helps you assess your business results and further the crafting of your strategic plan. The Action Toolkit at the end of this chapter contains links to several reputable websites that publish valuable market research on an ongoing basis. As with all research findings, you must be cautious and consider the sources;[2] however, a managerial routine of data collection and evaluation of research will enhance the likelihood of accurate decision making and informed forecasting.

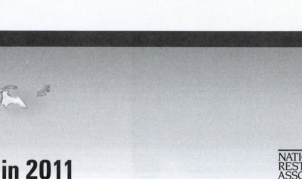

Additional Questions

What has been the most successful strategy for maintaining and building business during the recession?

Offering value specials (e.g. discounts, coupons, prix fixe menus)	38%
Simplifying menus to save on prep labor and ingredients	26%
Increased marketing efforts (including social media marketing)	15%
More portion size offerings	6%
Other	6%
Conservation efforts (e.g. reduce energy/water use, use less packaging)	6%
Negotiating with/changing suppliers	3%

What will be the hottest restaurant operational trend in 2011?

Mobile food trucks and pop-up restaurants	30%
Restaurants with gardens (e.g. rooftop, backyard, communal)	18%
Social media-based marketing	17%
Cooking classes/demonstrations	12%
Electronic/iPad/smartphone application menus and wine lists	12%
Customer DIY (e.g. build-it-yourself menus, customization)	8%
Other	3%

How can chefs/restaurateurs best promote health and nutrition?

Create diet-conscious menu sections (e.g. lower sodium, lower calorie, lower fat)	21%
Increase fresh produce options on menus	19%
Get involved in school nutrition/children's education efforts	17%
Provide nutritional information to guests to make their own decisions	16%
Reduce portion sizes	16%
Get involved in national campaigns/programs on nutrition and physical activity	8%
Other	4%

Do you use social media (e.g. Facebook, Twitter, YouTube) for professional purposes?

Yes	55%
No	29%
Not yet, but I plan to	16%

Watch the "What's Hot in 2011" video on the National Restaurant Association's website:
www.restaurant.org/foodtrends

Join the National Restaurant Association on Facebook and Twitter for additional restaurant industry updates and information.
www.facebook.com/NationalRestaurantAssociation
www.twitter.com/WeRRestaurants

Methodology:

The National Restaurant Association conducted an on-line survey of 1,527 members of the American Culinary Federation in October 2010. The chefs were given a list of 226 food and beverage items, cuisines, culinary themes and preparation methods, and were asked to rate each item as a "hot trend," "yesterday's news" or "perennial favorite" on restaurant menus in 2011. Note: Figures may not add to 100% due to rounding.

 Founded in 1919, the National Restaurant Association is the leading business association for the restaurant industry, which comprises 945,000 restaurant and foodservice outlets and a workforce of nearly 13 million employees. Together with the National Restaurant Association Educational Foundation, the Association works to lead America's restaurant industry into a new era of prosperity, prominence, and participation, enhancing the quality of life for all we serve. For more information, visit our website at www.restaurant.org.

 The American Culinary Federation, Inc., established in 1929, is the premier professional organization for culinarians in North America. With more than 22,000 members spanning 230 chapters nationwide, ACF is the culinary leader in offering educational resources, training, apprenticeship and accreditation. In addition, ACF operates the most comprehensive certification program for chefs in the United States. ACF is home to ACF Culinary Team USA, the official representative for the United States in major international culinary competitions, and to the Chef & Child Foundation, founded in 1989 to promote proper nutrition in children and to combat childhood obesity. For more information, visit www.acfchefs.org.

Figure 1-2
Example of Industry Data (*Source:* Reprinted by permission of the National Restaurant Association)

(*Source:* John Wollwerth/Shutterstock)

YOUR MENU AS THE CENTRAL PLANNING DOCUMENT

Your choice of menu offerings has far-reaching implications with an impact on operational criteria, facilities design, and ultimately the potential for earning profit over the long term. When you select a menu item, you commit to the following conditions:

- I will construct, maintain, and equip my facility to accurately prepare, cook, and serve this menu item.
- I have reliable and affordable sources of ingredients to prepare this item.
- I am prepared to store the ingredients to preserve quality and protect the food from contamination and growth of pathogens.
- I can recruit and train staff to prepare this item consistently.
- I can standardize the recipe to achieve consistent results.
- I will maintain an adequate inventory of china, glassware, and flatware to serve this item.

Each of these decisions carries a financial commitment that may or may not be a wise business decision. For example, the decision to invest in a wood-burning oven may position your pizza business above competitors, but at what cost? The build-out to meet fire code and insulate the structure exceeds the cost of using a standard deck oven. The handling of wood and ashes is labor intensive. Electric and gas-fired ovens use thermostats to control cooking temperatures, but wood fuel requires experience and skill. Finally, are there other items you can cook in the hearth that justify the investment?

The aforementioned example is one hypothetical case, yet it illustrates the complexities that arise when you designate a menu item or preparation method. Even apparently simple choices may present challenges. Can you sell blended cocktails in your intimate dining room without creating noise levels that prompt customer complaints? Is the electric circuit and 10 square feet you dedicate to an espresso machine paid for by the profit from selling *lattes* and *cappuccinos*?

THE MENU LIFE CYCLE

"If nothing ever changed, there'd be no butterflies."

—AUTHOR UNKNOWN[3]

The criteria that led you to offer your menus are certain to change, and so should your menu selections. Certain of these criteria are external to your control, and others are based on internal strategic decisions you elect to make.

EXERCISE 1-2
A NIGHTMARE FROM THE SEAS

The chef–owner of "Mar Azure" decided to specialize in sustainably harvested fish and seafood. She dedicated 75 percent of her lunch and dinner menus to her vision of the best seafood in the market. Within one year's time, she experienced irregular supplies of shellfish, restrictions on protected fish species, and was often without a variety of menu items to offer. Her only walk-in refrigerator increasingly smelled like the ocean—as did the pastries, dairy items, and other foods stored near the crustacea, mollusks, and whole fish. The crushed ice used to preserve the seafood created extra labor, and the handling of water once the ice melted increased the potential for cross contamination of food and work surfaces.

Suggest a comprehensive list of decision criteria that the chef–owner should have used when originally exploring this menu concept.

Changing Tastes

American restaurant cooking has demonstrated an amazing transformation, both in ingredients and cooking methods. Beginning with the British colonial presence and persisting into the twentieth century, fine dining in America was defined by European ingredients, recipes, and preparation methods. Figure 1-3, the 1899 menu from Delmonico's restaurant in New York City, illustrates then-prevailing tastes in upscale city dining.

Fast forward to more recent times, when a cultural self-awareness of sorts occurred during the 1970s and several influential chefs declared a contemporary culinary identity. Across America, a focus on braising and slow-cooking in the late 1960s yielded to wood-fired grilling and other rapid methods in the 1970s and 1980s. Hickory and oak smoke was soon replaced by mesquite, and then fruitwoods. Many wine lists in the 1980s rapidly shifted from German, French, and Italian wines to embrace the wines

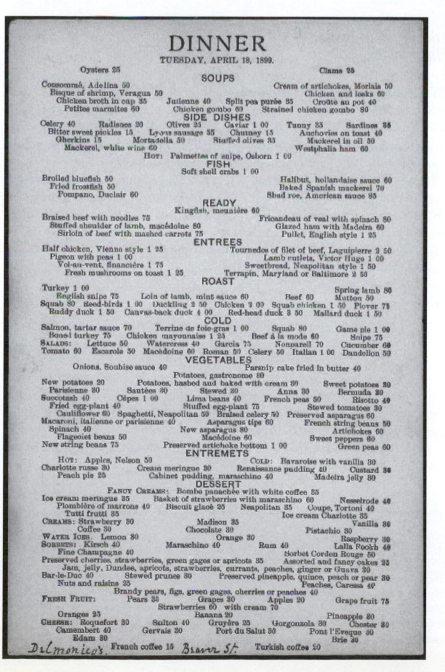

Figure 1-3

Delmonico's Dinner Menu, 1899, New York City, New York   (*Source:* en.wikipedia.org/wiki/Delmonico%27s; accessed May 1, 2011.)

emerging from California, and later from New York, Oregon, and Washington state. American tastes cycled through generic Rhine-style wines and American Burgandy-esque wines, to effervescent wine coolers, white zinfandels, and a more recent awakening to Malbec, Torrontés, and Grüner Veltliner wines. Today's culinary landscape, although influenced by two centuries of continental styles and practices, is vibrant and unapologetically pioneering.

Changing Customer Perceptions

Some operators likely placed *foi gras* on their menus as a means of proclaiming worldliness and excellence; however, the contemporary business climate subsequently has shifted to include greater emphasis on ethical responsibilities. Practices such as force-feeding geese and ducks to produce a fattened *foi* (liver) are now viewed as a liability rather than a measure of quality. This and other societal taboos should prompt operators to question their menu selections and assess whether they are still valued by present and future clientele.

Changing Food Supplies

By definition, the supply chain is composed of multiple circuits, each subject to regulatory and cost impacts. Consequently, the availability of ingredients has an impact on menu items offered by restaurants and other food services. The range of ingredients with which chefs create their artistry is constantly changing. *Kobe* beef, once a prize savored only in Japan, has become readily available in American cities and suburbs from coast to coast. Absinthe, the mythical drink of European poets and artists that was banned in the United States for nearly a century, is now once again legalized for sale in the United States and can be used to complement backbars and enhance urbane restaurant concepts. Conversely, trans fats, once quite standard in bakeshops and commercial kitchens, have been outlawed in Boston, Philadelphia, Montgomery County (Maryland), Seattle, New York City, and the entire state of California. Simply stated, recipes using trans fats in those locations had to be modified or removed from menus.

Internal Strategic Decisions

As previously discussed, menus should be used to enliven your business vision. As your vision changes, so, too, should your menus and menu selections. Beginning sometime in the late 1980s, many American diners began dissociating the notion of fine dining from the traditional white-tablecloth concept. This defection continues, yet owners and operators have been able to enjoy respectable check averages even without tuxedoed staff, linens, and heavy silverplate. Contemporary diners still demand quality, but their definitions of *quality* have changed. Perceptive operators correctly read these trends and responded with changes in their menu

---

EXERCISE 1-3
MENU DEVELOPMENT

The companion website for this textbook is http://www. pearsonhighered.com/barrish, which contains all of the digital files that accompany this and other chapters. Using *Menu Engineering Worksheet 01*, create an *a la carte* menu for a theoretical concept of your choice. If appropriate, include wine, malt beverages, and a selection of spirit-based drinks. This will become the basis for future exercises in this course, so challenge yourself and craft your future business vision.

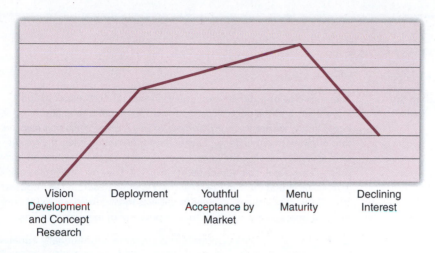

| Vision Development and Concept Research | Deployment | Youthful Acceptance by Market | Menu Maturity | Declining Interest |

Figure 1-4
Typical Menu Life Cycle

offerings. As the winds of culinary changes blow, chefs and menu planners must respond accordingly.

To varying degrees, the sum of these forces causes eventual obsolescence of menus (Figure 1-4). Certainly, there are items that weather time better than others; nonetheless, a signature item or favorite recipes may become dated and require retirement if you are to remain competitive. Knowing when to replace these items and the mechanics for engineering menus is discussed in Chapter 10.

SHIFTING PARADIGMS

"Your paradigm is so intrinsic to your mental process that you are hardly aware of its existence, until you try to communicate with someone with a different paradigm."

—DONELLA MEADOWS[5]

Those truisms that we seem to know and anchor our confidence with can betray us should we look away too long. For decades, we based our food-service concepts on all that we believed to be true. The rate of change has amplified and become complicated with global connectedness; thus, we must keep a watchful eye to that past, present, and future (Table 1-1).

AUTHOR'S INSIGHT

Not much surprises me anymore. Nonetheless, I was starting my day reading various news sources when I stumbled on an article that caused me quite a bit of distress.[4] Apparently, a new breed of chefs and owners are refusing customer requests for even the slightest accommodations. It seems that the customer is no longer "always right." Specifically,

- A fine-dining establishment in Chicago, assuming a purist stance, refuses to serve decaf coffee.

- A popular bistro cautions "No ketchup" is available with its french fries. (Don't even ask.)

- A well-respected gastropub in New York City serves a high-quality cheeseburger; however, there's a catch—the only cheese they allow you to have on it is Roquefort.

Although this is but a partial list, it compels me to wonder when chef whimsy (dogma?) trumps customer satisfaction. Is it possible that some restaurants are so self-righteous that they know better what the customers need, rather than hearing what the customers want? Only time will tell.

TABLE 1-1
SHIFTING PARADIGMS IN CONTEMPORARY DINING

What It Was	What It Has Become	What It Means
Dining value based on goods	Value based on the sum dining experience	There used to be a generalized equation that related cost of recipe ingredients and the price a customer paid for a menu selection. Increasingly, we are asking customers to pay higher prices that incorporate our investment in décor, cachet, and other intangibles. If a restaurant, lounge, or club is the latest place to be seen, then customers know they will pay for it, sometimes dearly. In 2011, the cost of a fruity cocktail in a plastic cup at the Tao Beach at the Venetian Resort in Las Vegas was $14.00, plus tax and tip. Elsewhere this was most certainly a $5.00 drink, but customers paid a stiff tariff for the privilege of experiencing Tao.
Quantity as a measure of value	Small yet stellar portions as a new measure of value	On the face of it, some operators and customers traditionally equated higher prices with larger portions. This is still true in value-priced and mid-markets, but there is a growing trend to offer exceptional ingredients and small portions at prices that otherwise would command large portions. Many customers understand that precious ingredients prepared with skill are worthy of premium prices.
White tablecloth	Upscale casual	Attractive **check averages** that customarily were associated with tablecloth dining now can be achieved with upscale casual concepts. Customers are less interested in traditional formality, yet still are willing to pay for memorable dining. A shift in focus to rarified ingredients or unique service concepts allows operators to obtain high check averages without the expense of linens, limited-use service pieces, and staffing of team service.
Animal-based protein as center-of-the-plate	Fewer rules. The entrée of meat, poultry, or fish accompanied by a starch and vegetable is no longer a universal of recipe and menu planning.	The concept of a meal anchored by a substantial portion of animal-based protein is no longer sacrosanct. Small-plate concepts (*tapas, mezze*, etc.) increasingly define the dining experience, particularly as a means of sampling a variety of dishes.
French cuisine as a benchmark for world-class dining	Recognition of other exemplary cuisines that are adaptable for today's restaurants	Beginning with Thomas Jefferson and followed by experiences gleaned from international travel, Americans accepted French cuisine as the benchmark for fine dining. Our recent shift from Eurocentrism and our enhanced understanding of global societies has informed us of the noble cuisines from Russia, the Orient, and other nations of historical import.
Red wine with meat; white wine with fish	A thoughtfully selected range of beverages to partner with our food offerings	As wines increasingly found their way onto American restaurant tables, we developed overly simplified rules to help customers navigate. Often, the simple rules failed to recognize the broad spectrum of preparation methods and intensity of ingredient combinations. For example, the rich thigh meat of an older roaster is flavored differently than the breast meat of a young hen. Breaded *scallopini di vitello* requires a different beverage accompaniment than a rich *osso buco* of veal shank. How can we believe that poaching, grilling, charbroiling, or roasting will not complicate these basic rules? And what of the grain- and fruit-based beverages? Beers and spirits may play a valuable role in creating an outstanding course or a memorable meal. Now we have refined our guidance by tasting our recipes with a variety of beverages that synergize and bring out the best elements in the ingredients and preparations. A dish cooked *à la Normande* is well suited to the dry *cidres* of Normandy, and the briny oysters of the Pacific Northwest are well served with a rich porter flavored with Cascade hops.

TABLE 1-1
CONTINUED

What It Was	What It Has Become	What It Means
Breakfast, lunch, dinner as the three traditional dayparts	Anytime snacks and meals	The notion of three typical dayparts made sense to a society that moved in a relatively synchronized manner. Business life has changed dramatically, and the "9 to 5" regimen is joined by flex schedules and other variants that prompt us to wake earlier or later and dine throughout the day. Not all restaurants are staffed for continuous dining; however, those markets that serve a heterogeneous population of workers, neighbors, and visitors understand the importance of menus that are available throughout the day.
Skilled kitchen staff	Convenience ingredients	For a variety of reasons, it has become difficult for some operators to recruit and retain skilled culinary staff. The talent required to fabricate portion cuts of meat and fish, to prepare sauces, and to create attractive desserts has been partially replaced by reliance on convenience ingredients. Many foodservices now purchase semi- or fully prepared items that reduce our need for skilled employees and enable us to serve menu items that exceed the abilities of our staff.
Food as sustenance	Food as art	Surely, we must eat to survive, but the role of food in supporting physical well-being is increasingly complimented by the aesthetic power of dining. The pantheon of theater, music, and visual arts has been joined effectively by culinary arts. The oversize white platters that many chefs now use as the palettes for their creative designs exemplify the artistic nature of culinary preparation.

EXERCISE 1-4

MENUS OVER TIME

Identify a restaurant or foodservice that has been in operation for at least 10 years. Interview the owner and catalog the changes in menu and dining trends that he or she has survived. What do these changes say about shifts in market demands and consumer behavior?

(*Source:* Michelangelo Gratton/Shutterstock

ACTION TOOLKIT

Customer data can be obtained by contract with local or national market-research firms; however, there is a wealth of free statistical information available from federal, state, and municipal governments.

- **American FactFinder from the U.S. Census Bureau:** U.S. Census Bureau database for population, housing, economic, and geographic data. www.factfinder.census.gov/home/saff/main.html?_lang=en
- **FedStats:** Statistics from more than 100 U.S. federal agencies, including national, state, county, and local statistical profiles. www.fedstats.gov/
- **Statistical Abstracts of the United States:** Online version of the National Data Book published by the U.S. Census Bureau. www.census.gov/compendia/statab/
- **Statistical Resources on the Web:** Directory of links to statistical resources on the Web, including agriculture, business and industry, cost of living, **demographics**, economics, energy, foreign economics, foreign trade, health, housing, labor, military, science, sociology, and weather. www.lib.umich.edu/govdocs/statsnew.html

There are several sources of industry data, including the following websites:

- **National Restaurant Association:** www.restaurant.org/research/
- **Restaurant Hospitality:** www.restaurant-hospitality.com/
- **Restaurant Management:** www.rmgtmagazine.com/
- **Nation's Restaurant News:** www.nrn.com/
- **The Beverage Information Group:** www.beveragenet.net

GLOSSARY

À la carte menu—A menu where each selection is individually priced. A diner may customize his or her meal by making personal selections from the *à la carte* menu.

Check average—The average amount each customer spends on food and beverage, calculated by dividing sales by the number of customers it took to generate those sales. Also referred to as *average cover* or *average check*.

Consumer behavior—The actions that customers and potential customers choose to take in response to the goods and services you offer.

Degustation menu—A tasting menu designed to provide diners with an integrated succession of small but exemplary courses.

Demographics—Age, gender, race, income, disability, education attainment, employment status, geographic location, home ownership, and other data used to understand and predict behavior of social and economic systems, including market demand for hospitality and food services.

Incidental market—The customers that choose to patronize your establishment even though you did not expressly market to them.

Intended market—The population on which you focus your marketing efforts. Also referred to as the *target market*.

Market—An economic relationship in which buyers drive commerce by seeking goods and services from sellers. In the food service industry, the most typical goods and services are prepared meals and beverages sold by the glass.

Prix fixe—A menu of several courses offered at one set price. Also referred to as *table d'hôte*.

Value decisions—Decisions made by customers that indicate which goods and services they find important enough to spend their money on. In a restaurant setting, these decisions include portion size, exclusive ingredients, and culinary artistry.

Vision statement—A verbal expression that states how a business would like to see itself.

ENDNOTES

1. thinkexist.com/quotation/the_best_vision_is_insight/295115.html; accessed May 1, 2011.

2. Rubrics and criteria for evaluating Web pages are available at www.library.cornell.edu/olinuris/ref/research/webcrit.html and www.library.cornell.edu/olinuris/ref/research/webeval.html.

3. thinkexist.com/quotation/if_nothing_ever_changed-there-d_be_no/188679.html; accessed May 1, 2011.

4. www.nytimes.com/2011/03/05/nyregion/05puritans.html; accessed May 1, 2011.

5. thinkexist.com/quotation/yourdigm_is_so_intrinsic_to_your_mental/10622.html; accessed May 1, 2011.

2

Where Food and Beverages Are Served

(*Source:* brodtcast/Fotolia)

Objectives

Upon completion of this chapter, you should be able to:

2.1   Discuss key concepts of restaurant menus.

2.2   Discuss key concepts of menus for take away dining.

2.3   Discuss key concepts of food truck menus.

2.4   Discuss key concepts of banquet and event menus.

2.5   Discuss key concepts of hotel in-room dining menus.

2.6   Discuss key concepts of employee feeding menus.

2.7   Discuss key concepts of menus for school and campus dining.

2.8   Discuss key concepts of hospital menus.

2.9   Discuss key concepts of long-term care menus.

Key Terms

Aperitifs

Buffet style

Contribution margin

Cycle menu

Digestifs

Eaux-de-vie

Guarantee

Malt beverages

Microbrews

Menu

Mise en place

On-site food service

Restaurant

Revenue

Spirits

Turndown service

Wine

MENUS IN RESTAURANTS

"I learned more from the one restaurant that didn't work than from all the ones that were successes."

—WOLFGANG PUCK[1]

Historical records suggest that restaurants emerged in the Western world during the 16th century, when Boulanger, a French soup seller, offered his savory elixirs as a restorative, hence the name **restaurant**. The forebear of today's operating model was the Grand Tavern de Londres (the "Great

Tavern of London") founded in Paris in 1782 by Antoine Beauvilliers. This enterprise introduced the concepts of individual food portions to diners who ate seated at tables during fixed operating hours (dayparts). Most notably, the guests were able to select from a **menu** ("small list") enabling accommodation of individual preferences. Thus did the heritage of commercial food service begin. The majority of clientele continue to patronize the world's restaurants to enjoy food and accompanying beverages. As discussed in Chapter 1, food and beverages serve a variety of customer needs. Depending on the items offered and selections made, restaurant food can provide a share of daily nourishment, as well as afford the satisfaction of social and psychological needs. It cannot be overstated how important a menu is to defining the personality, guest experience, and, ultimately, the success of a restaurant.

When compared to nearly all other commercial dining options, restaurants offer the greatest degree of choices for guests. Restaurants are where recipe innovations occur and "dining as entertainment" takes place. Despite the challenges of operating a profitable restaurant, thousands of entrepreneurs choose this form of business venture to express their creativity, and we look to small- to medium-size privately owned restaurants for tomorrow's concepts. Figure 2-1 illustrates a contemporary restaurant menu that exhibits broad appeal and a balance of selections.

As was discussed in Chapter 1, customers patronize restaurants to satisfy a wide range of needs, and menus are a primary attractant and tangible dimension. Consequently, there are countless variations of restaurant menus that appeal to every market segment. The structure and components of restaurant food menus are discussed in detail in Chapter 3.

Restaurants offer a spectrum of alcoholic and non-alcoholic beverages to provide thirst-quenching accompaniment to meals. Nonalcoholic beverages appeal to a large percentage of restaurant patrons and may include

- still or effervescent waters (bottled, or filtered/drawn from the tap in-house)
- sodas ("pop")
- fruit-based beverages, including juices
- energy drinks
- milk
- hot and cold tea and tea-based beverages
- hot and cold coffee and coffee-based beverages
- "virgin" cocktails, or *mocktails*

The broad classification of alcoholic beverages includes

- wine
- malt beverages
- distilled spirits

Wine is the product of fermented fruit juice, typically from varieties of the *Vitis vinifera* grape, and provides the complexity to turn good food into a memorable meal. Wine may be sold at the beginning of the meal (***aperitifs***), or consumed during the meal, and may also be enjoyed at the end of the meal. Figures 2-2 and 2-3 illustrate two different approaches to merchandising wine in restaurants. Whereas Figure 2-2 uses a modern communications approach to merchandise wines in the restaurant, Figure 2-3 illustrates a time-honored means that many customers are comfortable with and still expect. As this textbook unfolds, you will be provided with theory and tools for creating and merchandising your own wine lists. Nonetheless, as previously discussed in Chapter 1, you must constantly consider the collective needs and wants of your target market when selecting wine or any other beverage to be included on your menus.

All Oysters
— Hand Shucked —
To Order

CRAB HOUSE

Oyster Hour
— 4:00 to 6:00 PM Daily —
Shaw's Oyster Bar

TODAY'S HALF SHELL OYSTERS

	½ Doz
Whitecap (*Crassostrea virginica*), Dennis Port, Massachusetts	13.99
Otter Cove (*Crassostrea gigas*), Discovery Bay, Washington	13.99
Chincoteague Salts (*Crassostrea virginica*), Chincoteague Bay, Virginia	13.99
Barron Point (*Crassostrea gigas*), Skookum Inlet, Washington	13.99
Wellfleet (*Crassostrea virginica*), Wellfeet Harbor, Massachusetts	13.99
Blue Pool (*Crassostrea gigas*), Hamma Hamma River, Washington	13.99
Oyster Sampler	13.99

— SHAW'S SUSHI MENU —

SHAW'S SIGNATURES
Salmon Tataki	8.00
King Crab Mikado	10.00
Tuna, Guacamole & Chips	13.00
Shaw's Charred Sashimi Tuna	14.00

NIGIRI - SASHIMI
	Per Piece
Shrimp (Ebi)	2.50
Spicy Shrimp (Ebi)	2.50
Salmon (Sake)	2.50
BBQ Eel (Unagi)	3.00
Tuna (Maguro)	3.50
Spicy Tuna (Maguro)	3.50
Yellowtail (Hamachi)	4.00
Spicy King Crab (Kani)	4.00
King Crab (Kani)	4.00
Fatty Tuna (Toro)	10.00

SHARI - NASHI
Spicy No Rice Rolls
Spicy Shrimp	8.00
Spicy Tuna	10.00
Spicy California	12.00
Spicy Lobster	14.00
Spicy Yellowtail & Scallion	15.00

COMBINATIONS
Nigiri Combination (5 pcs)	14.00
Maki Combination (serves 2)	16.00
Sashimi Combination Tuna, Salmon & Yellowtail	17.00

MAKI SUSHI
Sweet Potato Roll	8.00
BBQ Eel & Avocado	9.00
Shrimp Tempura	9.00
Tuna & Avocado	10.00
Acapulco Roll	10.00
Spicy Tuna	10.00
King Crab California	12.00
Lobster, Avocado & Cucumber	14.00
Spicy Shrimp & Red King Crab	15.00
Spicy Crab, Salmon & Lemon	15.00
Rainbow Roll	15.00
Chicago Crazy Roll	17.00

SUSHI PLATTERS
Shellfish Maki	43.00

Shrimp Tempura, California, Vegetable, Spicy Shrimp & King Crab, Lobster, Avocado & Cucumber

Tuna & Salmon	52.00

Tuna Nigiri (4), Salmon Nigiri (4), Spicy Tuna Maki, Tuna on Top Maki, Tuna & Salmon Maki, Acapulco Maki

Grand Sushi	70.00

Maki - Lobster, Acapulco, California, Spicy Tuna
Sashimi - Tuna, Salmon, Yellowtail
Nigiri - BBQ Eel, Shrimp

STARTERS
Fried Lake Michigan Smelt	7.99
Shrimp & Vegetable Tempura	7.99
Wild Maine Blue Mussels Red Curry Broth	8.99
Crispy Calamari	9.99
Baked Blue Crab & Artichoke Dip	11.99
Jumbo Shrimp Cocktail (6)	11.99
Oysters Rockefeller	12.99
Blue Crab Spring Rolls	(4)13.99
Maryland Style Crab Cake	14.99
Chilled Alaskan Red King Crab Bites	24.99

Chilled Florida Stone Crab Claws
Fresh Caught from Islamorada, Florida Keys
Expertly Cracked - Served with Mustard Mayonnaise
1pc Medium...7.25   1pc Large...12.25

SMALL SALADS
Cole Slaw	4.99
Organic Mixed Greens	6.99
Caesar Salad White Anchovies	6.99

SOUPS
	Cup	Bowl
New England Clam Chowder	5.99	6.99
Seafood Gumbo	5.99	6.99
Lobster Bisque	6.99	8.99
Jambalaya	7.99	9.99

APPETIZER PLATTERS

Hot Appetizer Combination Mini Crab Cake, Crispy Calamari & Fried Shrimp	(Per Person)	13.99
Cold Appetizer Combination Half Shell Oysters, Cocktail Shrimp, Alaskan King Crab Bites	(Per Person)	14.99

Alert Your Server For Food Intolerances or Special Dietary Needs
— Personal Checks & Traveller's Checks Are Not Accepted —
An 18% Gratuity Will Be Added To Parties of 6 or Larger

Figure 2-1
Shaw's Crab House Lunch Menu, Chicago, Illinois   (*Source:* Reprinted by permission of Shaw's Crab House)

Shaw's
CRAB HOUSE

LUNCHEON SALADS

	Small	Large
Iceberg Wedge Salad Maytag Blue Cheese Dressing & Herb Vinaigrette	6.99	8.99
Chopped Bacon, Tomatoes, Chopped Egg, Chives, Migas		
Chopped Salad Avocado, Egg, Cucumber, Bacon, Scallion, Tomato, Blue Cheese	8.99	12.99
Chicken Cobb Salad Tomatoes, Bacon, Maytag Blue Cheese, Avocado, Scallions		12.99
Tuna Sushi & Asian Salad Combination Spicy Tuna Maki, Tuna Nigiri, Asian Salad		14.99
Crab Cake & Caesar Salad Platter White Anchovies, Mustard Mayonnaise		17.99
Shaw's Signature Chopped Seafood Salad Louis Dressing & Vinaigrette		19.99
King Crab, Shrimp, Dungeness Crab, Lobster, Hearts of Palm, Avocado, Egg, Cucumber, Olives, Tomatoes, Scallions		

Add Cup of Clam Chowder or Seafood Gumbo to Large Luncheon Salad..2.99

CRAB HOUSE SANDWICHES

Charbroiled Cheddar Burger Lettuce, Tomato, Hand Cut French Fries & Pickle	11.99
Tuna Salad Sandwich Tuscan Roll, Albacore Tuna Salad, Lettuce, Hand Cut French Fries & Pickle	11.99
Grilled Chicken B.L.T. Hellmann's Mayonnaise, Hand Cut French Fries & Pickle	12.99
Battered Alaskan Halibut Tacos Salsa Cruda, Chipotle Salsa, Tomatillo Salsa	15.99
Grilled Atlantic Yellowfin Tuna Tacos Salsa Cruda, Chipotle Salsa, Tomatillo Salsa	13.99
New England Lobster Roll Maine Lobster Meat, Hellmann's Mayonnaise, Homemade Potato Chips	18.99
Crab Cake Burger Blue Crab Meat, Lettuce, Tomato, Mustard Mayonnaise, Hand Cut French Fries	20.99

Add Cup of Clam Chowder or Seafood Gumbo to Crab House Sandwich..2.99

DAILY SPECIALS

DAILY:	**THE KING OF CRAB** - Steamed Alaskan Red King Crab Legs - 12oz. Drawn Butter	34.99
MON:	**Sauteed Lake Erie Yellow Perch** Lemon Butter, Cole Slaw	19.99
TUE:	**Baked George's Bank Haddock Diavola** Parmesan Crusted, Mashed Potatoes, Diavola Sauce	18.99
WED:	**Grilled Skirt Steak** Sweet Ginger Soy Marinade, Mashed Potatoes, Crispy Shallots	18.99
THU:	**Seafood Pot Pie** Maine Lobster Meat, Alaskan Red King Crab, Rock Shrimp, Sweet Pastry Crust	19.99
FRI:	**Fried Fisherman's Platter** George's Bank Haddock, Shrimp, Calamari, French Fries & Cole Slaw	18.99

Daily Specials Served with Cup of Clam Chowder or Caesar Salad & Mini Key Lime Pie

FRESH FISH

Fried Lake Michigan Smelt Platter Hand Cut French Fries, Cole Slaw, Tarar Sauce	12.99
Broiled Lake Superior Whitefish Parmesan & Garlic Crust, Grilled Tomato, Bell Pepper & Caper Vinaigrette	15.99
Sauteed George's Bank Yellowtail Flounder Lemon Butter, Tartar Sauce, Cole Slaw	16.99
Fish & Chips George's Bank Haddock, Hand Cut French Fries, Cole Slaw, Tartar Sauce	17.99
Parmesan Crusted George's Bank Haddock Sauteed Spinach, Lemon Butter	17.99
Oven Roasted Lake Erie Walleye Horseradish Crust, Green Beans, Dijon Mustard Vinaigrette	18.99
Sauteed Virginia Striped Bass Ginger-Scallion Crust, Asian Stir-Fry Vegetables, Ginger-Soy Vinaigrette	18.99
Sauteed Lake Erie Yellow Perch Lemon Butter, Tartar Sauce, Cole Slaw	19.99
Grilled Atlantic Yellowfin Tuna Crispy Rice Noodles, Scallions, Roasted Peanuts, Ginger-Soy Vinaigrette	21.99
Grilled Alaskan Halibut Roasted Baby Artichokes & Tomatoes, Gribiche Sauce	22.99
Grilled Wild Alaskan King Salmon Baby Arugula, Shaved Parmesan, Fingerling Potatoes, Herb Vinaigrette	25.99

SEAFOOD

French Fried Shrimp Hand Breaded Shrimp, French Fries, Cocktail Sauce	16.99
Lobster, Brie & Penne Pasta Maine Lobster, Spinach, Brie & Cheddar Sauce	18.99
Sauteed George's Bank Sea Scallops Shaw's Signature Rice, Sauteed Spinach, Lemon or Garlic Butter	21.99
Shaw's Seafood Platter Garlic Shrimp, Sea Scallops, Maryland Style Crab Cake	25.99
Maryland Style Crab Cakes Blue Crab Meat Hand Picked Exclusively for Shaw's .... (2)	25.99
Chilled Florida Stone Crab Claws (1lb) Mustard Mayonnaise .... Medium 42.99 Large	56.99
Parmesan Crusted Chicken Breast All Natural Chicken Breast, Sauteed Spinach, Lemon Butter	12.99

Shaw's Crab House proudly partners with Shedd Aquarium
to promote healthy oceans. Ask your server for a sustainable
seafood menu and Shedd Aquarium's Right Bite Card.

Figure 2-1
Continued

16

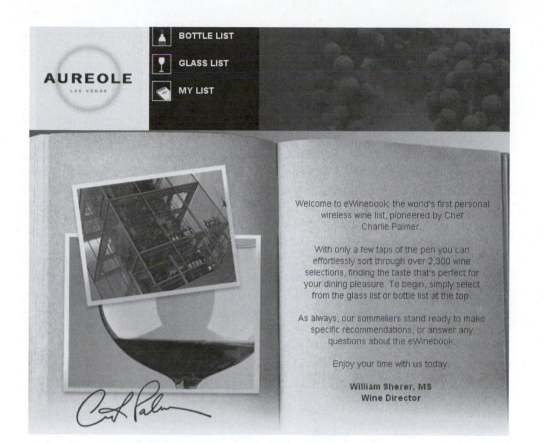

Figure 2-2
eWinebook—Aureole,
Las Vegas, Nevada
(*Source:* Courtesy of Charlie Palmer
Group)

Malt beverages, typically referred to as *beer*, include ale, porter, lager, and stout. These beverages are sold by the glass, bottle, or pitcher. Brewing and production of malt beverages does not require the expensive ingredients (*Vitis vinifera* grape juice) and lengthy production/inventory time commitment as does wine. Malt beverages have a history of lower prices than other alcoholic beverages; consequently, they have

Dessert Wine

FRANCE

Bin No.		Vintage	Bottle	
147	Château d'Yquem	1988	750	
24	Château d'Yquem	1990	575	
523	Château La Faurie-Peyraquey	1989	140	
22	Château Suduiraut	1990	135	
522	Château Suduiraut	2000	70	375 ml
116	René Renou, "Cuvée Anne," Bonnezaux	1997	100	375 ml
81	Gewürztraminer, Hugel, Selection-De-Grains-Nobles	1986	225	
166	Gewürztraminer, Hugel, Selection-De-Grains-Nobles	1989	200	
82	Hugel, Riesling-Selection-De-Grains-Nobles	1988	210	

Figure 2-3
Excerpt from the
Williamsburg Inn Regency
Room Wine List. (*Source:* The
Colonial Williamsburg Foundation)

achieved a niche as an affordable recreational beverage. Not until recently have more complex malt beverages such as cask-conditioned ales and Belgium *lambics* earned their rightful place as respectable accompaniments and memorable meal components. In fact, the quality and variety of malt beverages has become so established that "beer dinners" featuring the brewer's craft are quite commonplace.

In the mid-1980s, a movement began in the United States ("craft brews") and United Kingdom ("real ales") that heralded hundreds of new labels, effectively energizing an otherwise stolid market. Small-batch production and unique character quickly became the hallmarks of these beverages. The rapid growth of distinctive malt beverages made beer and ale menus feasible and highly profitable. Figure 2-4 is an example of a malt beverage list. As discussed in Chapter 7, craft brews and **microbrews** help define regional cuisine across the whole of the United States.

Spirits result from distillation of fruit, grain, or vegetable bases. Spirits listed on menus may be consumed undiluted as high-proof beverages, or mixed with a variety of ingredients to create a less-concentrated drink. Cocktails and other spirit-based drinks are a popular beginning to meals and are also central to social and recreational activities. Certain mixed drinks are associated with particular cuisines (*mojitos* with Cuban cuisine; *margaritas* with Mexican cuisine, etc.), as are straight spirits (*vodka* with Russian cuisine;

Sycamore Beer List

DRAFT BEERS:
Avery "Maharaja", Imperial I.P.A., Boulder Colorado, 10% abv — 6.00
Bear Republic "Ryevalry", Belgian Style Double Rye I.P.A., 8.2% — 6.00
Boulevard Amber Ale, Kansas City Missouri, 5.1% abv — 3.50
New Belgium "Dunkel Weiss", Fort Collins, CO, 9% abv — 5.00
Schlafly Hefeweizin, Unfiltered Wheat, Saint Louis Missouri — 3.50
Sierra Nevada "Bigfoot", Barley Wine, Chico California, 9.6% abv — 4.00

BELGIAN AND BELGIAN STYLE BEERS:
Boulevard Bourbon Barrel Quad, Belgian Style Ale, K.C.MO, 750 ml., 11.8% — 18.00
Cantillon Cherry Lambic, Belgium, 750 ml., 5% abv — 18.00
Castle Brewery Gueuze, "Fond Tradition", Belgium, 375 ml., 5% — 10.00
Cathedral Square "Hail Mary" Belgian Style I.P.A., Weston/St. Louis MO 22oz — 7.00
Charleville "Half-Wit Wheat", Belgian Style Ale, St. Genevieve MO, 22 oz. 4.5 — 7.00
Chimay Blue, Belgian Trappist Strong Dark Ale, 11.2 oz., 9% abv — 8.00
Duvel, Belgian Strong Pale Ale, 11.2 oz., 8.5% abv — 5.50
Fantôme Saison, Belgian Farmhouse Ale, 8% abv, 750 ml. — 18.00
Hitachino Nest "White", Belgian Style Wit, with Ginger, Japan, 5%, 11.3 oz. — 6.50
Houblon Chouffe, Tripel, Double I.P.A., Belgium, 750 ml., 9% abv — 15.00
Jolly Pumpkin "La Parcela", Sour Pumpkin Ale w/Cacao + Spices, MI, 750 ml, 5.9 — 18.00
New Belgium "Terroir", Dry Hopped Sour Ale, CO, 22 oz., 7.5% abv — 17.00
North Coast "Pranqster", Belgian Style Golden Ale, Ft. Bragg CA, 750 ml, 7.6% — 10.00
Scaldis, Brasserie Dubuisson, Belgian Ale, 12% abv, 8.48 oz. — 6.00
Schlafly "Grand Cru", Belgian Style Strong Golden Ale, St. Louis MO 9%, 750 ml — 14.00
Straffe Hendrik Bruges Triple, Bruges Belgium, 11.2 oz. 9% abv — 6.00
St. Bernardus Tripel, Watou Belgium, 750 ml., 8% abv — 16.00
Westmalle Trappist Dubbel, Belgium, 330 ml., 7% abv — 7.00
Unibroue "La Fin du Monde", Belgian Style Tripel, Canada, 750 ml., 9% — 12.00

PALE ALE:
Arcadia "Hop Rocket" Double I.P.A., Battle Creek MI, 12 oz., 9% — 6.00
Bear Republic "Hop Rod Rye", Healdsburg CA, 8% abv — 4.00
Boulevard "Doublewide" I.P.A., Kansas City Missouri, 8.5%, 750 ml — 13.00
Caldera India Pale Ale, Ashland Oregon, 12 oz. Can, 6.1% — 4.50
Firestone Walker "Double Jack", Dbl. I.P.A., Paso Robles CA 22 oz, 9.5% — 12.00
Founders "Centennial", I.P.A., Grand Rapids Michigan, 7.2%, 12 oz. — 4.00
Mikkeller "1000 I.B.U." Imperial I.P.A., Denmark/Belgium, 375 ml., 9.6% — 18.00
Odell "Myrcenary" Double I.P.A., Fort Collins CO, 9.3% — 5.00
R.J. Rocker "Black Perle", Black Double I.P.A., Spartanburg S.C., 9.5%, 22 oz — 14.00
Sierra Nevada Pale Ale, Chico California, 12 oz., 5.6% abv — 3.50

LAGER
Amstel Light, The Netherlands, 3.5%, 12 oz. bottle, 95 calories — 3.75
Budweiser 4.9 % abv, Bud Lite 110 cal., 12 oz., Miller Light 96 cal., 12 oz — 2.75
Clausthaler NA, Germany, 12 oz. — 3.50
Heineken, Holland, 12 oz. CAN, 5% abv. — 3.75
Lagunitas "PILS", Czech Style Pilsner, Petaluma CA, 6.2%, 12 oz. — 3.50
Schlafly Pilsner, Saint Louis Missouri, 12 oz., 4.8% abv — 3.00
Tecate, Mexican Lager, 12 oz. CAN, 4.5% — 2.75
Timisoreana Lager, Romania, 500 ml., 5% abv — 5.00
Tin Mill Doppelbock, Lager, Hermann MO, 12 oz., 5% — 3.50

STOUT AND PORTER:
Arcadia Barrel-Aged "Shipwreck" Porter, Battle Creek Michigan, 12%, 12 oz. — 9.00
Boulevard 'Bully!' Porter, Kansas City, MO, 12 oz., 5.2% abv — 3.50
De Struise "Black Albert" Imperial Stout, Belgium, 11 oz., 13% abv — 10.00
Goose Island "Night Stalker", Imperial Stout, Chicago Ill., 22 oz., 11.7% abv — 15.00
Great Divide 2010 Oak-Aged "Yeti", Imperial Stout, Denver CO, 9.5%, 22 oz. — 13.00
Guinness Irish Stout, the original light beer, 14.9 oz. can with nitro widget, 4.2% — 4.50
Left Hand Milk Stout, Longmont Colorado, 12 oz., 5.2% — 4.00
Mikkeller "Black", Imperial Stout, Denmark/Belgium, 16%, 12.7 oz. — 20.00
N. Coast "Rasputin XII", Barrel-Aged Imperial Stout, Ft. Bragg CA, .5L., 11.2% — 20.00

OTHER STYLES:
Anchor Steam, "California Common" San Francisco, CA, 12 oz., 4.9% — 3.75
Bell's "Third Coast" Old Ale, English Style Strong Ale, Michigan, 12 oz., 10.2% — 5.00
Boulevard Chocolate Ale, Christopher Elbow Collaboration, 9.1%, 750 ml. — 18.00
Crispin "Original" CIDER, California/Minnesota, 5% abv — 4.00
Dupont CIDER, '09, Normandy France, 5.5% abv, 750 ml. — 17.00
La Choulette Ambrée, Biere de Garde, France, 8% abv, 750 ml. — 15.00
Lagunitas "Hairy Eyeball", American Strong Ale, 9%,12 oz.,'09 or '11 vintage — 5.00
Lakefront "Bridgeburner", American Strong Ale, Milwaukee Wisc., 22 oz., 8% — 10.00
Moylan's "Kilt Lifter", Scottish Style Ale, "Wee Heavy", Novato CA, 8%, 22 oz. — 9.00
Nøgne-ø #100, Barley Wine, 500 ml., Norway, 10% abv — 11.00
Reissdorf Kölsch, Koln Germany, 500 ml., 4.8% — 6.00
Sam Smith "Yorkshire Stingo", Barrel-Aged Strong Ale, England, 550 ml., 9% — 16.00
Schlafly Barrel Aged Barley Wine, 2010 vintage, 750 ml., 10.2% abv — 16.00
Sierra Nevada "Bigfoot", Barley Wine, Chico CA, 12 oz., 9.6% abv — 4.00
Tallgrass Brewing "Oasis", Imperial E.S.B., Manhattan KS, 16 oz. can, 7.2% — 4.50
Unibroue, 'Ephemere' Apple Ale, Canada, 12 oz., 5.5% abv — 5.00
Weihenstephaner "Vitus", Weizenbock, Freising Germany, 7.7%, 500 ml. — 6.00

Figure 2-4
Sycamore Beer List, Colombia, Missouri   (*Source:* Courtesy of Sycamore Restaurant, Columbia, Missouri)

Figure 2-5
Atlanta Fish Market Cocktail
List, Atlanta, Georgia
(*Source:* Reprinted by permission of
Buckhead Life Restaurant Group)

aquavit with Swedish cuisine, etc.). As is the case with dessert wine served at the end of a meal, certain spirit-based drinks are traditional as **digestifs**. Cordials and **eaux-de-vie** are examples of spirits used to punctuate a meal's end. Figure 2-5 is an excerpt from a cocktail list.

MENUS FOR TAKE-AWAY DINING

Whether referred to as *carryout* or *take-away,* meals prepared in commercial kitchens and packaged for customers to eat at home possess a proven track record. Coupled with drive-through or online ordering and curbside pickup, these menus are a formidable option when convenience is desired. Quick-service restaurants dominate this segment with familiar brand names such as McDonald's, Pizza Hut, and Taco Bell. Whereas these restaurants typically provide functional on-premise dining rooms, their menu items are highly portable and well suited for carryout dining. In fact, this segment pioneered store design and point-of-sale technologies to expedite the ordering and service of their menu items. This does not suggest that traditional dine-in concepts do not provide take-away meals. On the contrary, some of the nation's most successful full-service restaurants have strategically entered the carryout market with great success. Figure 2-6 illustrates the scope and sophistication of menu items available for convenient take-away dining.

Certain menu items lend themselves to take-away dining, including soups and items that are moist or sauced. Salads also perform well, particularly if they are packaged "undressed" so they don't wilt or become stained. Sandwiches are particularly

Figure 2-6
Excerpt from Outback
Steakhouse Curbside
Take-Away Menu
(*Source:* Reprinted by permission of
OSI Restaurant Partners, LLC)

Figure 2-7
Excerpt from Wegmans Takeout Menu   (*Source*: Reprinted with permission from Wegmans Food Markets)

successful and are the most popular carryout items. Alternately, the most problematic items are those that rely on intricate presentation/garnishing, or contain ingredients that quickly melt, congeal, discolor, or lose texture. During planning and development stages, all recipes should be tested under field conditions to assure the product integrity meets customer expectations.

Space utilization can be maximized when facilities are used to serve meals off premise. Take-away dining effectively expands service capacity without the cost of dedicating additional seating space. Finally, from a psychological marketing perspective, carryout meals, once within the home, extend branding and persistence of marketing messages. Condiments, packaging, and printed collateral material all have shelf life and can provide a subtle yet effective reminder that can prompt return visits and future purchases.

MENUS IN SUPERMARKETS

Historically, supermarkets were used by consumers to obtain ingredients to prepare meals at home. During the late-1980s, restaurants were confronted with competition from supermarkets in the form of home-meal replacement. In an increasingly astute fashion, supermarkets began to package and sell ready-to-eat portions of entrées, appetizers, and desserts. Thus it became possible to enjoy restaurant-quality meals at home with a minimum of effort (or a dearth of culinary skills). To appreciate the paradigm shift, it should be noted that Americans once visited pizzeria restaurants to dine in or take away their favorite pies, yet today nearly half of the pizzas consumed are now baked fresh in grocery stores rather than restaurants. Figure 2-7 illustrates seasonal and family meals available from a regional grocery chain.

Supermarkets aren't the only retailers that encroach on restaurant market share. Convenience stores, gas stations, and drug stores such as Walgreens have deployed made-to-order and prepackaged concepts to capture customers that might otherwise patronize traditional dining rooms and food-service options. Whether prepared and served by a traditional restaurant, supermarket, or retail store, a primary challenge is to retain palatability and food quality. For certain recipes, this translates to fully cooked foods sold chilled that must be reheated prior to service; other foods are sold hot and are ready to eat on purchase. Careful menu selection by operators and skilled recipe development by chefs ensures that the right items are merchandised for transit and off-premise consumption.

To further illuminate the inventive competition for customer patronage, in a strategic twist that blurs definitions, today's supermarkets increasingly provide

---

EXERCISE 2-1
PLANNING MENUS FOR SPECIFIC DEMOGRAPHICS

1. Select a hyperlink listed in the Chapter 1 Action Toolkit to research zip (postal) code 33027. Based on this population and their specific demographics, create a list of 10 menu items appropriate for a take-away menu at a restaurant, supermarket, or other foodservice in that area.

2. Select a hyperlink listed in the Chapter 1 Action Toolkit to research zip (postal) code 95448. Based on this population

and their specific demographics, create a list of 10 menu items appropriate for a take-away menu at a restaurant, supermarket, or other foodservice in that area.

3. Compare and contrast the two menus and explain the impact of market characteristics on your decision making. What features are unique among your 20 menu items? What features do the items have in common?

(*Source:* SVLuma/Shutterstock)

aesthetic dining space not unlike a restaurant. As discussed in Chapter 7, these enhanced dining experiences are increasingly complemented with music and other entertainment and lifestyle events, with the result of redefining the role of supermarkets in the consumer visitation routine.

FOOD TRUCKS

For decades, mobile food trucks have provided hot meals to construction sites, fairgrounds, and various other outdoor events. Much of the food has been modest in scope; however, recent trends illustrate the public's eagerness to explore exotic, if not cutting-edge menu items sold across the counters of next-generation food trucks. In fact, in 2010, *Food and Wine* magazine named a California food truck owner one of the 10 best new chefs of the year. The trend in upscale food trucks began on the West Coast in Los Angeles, San Francisco, and Portland, and soon spread east to Chicago, New York City, and points in between. Chef–operators find the venture appealing, because they do not have to establish restaurants in traditional high-rent corridors; rather, they can lease commissary space and bring their trucks to the customers. The startup costs for these businesses are considerably less than a brick-and-mortar establishment, and this mode of food service is increasingly attractive to entrepreneurs. The relatively low capital and operating costs invite culinary risk-taking that might otherwise not occur in more traditional establishments.

Customers follow the businesses on Twitter and other social media to obtain real-time updates (*tweets*) on the whereabouts of these rolling kitchens. The menus are varied, yet exhibit playfulness and a desire to break culinary rules. Perhaps the defining culinary characteristic of food trucks relates to the need for uncompromising food quality. Whereas traditional restaurants provide a blend of table service and surroundings designed for a hospitable experience, the food truck transaction solely involves food-to-go. Consequently, the quality of the food must be impeccable. The food need not be gourmet in the traditional sense; however, many operators have elected to build their menus around specialty ingredients or juxtaposed gastronomic genres. A recent scan of menus includes kosher tacos, Korean barbeque short ribs, Taiwanese bubble tea, South American *arepas*, organic vegan soups and entrees, Jamaican jerk chicken *dosas*, Vietnamese *banh mi* sandwiches, *shawarma*, artisanal hamburgers, *falafel*, and brochettes of every conceivable ingredient. If there is a unifying menu theme, it is the appeal of street foods that lend themselves to simplicity and casual dining. The nonconformist nature of the food-truck movement points to a retreat from formality and an embrace of bold tastes that prevail without the trappings of traditional table service.

Lest you think that the food-truck domain belongs solely to independent operators, it is important to acknowledge the entry into this niche by chains such as Qdoba, Sizzler, Dairy Queen, and Gold Star Chili. As is the case with upstart chef–operators, these chains strive to extend their presence by selling selected items around and about the avenues, *sans* walls and physical addresses.

MENUS FOR BANQUETS AND EVENTS

Banquets allow diners with a common bond to enjoy collegial or celebratory meals together. The bond may involve being on the same sports team, attending a meeting or conference together, or celebrating a life-cycle event with friends and family. For example, the lucrative business of catering to weddings, bar/bat mitzvahs, and graduations is one of the most competitive segments of the hospitality industry.

Regardless of the occasion, there are several commonalities:

- Typically 8 or 10 diners are seated at round tables or at a conference-style banquet table, and the number of tables may range from a few to more than a hundred.
- If the menu is plated in the kitchen (as opposed to buffet style), then there are limits to personal decisions, and guests will likely have only the choice between two or three entrées. Generally, that is the only decision to be made, because only one appetizer selection and only one dessert selection typically is made available to the group.
- If the menu is served **buffet style**, there may be a greater range of selections; however, this is not always the case.
- From an operational point of view, there are economies of scale when preparing a limited selection of recipes.
- From a production planning point of view, a **guarantee** made by the client informs you of exactly how much food to purchase and prepare. As opposed to an *à la carte* restaurant menu where *mise en place* must be assembled in hopes that guest traffic will result in forecasted sales, banquets enable food preparation based on fairly exacting calculations.
- From a profit perspective, the guarantee made by the client assures agreed-on **revenue** regardless of how many guests attend the event.

Banquets may be served in restaurants and any other location permitted to accommodate groups. Large gatherings of hundreds or thousands of guests require specialized spaces, such as hotel ballrooms; convention centers; and tented, off-premise locations. These venues often charge a premium price because of their relative monopoly on large function space. Although this is not always the case, it is common for higher than market rate pricing to be charged by large banquet facilities. Outwardly, it may appear that banquets are a treasure trove for profit-minded operators; however, the challenge of serving quality food and beverage to large numbers of guests is formidable. Certain foods that are suitable for *a la carte* menus are too fragile or require unrealistically high levels of handwork for banquet service. Logistical planning is intricate, requiring production of large batches and assembly line plate-up.

Banquet meals are often preceded by receptions that encourage socialization and permit attendees to filter in and gather. Many reception foods are bite-size and easy to carry, which is particularly important when guests are circulating and holding a beverage in one hand. Other reception items are selected because the large (i.e., batch) quantity lends itself to dramatic presentation not achievable in *a la carte* service. Whole fish, entire bone-in roasts of poultry or meat, and themed stations generate excitement and provide an outlet for creativity. Consequently, reception menus are an important dimension of banquet catering. Figure 2-8 contains an excerpt from a banquet reception menu.

Popular reception menu items include:

- chilled shellfish on ice, including shrimp, oysters, clams, and crab
- caviar on ice
- smoked seafood, including shrimp, trout, or scallops
- garnished platters of smoked salmon fillets
- warm dips often blending vegetables and proteins such as seafood, poultry or ham
- tartlets, *barquettes,* or baked shells filled with savory mixtures
- skewered foods, including *brochettes* and *kebabs*
- scallops or water chestnuts wrapped in bacon
- *charcouterie*, including sliced sausages and ham, pâtés, and other cooked or processed meats
- domestic and imported cheese displays
- baked *brie en croute* with garnishes
- savory *strudel*
- stuffed mushroom caps
- globally themed displays, including potstickers, dumplings, *antipasti, tapas,* and *mezze*
- *Sushi* and *sashimi*
- miniature crab cakes
- puff pastry or *filo* wrapped around a savory filling
- raw or blanched vegetables, often referred to as *crudité*
- flatbreads and *bruschetta*
- petite sandwiches
- live-action stations, where food is carved, including bone-in ham and roast meats or poultry
- raw bars, where shellfish are shucked and cracked to order
- regionally themed displays that are location appropriate (low-country coastal cuisine, California wine country fare, etc.)

The preceding list includes fairly typical reception foods; however, this is an area where creativity and drama may also be invited. Dialogue with the client during planning stages is the key to creating an effective and memorable reception menu. Ambitious caterers often approach clientele without specific menus and develop the event through client-driven discourse. Certainly, clients must be guided lest they stray toward menus that are susceptible to failures; however, collaboration can result in customized solutions that produce delicious and memorable results.

The creativity often found in banquet receptions is typically more restrained during the meal proper because of the need for a generally popular and acceptable menu that appeals to a broad audience of diners. The larger the group, the more diverse are the food likes and dislikes; consequently, the more conservative the menu will be. Whereas banquet meals certainly call for quality, they do not demand unbridled inventiveness, unless the group is relatively homogeneous (and adventurous) in

reception

Meal Additions

(Reception Station pricing is based upon a 60 minute service period)

Butler Passed Hot Hors D'oeuvres
Vegetable Spring Roll
Mini Beef Wellington
Teriyaki Glazed Beef Satay
Brie and Almond in Puff Pastry
Chicken Satay with Thai Peanut Sauce
Spanakopita
Pecan Chicken Tender
$6 Each

Coconut Shrimp
Shrimp Quesadilla
Rueben Mini
Crispy Bacon Wrapped Scallop
Spicy Beef Empanada
Fresh Vegetable Empanada
Portobello Mushroom Tart
$6.50 Each

Vidalia Onion Bisque Shooter
Butternut Squash Shooter
Roasted Tomato Bisque Shooter
Chili-Lime Salmon Skewer
Petite Lamb Chops with Fresh Rosemary
BBQ Duck Roll in Chinese Pancake
Mini Jumbo Lump Crab Cake
$7 Each

Butler Passed Chilled Canapés
Chicken Mango in Endive
Bruschetta Rosso
Boursin Cheese Crisp
Mini Potato Pancake with Sour Cream and Caviar
Red Pepper Hummus on Pita Chip
Asparagus Wrapped Prosciutto Ham
Beef Carpaccio with Horseradish Cream
$6 Each

Shrimp BLT's on Crostini
Chilled California Roll
Smoked Salmon on Pumpernickel and Dill CreamCheese
Petite Caesar Salad in Filo Cup
Peking Duck Roll
Risotto Arancini with Spicy Marinara
$6.50 Each

Pepper Crusted Ahi Tuna with Wasabi Crème
Honeydew Melon with Blueberry Shooter
Strawberry Mint Shooter
Ceviche Shooter
Gazpacho Shooter with Vodka-Lime Marinated Shrimp
Jumbo Shrimp Cocktail
Lobster Club
$7 Each

All prices are subject to a taxable 22% Service Charge
and 10% DC Sales Tax

OMNI ❖ HOTELS & RESORTS
shoreham | washington dc
20

reception

Reception A La Carte

(Reception Station pricing is based upon a 60 minute service period)

International Cheese Display

Assorted Cheeses to Include:

Large Display $1250 (Serves 100 Guests)

Medium Display $625 (Serves 50 Guests)

Saga Blue, Port-Salute, Bel Paese, Jarlsberg, Havarti, Brie, Boursin, Goat Cheese and Gouda

Decorated with Grapes and Strawberries

Served with Assorted Water Crackers and Sliced French Baguettes

Display of Artesian American Cheese

Medium Display $750 (Serves 50 Guests)

Iowa Maytag Blue, Vermont Goat, Grafton Two Year Old Cheddar

Maryland's Talbot Reserve, California's Winchester Cumin Gouda

Decorated with Dry Fruit, Mixed Nuts and Honey

Market Display of Fresh Vegetables Crudités

Large Display $1000 (Serves 100 Guests)

Medium Display $500 (Serves 50 Guests)

Zucchini, Broccoli, Radishes, Peppers, Celery, Cauliflower, Baby Carrots and Cucumbers

Served with Curried Yogurt Dip and Blue Cheese Dip

Mosaic of Fresh Fruit

Large Display $900 (Serves 100 Guests)

Medium Display $450 (Serves 50 Guests)

Golden Pineapple, Honeydew, Cantaloupe, Strawberries And Seasonal Fruits and Berries

Mezze

Large Display $1300 (Serves 100 Guests)

Medium Display $650 (Serves 50 Guests)

Grilled Eggplant, Summer Squash with Roasted Peppers, Artichoke Salad and Stuffed Grape Leaves, Tabbouleh Salad, Kalamata Olives, Hummus and Baba Ghanoush with Pita Crisps

All prices are subject to a taxable 22% Service Charge
and 10% DC Sales Tax

OMNI ❖ HOTELS & RESORTS
shoreham | washington dc
21

Figure 2-8
Omni Shoreham Hotel Banquet Reception Menu, Washington, DC   (*Source:* Reprinted by permission of Omni Shoreham Hotel)

reception

Reception A La Carte

Service Periods are One Hour and a Half to Two Hours

All Carving Stations will have appropriate Rolls and Condiments. Carving Stations require One Attendant per 100 Guests at $175 per Attendant

Steamship of Beef $1400 (Serves 100 Guests)

Beef Strip Loin $800 (Serves 50 Guests)

Bone-In Prime Rib $725 (Serves 35 Guests)

Peppercorn Crusted Whole Tenderloin $625 (Serves 25 Guests)

Sage Rubbed Whole Turkey $800 (Serves 50 Guests)

Honey Glazed Ham $600 (Serves 50 Guests)

Maple Glazed Pork Loin $500 (Serves 40 Guests)

Sesame Seared Tuna Loin $600 (Serves 40 Guests)

Mediterranean Stuffed Salmon Roulade with Kalamata Olives, Feta Cheese, Spinach and Artichoke $275 (Serves 15 Guests)

All prices are subject to a taxable 22% Service Charge and 10% DC Sales Tax

OMNI HOTELS & RESORTS
shoreham | washington dc

23

reception

Meal Additions

Chef Attended Stations

Reception Station pricing is based upon 1 Hour of Service

Chef Attended Stations Requires 1 Attendant per 100 Guests at $175 per Attendant

Chesapeake Station $32 per Guest

Based Upon One (1) Piece per Person

Cold Display of Shrimp Cocktail and Oysters on the Half Shell

Hot Display of Mini Crab Cakes and Clams Casino

Cocktail Sauce, Remoulade and Mignonette

New York, New York $24 per Guest

Make Your Own Deli Sandwiches with:

New York Deli Hot Dogs

Hand Carved Corned Beef and Pastrami

Also served with Warm Sauerkraut, Thousand Island, Hot Mustard, Swiss Cheese,

Crisp Dill Pickles and Rye Rolls

Cole Slaw and Potato Salad

All prices are subject to a taxable 22% Service Charge and 10% DC Sales Tax

OMNI HOTELS & RESORTS
shoreham | washington dc

24

Figure 2-8
Continued

food preferences. In addition, food may be thought of as fashion, and fashions change over time, so it is unwise to be overly prescriptive. Balance is the key when planning banquet meals. Recipes containing lamb, game, and seafood are less typical, whereas poultry and beef appeal to a broader audience. Vegan and vegetarian options should also be available, because there are often diners who choose not to eat animal proteins. Banquet staff should be knowledgeable of the ingredients in the recipes they are serving, in case they must respond to questions relating to food allergies and sensitivities.

Menus for banquet meals are highly influenced by daypart as well as the function they are to support. Whereas most banquet breakfasts require speed and short duration (to facilitate conduct of meetings), other catered breakfasts may involve award ceremonies or support presentations by keynote speakers. Consequently, a variety of breakfast menus should be made available for clients to choose from. Breakfast menus often include eggs, pancakes, waffles, french toast, and meats such as bacon ham or sausage. Potatoes and grains such as grits or oatmeal are also popular. Fresh fruit juices and yogurt are typical in banquet breakfasts, as are coffee and hot tea. These items are breakfast classics and don't challenge the sensibilities of large groups and their inherent diversity. Embellishments may be appropriate, including made-to-order espresso drinks and Belgian waffle stations; however, variety often translates to greater service demands and possibility of slower service patterns. Figure 2-9 illustrates a typical banquet breakfast menu.

Menus for banquet lunches are governed by similar logic. Often, banquet lunches follow morning meetings and are, in turn, followed by afternoon meetings. Because their purpose is sustenance and respite, more so than celebration, practical function is the rule. As with banquet breakfasts, creativity and quality are appropriate, but adventurous selections usually take a back seat to established crowd pleasers (Figure 2-10).

Popular banquet lunches include:

- sandwiches on bread or croissants
- boxed lunches that allow for busy agendas
- pasta dishes
- chicken-based dishes
- deli-style meat and cheese platters
- creative vegetarian entrées
- entrée salads, often including cooked proteins such as chicken or beef
- smaller-size portions of dinner entrees

Often, banquet lunches include a soup, salad, or other appetizer that precedes the entrée, and pie, cake, or a fruit dessert that follows the entrée.

Banquet dinners typically end a day's activities, and are often more celebratory in nature than breakfast or lunch. If we think of lunches as functional, then dinners should be positioned as memorable. There is usually less of an agenda-based time demand, and more elaborate courses may be appropriate. Popular banquet dinner menus include:

- creative appetizers
- soups
- salads
- chicken-based entrées
- beef entrées
- fish entrées
- protein combinations such as "surf and turf" or mixed grills
- live-action stations where food is carved, including bone-in ham and roast meats or poultry
- regionally themed plated meals and buffets that are location appropriate

Breakfast Buffets

Morning Glory
Orange and Grapefruit Juices
Seasonal Fresh Fruit
Assortment of Breakfast Pastries and Bagels
Sweet Butter, Fruit Preserves, Whipped Cream Cheeses
Freshly Brewed Regular and Decaffeinated Illy Coffee
Assortment of Gourmet Teas
18 per person
(10 person minimum)

Calm Water Spa
Orange and Grapefruit Juices
Juice (select one): Cantaloupe or Watermelon
Seasonal Soymilk Bichermuesli
Fruit and Berries (in season)
Individual Plain, Low Fat and Fruit Yogurts
Hard Boiled Eggs
Assorted Harvest Cereals with Whole and Skim Milk
Assorted Bagels
Sweet Butter, Fruit Preserves, Whipped Cream Cheeses
Freshly Brewed Regular and Decaffeinated Illy Coffee
Assortment of Gourmet Teas
20 per person
(10 person minimum)

Bagel Bar
Orange, Grapefruit and Cranberry Juice
Fresh Fruit Salad
Assorted Bagels
Smoked Salmon Accoutrements of Capers, Shaved Red Onion, Hard Boiled Egg
and Snipped Chives
Flavored Cream Cheeses to include: Chive, Seasonal Berry and Lowfat
Margarine and Fruit Preserves
Freshly Brewed Regular and Decaffeinated Illy Coffee
Assortment of Gourmet Teas
22 per person
(10 person minimum)

All menus are subject to 21% service charge and 7.5% tax

Figure 2-9
Hawks Cay Banquet Breakfast Menu, Duck Key, Florida   (*Source:* Reprinted by permission of Hawks Cay)

Breakfast Enhancements
Hot Oatmeal, Candied Pecans, Light Cream, Soft Brown Sugar, Raisins
6 per person

"The Baked Three Potato Hash Brown"
8 per person

Omelet Station
Fresh Farm Eggs, Egg Beaters and Egg Whites,
Country Ham, Bell Peppers, Scallions, Wild Mushrooms, Tomatoes, Swiss and Cheddar Cheeses
$150 Chef Fee
14 per person

Ginger Cinnamon Spiced French Toast or
Buttermilk and Blueberry Pancakes
Strawberry Whipped Cream, Maple Syrup
12 per person

Trio of Smoked Salmon, Accoutrements of Capers
Shaved Red Onion, Flavored Cream Cheeses
Hard Boiled Egg, Snipped Chives
Assorted Bagels
14 per person

Granola Yogurt Parfaits with Seasonal Berries
8 per person

Belgian Waffle Bar
Chocolate Chips, Fruit Compote, Maple Syrup
Whipped Cream
12 per person

All menus are subject to 21% service charge and 7.5% tax

Figure 2-9
Continued

Lunch Buffets
20 person minimum

Key Colony
Caprese Salad
Antipasto Platter

Pasta: Choice of Two
Cheese Tortellini, Whole Wheat Penne or Mushroom Ravioli
Sauces: Choice of Two
Tomato-Basil, Alfredo with Snipped Chives, Genovese Pesto
with Sun-dried Tomatoes or Veal Bolognese

Roasted Chicken, Eggplant Caponata

Broccoli and Fennel Sausage

Olive and Tomato Focaccia

Tiramisu, and Panna Cotta

Freshly Brewed Regular and Decaffeinated Illy Coffee
Assortment of Gourmet Teas
40 per person

Grassy Key
Salad of Baby Greens, Candied Pecans, Dried Cherries, Goat Cheese
Passion Fruit Papaya Vinaigrette

Marinated Chicken Breast
Pearl Onions, Field Mushrooms and Green Beans in a Chicken Jus

Gulf Snapper Almondine

Provencal Herb-Roasted Potatoes

Butter-Braised Carrots and Haricot Verte

Grand Marnier Marinated Red Fruits and Crème Chantilly
Dark Chocolate Tart

Freshly Brewed Regular and Decaffeinated Illy Coffee
Assortment of Gourmet Teas
42 per person

All menus are subject to 21% service charge and 7.5% tax

Figure 2-10
Hawks Cay Banquet Lunch Menu, Duck Key, Florida   (*Source:* Reprinted by permission of Hawks Cay)

Plated Lunch
Luncheons include Freshly Baked Bread Basket with Butter
Three Course 48 per person

Soups (Please Choose One)
Yellow Tomato and Mango Gazpacho

Bone Island Chowder

Black Bean Soup

Florida Lobster Bisque

Salads (Please Choose One)
Seasonal Local Farmer Greens, Cured Tomato, Aged Red Wine Vinaigrette

Romaine Hearts, Caesar Dressing, Parmesan, Black Pepper Crouton

Iceberg Wedge BLT Salad, Blue Cheese Dressing

Tropical Fruit Salad, Mango, Papaya, and Pineapple
Cherry Tomato, Arugula and Frisee, Key Lime Vinaigrette

Entrees (Please Choose One)
Mushroom Ravioli, Baby Vegetables, Crushed Tomato, Shallots

Teriyaki Snapper, Steamed Gingered Bok Choy in Oyster Sauce, Coconut Jasmine Rice

Crispy Bacon Wrapped Mahi Mahi, Conch and Chorizo Fried Rice, Key Lime Beurre Blanc

Honey Thyme-Roasted Chicken Supreme, Chive Mashed Potatoes, Garden Vegetables

Four Pepper Crusted Petit Tenderloin, Basil Pesto Roasted Potato, Pearl Onions,
Buttered Asparagus, Pinot Noir Jus

Dessert (Please Choose One)
Key Lime Pie
Fresh Berry Tart with Chocolate Sauce
Praline Chocolate Crunch, Vanilla Anglaise
Freshly Brewed Regular and Decaffeinated Illy Coffee
Assortment of Gourmet Teas

Figure 2-10
Continued

Figure 2-11
Viennese table
(*Source:* giemmephoto/Fotolia)

Large numbers of assembled diners present unique options for creative desserts that might otherwise not be feasible. Examples of banquet desserts include:

- buffets with fountains of molten chocolate accompanied by fruit and cake for dipping
- *Viennese tables* and buffets of petite desserts (Figure 2-11)
- action stations with the drama of flambé and culinary theater

Desserts of this nature serve the additional function of reinvigorating socialization, as diners arise and visit the stations along with guests from other dinner tables.

The need for diversion and rest periods during meetings and conferences offers the opportunity to sell coffee breaks and other between-meal menus. Figure 2-12 illustrates a full spectrum of break options. The potential for break revenue cannot be underestimated. Breaks are sold in two ways:

- *Per person*, where beverages and food items are sold based on a guaranteed number of guests. Breaks of this nature provide operators with set amount of revenue, and allow clients unlimited quantities.
- *By the unit*, such as gallons of coffee or dozens of muffins. This arrangement requires monitoring of consumption, and sales are not known until all consumed quantities are calculated.

Both approaches have their merits, and the choice of options may be important to the client who requires the certainty of guaranteed charges, prefers to pay only for what is consumed, or is otherwise predisposed because of personal preferences.

The most popular non-alcoholic beverages for banquets are cold and hot teas, sodas (pop), and coffee.

Alcoholic beverage selections for banquets are similar to those in restaurants; however, the breadth and scope of any one banquet bar is considerably more limited. Whereas a restaurant may offer upward of 20 beer varieties, most banquets limit selections to less than five. Similarly, clients may choose two or three wines to pour

breaks

Break Packages

(Break Packages are designed for a 60 minute service period.)

Georgetown Park $24 Per Guest

Homemade Scones Served with Whipped Butter and Preserves

Assorted Finger Sandwiches to Include:

Chicken Salad

Smoked Turkey

Smoked Salmon

Vegetable with Cream Cheese

French Pastries and Chocolate Dipped Strawberries

A Selection of Tazo® and Herbal Teas with Lemon & Honey

Dupont Circle $19 Per Guest

Mixed Nuts, Granola Bars, Terra Chips

Crisp Vegetable Crudités with Low Fat Yogurt Dip

Sliced Seasonal Fruits and Berries

Assorted Mineral Waters, Bottled Fruit and Vegetable Juices

Woodley Park Zoo $18 Per Guest

Individually Bagged Animal Crackers

White Cheddar and Caramel Flavored Popcorn

Warm Soft Pretzels with Gourmet Deli Mustard and Spicy Cheese Dip

Tortilla Chips with Salsa

Assorted Soft Drinks

Sweet Treat $17 Per Guest

Chef's Selection of Assorted Cookies

Freshly Brewed Starbucks® Organic Shade Grown Regular and Decaffeinated Coffee

A Selection of Tazo® Teas with Lemon and Honey

Assorted Soft Drinks

All prices are subject to a taxable 22% Service Charge and 10% DC Sales Tax

OMNI HOTELS & RESORTS
shoreham | washington dc

8

---

breaks

Refreshment Breaks

A la Carte Items

(A la carte Breaks are designed for a 30 minute service period.)

Break items must be ordered for the entire group

Assorted Breakfast Pastries $58 per dozen

Variety of Bagels with Toaster Station and Cream Cheese Trio $58 per dozen

Freshly Baked Blueberry Scones with Sweet Butter and Preserves $58 per dozen

Homemade Coconut Ginger Granola Bars or Warm Cinnamon Buns $48 per Dozen

French Pastries and Miniature Fruit Tarts $60 per Dozen

Kitchen Sink Brownies
Caramel, Chocolate Chip, White Chocolate Chip and Chocolate Fudge $56 per Dozen

Chef's Selection of Assorted Cookies $56 per Dozen

Soft Bavarian Pretzels Served Warm with Assorted Gourmet Mustards $54 per Dozen

Beverage Selection

Freshly Brewed Starbucks® Organic Shade Grown Coffee and Assorted Tazo® Teas $87 per Gallon

Hot Chocolate served with Gourmet Marshmallows and Chocolate Shavings $85 per Gallon

Tropical Fruit Punch, Iced Tea, or Lemonade $65 per Gallon

Freshly Squeezed Orange and Grapefruit Juices $90 Gallon

Whole, Skim and Chocolate Milk $4.50 Each

Assorted Coca-Cola® Soft Drinks $5 Each

Gatorade®, Red Bull or Energy Drink $6.25 Each

Still Water - Deer Park $5 Each

Still Water - Aqua Panna, Sparkling- San Pellegrino $6.25 Each

All prices are subject to a taxable 22% Service Charge and 10% DC Sales Tax

OMNI HOTELS & RESORTS
shoreham | washington dc

9

Figure 2-12
Omni Shoreham Hotel Break Menu, Washington, DC   (*Source:* Reprinted by permission of Omni Shoreham Hotel)

Figure 2-12
Continued

(*Source:* Lucky Dragon/Fotolia)

AUTHOR'S INSIGHT

Savvy operators have capitalized on opportunities to pro-vide memorable beverage menus at banquets. One of my favorite presentations involved a massive bar constructed solely of ice from which a variety of chilled vodkas were served. Reservoirs were bored into the bar and the contents of the bottles themselves flowed through the ice, ultimately delivering chilled shots to amazed guests. The mist, the backlighting, and sheer spectacle of the bar demonstrate the potential for creative banquet beverage service.

for the entire group. When spirits are served, they likely feature five or six choices with a few mixers. It is not practical to replicate a full bar in a banquet setting.

Alcoholic beverages served at banquets may be paid for by the client or by the guests. General classifications of banquet bars are as follows:

- *Host bars,* where clients are charged by the person times the duration of the event. The client pays fixed charges regardless of how much is consumed and clients can be certain of their bill prior to the event.
- *Consumption bars,* where hosts are charged by the number of bottles or ounces consumed.
- *Cash bars,* where guests purchase their own drinks.

Not surprisingly, the same beverages can be used on any of these bars; only the billing arrangement varies.

Popular banquet bars include:

- sparkling wine and champagne fountains
- wine bars
- beer-centric themes for sports banquets
- "martini" bars using stemmed cocktail glasses to serve all types of spirits
- globally themed bars featuring *sake* or *soju, caiprihinas,* and rum-based tropical drinks

EXERCISE 2-2
PLANNING THEMED BANQUET MENUS

Research the foodways of one of the following countries, and create a reception and banquet buffet menu (food and beverages). Explain your rationale for selections.

- Switzerland
- Morocco
- Scotland

EXERCISE 2-3
PLANNING MEETING BREAKS

Create an appropriate 2-day set of break menus to support a business meeting for 75 male and female attendees. Assume the following meeting scenario:

- Monday plated breakfast   7:30 AM to 8:15 AM
- Monday box lunch   12:00 PM to 1:00 PM
- Monday cocktail reception   6:30 PM to 7:15 PM
- Monday buffet dinner   7:15 PM to 8:30 PM

- Tuesday continental breakfast   7:30 AM to 8:15 AM
- Tuesday awards luncheon   12:00 PM to 1:30 PM

The 75 attendees are a group of executive men and women between the ages of 27 and 60. In addition to planning the break menus, explain the rationale for your selections and how they fit into the entire 2-day activities.

(*Source:* stefanolunardi/Shutterstock)

MENUS FOR HOTEL IN-ROOM DINING

Whether referred to as *room service* or *in-room dining,* the attempt to provide food and beverage in guestrooms is an ambitious endeavor. Hotel guest rooms and suites are purpose built for sleeping, lounging, dressing, and other lodging functions. Whereas some suites are furnished with tables and chairs that approximate those found in restaurant dining rooms, most rooms are furnished with a modest desk that serves multiple purposes, with dining not particularly high on the list. A dining room facsimile must be created by delivering food and beverages and all service *mise en place* to provide a seamless dining experience. Figure 2-13 illustrates an effective upscale in-room dining menu that relies on a minimum of verbiage and graphics. Figure 2-14 shows photos and flourished language to merchandise room service.

Food recipes and food items that may be appropriate for dining room service may not be suitable for in-room dining. Although not comprehensive, Table 2-1 identifies concerns that must be managed if quality is to be provided consistently.

Because hunger strikes different guests at different times, it is necessary to provide room service menus for each daypart. Tastes change and business concepts are highly individualized, so this text does not prescribe specific menu items. Nonetheless, because of their widespread appeal and stability for delivery to rooms, there are certain ingredients and preparations that are better suited for in-room dining:

- salads and raw vegetables—sturdy ingredients, including root vegetables, tubers, and tomatoes

EXERCISE 2-4
CONTROLLING QUALITY OF IN-ROOM DINING MENU ITEMS

For each of the potential problems listed in Table 2-1, identify how you can serve these foods successfully by implementing creative and verifiable controls.

IN-ROOM DINING BREAKFAST (6:30 AM - 11:00 AM)

CONTINENTAL BREAKFAST   16
*Choice of chilled fruit juices, three pastry items, cereal,
fruit cup and coffee or tea*

AMERICAN BREAKFAST   21
*Choice of chilled fruit juices, to eggs any style, choice of
breakfast meat, breakfast potatoes, muffin, Danish or
toast with coffee or tea*

COFFEE & MORE

THE JUICE BAR   5
*Kennesaw Fresh Florida Orange,
Kennesaw Fresh Grapefruit, Cranberry,
Tomato and Pineapple*

A Pot of Regular or Decaf Coffee   12

Espresso   4

Assorted Gourmet Teas   4

Soft Drinks & Iced Tea   4

Fiji Water   4/9

San Pellegrino   4/9

Red Bull Energy Drink   5

Milk   4

EYE OPENING COCKTAILS

Mimosa   10
Prosecco sparking wine, fresh florida orange juice

Bloody Mary   10
*Absolut vodka accompanied by traditional
bloody mary mix*

Seabreeze   10
Absolut vodka, cranberry and grapefruit Juice

Screwdriver   10
Absolut vodka, fresh florida orange juice

Irish Coffee   8
Irish whiskey with regular or decaffeinated coffee

STARTERS

Assorted Cereals and Organic Kashi   6

Steel Cut Irish Oatmeal   11
Raisins and brown sugar

Bircher Muesli   9
Banana and berries

Seasonal Fruit Bowl with Yogurt   12

Banana Split   9
Berries, vanilla bean yogurt, granola sprinkles

Artisanal Smoked Salmon   18
Toasted bagel and traditional accompaniments

W.O.W. INSPIRATIONS

Power Breakfast Smoothie   8
*Non fat yogurt, acai, soy milk, blueberries,
banana, protein burst, organic agave syrup*

Tropical Smoothie   8
Soymilk, pineapple, banana, coconut

Homemade Granola   9
Berries, yogurt, milk

Organic Herb Garden Egg White Omlete   15

Whole Wheat Breakfast Wrap   15
Scrambled egg whites, turkey, low fat cheese, greens

Complete Spa Breakfast   17
*Organic herb garden egg white omelet with choice of
fresh fruit or yogurt, multigrain toast, juice and small pot
of coffee or tea*

Special Dietary needs can be accommodated

Figure 2-13
PGA National Resort and Spa In-Room Dining Menu, Palm Beach Gardens, Florida   (*Source:* Reprinted by permission of PGA National Resort & Spa)

MAINS

Turkey Pot Pie   17
Flaky puff pastry, vegetables, spinach,

Bear Trap Fish and Chips   19
Remoulade, malt vinegar, hand cut fries

Shepherd's Pie   22
Chef Gordon's family recipe

Catch of the Day   24

Half Roast Chicken   22
Baked potatoe, tomato gratin

Steak Frites   34
*Grilled 12oz NY steak, Tuscan hand cut fries,
Tomato gratin*

DESSERT

Layer Chocolate Cake, Chocolate Sauce   7

Strawberry Cheese Cake   7

Warm Apple Pie, Caramel Sauce   7

Key Lime Pie, Mango Passion Fruit Sauce 7

Warm Brownie, Vanilla Ice Cream   7

Ice Cream and sorbets   7

KIDS ALL DAY MENU
All served with apple sauce and side of broccoli

Chicken or Cheese Quesadillas   7
 sour cream, salsa and guacamole

Chicken Tenders   7
(Baked or Fried), french fries, BBQ

Cheese or Pepperoni Pizza   7

Macaroni and Cheese   7

Grilled Cheese Sandwich   7

Kids Burger   7

Hot Dog   7

Peanut Butter & Jelly Sandwich   7

Milk or Chocolate Milk   4

Milk Shake   6
(Strawberry, vanilla or chocolate)

Soft Drinks & Iced Tea   4

Juices   4
Orange, grapefruit, apple, cranberry,

Please inform us of any dietary restrictions so we may do our best to accommodate your needs.

18% Gratuity, $3.00 per room surcharge and 6.0% Florida Sales Tax will be added to all guests checks

Consuming raw or undercooked meats, poultry, seafood, shellfish or eggs may increase your risk of food borne illness, especially if you have certain medical conditions

Figure 2-13
Continued

IDAHO SIGNATURES

We are proud to support our community by serving products produced in our region.
ADD TWO EGGS TO ANY ORDER ~ 3.00

IDAHO HUCKLEBERRY PANCAKES

Our signature breakfast item offers a delightful taste of Idaho's mountain fruit - the wild huckleberry. Accompanied by your choice of bacon or sausage. ~14.00

POTATO BENEDICT

Idaho potato skins topped with scrambled eggs, ham, bacon, sausage, Cheddar cheese and Hollandaise sauce. Served with hash browns. ~ 17.00

FRENCH TOAST COEUR D'ALENE

Thick-cut cinnamon-swirled bread grilled with shaved almonds, sweetened flakes and topped with wild huckleberry-raspberry purée. Served with your choice of sausage or bacon. ~ 14.50
Traditional French Toast also available. ~ 12.00

RUBY RED TROUT

Potato-crusted and served with hash browns and two eggs prepared to your specifications. ~ 17.00

MULTI-GRAIN PANCAKES

Produced right here in Coeur d'Alene by Heidi's Pancakes, these coarse-ground multi-grain pancakes have a nutty texture and full flavor with a hint of brown sugar. Rich with flax seeds and high-protein blue corn. ~ 12.00

CONTINENTAL BREAKFAST

Fresh-squeezed orange juice, fresh fruit plate, huckleberry muffin, strawberry cream cheese coffee cake and a pot of Starbucks® coffee. ~ 13.50

ON THE LIGHTER SIDE

HEALTHY START

Fresh-squeezed orange juice, choice of cold cereal or hot oatmeal with sun-dried cherries, apricots, raisins, brown sugar and 2% milk. Served with a fresh fruit plate and a pot of Starbucks® coffee. ~ 13.00

BAKERY FRESH BREAKFAST PASTRIES

Three Beverly's signature orange rolls
OR a muffin *(Your choice of huckleberry cream cheese, morning glory, cranberry bran with flax seed or blueberry)*
OR a bagel with cream cheese
OR two slices of toast. ~ 5.00

FRUIT AND YOGURT PARFAIT

Layers of fresh berries, organic almond granola and low fat yogurt. ~ 9.50

COEUR D'ALENE FRUIT PLATE

Pineapple, cantaloupe, honeydew, seasonal berries and fruit yogurt. ~ 9.50

CEREALS

Choose from homemade steel-cut oatmeal, Mueslix, Raisin Bran, Special K, Cocoa Puffs, Lucky Charms or Frosted Flakes. Accompanied by your choice of seasonal berries or sliced banana. ~ 8.00

A 3.50 service charge, 6% tax and 18% gratuity will be added to each order.

Figure 2-14
Coeur d'Alene Resort Room Service Menu, Coeur d'Alene, Idaho   *(Source: Reprinted by permission of Coeur d'Alene Resort)*

DINNER SELECTIONS

All selections are served with warm sourdough rolls and butter.
ADD AN ORGANIC FIELD GREENS SALAD TO ANY ENTRÉE ~ 4.00

RIB EYE STEAK
14 ounce steak with maitre d' butter, Idaho mashed potatoes and seasonal vegetables. ~ 36.00

NEW YORK STRIP STEAK
8 ounce steak grilled with a peppercorn demi glaze, rosemary red potatoes and seasonal vegetables. ~ 24.00

ALASKAN HALIBUT
Alaskan halibut with a Dungeness crab cake pan-seared with Yukon Gold potatoes, seasonal vegetables and lemon beurre blanc sauce. ~ 34.00

FRESH ATLANTIC SALMON
Served with fresh herb beurre blanc, jasmine rice and fresh seasonal vegetables. ~ 28.00

BEVERLY'S DUNGENESS CRAB CAKES
Two large crab cakes made with fresh Dungeness crab, accompanied by organic greens and a light citrus vinaigrette. ~ 20.00

MEDITERRANEAN CHICKEN
Marinated grilled chicken with our jasmine rice blend, combined with baby garbanzo beans, tomatoes, red onion and Kalamata olives. Served with grilled pita. ~ 22.00

SIGNATURE DESSERTS

IDAHO HUCKLEBERRY COBBLER
Baked with a strudel topping and served with vanilla ice cream. ~ 9.50

WARM SIGNATURE APPLE PIE
An individual deep dish apple pie with cinnamon streusel topping. Served warm with a scoop of vanilla ice cream. ~ 9.00

COEUR D'ALENE CHEESECAKE
Fresh from our Resort bakery, choice of huckleberry topping or fresh strawberries. ~ 9.00

TOLL HOUSE PIE
Warm chocolate chip pie, with M&M's®, walnuts, vanilla ice cream and Hershey's chocolate sauce. ~ 8.50

BUTTERFINGER SUNDAE
A really big treat for all ages. Chocolate and vanilla ice cream, topped with chocolate sauce, crushed Butterfinger® and whipped cream. ~ 8.50

HÄAGEN-DAZS® ICE CREAM
A full pint served in a silver bag. Ask for today's selections. ~ 8.00

CRÈME BRULEE
Creamy custard made with real vanilla beans and a caramelized sugar crust. ~ 8.00

"SIN-LESS" CHEESECAKE
"No Sugar Added" cheesecake, sweetened with Splenda® and baked in the Resort bakery. ~5.50

A 3.50 service charge, 6% tax and 18% gratuity will be added to each order.

Figure 2-14
Continued

ON THE GO

Get out and enjoy all Idaho has to offer and we will pack a picnic lunch for your adventure.
Allow one hour preparation time for your picnic.

ALL-AMERICAN PICNIC LUNCH

Choose from our selection of sandwiches or wraps. All selections will be
accompanied by Idaho potato salad, sliced fresh fruit, chocolate-dipped strawberries
and choice of bottled water or soft drink. ~ 19.99

CLASSIC SANDWICHES

Select Albacore tuna salad, smoked turkey,
roast beef or baked ham. Choose from Cheddar,
Swiss, Pepper Jack or American cheese on white,
wheat, sourdough or rye bread.

WRAPS

MEDITERRANEAN

Organic field greens, cucumber, Kalamata olives,
red onion, artichoke hearts, grilled peppers, Feta cheese,
olive tapenade, hummus and balsamic glaze.

CHICKEN CAESAR

Crisp hearts of romaine, grilled chicken breast, croutons
and Parmesan cheese tossed with Caesar dressing.

SMOKED TURKEY

Turkey, cheese, lettuce, tomato and mayo.

TURKEY, BACON, AVOCADO

Turkey, bacon, lettuce, tomato, sliced avocado and mayo.

ROASTED VEGGIE

Roasted peppers and zucchini with organic field greens
and green garbanzo bean hummus.

A PICNIC BY THE LAKE

A picnic lunch for two packed in a take-along basket complete with plastic tablecloth
Smoked buffalo sausage, venison smoked Cheddar salami, grilled pita with green garbanzo hummus,
romesco, olive tapenade, roasted garlic and caper berries, Gouda, Swiss, Cheddar and Boursin cheeses
and sliced baguette bread. Accompanied by two bottles of San Pellegrino and your choice of
two soft drinks or two bottled waters. ~ 38.00
ADD A BOTTLE OF OUR HOUSE-LABELED WINE FOR 15.00

KIDS' PICNIC LUNCH

Choose from ham, turkey, roast beef or peanut butter and jelly on white or wheat bread.
All selections are accompanied by fruit yogurt, snack apple, string cheese, fruit snacks,
choice of juice and an Idaho huckleberry chocolate bar. ~ 16.00

A 3.50 service charge, 6% tax and 18% gratuity will be added to each order.

Figure 2-14
Continued

TABLE 2-1
FOODS THAT MAY BE PROBLEMATIC FOR IN-ROOM DINING

Foods That May Be Problematic	Potential Problems
Starch-thickened sauces and soups	These items may congeal in transit from kitchen to guest room.
Thinly sliced protein items	The relatively high proportion of surface area cools rapidly and is prone to oxidative color changes and drying.
Strong-scented ingredients	Although desirable during one's meal, the aromas of garlic, onions, seafood, and other assertive foods may linger in an undesirable manner (above all, this is a sleeping room, too).
Intricately plated foods	Transport from the kitchen to guest rooms is likely to involve varying degrees of jiggling, bumping, and agitation. Intricately plated presentations may suffer, and although flavors may not be compromised, the appearance may not present as intended.
Poached, scrambled, or fried eggs	The tender nature of these items cannot be subjected to additional heat beyond the initial cooking.
Foams, such as whipped cream	The air beaten into these items may be lost over time and the foam may lose volume.
Emulsions	Unstable emulsions may separate.
Frozen desserts	Ice cream, sorbet, and frozen desserts may soften, melt, and run.

- solid cuts of proteins, rather than thin slices of meats and poultry
- moist-cooked recipes served as braises, stews, or casseroles
- frosted or iced desserts
- foods designed to be served at tepid temperatures, neither hot nor chilled

Often, pioneering trends found on restaurant tables are late to arrive on room-service menus. In fact, many room-service menus intentionally avoid novel food items so as to attract a middle market with "safe" items. Whereas this may not alienate large numbers of potential customers, it may fail to generate significant business and pales in comparison to progressive restaurant menus. Particularly at dinner, many hotel guests elect not to use room service, preferring to enjoy local tastes that are more prevalent in neighboring restaurants. Consequently, when conceiving tactics to increase sales per guest, hotel managers have begun to benchmark against best practices in restaurants and other foodservices. For example, many restaurant operators source organic ingredients and locally raised meat and poultry. The same ingredients are now finding their way onto in-room dining menus. In fact, during 2010, the Trump International Hotel & Tower Chicago became the first lodging property in the United States to introduce a certified organic room-service menu.

Although it is a concept that began in limited-service hotels, *grab-and-go* as a room service alternative has found its way into the entire spectrum of lodging properties, including luxury hotels and resorts. Whereas traditional in-room dining may be appropriate for certain properties, it is not without its problems. Operators struggle with inconsistent traffic volume and the cost of maintaining quality in-house delivery services. Guests bemoan the length of time required to obtain their meals and the often compromised food quality. Hotels and resorts historically have added service fees and gratuities that result in very expensive room-service food and beverage purchases. Many customers view this form of dining as a luxury, rather than a reasonable option. Alternatively, grab-and-go concepts offer hotel guests (and non-guests) opportunities to peruse the shelves of an in-house culinary marketplace for reasonably priced, ready-to-eat food and beverages that are suitable for in-room dining or enjoying elsewhere throughout the property. Aesthetic in-house marketplaces have emerged as a viable alternative to traditional in-room dining. For example, the Hyatt Corporation introduced "The Market" in the Grand Hyatt New York, as its foray into new in-room dining options. Its research indicated that customers preferred alternatives to traditional room service, and the hotel responded with an elegant space offering locally sourced, high-quality menu items. The proximity of the property to adjacent offices and residences enables the market to also serve non-guests seeking light meals, snacks, and home-meal replacement options at attractive price points throughout the day.

During the 1970s, many hotels invested in mini-bars/in-room entertainment centers. These credenzas with enclosed refrigerators provided on-demand snack foods as well as beverages and sundries. This merchandising method is not without problems. The privacy of the guest room allows tampering, and there are reported cases where packages have been opened and contents consumed, then the packaging was made to look as if no consumption occurred. Obviously, a thorough inventory is called for, which creates a significant problem—the marginal revenue from those sales does not always cover the time and expense of counting inventory. To reduce labor, technologies emerged whereby sensors indicated if products had been handled by guests, ostensibly equating to a sale. The manual or automated inventory recordkeeping is a significant consideration that operators must evaluate prior to investing capital for in-room mini-bars and entertainment centers.

An additional concern involves the unsupervised access to myriad alcoholic beverages. Most hotels restrict minors from access by not issuing a mini-bar key or code to underage guests; however, adults have unfettered access should they choose. The wisdom of stocking dozens of bottles of beer, wine, and spirits in guestrooms raises questions of legal liability should a guest hurt themselves or others. Since the early part of this century, several major hotel operators have made the decision to remove in-room entertainment centers from their properties for a variety of reasons. The reason most frequently cited was unsatisfactory **contribution margin**.

Hotels electing not to equip guestrooms with mini-bar supplies of snacks or beverages should investigate alternative revenue-producing opportunities. By definition, hotels receive travelers, and their arrivals may occur any time during the day or night. If the arrivals and check-in are coordinated with typical meal periods, then breakfast, lunch, or dinner menus suit nicely. Nonetheless, some guests arrive at non-mealtime hours or seek alternatives to conventional meals, which presents opportunities for sales of other profitable menu items, such as appetizer items and snacks. The Walt Disney World Swan and Dolphin Resort in Orlando, Florida, capitalizes on this revenue opportunity by providing guests with a customized shopping list specially selected by guests for their stay. The 24-hour *Personal Pantry* service enables guests to place orders for beverages, cereals, milk, and snack foods prior to their arrival or during their stay. Hotel staff stocks the room at a pre-designated time, permitting guests to enjoy their vacation without the need to venture to off-premise convenience stores. Competitive prices and freedom from service fees or delivery charges motivate customer purchases.

Even if beverages are not provided by an in-room mini-bar, there are other opportunities for alcoholic and nonalcoholic beverage sales to guestrooms. Menu planners should provide alternatives for guests who desire one drink or entire bottles. Figure 2-15 illustrates an in-room dining alcoholic beverage menu.

Figure 2-15
Coeur d'Alene Resort Room
Service Beverage and
Catering Menu, Coeur
d'Alene, Idaho
(*Source:* Reprinted by permission of
Coeur d'Alene Resort)

BEVERAGE & CATERING MENU

If you are entertaining in your room, our professional Room Service team can provide both
food and refreshments for any occasion. Dial 27 for assistance.

COCKTAILS

COEUR D'ALENE RUM RUNNER
Rum, blackberry juice, Peach Schnapps, pineapple and orange juice with a float of Myers Rum.

BREEZY COLADA
A frozen creamy colada with Malibu Rum.

THE CUCUMBER WHITE COSMOPOLITON
This cocktail adds new flavor to an old favorite. Fressh cucumber muddled with
Kettle 1 Citroen vodka and white cranberry juice. Very refreshing and unique.

BEVERLY'S SPLASH
Grey Goose L 'Orange mixed with peach schnapps and cranberry juice. Orange as a garnish.

THE FUITINI
A melody of infused vodka and fresh squeezed orange juice, and cranberry juice.

HUCKLEBERRY SPARKLER
Moet & Chandon "white Star" champagne adorned with fresh huckleberry, dancing to the bubbles.

COEUR D'ALENE SUNRISE
Malibu Rum, Triple Sec, orange and pineapple juice with a floater of grenadine.

SHAKERS

TRADITIONAL COSMOPOLITAN
Absolut, Triple Sec, cranberry juice and a hint of lime.

PEPPERMINT TWIST
Peppermint Schnapps, Kahlua, Crème de Cacao shaken and strained into a martini glass.

APPLETINI
Apple Pucker, vodka and a splash of sprite.

CHOCOLATE MARTINI
Kahlua, Stolichnaya Vanil Vodka, Godiva and a splash of cream.

BOTTLED BEER

MICRO BREWS	IMPORTED	MACRO BREWS
ALASKAN AMBER	HEINEKEN—Holland	BUDWEISER
BLACK BUTTE PORTER	AMSTEL LIGHT—Holland	BUD LIGHT
PYRAMID HEFEWEIZEN	CORONA—Mexico	COORS LIGHT
BRIDGEPORT IPA	KOKANEE—Canada	MILLER LITE
FAT TIRE	MODELO ESPECIAL—Mexcio	MICHELOB ULTRA

WINES BY THE GLASS

WHITE WINES	RED WINES
LATAH CREEK "HUCKLEBERRY RIESLING" 7 Glass 26 Bottle	PARKER STATION PINOT NOIR, California 7 Glass 26 Bottle
DR. LOOSEN RIESLING QBA, Mosel, Germany 2005 9 Glass 34 Bottle	ELK COVE PINOT NOIR, Willamette Valley 2004 16 Glass 52 Bottle
COEUR D'ALENE CELLARS BARREL ROOM WHITE, Columbia Valley 2004 9 Glass 34 Bottle	JIM BARRY SHIRAZ, Clare Valley Australia 10 Glass 38 Bottle
TENUTA SETTEN PINOT GRIGIO, Fiuiano, Italy 8 Glass 30 Bottle	WALLA WALLA VINTNER'S MERLOT, Columbia Valley 15 Glass 58 Bottle
GORDON BROTHERS CHARDONNAY, Columbia Valley 2004 8 Glass 30 Bottle	BERINGER MERLOT, Napa Valley 9 Glass 34 Bottle
FREI BROTHERS CHARDONNAY, Russian River 2004 11 Glass 42 Bottle	J. LOHR CABERNET SAUVIGNON, Paso Robles 9 Glass 34 Bottle
CLOS DU VAL CHARDONNAY, Carneros 2004 14 Glass 54 Bottle	NELM'S ROAD, Cabernet, Columbia Valley 14 Glass 54 Bottle
DROUHIN POUILLY-FUISSE, Burgundy 2004 10 Glass 38 Bottle	LA MASSA GIOEGIO PRIMO CHIANTI CLASSICCO 15 Glass 58 Bottle

WINES WITH BUBBLES

MOUNTAIN DOME BRUT, Columbia Valley ~ 30 Bottle
MOET & CHANDON "WHITE STAR" EXTRA DRY CHAMPAGNE ~ 85 Bottle

For more wine selections by the bottle, please dial 27 for Beverly's Full Wine List.

AUTHOR'S INSIGHT

Creativity is key to successful marketing of in-room food and beverages. I recall experiencing an important "ah-ha" moment working in a five-star resort in South Florida. The high-end incentive market made up a significant percentage of our business. We filled guestrooms and function spaces with the world's highest-achieving sales people. For quite some time, our normal practice involved nightly **turndown service**, including placement of imported cheeses and tawny port, or Belgian chocolates and champagne, in each guest room. After several days of this luxury treatment, it became apparent that "the pampered factor" bordered on overkill. Most conference feedback indicated that our guests were overwhelmed with service in excess of their typical lifestyles. Our response was modification of luxury turndown menus to include a carafe of fresh milk and a simple peanut butter and jelly sandwich. Much to everyone's delight, this became our most requested turndown item. I learned that variety and simplicity provide balance where excess might otherwise create imbalance.

MENUS FOR EMPLOYEE DINING

All employers, whether in the public or private sectors, hire their staff members to contribute to the collective work effort, so efficient breaks are critical. By logic and by law, employees are scheduled periodic breaks for personal needs and hunger relief. Typical breaks range between 15 minutes and 1 hour, but the one constant is the need to make the break convenient for employees to obtain their meals and return to work in a timely manner. Whereas each employer's accommodations vary to suit their business needs, inevitably the intent is to provide efficient transitions from work to break and back to work. Employees who work in retail or commercial areas may walk or commute to nearby restaurants or street vendors. This arrangement provides local foodservices with a relatively captive market. When convenient options such as these are not available, then other alternatives must be arranged by top management.

Many employers provide an alternative in the form of **on-site food service** (also referred to as *business dining*) within the workplace. Such food service may be self-operated by the employer or contracted with a regional company, a national firm, or global conglomerate. Companies such as Compass, ARAMARK, and Sodexho are industry leaders in this field. There are several features that distinguish on-site food service from restaurants:

- On-site food service is directly correlated with return-to-work and shift efficiency. Consequently, while it may provide aesthetic dining, it primarily serves as a convenience for employees and employers, rather than as a culinary statement.
- Food quality can coexist with workplace convenience. In fact, a key factor in regular employee participation is the provision of satisfying meals and snacks. Ideally, an employee working four or five days per week is targeted for 4 or 5 days of meal transactions. This occurs only if the menus are varied, affordable, and consistently of high quality.
- Affordability has an important impact on menu selections and pricing of these selections. Menu items are often priced lower than the prevailing market prices of local businesses.
- To enable the lower menu pricing, on-site dining is frequently subsidized by the employer (client). Certainly, it is possible to price certain menu items to achieve profit or break even, but often the established operating budget allows net loss that is offset by a negotiated subsidy.
- A significant percentage of the menu is cyclical, inasmuch as it changes daily. This practice keeps interest levels high.

The challenge for menu planners is to maintain an attractive product mix that incorporates cyclical menu items and an ever-present core menu, both of which foster repeat traffic and a reasonable net profit or break even.

MENUS FOR SCHOOL AND CAMPUS DINING

Menu planning for feeding students shares similarities with that of employee dining. Regional, national, and global foodservice operators often partner as contractors, with schools, colleges, and universities to provide expertise and management of campus dining. Alternatively, some schools elect to retain control and operate their foodservices on their own. The primary interest is efficient and prompt service that provides nourishing options at minimum expense to the school and reasonable cost to the student. This is particularly important in kindergarten through 12th grade (K–12) schools, where schedules are closely synchronized. Planning menus for K–12 schools is an ongoing challenge insomuch as younger students have distinct likes and dislikes that are highly influenced by their peers and by brand advertising. Although this isn't unique to that age group, children in kindergarten through 12th grade are highly impressionable, and this may present obstacles to menu variety and preparation methods. Although some schools have succumbed and simply offer perennial favorites such as pizza and fried foods, other systems have chosen the more difficult path and have made concerted efforts to offer nutritionally sound options. Ultimately, the students decide whether to participate in meals, so there is wisdom in forming student advisory councils to provide input on menu selections and other criteria with an impact on the program. One key to improving interest is the use of **cycle menus**, which are used to plan the offerings for all meals over the course of several weeks. This disciplined planning approach requires menu developers to consider variety, repetition, and compatibility of ingredients, all within the context of diner likes/dislikes.

It must be noted that cycle menus are not relegated to school food service only. An essential benefit of these menus is their ability to satisfy a captive audience, and they are widely used in health care, the military, and penal food service, as well as school and campus dining. In fact, some commercial operations use abbreviated cycle menus in the form of "daily specials."

Some K–12 school systems have opted to participate in the National School Lunch Program (NSLP), which is a federally assisted meal program providing nutritionally sound lunches and milk at no personal cost or at reduced prices to qualifying students. Participation in this program also involves mandated menu guidelines and significant process/outcomes reporting. As a result of the highly institutionalized nature of these programs, they are frequently managed by registered dietitians and other professionals with specialized knowledge of institutional food service, public policy, and wellness.

The emphasis on speed of service is not as critical in college campus dining because of the varied schedules of students. Nonetheless, there are peak times where menus must support operational urgency. Colleges with residence and dining services frequently require freshman and other students living on campus to purchase a meal plan. Because of this forced meal participation, it is imperative that colleges provide high levels of student satisfaction both in menu selections and in service. Figure 2-16 illustrates the variety and creativity that can be achieved in a student-centered dining program. More often than not, dining plans are sold as a declining balance package, whereby a finite number of meals are purchased. Where allowed, students select the package that best suits their meal demand, campus usage patterns, and dining habits. Other typical features involve paying into elective credit balances that may be used campus-wide for dining as well as sundry purchases on campus and at neighboring merchants.

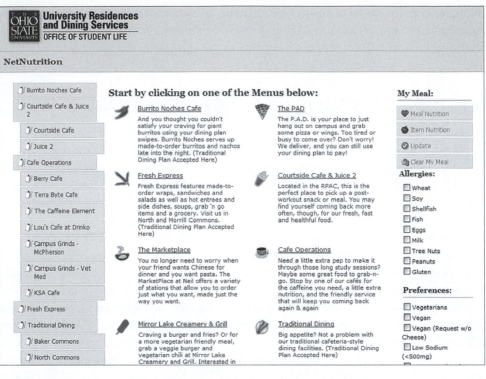

Figure 2-16
Campus Dining at The Ohio State University, Columbus, Ohio   (*Source:* Reprinted by permission of The
Ohio State University)

MENUS FOR HOSPITALS

Menu planning for patient feeding should be viewed as a component of an integrated care plan. Hospitals provide acute care based on the collaborative input of physicians, dietitians, and other healthcare professionals. Patient meals served in hospitals are frequently paid through major medical insurance plans, so along with palatability, cost containment and operational efficiency are an ever-present focus of management.

As is the case in on-site dining and school/campus dining, hospital menus are based on multi-week cycles, possibly anchored with a core of non-cyclical menu items.

Many hospitals have developed enhanced food service options where patients may pay an out-of-pocket surcharge to enjoy chef-prepared meals that parallel the creativity and quality of restaurant meals. Whereas these enhanced meals are seldom covered by insurance plans, it can be argued that the therapeutic value of pleasing cuisine is an important part of a comprehensive care plan.

In addition to meals delivered to patient rooms, most hospitals provide food service for visitors and staff. These dining options vary dramatically, and in recent years have included bistro-style food concepts and upscale coffee bars.

MENUS FOR LONG-TERM CARE

Continuing care retirement communities provide a home and wide array of services for seniors who seek a nurturing social environment or who may require specialized care. A continuum of care, including independent living, assisted-living, and skilled nursing, provides for long-term residency. Although personal choices (gardening, parlor games, shopping excursions, religious worship, etc.) enable individuals to extend the lifestyles they have come to enjoy, congregate dining serves as the preeminent social event of every day. Because many residents partake all or most of their meals on property, variety and choices to suit a captive audience must be managed creatively. Whereas a core of favorite items is easily identified, it is necessary to provide a cycle menu that marries these favorites with seasonal variety selections. Nourishment, palatability, and cost containment are typical management foci. Quality levels vary based on the business structure and parties paying for the services. In fact, some private-pay communities mirror the quality levels of country clubs and resort hotels.

ACTION TOOLKIT

Many restaurants and other foodservices make their menus available on their website. In addition, there are formal and informal (Wiki) websites where the menus and service are profiled or reviewed. Useful sites include:

- **Gayot** www.gayot.com
- **Fodors** www.fodors.com
- **Urbanspoon** www.urbanspoon.com
- **Menuism** www.menuism.com

There are several sources of industry news and data to help you plan your menus in an informed manner, including the following websites:

- **National Restaurant Association** www.restaurant.org/research
- **Nations Restaurant News** www.nrn.com
- **Progressive Grocer** www.progressivegrocer.com

GLOSSARY

Aperitifs—Alcoholic beverages, typically wine or spirits, consumed at the start of a meal, so as to stimulate the appetite.

Buffet style—A style of foodservice in which customers serve themselves from menu items on display in an area other than the kitchen.

Contribution margin—The fraction of sales revenue that remains after the direct variable cost of goods are subtracted. As related to menu management, this is most often defined as menu price minus food or beverage costs.

Cycle menu—A menu planned for 2 or more weeks that provides structure and coordinated variety of choices that repeats in a continuous manner for a fixed time, typically within the context of a captive audience.

Digestifs—Alcoholic beverages, typically wine or spirits, consumed at the end of a meal, so as to promote digestion and close the procession of food and beverage.

Eaux-de-vie—("water of life") Spirits distilled from fermented fruit juices, including grapes, soft fruit, and stone fruit.

Guarantee—A contractual agreement between a foodservice and client to prepare, and thus sell to the client, a specific number of banquet meals.

Malt beverages—Alcoholic beverages produced from the fermentation of a malted grain combined with yeast and water. Popular malt beverages include beer, ale, porter, lager, and stout.

Menu—("a small list") The list of food and beverage items available for purchase. Several menus may be developed, each focusing on a specific category (desserts, bar snacks, carry out items, etc.).

Microbrews—Malt beverages created in small breweries producing 15,000 barrels or less per year. These limited production runs are intended to enable brewmasters to control nuances of the final product, thus yielding distinctive quality beverages.

Mise en place—("put in place") To have all items and ingredients at the ready in anticipation of their use in meal service, so as to facilitate unimpeded workflow.

On-site food service—Meal service provided to employees within their workplace.

Restaurant—A commercial enterprise that sells prepared food and beverages and provides hospitality to diners; derived from *restorative*.

Revenue—Business income derived from the sale of goods and services to customers.

Spirits—Alcoholic beverages produced by distillation of fruit, grain, or vegetable bases.

Turndown service—An activity conducted by staff to freshen and prepare occupied hotel guest rooms for evening retirement. Often this includes providing fresh towels, readying bed linens, and delivering modest food and beverages as an act of hospitality.

Wine—An alcoholic beverage obtained from the fermentation of fruit juice, most typically *Vitis vinifera* grapes.

ENDNOTE

1. thinkexist.com/quotation/i_learned_more_from_the_one_restaurant_that_didn/227464.html; accessed May 1, 2011.

3

How Customers Buy Your Product

Key Terms

American Viticultural Area (AVA)

Amuse bouche

Apéritif (*Aperitif*)

Continental breakfast menu

Dayparts

Dégustation menu

Full breakfast menu

Intermezzo

Price resistance

Prix fixe menu

Small-plate menu

Tasting menu

Wine list

(*Source:* Blend Images/Shutterstock)

Objectives

Upon completion of this chapter, you should be able to:

3.1   Create *à la carte* menus

3.2   Create small plate menus

3.3   Create *prix fixe*, *table d'hôte*, and *dégustation* menus

3.4   Create non-alcoholic beverage menus

3.5   Create menus of alcoholic beverages sold by the glass

3.6   Create wine lists and menus of alcoholic beverages sold by the bottle

NOT QUITE BUSINESS AS USUAL

"Hell, there are no rules here—we're trying to accomplish something."

—THOMAS A. EDISON[1]

There was a time when menu-writing guidelines were sacrosanct and functioned as fairly rigid doctrine. Many diners accepted the direction and were happily led by chefs and *sommeliers* and their expertise. Conventional wisdom divided menus into two broad stylistic classifications: ***à la carte*** and ***prix fixe***. This simplified model inferred that diners either chose their own meal selections, or it was done for them by the restaurant. This arrangement perseveres today, but is manifest in numerous variations. Traditional menu-planning practices are typical in low- to mid-price restaurants; however, new

AUTHOR'S INSIGHT

As I write this paragraph, I think back to last night's dinner at a bustling independent restaurant in Cleveland's revitalized arts corridor. We drank a private-label *sauvignon blanc* bottled exclusively for the restaurant, and were later treated to a brilliant private-label *meritage*, once again, bottled exclusively for the house. In addition to a creative *à la carte* menu, there was a "Family Meal" designed on the spot by the chefs. To enjoy this option, the entire table was required to order this reasonably priced option. One of the chefs visited our table and surveyed our food preferences, sensitivities, and allergies. He seemed to be sizing us up in the best sense possible. Soon, a procession of filled bowls, crusty loaves, and savory platters were delivered to our table. Every dish was delicious, creative, and a fun way for our party to dine. I could not have asked for a better dinner. After coffee and dessert, we chatted with the table across from us. They too had selected the Family Meal; however, the dishes they received were entirely different, yet equally satisfying. The lessons here are poignant:

- Private labeling to reinforce culinary and marketing strategies is available to even small operators.
- Depending on your market niche, customers may be receptive to imaginative table service, such as family-style, tasting menus, and other creative options.
- Consistent quality is important, but variation is a means of instilling excitement for customers and staff.

rules have found a most welcome arena in the moderate- to high-price dining concepts. In those restaurants that dare to break the mold, customers can experience the forefront of culinary discovery.

Menu planners have never been more attuned and responsive to the wants and desires of their clientele. The adventurousness of today's customers allows for novel revenue opportunities, repeat business potential, tenacious brand loyalty, and sustained profit. Nonetheless, there are fine nuances that connect consumer behavior and value decisions with informed operational strategy.

A unique feature of this chapter (and indeed, the entire textbook) is the lack of prescription or strict decrees. In fact, the only rule is to know your target market's desires and parallel your offerings to capitalize on this demand.

STEPS IN CREATING *À LA CARTE* MENUS

À la carte menus make it possible for your customers to choose one, two, or several menu selections during their visit. Of all the menu styles, they permit your customers the greatest opportunity for personal choices. Consequently, they represent the most

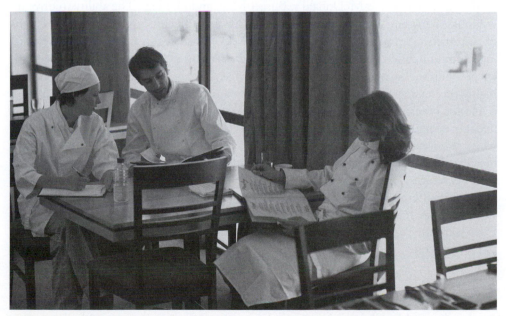

(*Source:* Nick White/Thinkstock)

prevalent menu style in commercial foodservices. Guests may select a single beverage, such as a coffee enjoyed at a counter or table, or a cocktail enjoyed at the bar. Two or more selections, such as a soup and sandwich, or a goblet of wine and a composed salad, may more closely represent a meal. *Choice* is the operative word. As a business planner, your understanding of how to influence customer choices is a primary key to business success. Figures 1-3, 2-1, 2-13, and 2-14 provide varied glimpses of *à la carte* food menus.

Menus should be created in a deliberate sequential manner, as follows:

The first step in creating an *à la carte* menu is to identify customer wishes and their assumed value decisions for the **daypart** in question.

The second step in creating an *à la carte* menu is to create a menu structure and populate the structure with items for your guests to select.

The third step in creating an *à la carte* menu is to price the selections and forecast contribution to profit, and make adjustments prior to deploying the menu. (This step is covered in more detail in Chapters 5 and 8.)

The fourth step in creating an *à la carte* menu is to develop a marketing strategy to generate sales of forecasted items at required levels. (Marketing of menus is in fact a subset of the overall marketing plan, and the topic of internal merchandising is discussed in Chapter 9.)

CREATING *À LA CARTE* BREAKFAST MENUS

Speed

Customers seeking nourishment at breakfast typically cite speedy service as their ultimate deciding factor. This customer preference fueled the rapid expansion of breakfast at fast-food restaurants such as McDonald's, Burger King, and Hardees. The ability to drive up without leaving one's vehicle and receive a hot breakfast fits the busy lifestyles of millions of customers. Starbucks pointed the quick service of breakfast in a new direction, featuring premium coffee and tea beverages and "grab-and-go" pastries and breakfast sandwiches. Starbucks capitalized on speed-of-service, but also was able to sell products at highly profitable price points because of variety and perceived quality. During 2008, as economic pressures spread throughout the American consumer markets, Starbucks revisited its pricing strategy, and began offering breakfast pairings that were comparably priced with traditional quick-service restaurants. Shortly thereafter, in a bid to claim/reclaim breakfast business from competitors, McDonald's introduced their own line of premium coffee beverages ("Premium Roast Coffee" and "McCafé©" espresso-based drinks).

Certain ethnic foods are suitable for quick breakfast service. Cuban *pasteles* and *café con leche*, Jewish-American bagels with lox and cream cheese ("a *schmear*"), or a French-inspired *pain au chocolat* are but a few examples that lend themselves to breakfast on the run.

Substance

When speedy service is somewhat important but a more substantial meal is desired, the **continental breakfast** is an appropriate menu offering. Based on Mediterranean traditions, this breakfast includes a hot beverage, such as drinking chocolate or hot cocoa, or coffee with milk, such as *cappuccino* or *latte*, and sweet baked items such as *croissants* or *brioche*. Fruit juices are frequently part of a continental breakfast, as is yogurt and *muesli*. Occasionally it includes cured meats (ham, salami) and cheeses.

Many American foodways evolved from the Anglo heritage of the British colonists. High caloric intake provided sustenance for a laborious lifestyle, and breakfast "primed the engine," as it were. Although less frequently eaten, the English, Welsh, and Irish **full breakfast menu** remains the benchmark for a substantial morning meal, and typically includes eggs, bacon (cured from the pork loin), sausages and puddings, grilled tomatoes, sautéed mushrooms, baked beans, toast or fried bread, and tea or coffee. The traditional American breakfast of eggs, bacon, and sausage is rooted in these British breakfasts, albeit less extensive. As America became less of a labor-based society, the need for these breakfasts diminished, and now a more contemporary breakfast may include egg-white omelets, turkey bacon, low-fat yogurt, granola, and fresh fruit. In nearly all instances, cooking to order is the key to quality for this type of breakfast; consequently, it is best reserved for markets willing to devote adequate time for this personalized preparation and service.

The Nutritional Importance of Breakfast

Because food is, above all else, the body's source of energy and nutrients, we must be sensitive to the nutrition desires of our clientele. Understanding your target market and responding in a balanced manner is the key to successfully addressing the issue of nutritious menus. It is misguided to act in an overtly dogmatic fashion and dictate your guests' nutrition regimen.[2] Nor should you dismiss opportunities to provide healthy

---

CASE STUDY 3-1 *BREAKFAST MENU*

Browse the Boar's Head Inn Web site at www.boarsheadinn.com/. The AAA Four Diamond Resort and Spa features 170 guest rooms, championship golf, tennis, and modern meeting facilities. Study the Old Mill Room Restaurant breakfast menu. The Old Mill Room is the resort's signature restaurant, and is one of five dining options at the Inn.

Range of Breakfast Menu Selections

This menu is relatively compact, offering a handful of *à la carte* selections (a full buffet is also available). The choices range from relatively light to rich and filling.

Nutrition Options

Health-conscious customers are accommodated, as are vegans. This menu is compatible with a variety of diets and supports the United States Department of Agriculture's *MyPlate Plan* (discussed in greater detail in Chapter 7).

Operational Practices

The *à la carte* breakfast offered at the Old Mill Room is easily produced. A culinary staff member must be dedicated to the omelet station.

Uniqueness

This is a high-quality menu that appeals to a broad audience without particularly distinctive selections.

Summary

This menu is conservative in approach, yet befits the quality of a world-class resort. Ingredients such as prime rib and imported smoked salmon infer excellence and direct customers' value decisions. The limited choices run the gamut of healthy to traditional, and include meat, fish, eggs, and grains. Skilled staff is required; however, none of the recipes or presentations are so complex as to present at unusual operational hurdles.

EXERCISE 3-1
CREATING AN *À LA CARTE* BREAKFAST MENU

Q1. Select a hyperlink listed in the Chapter 1 Action Toolkit to research zip (postal) code 02901. Based on this population and their specific demographics, create a breakfast menu that will appeal to the local market, can be prepared by a relatively unskilled staff, and possesses at least one signature item. Use the following categories as your structural guide:

- Juices
- Fruits
- Cereals
- Griddle-baked items

- Oven-baked items
- Egg dishes
- Meats
- Signature dish
- Combination dishes
- Side dishes
- Cold beverages
- Hot beverages

Q2. Explain the reasoning behind your selections.

---

and marketable menu selections. There is a wide behavioral gap between customers who eat wisely and those who eat with little regard for the consequences of their choices. A wellness-minded market that views your breakfast food as unhealthy will not likely become your core of repeat clientele. Conversely, a market that seeks convenient dining will be more tolerant of fats and sodium content.

Diversity as a Marketable Asset

Globalization is a reality of our society. As the population of the United States continues to receive individuals from across the globe, breakfast menus change to satisfy the increasingly varied demands of the market. Asian breakfasts contrast widely, and include Vietnamese *pho*, Chinese *congee* and *dim sum*, and Japanese *miso* soup and green tea. Just as certain items are local specialties in the United States, these Asian items are also regional and may be popular in one province and unknown in another. Hispanic menus often include sweet espresso-based coffee, toasted breads, and pastries such as *arepas* or *churros*. *Huevos rancheros*, originating from Mexico, have crossed over to many North American menus with much success. This is a snapshot of a much grander gastronomic montage, yet it serves as an important introduction to world cuisines on the breakfast menu. These international menu items serve a multifold purpose. First, they provide familiar foods that individuals grew up with in their own cultures. Second, they expand our own foodways and create a richer mosaic of dining as cultural expression. Finally, these items, when introduced, provide a marketing catalyst to keep customer interest at necessary levels.

CREATING *À LA CARTE* LUNCH MENUS

Lunch represents a significant break in the day, and for millions of individuals it must be timely and sustain them for the remainder of their workday. It also provides a social juncture where friends, family, and colleagues can spend quality time together. When developing lunch menus, you must be cognizant of the same concerns as in planning breakfast menus (customer needs/wishes and assumed value decisions).

As discussed in Chapter 1, there are a multitude of reasons that motivate customers to dine away from home. At lunchtime, the most common reasons include:

- to save time or reduce travel
- to obtain nourishment
- to conduct business or business-related entertainment

EXERCISE 3-2

EXPLORING ALTERNATIVE PREPARATION METHODS

Scenario: The "Gallery Café" will be the first and only dining option at a contemporary art museum in the cultural corridor of a vibrant tourist destination. Hundreds of museum visitors pay to view the galleries and exhibits. The soon-to-be opened café is intended as a convenience for the visitors and a revenue source for the museum. Guest feedback clearly indicates that service must be prompt, and guests want to view the art, not sit and wait for their meals. The cycle time between ordering and table turnover should be no more than 30 minutes. Management is convinced that they can position lunch entrées for an average of $9.00 to $16.00, but they must deliver consistent culinary quality to do so. Preliminary planning suggests the following entrees as part of the menu:

- Wood-Grilled Duck Tacos with Caramelized Red Onions and Made-to-Order Guacamole
- Calzones Filled with Lamb Sausage, *Fontina*, and Roasted Delicato Squash
- *Frisee* Salad with *Lardons*, Garlic Croutons, and a Poached Free-Range Quail Egg

Q1. Evaluate the suggested entrées and discuss your impressions. Are the items feasible from a prompt production and service perspective? What alterations might you suggest? How could you test your suggested modifications?

- traveling as tourists away from homes
- networking and dining as a social and recreational act

The lunch menus you create must satisfy these motivations and needs.

Speed

Lunch customers seeking to save time or reduce travel can be satisfied by *à la carte* menus that facilitate a quick cycle from point-of-ordering to service and payment. This is best illustrated by extremes. A lunch menu that involves prepared-to-order items requiring inordinate cooking times generally is not feasible. For example, a Cornish hen roasted to order, which might be a suitable entrée on a leisurely dinner menu, takes too long to prepare at lunchtime and does not enable prompt service. Conversely, a char-grilled salmon fillet or a high-quality *bento box* can be prepared in less than 10 minutes, thus allowing rapid service and efficient customer turnover. These examples represent opposite extremes, but should illustrate the wide range that your menu planning should occur within. If your research

(*Source:* Jupiterimages/Thinkstock)

CASE STUDY 3-2 *LUNCH MENU*

Sweatman's Bar-b-que in Holly Hill, South Carolina, delivers the ultimate Southern barbeque experience. They are open only two days a week, but any visit to Charleston merits an excursion to this regional shrine.

Range of Lunch Menu Selections

This menu couldn't be much more compact. Pulled pork barbeque from whole hogs cooked over a smoldering grill is the attraction. *À la carte* items are available, but the less than $10.00 buffet is what draws diners from across the country. Selections include smoky pulled lean pork, bronzed dark meat, fall-off-the-bone ribs, crispy pork skins, a pork gravy hash, homemade pickles, tart cole slaw, perfectly cooked white rice, and banana pudding. Sweet tea completes the experience.

Nutrition Options

Health-conscious customers are accommodated, as are those who prefer to "pig out" (pun intended). True barbeque, such as this, is slow-cooked, allowing a lot of the meat's fat to render, leaving a slightly leaner finished product. Wise choice of side dishes keeps diners on the right side of the calorie count.

Operational Practices

This menu is a true artisan endeavor. Craftsmanship and close supervision by the proprietor create sublime food and consistent quality. This is lowcountry soul food *par excellence*, and demonstrates how a simple operational concept can yield business success and a reputation that draws in repeat clientele.

Uniqueness

This is one of several regional barbeque "joints," each featuring similar items within the lowcountry culinary context.

Summary

This menu succeeds because it is built on simple items that are expertly prepared. Familiar foods are available and the unfussy approach appeals to a broad market.

indicates that roasted poultry truly appeals to your lunch clientele, then you must investigate recipe changes or altered preparation steps. For example, a slight modification whereby the birds are par-cooked in the morning and finished when ordered could provide a balance of speed and culinary quality. The same adaptive approach is not always possible with other ingredients, but the inquisitive culinary team should collaborate during all phases of the planning and development process to assure that prompt service can be achieved.

Substance

À la carte lunch menus vary widely, so it is difficult to be prescriptive. As was discussed in Chapter 2, sandwiches and substantial salads are perennial favorites. Aside from those items, the menu can encompass cooked proteins, soups, vegan and vegetarian items, desserts, and beverages.

CREATING *À LA CARTE* DINNER MENUS

Speed

Dinner menus are typically less hurried than all other dayparts, and this allows for a progression of courses.

Substance

Operators who determine their clientele seeks multiple courses must start by creating a dinner menu structure. No one structure is appropriate until the context and target

THE SPOTTED PIG
314 W. 11th St. @ Greenwich St.
New York, NY 10014
(212) 620-0393

Bar Snacks	
Deviled Eggs	$4
Devils on Horseback	$7
Marinated Olives	$4
Roasted Almonds	$4
Roll Mops	$8
Pot of Pickles	$6
Chicken Liver Toast	$6

Plates	
Hog Island Oysters with Mignonette	6 for $18/12 for $36
Smoked Haddock Chowder with House-made Crackers	$15
Fried Duck Egg with Ramps & Sherry Vinegar	$16
Boston's Bibb Lettuce with Tarragon & Mustard Dressing	$14
Sheep's Milk Ricotta Gnudi with Basil Pesto	$16
Beet Salad with Spring Onions & Goat Cheese	$16
Beer Steamed Cockles with Tomatoes & Spring Garlic	$16
Pan Seared Arctic Char with Ramps & Bacon Vinaigrette	$17
Roasted Asparagus with Parmesean Custard & Proscuitto	$18
Crispy Pig's Ear with Lemon Caper Dressing	$15

Entrees	
Grilled Max Creek Trout with Fiddle Head Ferns & New Potatoes	$29
Pan Roasted Veal Chop with Baby Artichokes & Dandelion	$35
Chargrilled Burger with Roquefort Cheese & Shoestrings	$17
Braised Oxtail with Olive Oil Mashed Potatoes	$29
Pan Seared Scallops with Ramps & Chili	$32

Sides	
Duck Fat Roasted Potatoes	$8
Beets & Greens	$8
Roasted Carrots	$8
Chard with Olives	$8
Creamed Spinach	$8
Shoestring Fries	$8
Plate of Five Vegetables	$24

Desserts	**$8**
Walnut, Chocolate & Amaretto Cake	
Flourless Chocolate Cake	
Ginger Cake	
Crème Caramel	
Cheese Plate	2 for $ 10/3 for $ 15

Figure 3-1
Spotted Pig Menu, New York City, New York (*Source:* Reprinted by permission of The Spotted Pig)

market have been identified. Some structures imply a progression of courses; other menus are relatively unstructured, suggesting a meal composed of one or more selections that satisfy each diner's particular appetite and budget.

Figure 3-1 illustrates a menu featuring Italian and British cuisine. This restaurant is one of America's pioneering gastropubs (more on this in Chapter 7) dedicated to local seasonal ingredients prepared with uncompromising quality. Like many *à la carte* menus, entrées, sides, and desserts are offered. In addition, a robust selection of "Bar Snacks" and "Plates" is available. The creativity of these items defies simple classification, and because of the spectrum of delicious options, diners will be hard pressed when trying to decide on their meal choices.

Figure 3-2 illustrates a menu of equally high quality with many choices that is quite likely to challenge guests with tough decisions (in the best possible way). Menus such as this possess two inherent advantages:

- Rather than conforming to a conventional pattern, they subtly compel diners to make lots of choices before and after their entrée.
- They almost guarantee a repeat visit so that further exploration can occur.

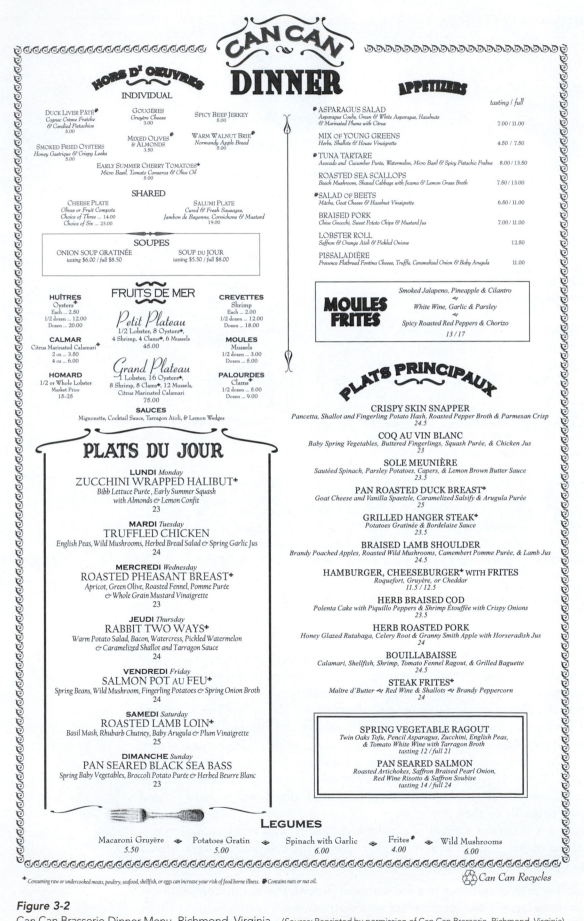

Figure 3-2
Can Can Brasserie Dinner Menu, Richmond, Virginia   (*Source:* Reprinted by permission of Can Can Brasserie, Richmond, Virginia)

The lesson to be learned involves how menu structure can guide the number of selections (breadth) a guest will choose as their meal. Table 3-1 compares the structure of the *à la carte* dinner menus previously illustrated in Figures 3-1 and 3-2. It is readily evident that a simple comparison is impossible, because each of these menus is uniquely structured.

Certainly, guests possess a sense of how much they want to eat, but that may be highly influenced by an array of creative choices. As a menu planner, you must assess how prone your market is to such influence, and then provide choices in a persuasive fashion. It is important to note that categorization and grouping leads customers to purchase decisions. If you are intuitive and strategic in the communication of your *à la carte* offerings, then your desired sales objectives become synchronized with customer purchase behavior.

TABLE 3-1 COMPARISON OF MENU STRUCTURE	
Spotted Pig	**Can Can Brasserie**
Bar snacks	Appetizers
	Hors d'oeuvres
	Fruits de Mer
Plates	Plates du jour
Entrées	Plates Principaux
Sides	Legumes

CREATING SMALL-PLATE MENUS

In the late 1980s, a dining pattern emerged that was referred to as *grazing*. This trend expanded with the greater prevalence of innovative appetizers across American menus. Many customers opted to order or share two or more appetizers rather than select a customary entrée. The underlying message was, "We want new choices and we want smaller." Attentive operators interpreted these messages as the market's interest in alternative menu structures. The primary concern questioned the necessity of an entrée to anchor the dining experience. A second and equally important concern involved reconsideration of portion sizes.

Wrongly conceived, a succession of courses can create fullness too soon in the meal. It is important to visualize the likely progression of guest selections and create portion sizes that deliver a filling but manageable meal. A relatively recent adaptation of European and Asian menus involves the offering of **small plates**. These diminutive but satisfying menu items can be found throughout Vietnam, India, China, Morocco, Greece, Portugal, Spain, Russia, and many other nations. Perhaps the most popular small plates are found in authentic Chinese *dim sum* and Japanese *sushi* restaurants. The Chinese *dim sum* concept features one-, two-, and three-bite plates that lend themselves to multiple selections. Similarly, the Japanese sushi menu allows diners to select from dozens of choices of sushi styles as part of their dinner.

Whereas the preceding examples illustrate ethnic menu themes, small plates can be developed for nearly any culinary concept. Purchasing patterns of American diners seeking less-filling plates have affirmed their support for smaller portions and movement away from large portions as an inferred measure of quality. As discussed earlier, changes in earnings and household wealth influence the frequency with which customers use food services. In the latter part of 2007, recessionary pressures created a significant downturn in guest traffic across all restaurant segments. Operators responded with a variety of strategies, including the introduction of snack-size portions. In retrospect, this was a successful strategy, as it created customer traffic during non-peak hours and in between typical dayparts, and allowed for some degree of sustaining cash flow. Customers seeking reduced portion sizes increasingly have been visiting restaurants between 3:00 PM and 6:00 PM. In 2010, McDonald's executives indicated that sales in between traditional meal periods represented the daily segment with the greatest revenue increase for three years in a row. The sharp drop in discretionary consumer spending, the customer propensity to snack (and pay lower check

EXERCISE 3-3
DEVELOPING A SMALL-PLATE MENU

Q1. Select a hyperlink listed in the Chapter 1 Action Toolkit to research zip (postal) code 33040. Based on this location and their business drivers, create a small-plate menu that features ingredients, preparation methods, and recipes representative of the location. Your menu should satisfy guests seeking a light snack, but also satisfy diners seeking an entire evening meal.

averages), and operator's willingness to offer reduced portions align quite well. In 2010, menu items termed *snack, snackable,* or *snacker* increased by 185% over 2007, and items described on menus as *mini* increased by nearly 400%.[3] When measured in calories, a distinct trend is evident. In the 1970s, Americans consumed an average of 200 daily calories from snacks. By the 1990s, this number was 360 calories. As of 2010, the average American claimed to consume 470 calories of snacks on a daily basis. These increased calorie counts do not necessarily suggest that Americans are consuming more calories in restaurants. In fact, some customers are replacing full-size meals with these small plates and reduced portions. Independent and chain operators spanning all industry segments have responded in a creative manner. The Cheesecake Factory introduced a line of "pre-appetizers." Many bar menus have been expanded by offering portion sizes that elude definition. *Sliders,* in the form of miniature sandwiches, proliferate in all permutations conceivable. These trends bode well for creative operators. You would be wise to study your intended market to assess their interest in small plates and reduced portion sizes. Whether prompted by diner interest in global cuisine, nutritionally motivated trade off from full-size portions, or interest in saving discretionary dollars, it appears that small plates will continue to offer valued alternatives to various market segments.

CREATING *PRIX FIXE* AND *TABLE D'HÔTE* MENUS

Prix fixe and *table d'hôte* menus are meals composed of two or more courses sold at a set price. Diners opting for this type of menu make very limited choices within a series of courses selected by the menu planning team. These menus may range from the commonplace to the exotic, as revealed throughout this section of the chapter. In its strictest reading, *prix fixe* provides a complete menu with all options for one price. Typically, within this menu, diners may choose from several appetizers, entrées, and desserts. Occasionally, there are various price ranges (for example, a $15.00 *prix fixe* lunch and a $25.00 *prix fixe* lunch, with respective selections). *Table d'hôte* is a meal based on the price of the entrée. Each entrée is assigned its own price, and the entrée selection entitles guests to select from a list of appetizers and from a list of desserts to complete the meal. Because these two menu formats share similarities, they are treated interchangeably throughout this textbook.

Banquets feature the most frequently encountered *prix fixe* menus. In all but the rarest settings, it would be unimaginable to conduct a banquet with a full *à la carte* menu. The relatively large number of guests coupled with too many choices becomes an unwieldy and inefficient production and service challenge. Despite their prevalence in banquet and restaurant settings, *prix fixe* menus are found during all dayparts and in nearly all food-service segments, including campus dining, airlines, and resorts.

Reasons to offer *prix fixe* menus include:

- Providing a meal where the set price offers perceived value for customers
- Serving as an operational means for production planning and batch preparation. *Prix fixe* and *table d'hôte* menus often involve less *mise en place* for kitchen staff, and with fewer choices, purchasing and preparation can be conducted in

Figure 3-3
Extract from Tujague's
Menu, New Orleans,
Louisiana   (*Source:* Reprinted by
permission of Tujague's Restaurant)

Creole Menu

Tujague's six course, table d'hote menu is built around
such staples as savory Shrimp Remoulade and Tujague's
own traditional beef brisket with Creole sauce -- a piquant
remoulade sauce flavoring spicy cold shrimp and
succulent chunks of beef brisket boiled with aromatic
vegetables served with horseradish sauce topped off with
warm bread.

Our menu selections also include the daily offering of
nearby market vendors in an effort to use only the freshest
ingredients.

On a sweeter note, the bread pudding and pecan pie harken
one back to grandmother's kitchen, along with the aroma
of rich dark-roast coffee.

All meals are served in the traditional Creole manner, from
appetizer through dessert, with a choice of entrees.

For Creole chefs, only the day's freshest produce is put on
the table. All meals are served with hot French bread. Fine
wines, cocktails, and beers are available including our own
micro-brewed Tujague's Beer.

We offer Filet Mignon, 2 Fresh seafood, and a fourth non-
seafood entree daily.

Dinner Menu

Appetizer
Shrimp Remoulade

Soup du Jour

House Specialty
Beef Brisket with Creole Sauce

Entree
A choice of 4 entrees du Jour

Dessert

Beverage

a more efficient manner. Conversely, *à la carte* menus offer more customer
choices and are less suitable for exacting production forecasting

- Your menu planning team may understand sensory/culinary synergies of the
  various food and beverage menu items and elect to provide firm guidance to
  customers. Often this becomes a signature for the operation. Figure 3-3 is an
  example of a signature *prix fixe* menu.

Prix fixe and *Table d'hôte* at Breakfast

Breakfast buffets satisfy multiple customer needs. Foods typically associated with full
breakfasts (eggs, potatoes, sausages, etc.) are the foundation of most breakfast buffets.
With sufficient business volume, these and other foods can be prepared in advance and
merchandized under temperature control with minimal quality loss. In addition, these
buffets allow relatively quick service and reduce the labor cost involved in *à la carte*
service. When expanded to include a multitude of items that straddle the breakfast and

lunch dayparts, these buffets transform into brunch. Lunch and dinner buffets provide similar solutions for customers and operators.

Prix fixe and *Table d'hôte* at Lunch and Dinner

Centuries ago, customs and conventional wisdom prompted *gastronomes* to feature a robust succession of courses featuring diverse ingredients. For example, a menu might begin with a piquant **amuse-bouche** ("mouth amuser"), a first course of iced shellfish, then a vegetable-based soup, a palate cleanser **intermezzo** or *trou normand*, perhaps followed by roasted fowl or a red meat entrée. European tradition follows this entrée with a refreshing salad, then a cheese course. Ultimately, the meal finishes with a dessert course and coffee. Whereas most modern diners do not choose meals featuring marathon successions of courses, at least one dimension is relevant today. This example ascribes to the logic of minimal repetition, thoughtfully planned variety, and an orchestrated flow of tastes and textures. There is a logical marketing basis for planned variety. Imagine the case of a diner with an aversion to fungus ingredients. If she or he sat down to a *table d'hôte* menu with course-after-course of mushrooms and truffles, the dinner would be a forgettable if not miserable experience. Variety of ingredients reduces the likelihood of disappointing your guests. In addition, it is typical and wise to utilize a range of preparation methods in a *prix fixe* or *table d'hôte* menu. If every course were poached, the lack of textural variety would likely result in palate fatigue. Similar undesirable results also occur with a succession of fried courses. This principle notwithstanding, you shouldn't be slavish to rules. In fact, certain chefs and restaurateurs work at being iconoclastic in their menu design. Figure 3-4 illustrates a *prix fixe* menu that

Figure 3-4
Incanto Head to Tail Dinner Menu, San ancisco, California *(Source:* Reprinted by permission of Incanto)

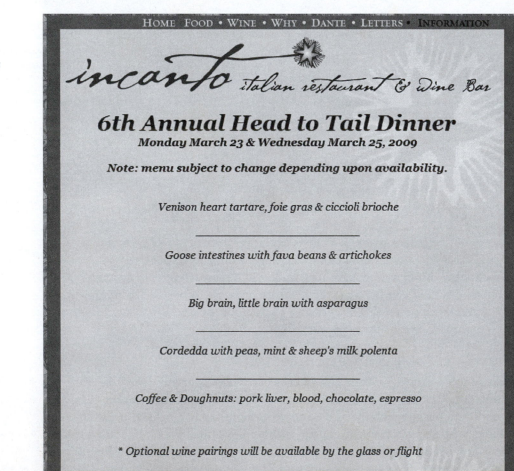

seemingly breaks all the rules. A majority of diners approach offal and variety meats with trepidation; however, the menu in Figure 3-4 assumes an unapologetic posture by offering a succession of these organ meats. Obviously, the operator has made a conscious decision to attract one market segment at the expense of others. As previously discussed, you must understand your market and assess their acceptance of daring menu offerings. When properly prepared and merchandised, the drama and word-of-mouth will have long-lasting positive impact that may yield benefits in the form of celebrity and attraction of new clientele.

A variation of prix fixe menus is the **degustation menu**, which are based on decidedly small portions, each delivering memorable impact, hence the interchangeable title of **tasting menu**. Degustation menus are labor-intensive propositions in that the *mise en place* of ingredients is extensive and the number of recipes is expansive. Consequently, these menus often carry a premium price tag; however, it is possible to offer low- and moderately priced degustation menus as well. The underlying premise in offering degustation menus assumes a highly skilled culinary team will deliver an unparalleled succession of courses. Adventurous diners are the target market, and this segment is particularly inclined to purchase fine wine as an accompaniment to their meals. Because of the wide range of foods, it becomes difficult for one or two wines to complement an entire degustation menu. Thus, it is common for managers to pair each course with a different wine. A surcharge for a matched flight of accompanying wines is typical. Figure 3-5 illustrates an example of a moderately priced tasting menu matched with a flight of complementary wines.

When all is said and done, a sequence of food and wine is served with the promise of a uniquely memorable dining experience. These occasions, when properly executed, can generate significant check averages yet still indoctrinate repeat visitation by satisfied customers. In fact, some chef–operators such as Charlie Trotter only offer degustation menus at their restaurants. In summary, a *table d'hôte* or *prix fixe* menu, while relieving customers of some degree of personal choice, enables you to design an integrated menu that

Tobin James Winemaker Dinner with Tobin James

When	Mon, March 28, 6:30pm – 9:00pm
Where	3731-A India Street, San Diego, CA 92103 (map)
Description	RSVP: (619) 295-3939
	$59.50 + tax and gratuity

STANDARD WINES DINNER WITH TOBIN JAMES
Pre-dinner reception with Tobin James from 5:45 to 6:30
Dinner starts promptly at 6:30

For the fourth year in a row, Wine Vault & Bistro is pleased to announce the long awaited Tobin James winemaker dinner. Legendary Tobin James will be here in person down from Paso Robles to host the dinner. The wine line-up will feature his more readily available favorites. We're serving a great 5-course dinner for this event. We hope you'll be able to join us for a fun time of tasting some great wine paired with some great food while spending time with Paso's hands down most colorful icon! Here's the line-up:

Wild Greens | Radishes | Smoked Burrata | Preserved Lemon | Hazelnuts | Ramp Nage
NV Tobin James "Dream Weaver" Sparkling Wine

Roast Suckling Pig | Bacon Jam | Charred Onion Purée | Marble Potatoes | Bourbon Glaze | Crispy Broccolini
2008 Tobin James "Ballistic" Zinfandel
2007 Tobin James "James Gang Reserve" Zinf

Seared Duck Breast | Sunchoke Purée | Crispy Confit | Puntarelle | XO Sherry | Romanesco
2006 Tobin James "James Gang Reserve" Cabernet Sauvignon

Braised Leg of Lamb | Apricot Purée | Minted Yogurt | Cous Cous | Guanciale | Curry
2007 Tobin James "Rock 'n' Roll" Syrah

NY Strip Loin | Pommes Paille | Roasted Maitakes | Parmesan Cream | Mustard Greens
2006 Tobin James "Black Magic" Petite Sirah

Figure 3-5
Wine Vault & Bistro Chef's Five-Course Tasting Menu with Paired Wines, San Diego, California   (*Source*: Reprinted by permission of Wine Vault & Bistro)

EXERCISE 3-4
CREATING A *PRIX FIXE* MENU

Q1. Create a five-course *prix fixe* menu based upon a theme. Examples of themes include:

- Seasonal vegetable harvest
- Heirloom produce
- Historical foodways
- Regional favorites
- Winemaker's dinner

However, you are encouraged to conceive a theme of your own.

Q2. Create a five-wine/beer flight to accompany your menu.

Q3. Identify the intended market for your menu and explain why the concept will succeed.

capitalizes on operational planning and execution, and generates marketing value through creative and informed construction.

NON-ALCOHOLIC BEVERAGE MENUS

The majority of alcoholic beverages are sold after 5:00 PM; thus, there is a lengthy period of time during the day when non-alcoholic beverages are appropriate for menu inclusion. Non-alcoholic beverages present a significant profit opportunity.

Certainly, tap water should be available at no cost to your diners. One can argue that all other non-alcoholic beverages compete with tap water. The challenge thus becomes, "What value can you add to other non-alcoholic beverages to position them for purchase?" Many of these items are either proprietary formulations (Pepsi, Red Bull, etc.) or simple recipes that are frequently consumed by customers at their homes (iced tea, milk, etc.). It is sometimes difficult to command high contribution margins on these items because of their relative familiarity and generally recognized costs. For example, many customers know that they can purchase a two-liter bottle of national brand soda pop (Coca Cola, 7-Up, etc.) for less than $2.00 at most grocery and convenience stores, yielding a 6-ounce beverage costing $0.18. Shift now from your customers' homes to a restaurant dining room. In restaurants, we provide a glass (or disposable cup), maybe some ice cubes, and serve a chilled beverage that is marked up above our cost. Customers expect a markup, but how much is appropriate? The concept of **price resistance** explains the inverse relationship between prices and customer demand that eventually drives away purchases. As prices for an item increase, customers are less inclined to purchase that item. Price resistance is the tension that occurs and its ultimate effect prompts customers to settle for lesser goods (complementary tap water, in this case). Figure 3-6 illustrates the relationship between unit pricing of non-alcoholic beverages and the demand (as measured in unit sales).

There are three approaches to this dilemma, each with their own strategic nuances. One approach is to sell what you deem appropriate and merchandize it without regard to price-resistance behaviors. Whereas you may encounter diminished sales, you might also enjoy the high profit margins that accrue from those customers who do order your non-alcoholic beverages. An alternate approach is to sell these items for a modest markup and forgo excessive per-unit contribution margins. You will likely sell more units; however, the primary benefit is the goodwill created when customers realize the value you are extending. A third and wholly different approach involves the crafting of distinctive beverage lists that defy simple value decisions. By focusing customer attention on product attributes, the perceived worth of the items becomes a more attractive consideration. Examples include beverages that are unique to the market or contain ingredients with contemporary (or nostalgic) marketing cachet.

Figure 3-6
Price Resistance in Non-alcoholic Beverage Purchases

EXERCISE 3-5
CREATING SIGNATURE NONALCOHOLIC BEVERAGE MENUS

Q1. Decide on a theme (loose-leaf teas, spring/mineral waters, homemade sodas, etc.) and develop a signature menu to attract clientele.

Q2. In what types of venues could these menus find a market? Explain your reasoning.

The same approach can be used when developing unique tea or coffee menus, by creating a concept where the whole is greater than the sum of its parts. Origin, rarity, and method of preparation all connote value, and if used to frame the merchandizing, customers may be attracted regardless of the price points. In addition to creative water, tea, and coffee menus, restaurants can also offer unique soft-drink formulations. Hand-crafted syrups can be mixed with carbonated water to create signature soft drinks at the bar or tableside. Fresh ginger root, hibiscus, pomegranate, celery, cucumber, sassafrass, and other flavors can be used to flavor non-alcoholic beverages or mixers for signature bar drinks. Stevia or agave nectar can be used as an alternative to traditional processed sugar or corn-syrup sweeteners. If you are creating signature drinks of this nature, it is unlikely that your customers will have a basis for evaluating their relative worth, hence greater freedom for you to mark up the price.

GLASSES OF ALCOHOLIC BEVERAGES

Wine sold by the glass is a popular beverage at the bar and enables restaurant diners the opportunity to match several beverages to the several courses of their meals. As discussed in Chapter 2, a good meal can be elevated to a great dining experience with the appropriate wines. Undoubtedly, bottled wine sales constitute an important focus for many restaurants; however, it is imperative—if not critical—to offer a strategically conceived selection of wines by the glass as well, for two compelling reasons:

- Individuals may have different preferences and one bottle will not satisfy all tastes. The opportunity to order glasses of wine solves this problem,
- Wine is intoxicating, and a bottle may contain more wine than the diner(s) are prepared to drink.

The goal in designing a wine-by-the-glass list (the same is true for a bottle list) is to reinforce the dining experience you want to provide. Envision the courses that your guests will likely choose. As discussed earlier in this chapter, typical courses in a mid-market restaurant include:

- Appetizers (small plates, soups)
- Salads
- Entrées
- Desserts and coffee

Be prepared to offer glass selections appropriate for each of these courses. To begin the planning process, your team should create a sensory list that catalogs the gastronomic sensations of your various foods you sell. Although this is a subjective exercise, it helps direct your team as they designate wine selections. For example, if your sensory list includes such terms as *spicy, herbal, rich, unctuous,* or *meaty,* then you should offer wines that have sufficient character as to complement these items. Conversely, if your sensory list includes such terms as *lean, clean, pure,* or *scented,* then a list of less assertive wines must be identified. The nuances of your food should not be dominated by wines;

EXERCISE 3-6
MATCHING FOOD AND WINE SENSATIONS

Q1. Create a "raw bar" seafood (chilled, lightly cooked, or raw shellfish) menu of at least 10 selections. Research the selections and create a sensory profile for each item. Two such examples:

- Abalone—briny; chewy, mineral aftertaste
- Sea Urchin—creamy, sweet, briny

Q2. Create a wine-by-the-glass list to accompany your seafood menu.

Q3. Explain the reasoning that governed your food and wine selections.

Q4. What target market do you expect for this menu?

If possible (and you are of legal drinking age), taste a variety of wines with your selections to complement your research.

---

nor should the wines be overpowered by the foods they are consumed with. Obviously, your team must taste food and wine together as part of the planning process. Understanding what is in the bottle is a daunting feat and comes only with research, consultation, and tasting. One example: *Zinfandel* is a popular American red wine grape. The best producers bottle zinfandel in various styles, ranging from fruit-forward to structured and austere. A well-intended menu planner might erroneously be inclined to recommend a particular zinfandel by the glass without considering its particular sensory profile. Certain zinfandels are rather light, whereas others are deep and brooding; consequently, the pairing of food and wine is not a simple matter. As with all foods, wine possesses aromas, layers of flavors, mouth-coating body, and aftertastes (finish). Just as you would select one type of peppercorn or chocolate for a recipe, you should practice informed selectivity in specifying wine (and all beverages). You must offer the wines that best fit your cuisine and overall menu concept. Riesling wines offer another example. Wines produced from this grape range from very dry to very sweet. In most cases, it would be a mistake to offer glasses of sweet Riesling at the start of a meal. This would be akin to serving dessert before the other courses, and palate fatigue could set in. In most states, wine distributors are allowed to sample their products to licensees so that exploratory tastings can be conducted by the menu planning team. There is no substitute for tasting wines before they are added to your wine list. Once selections are made, the service staff should also taste the wines so they can sell them based on actual knowledge and experience.

Wine is also decanted from bottles and sold in *carafes* and *quartinos*. These portions offer alternatives to customers who don't want a bottle, yet desire greater value than a single glass may deliver.

It is difficult to identify a universal portion size for wines served by the glass. Every business decides what is best for its own operational plan. Nonetheless, rule of thumb suggests that five glasses can be poured from a standard 750-milliliter bottle, thus producing an approximate 5-ounce portion. It must be impressed that this is merely a common practice, not an ironclad rule. Certain **apéritif** (appetizer) wines are served in small portions so as to parallel the smaller portion size of the appetizer foods. Dessert wines are also served in small portions. Creative concepts where flights of multiple wines are served will certainly consist of a series of less than 5-ounce pours. Table 3-2 illustrates typical sizes for wines served by the glass and carafe.

TABLE 3-2
TYPICAL PORTION SIZES FOR WINES BY THE GLASS

Wine Portion Size	Ounces
Glass—to accompany appetizers	2 to 4
Glass—to accompany dessert	2 to 5
Glass—to accompany entrées	3 to 6
Split of sparkling wine	6.3
Quartino	8.8
Half bottle	12.7
Half-liter carafe	17.6
Standard bottle	25.4
Full-liter carafe	33.81

As discussed in Chapter 2, malt beverages are also sold by the glass. Breweries package these products in bottles, cans, and kegs. When tapped from the keg, these beverages are the essence of the brewer's craft. A properly handled keg provides a fresh product that can be extremely profitable. Your beer selections should complement your foods. The same principles in sensory matching of wine to food also apply to malt beverages. In fact, several creative restaurants have successfully offered *prix fixe* beer dinners where flights of malt beverages have been matched with appropriate meal courses (Figure 3-7).

Figure 3-7
Beer Dinner Menu, TJ's, The Jefferson Hotel, Richmond, Virginia   (*Source:* Reprinted by permission of The Jefferson Hotel)

SIERRA NEVADA BEER DINNER

Friday, March 11, 2011 7pm
Executive Chef James Schroeder

"We wanted to pay tribute to the original pioneers who helped me and hundreds of others get started," said Sierra Nevada founder Ken Grossman. "Few people in the craft-brewing world have accomplished more than these guys, and we thought it might be fun to get the original crew together and make something special."

On **Friday, March 11th at 7pm**, find out what Ken Grossman is talking about at a very special beer dinner at TJ's hosted by Scott Hite from Sierra Nevada. Last year Sierra Nevada put out 4 very special beers to celebrate their 30th anniversary of brewing out in Chico, CA. We've been carefully stowing away cases and a keg to do a dinner featuring each brew. Don't miss this opportunity to try Chef Schroeder's amazing cuisine paired with some very special brews!

For more information on the Sierra 30 project, please visit their website at http://www.sierra30.com/

Please call 804-649-4672 or e-mail jonathan.kibiloski@jeffersonhotel.com for reservations.

$50 per person, plus tax and gratuity.

Sierra Nevada Beer Dinner Menu

Executive Chef James Schroeder

Chesapeake Bay Oyster Stew
Turnips, Benton's Bacon, Yukon Gold Potatoes, Parsley
Charlie, Fred and Ken's Bock - Imperial Helles Bock

Pan Seared Squab Breast with Crispy Leg
Blue Corn Polenta, Red Wine Braised Cabbage, Cherry Gastrique
Brewer's Reserve - Oak Aged Ale

Espresso Dusted Beef Tenderloin
Sweet Potato and Cipolin Onion Hash, Beef Short Ribs, Short Rib Jus
Jack and Ken's Ale - Black Barleywine

Black Berry Tart with Saint Andre Cheese
Whipped Cream, Vanilla Anglaise
Fritz and Ken's Ale - Imperial Stout

Cost is $50 per person, plus tax and gratuity.
Please call 804-649-4672 or e-mail jonathan.kibiloski@jeffersonhotel.com for reservations.

Malt beverages by the glass are typically sold in 10- to 22-ounce portions, with the size often influenced by the traditional glassware. Pilsners, tankards, steins, goblets, and so on vary in volume, and the appropriate glassware dictates how large or how small a portion is offered for sale. Beer is also sold in 32- and 60-ounce pitchers.

As discussed in Chapter 2, nearly all spirits are sold by the glass, either straight (undiluted), on ice ("on the rocks") or mixed as cocktails. Spirit-based drinks may be appropriate for certain meal courses; however, many customers are quite opinionated in their spirit preferences and may not be subject to merchandising efforts. Brand name spirits create loyalty ("I'm a Jack Daniel's man," "My tequila is Patron"), and customers may be less prone to suggestive selling efforts. Nonetheless, you should understand what spirit drinks compliment your food menu. Margaritas are well accepted as accompaniments to Mexican cuisine; Bloody Marys and Mimosas are popular brunch drinks; brandies and *eaux-de-vie* can be merchandized with dessert in many operations.

Mixed drinks (cocktails) where spirits are added to various ingredients ("mixers") have been enjoyed since the 17th century. Back then, certain recipes called for herbs, tinctures, and homemade ingredients. In more recent history, many operators accepted the homogeneity of bottled garnishes and commercially prepared mixers without much thought, resulting in consistent, albeit undistinguished, mixed drinks. Bartenders could prepare a seemingly endless variety of drinks that tasted fairly much the same from one operation to another. Fast forward to today, and you may observe a renaissance of sorts, where mixologists have returned to the craft of preparing homemade ingredients for use in their drinks. In fact, a *cocktail culture* is emerging, and these bartenders envision themselves as *bar chefs* or *culinary mixologists*, using a broad spectrum of vegetables, herbs, and aromatics, in addition to house-brewed bitters and artisan sodas (Figure 3-8). In essence, the gastronomic focus of the chef's kitchen has permeated the bar with the prospect of a new approach to delivering culinary drama.

In some quarters, the vision of artisan cocktails is so inspired that bartenders are mixing cocktails, then aging the beverages in port, sherry, or bourbon barrels for weeks or months. These barrel-aged cocktails become more nuanced and attain unique sensory profiles, much in the way that wine does while aging in wood.[4]

BOTTLES OF ALCOHOLIC BEVERAGES

Wine menus are referred to as **wine lists**. Wine, although perfectly acceptable as a rustic beverage served in simple tumblers, reaches its zenith when selected as an aged vintage poured into skillfully matched stemware. Wine sold by the bottle assures guests that they are the first to expose the beverage to air, hopefully enjoying the bottle at its peak (once a cork or closure is extracted, after a brief desirable period of *breathing*, all wines begin to oxidize and lose quality). Wines sold by the bottle are sealed and labeled so that specific identity can be assured.

Wine lists should be developed with an eye toward usability. Customers should be able to navigate the list in a manner that permits them to make informed selections. Simple lists are appropriate for mass markets, whereas sophisticated lists with broad and deep selections are appropriate for world-class dining concepts. Breadth on a wine list is achieved by including many varietals or bottles from many producers. Conversely, depth is achieved by including many horizontal and vertical selections. A horizontal selection features bottles from a single year from multiple producers or wineries. Vertical depth involves many selections from the same winery but from multiple vintages. In addition, customers should be able to purchase

Tomato Water Bloody Mary

Ingredients

1½ oz Citrus Vodka
Tomato water (*see below*)

Method:

Strain over ice.
Build cocktail in a Hi-ball glass over ice.
Roll in shaker.
Return to glass.
Garnish with a Cherry Tomato

Tomato Water

Ingredients

5 pounds fresh vine-on tomatoes (to yield 1–2 liters of tomato water)
1 Stalk of lemon grass
2 Serrano chilies
1 small Bermuda onion
Salt to taste
Cheese cloth

Method

Coarsely chop and purée tomatoes onion, lemon grass, and chilies in a food processor in several batches.

Add a small amount of salt in this process.

Transfer pulp to a cheesecloth and suspend over a large stockpot. Leave to strain until pulp volume has reduced by two thirds, about 12–24 hours. The liquid will be clear.

Figure 3-8
Todd Thrasher's Tomato Water Bloody Mary   (*Source:* Reprinted by permission of EatGoodFood Group)

bottles of various sizes, including splits of wine (187 ml), half bottles (375 ml), and standard wine bottles (750 ml). A wine list with various-size bottles allows customers to complement their food selections while controlling their alcohol intake. Smaller bottles bridge the gap between single glasses, and full-size (750 ml) bottles and allow a degree of restraint while enabling guests to enjoy the pleasure of their own bottle selection. Parties can enjoy various wines with multiple courses without drinking excessively. More so, diners can have access to precious wines without the big-ticket price tag of full-size bottles.

Some menu writers elect to organize their wine lists by country of origin. Some customers are challenged by this method, particularly when the names of the wines are printed in a foreign language, and the color (red, white, rosé) or style (still, effervescent, dry, sweet) of the wine is not clearly evident.

A more customer-friendly wine list may be organized as follows:

- *Apéritif* wines
- Sparkling/effervescent wines
- White wines
- Rosé wines
- Red wines
- Dessert wines

Each of these major categories is typically subdivided. Organization based on geographic origin at this level is less confusing, because primary categorization as illustrated in our list, is already established. For example, a sparkling/effervescent wine list section might include:

- Cava from Spain
- Prosecco from Italy
- Sekt from Austria or Germany
- Champagne from France
- Sparkling wine from California, New Mexico, and other states

Further delineation may include delimited regions within the geographic regions, such as this categorization of Napa Valley wines:[5]

- Atlas Peak AVA
- Chiles Valley AVA
- Diamond Mountain District AVA
- Howell Mountain AVA
- Los Carneros AVA
- Mt. Veeder AVA
- Oak Knoll District of Napa Valley AVA
- Oakville AVA
- Rutherford AVA
- Spring Mountain District AVA
- St. Helena AVA
- Stags Leap District AVA
- Wild Horse Valley AVA
- Yountville AVA

A different type of categorization is achieved when grape varietals are indicated, as is the case in this red wine section:

- Gamay
- Malbec
- Pinot Noir
- Cabernet Franc
- Petit Verdot
- Merlot
- Cabernet Franc
- Zinfandel
- Syrah

It should be evident that the complexity of wine origin and classification cannot be readily simplified and considerable knowledge of the subject must be possessed to design a moderate or extensive wine list. Figure 3-9 illustrates the nuances of a spectacular wine list from a superior restaurant. World-class lists such as this provide clear guidance to customers and are magnets to clientele seeking unforgettable dining experiences. The subject of wine list design and organization is further discussed in Chapter 9.

As previously discussed, draft beer provides a fresh-tasting and high profit margin means of selling malt beverages. A constraining factor for many operators involves the space and capital investment required to store kegs and install draft equipment. In addition, the beer does not remain fresh indefinitely, and American kegs contain 15.5 gallons, which requires a steady demand from customers if it is to remain acceptable. Many operators offer a limited selection of draft beers but also offer a variety of bottled beers. Because nearly all bottled beer is pasteurized, it possesses extended shelf life (up to 12 months). As such, your malt beverage menu can consist of a broad spectrum of

SAUVIGNON BLANC & SEMILLON

'07	Les Arums de Lagrange	Bordeaux	63
'06	Blanc de Lynch Bages *(limited supply)*	Bordeaux	155
'09	Sineann	Marlborugh, New Zealand	44
'09	Rochioli	Russian River Valley	82
'09	Peter Michael *'L'Après Midi'*	Sonoma County	110
'08	Stone Paddock	Hawkes Bay, New Zealand	38
'09	Hippolyte Reverdy	Sancerre, France	68
'08	Edmond Vatan *'Clos la Néore'*	Sancerre, France	148
'08	Pascal Cotat *'Les Monts Damnés'*	Sancerre, France	159
'09	Pascal Cotat *'La Grande Cote'*	Sancerre, France	141
'09	Pascal Cotat *'Les Monts Damnés'*	Sancerre, France	136
'09	Ojai *'Mcginley Vineyard'*	Santa Ynez Valley	57
'10	Yali *'Wetland'*	Valle de Lolol, Chile	35

ROSÉ

'08	k.furtado *'McGinley Vineyard'* Syrah	Santa Barbara County	62
'07	Simone	Palatte, France	149
'09	Knipser *'Clarette'*	Pfalz, Germany	51

WHITE RHÔNE

'08	Condrieu	Gangloff	240
'07	Châteauneuf-du-Pape Blanc *Clairette/Roussanne*	Saint Préfert	154
'07	Châteauneuf-du-Pape Blanc *Clairette/Roussanne*	Marcoux	127
'05	Châteauneuf-du-Pape Blanc *Clairette/Grenache Blanc* (limited supply)	Rayas	395
'06	Châteauneuf-du-Pape Blanc 1.5L *Clairette/Grenache Blanc/Roussanne*	Vieux Télégraphe	250
'01	Ermitage *'Le Méal'* Marsanne *(limited supply)*	M. Chapoutier	425
'04	Hermitage Blanc *Marsanne*	Betts & Scholl	145
'04	Hermitage *Marsanne/Rousanne*	Jean-Louis Chave	385
'05	Hermitage *Marsanne/Rousanne*	Jean-Louis Chave	465
'02	Hermitage *Marsanne/Rousanne* (limited supply)	Jean-Louis Chave	353
'03	Hermitage *Marsanne/Rousanne* (limited supply)	Jean-Louis Chave	508

ALSACE

'04	Gewurztraminer *'Clos Saint Urbain-Rangen de Thann'* Grand Cru *(limited*	Zind Humbrecht	133
'08	Sylvaner/Muscat/Auxerrois *'Tradition'*	Kuentz-Bas	46
'09	Riesling *'Cuvée Albert'*	Albert Mann	58
'08	Pinot Gris *'Barriques'*	Ostertag	57
'05	Pinot Gris *'Brand'* Grand Cru	Albert Boxler	131
'96	Tokay Pinot Gris *'Vendange Tardive'* (limited supply)	Schlumberger	129

RIESLING

'07	Christoffel Erben *'Ürziger Würzgarten'* Kabinett *(limited supply)*	Mosel, Germany	58
'08	Willi Schaefer *'Graacher Himmelreich'* Kabinett	Mosel, Germany	59
'08	Dr. Siemens *Spätlese*	Mosel, Germany	69
'08	Detonation *'Batterieberg'*	Mosel, Germany	36
'07	Peter Jakob Kühn *'Quartzit'* Trocken	Rheingau, Germany	76
'08	Smith Madrone	Spring Mountain District, Napa	61

Figure 3-9
Larkspur Restaurant Wine List, Vail, Colorado   (*Source:* Reprinted by permission of Larkspur Restaurant, Vail, CO)

BORDEAUX

'08	Chateau La Rame	Bordeaux	40
'07	Couronneau	Bordeaux	35

Left Bank

'06	Moulin de Tricot	Haut-Médoc	79
'06	Cambon La Pelouse	Haut-Médoc	62
'05	Cantermerle *(limited supply)*	Haut-Médoc	134
'05	Les Allées de Cantermerle	Haut-Médoc	63

Saint-Estèphe

'04	Cos d'Estournel	2ème Cru	300
'96	Cos d'Estournel	2ème Cru	499
'06	Ormes de Pez	Cru Bourgeois Exceptional	105

Pauillac

'06	Les Tourelles de Longueville	Pauillac	102
'96	Lafite Rothschild	1er Cru	1450
'06	Lacoste Borie	Pauillac	63
'07	Grand-Puy-Lacoste	Pauillac	173
'96	Latour	1er Cru	1160
'04	Latour	1er Cru	1572
'07	Clerc Milon	Pauillac	145
'08	Lynch Bages	5ème Cru	263
'06	Lynch Bages	5ème Cru	243
'95	Mouton Rothschild	1er Cru	1337
'06	Pichon-Longueville *'Comtesse de Lalande'*	2ème Cru	315
'03	Pichon-Longueville *'Comtesse de Lalande'* 1.5L (limited supply)	2ème Cru	814

Saint-Julien

'96	Léoville Poyferré	2ème Cru	357
'07	Amiral de Beychevelle	Saint-Julien	91

Margaux

'06	Prieuré-Lichine *(limited supply)*	Margaux	118
'99	Margaux	1er Cru	1572

Right Bank

Saint-Émilion

'03	Cheval Blanc *(limited supply)*	Grand Cru Classé	1000
'00	Figeac	Grand Cru Classé	750
'06	Laplagnotte-Bellevue	Saint-Émilion Grand Cru	63
'06	Fonbel	Saint-Émilion Grand Cru	79
'06	La Madeleine *(limited supply)*	Saint-Émilion Grand Cru	97
'04	L'Angelus	Grand Cru Classé	329
'01	Le Dôme *(limited supply)*	Grand Cru Classé	620

Figure 3-9
Continued

THE TAPHOUSE BOTTLED BEER LIST

SIERRA NEVADA TORPEDO....................ca/usa...4.95
if you like lots of hops...

DUCHESSE DE BURGOGNE.......................belgium...................................7.95
sweet, complex, sour, the absolute belgian ale.

BATEMAN'S...............................uk.........19.6 oz...........................7.95
packing an astonishing amount of flavor in a 5% abv beer, this is pure brit brilliance.

SCHNEIDER-BROOKLYNER HOPENWEISS....germany................................6.95
a hoppy wheat with biceps..oddly wonderful..shawn-approved.

DELIRIUM TREMENS...........................belgium...................................6.95
ya know, as in dt's, as in
MYGODDIDYOUSEETHOSEBATS!!THEYWEREMONNNNSTERBATS&...

REBEL CZECH..........................czech republic.......................................4.50
from the land with the highest per capita beer consumption on the plant. God's country.

DUVEL...........................belgium..6.95
the world's most dangerous beer.

BROTHER THELONIOUS.........................cali,usa.......................................6.95
extra hooverable take on the belgian thing man.

ADVENTINUS..................................germany.......................................6.95
theoretically, a big, big, wheat beer. actually, a religious experience.

HOEGAARDEN................................belgium...................................4.95
belgian wheat beer with a guzzleability factor of 1000% metric.

GOLDEN MONKEY...........................usofa...4.95
guaranteed to detonate your evening.

ST. LOUIS FRAMBOISE....................belgium...............750 ml...............10.95
fantastic dessert beer, with a light hint of raspberry & this price for a 750 looks like a mistake.

ACE PEAR CIDER.............ca..4.50
ditch the nestea, this is true refreshment. plus, it has alcohol.

PILSNER URQUELL.................czech republic.......................................4.25
lotsa' people who know more about beer than we do say this is the greatest beer on the planet.

CHIMAY GRANDE RESERVE...........belgium.........25 oz corked bottle......17.95
this is it! your chance to say: "I'm drinking the classiest beer in the world & you're not...peon."

LEGEND BROWN ALE............us...hey, richmond even...........22oz................5.95
one of richmond's all time favorites.

AMSTEL LIGHT.....................holland...................................4.25
a world class light beer.

BELHAVEN SCOTTISH ALE................duh............................5.25
haggis, bagpipes, & kilts - you deserve a good beer.

Figure 3-10
Commercial Taphouse Bottled Beer List, Richmond, Virginia   (*Source:* Courtesy of The Commercial Taphouse, Richmond, Virginia)

choices. With the availability of hundreds of draft and bottled beers, some operators elect to market variety. Others prefer to rotate a small but stellar selection that speaks to their intended market. Figure 3-10 illustrates a compact yet creative bottled beer list.

With two notable exceptions, spirits are not sold by the bottle for on-premise consumption. A full bottle dispensed to guests has high potential to intoxicate, and complicates the supervisory oversight and control by servers. Consequently, on-premise full-bottle sales are rare and highly regulated. The first exception is found in hotels. As illustrated in Chapter 2, hotel guests may purchase sealed bottles of spirits, which are delivered to their guestrooms with garnishes, mixers, glassware, and ice. A second exception, referred to as *bottle service*, is found in upscale clubs ("ultra lounges"). VIP service is provided in the form of reserved tables, with full bottles accompanied by garnishes, mixers and glassware. There is typically a minimum beverage tab required, and the cost for the reserved table can range from hundreds to thousands of dollars; however, bottle purchases usually offset the table reservation.

ACTION TOOLKIT

As a menu planner, you should assemble a professional resource library of recipes and technical information. The following textbooks are key essentials for all menu planners:

The Prentice Hall Essentials Dictionary of
Culinary Arts, 1/e.
Labensky & Ingram
2008; Prentice Hall; 288 pp.
ISBN-10: 013170463X | ISBN-13: 9780131704633

On Cooking: A Textbook of Culinary
Fundamentals, 5/E.
Hause, Labensky & Martel
2007; Prentice Hall; 1440 pp.
ISBN-10: 013715576X | ISBN-13: 9780137155767

Culinary Fundamentals, 1/e.
The American Culinary Federation
2006; Prentice Hall; 1104 pp.
ISBN-10: 0131180118 | ISBN-13: 9780131180116

Art of Nutritional Cooking
Baskette & Painter
2009; Prentice Hall; 336 pp.
ISBN-10: 0130457019 | ISBN-13 9780130457011

International Cooking: A Culinary Journey, 1/e.
Heyman
2003; Prentice Hall; 474 pp.
ISBN-10: 0130326593 | ISBN-13: 9780130326591

The Essentials of Wine With Food Pairing
Techniques, 1/e.
Laloganes
2010; Prentice Hall; 336 pp.
ISBN-10: 0132351722 | ISBN-13: 9780132351720

Sotheby's Wine Encyclopedia, 2/e.
Stevenson
2009; Prentice Hall; 664 pp.
ISBN-10: 0135044375 | ISBN-13: 9780135044377

Hospitality Manager's Guide to Wines, Beers,
and Spirits, 2/e.
Schmid
2008; Prentice Hall; 320 pp.
ISBN-10: 0132059681 | ISBN-13: 9780132059688

As you learn to create food and beverage menus, the following links may prove invaluable in your research:

- **Albert Uster Imports** The best worldwide ingredients for the pastry kitchen. www.aeb.org
- **American Egg Board** www.aeb.org
- **The American Lamb Board** www .americanlambboard.org
- **American Dietetic Association** The premier organization for nutrition research and dietetic professionals. www.eatright.org
- **Baking 911** Baking tips and recipes for all skill levels. www.baking911.com/
- **Breeds of Poultry** www.ansi.okstate.edu/ outreach-extension/poultry/poultry-resources
- **Cheese Information** A listing of several kinds of cheese. www.cheesesupply.com/
- **The Cook's Thesaurus** A cooking encyclopedia that covers thousands of ingredients and kitchen tools. www.foodsubs.com/
- **Epicurious** Recipes and everything about food. www.epicurious.com/

- **Escoffier on Line**   Culinary Web resources, culinary education and scholarship information and Culinary Career Center for the professional culinary community. www.escoffier.com/index.php
- **Food Network**   The lifestyle website. www.foodnetwork.com/
- **International Cake Exploration Societé (ICES)**   Great source of creative ideas for classic and contemporary cakes. www.ices.org/
- **Iowa Pork Producers**   www.iowapork.org/
- **Joy of Baking**   Recipes and tips for bakers. www.joyofbaking.com/
- **National Beef Council**   www.beef.org/
- **National Pork Producers Council**   www.nppc.org/

- **North American Meat Processors Association**   www.namp.com/namp/Default.asp
- **Pastry Chef Central**   Pastry supplies and ingredients. www.pastrychef.com/
- **Poultry Science Association**   www.poultryscience.org/index.asp?autotry=true&ULnotkn=true
- **Produce Packing Guidelines**   www.agmarketing.extension.psu.edu/Wholesale/ProdPkgGuide.html
- **Retail Bakers Association**   Useful info and newsletter. www.retailbakersofamerica.org/
- **Wisconsin Cheese Information**   www.eatwisconsincheese.com/

GLOSSARY

American Viticultural Area (AVA)—a designated wine grape-growing region in the United States defined by the United States Department of the Treasury. AVA designations infer winemaking characteristics and quality potential arising from specific geography, soil attributes, and climactic conditions.

Amuse-bouche—"to entertain the mouth"; a tiny, typically unannounced course preceding the appetizer. The course is seldom ever ordered by guests, but rather is sent to the table complements of the chef.

Apéritif (Aperitif)—a wine or spirit served at the beginning of a meal to stimulate the appetite.

Continental breakfast menu—a menu based on Mediterranean traditions, typically including a hot beverage, such as drinking chocolate or hot cocoa; or coffee with milk, such as *cappuccino* or *latte*; and sweet baked items such as *croissants* or *brioche*.

Daypart—functional division of the 24-hour time period. Typical dayparts in the foodservice industry are breakfast, lunch, and dinner.

Dégustation menu—a variation of *prix fixe* menus based on decidedly small portions, each delivering memorable impact; see also *tasting menu*.

Full breakfast menu—a substantial and traditional breakfast of English, Welsh, and Irish origin. Typically includes eggs, bacon (cured from the pork loin), sausages and puddings, grilled tomatoes, sautéed mushrooms, baked beans, toast or fried bread, and tea or coffee.

Intermezzo—a tiny yet purposeful course intended to cleanse the palate and refresh the appetite, typically served prior to the entrée. Tart frozen ices or *eaux-de-vie* are frequently used for this purpose.

Price resistance—the inverse relationship between prices and customer demand that will eventually drive away purchases.

Small-plate menu—a menu that is solely composed of small portions that, when ordered in combination, provide a meal. Examples include *mezze*, *tapas*, and *dim sum*.

Tasting menu—another term for degustation menus.

Wine List—a menu of wines served by the glass and by the bottle.

ENDNOTES

1. www.thinkexist.com/quotation/hell-there_are_no_rules_here-we-re_trying_to/12125.html; retrieved May 1, 2011.

2. The exceptions to this statement include (1) instances when you are asked your professional opinion by customers as to healthy choices, and (2) if you are employed in jobs where you are expected to be prescriptive in nutritional menu planning, such as in public schools, hospitals, and nursing homes.

3. Mintel Menu Insights, 2010. www.mintel.com/press-centre/press-releases/534/snacks-the-new-meal-restaurants-are-serving-up; retrieved May 1, 2011.

4. You must verify that premixing cocktails prior to customers ordering their drinks is permitted by law in your jurisdiction. Many statutes require the labels of spirits to be visible to customers while drinks are being prepared, to assure true identity of the brands.

5. American Viticultural Area, a system for classifying winegrowing regions in the United States.

4

The Strategic Value of Knowledge

Key Terms

Competitive set

Control states

Integrated foodservice management software suite

Locavore movement

Perpetual inventory

Point-of-sale system

Theoretical costs

SWOT analysis

(*Source:* Jack Hollingsworth/Thinkstock)

Objectives

Upon completion of this chapter, you should be able to:

4.1   Discuss the experience needed by menu planners.

4.2   Discuss the knowledge needed for effective menu planning.

4.3   Discuss the tactical value of on-demand market data.

4.4   Develop a digital information dashboard.

4.5   Discuss the strategic acquisition and use of customer data, including the value of on mined from customer loyalty clubs.

4.6   Assess the impact of competition.

4.7   Exercise informed menu-planning decisions within the context of ingredient availability, market prices, and vendor/distribution channels.

4.8   Understand the options for harnessing information technology in menu planning.

4.9   Explain the typical components of an integrated foodservice management software suite.

EXPERIENCE NEEDED BY MENU PLANNERS

"The difference between school and life? In school, you're taught a lesson and then given a test. In life, you're given a test that teaches you a lesson."

—TOM BODETT[1]

A quick scan or an in-depth study of hiring criteria for culinary management and hospitality leadership jobs points to the value of relevant work experience. Regardless of the series of jobs you will hold, each experience sheds light on the practice of menu planning. You should recognize that preparation for menu planning begins early in your career. For example, receiving deliveries and handling inventory may appear to be simple acts of labor, but in fact, they inform you of inventory items and their attributes. Front-line employees, including food runners and bartenders, interact directly with clientele and learn firsthand of customer cues, questions, and preferences. It must be recognized that sales history data only tells us what sold; it does not enhance understanding on customer pre-selection dynamics. Bartenders, for example, receive customer requests for certain spirits or liquors that are not stocked in inventory, and their insights on unmet demands should be captured for use in future menu planning. Similarly, servers regularly field questions from their guests that can help refine future menus. Servers understand the frequency of customers seeking other portion sizes, alternate preparation methods, or combinations not presently on the menu. The multitude of tasks within a food service provides insight on the menu development process.

Many individuals entering new professions are concerned that their lack of experience may be an impediment toward entry into management-level jobs, including those involving menu planning. There are merits to this concern; however, it should not be viewed as an insurmountable barrier. It is useful to focus on ways to position yourself for this new set of duties. Perhaps the best experience is to dine as your customers might. Visit a variety of food services to enable grounded comparisons. Taste a wide selection of foods (and alcoholic beverages if you are of legal age) to develop a sensory basis for menu planning. These experiences provide the culinary foundation that will be called on for years to come.

THE KNOWLEDGE NEEDED FOR EFFECTIVE MENU PLANNING

"A customer is the most important visitor on our premises. He is not dependent on us. We are dependent on him. He is not an interruption in our work. He is the purpose of it. He is not an outsider in our business. He is part of it. We are not doing him a favor by serving him. He is doing us a favor by giving us an opportunity to do so."

—MAHATMA GANDHI[2]

AUTHOR'S INSIGHT

The first menu I ever developed for commercial deployment occurred when I was an undergraduate at the Ohio State University. I was called on to convert a tired campus cafeteria concept into a high-volume Euro-themed delicatessen. Whereas I had operational experience from several restaurants and hotels, I was a novice manager, let alone menu developer. Nonetheless, the planets seemingly aligned and I created a profitable menu that was wildly popular among students and faculty. What could have been an unsuccessful venture succeeded because of market research, product development, clever merchandizing, and a healthy dose of intuition. I also was able to inspire a coalition of support among the staff, and everyone sensed a personal stake in the endeavor. If there is a lesson to be learned, it is that you are never too young or inexperienced to create a winning menu. Everyone starts somewhere.

Planning menus is a skilled activity and should be approached as such. Just as in any profession, you should possess a variety of knowledge and experiences as you approach your planning tasks.

SWOT Analysis

- You should develop a multidimensional understanding of your business and the environment it operates within by conducting a **SWOT analysis**, a common means of cataloging key business conditions (strengths, weaknesses, opportunities, threats), so you can recalibrate your tactics and strategies.

Internal

- **Strengths**—Positive attributes of your business that position you for success, including skilled culinary staff, access to superior ingredients, and an understanding of your market derived over time.
- **Weaknesses**—Areas in which your capacity or organizational characteristics impede higher levels of business success, including the size or location of your business, excessive staff turnover, and low productivity.

External

- **Opportunities**—Those areas you might capitalize on to increase sales volume, reduce costs/expenses, or reposition yourself within the market, including capturing business from competitors, redefining your concept, and relocating to a more viable address.
- **Threats**—Events that are typically out of your control that could have a negative impact on your business, including introduction of new competitors and a downturn in the economy.

You should understand the food and beverage preference trends of your market. Certainly, novel patterns will emerge; however, it is critical to understand the historical and current dining preferences of your target market. When do they like to dine out? What are the customary price points for menu categories? What foods and beverages are most popular? What items are least popular? Whereas national statistics are available, local market data is more difficult—yet not impossible—to obtain. For example, in addition to processing credit payment transactions for food and beverage merchants, American Express provides market intelligence in the form of business analytics, market reports, and advertising tools. For a modest fee, you can purchase quarterly *Local IQ Reports* that provide detailed statistical information on consumer and commercial spending for restaurants in your area.[3] This information does not address menu preferences specifically, but it does provide insight on dining spending, influences, origins and destinations of dining purchases, lifestyle profiles, and media preferences.

EXERCISE 4-1
SWOT ANALYSIS TO INFORM MENU PLANNING

Select a foodservice operation or restaurant and interview the management staff to conduct a simple SWOT analysis for the business. You may find it valuable to interview several managers individually to obtain a variety of perspectives.

Q1. Based on your findings, are the current menus appropriate for the business situation?

Q2. Based on the threats and opportunities, how might this business transform itself for future survival and success? What impact does this have on their menus?

AUTHOR'S INSIGHT

In my estimation, one of the most important positions in a kitchen is held by the dishwasher. How so? The remnants of a meal return to his or her workstation, and this provides the surest sign of guest acceptance. If a meal wasn't well received, the dishwasher is sure to know. If the portions are too large, this person can provide details. When empty plates return to the dishroom, this valued staff member can announce success of the menu item. From my perspective, every culinary and hospitality professional should experience a stint as a dishwasher if they are to appreciate the consultative importance of this position.

EXERCISE 4-2
DOES KNOWLEDGE ALWAYS MATTER?

Conduct a Socratic argument with the following prompt: "Menu planners do not need to know how to cook."

- Another method is to conduct **focus group** studies. A focus group discussion using scripted prompts can be administered to a representative sample of local residents, with greater local market comprehension as an outcome.
- Menu planners must understand product/flow and logistics as food and beverages are processed or cooked. As discussed in Chapter 3, timing is critical for seat turnover and customer satisfaction. Customer orders and tickets must be processed in a swift and coordinated manner. To achieve this objective, you must understand equipment capacity, cooking times, holding times, and balancing of staff workloads. Some of this knowledge is achieved through study, but much of it comes through experience working in the field.

ON-DEMAND MARKET DATA

The Chapter 1 Action Toolkit introduced several web resources to better help you understand your market. These resources can be augmented with additional information that applies specifically to your local market. Figure 4-1 illustrates an information dashboard that makes pertinent information convenient to menu planners. This example was developed for one particular regional market; however, it can easily be customized for other areas.

The links within the dashboard allow you to view some of the same resources used in prior studies (SWOT analyses, etc.), and are particularly valuable when placed at your (virtual) fingertips.

CUSTOMER DATA

Chapter 1 introduces the importance of aligning your business vision with suitable target markets. The notion of a *market* is a somewhat artificial construct in that *individuals* are a more appropriate unit of study. If you understand behaviors of persons, then you can begin to understand the markets they aggregate into. Previously in this chapter, you learned about the value of focus groups as related to menu

INFORMATION DASHBOARD
27 November, 2011   14:21 EST

NEWSPULSE
LOCAL WEATHER & NEWS
SPORTS
MARKETS

Markets Closed		CNNMoney.com »
Updated 5:30 pm ET Nov 27		Indexes My quotes
Dow 10,309.92	-154.48	(-1.48 %)
Nasdaq 2,138.44	-37.61	(-1.73 %)
S&P 1,091.49	-23.36	(-2.10 %)

- Refdesk.com
- keysnews.com
- Key West Travel Guide Calendar of Events
- Florida Traffic Warnings and Updates
- keywestmenu.com
- Key West International Airport Flight Information
- Local Crime Statistics
- National Restaurant Association SmartBrief

My Competitive Set

- El Siboney
- El Meson de Pepe
- Jose's Cantina

Figure 4-1
Information Dashboard

EXERCISE 4-3
CUSTOMIZING YOUR INFORMATION DASHBOARD

Save a copy of the file located at http://www.pearsonhigh-ered.com/barrish dashboard to your hard drive or another storage device. Rename the file "[Your Name] Dashboard." Replace or delete existing links that may not be of value to you or your concept, and add links that are relevant to your concept and region.

Q1. How and when do you see yourself using this tool for menu planning and forecasting?

Q2. Test the usability of the tool by attempting to access information to answer the following questions:

- Will local events cause my anticipated historical traffic to increase or decrease this week?
- What criminal activity is most prevalent in my market corridor?
- What local and national industry developments should I be aware of?

planning. It also helps to understand specific patterns exhibited by your actual clientele. There are blunt instruments for obtaining generalized data (regional demographic databases, etc.); however, you can create your own databases by obtaining information from your existing customers. Hotels and casinos excel at this through their customer loyalty ("club") and affinity programs. Some restaurants also do a commendable job in this arena. Figure 4-2 illustrates a Web-based registration form for a restaurant loyalty club.

The data collected through this type of effort can then be entered into a database and mined for strategic planning purposes. Figure 4-3 illustrates a sample customer database (affinity club) report prepared with Microsoft Access.

In addition, social media technology such as Facebook, Twitter, or Foursquare can be used to network with potential customers. When individuals accept your invitations into your network, they agree to receive future digital communications from you.

Using data collected from actual customers, you can obtain market intelligence on age, gender, family/marital status, and dining out habits. If the data serves as a representative sample, then you can generalize the findings to the larger population of

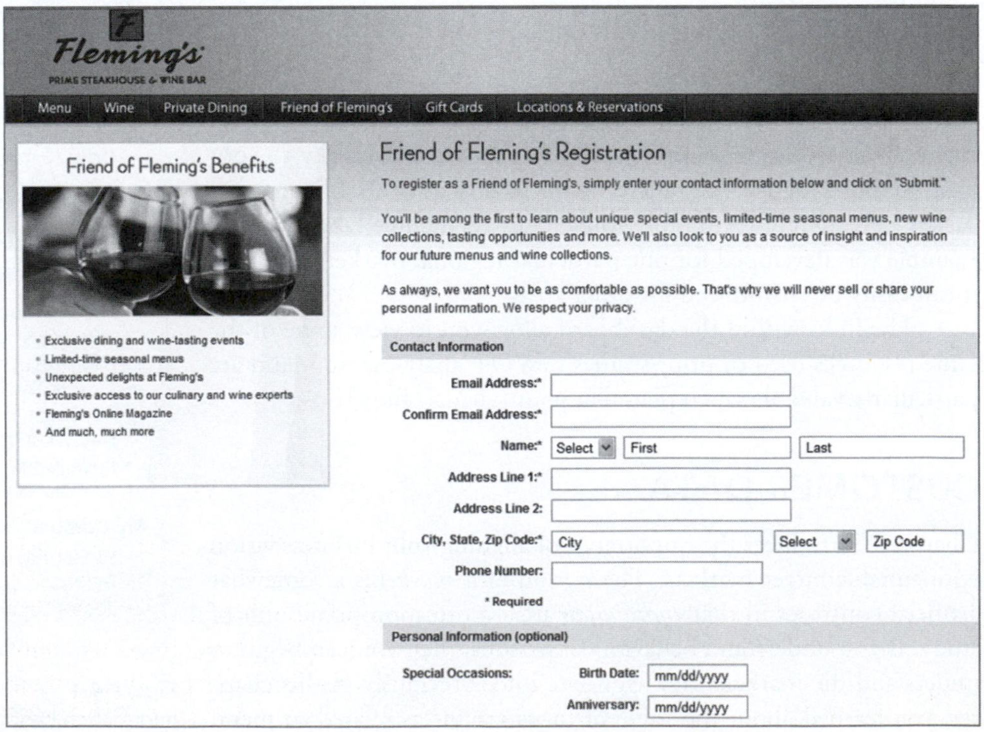

Figure 4-2
"Friend of Fleming's"
Registration Form
(*Source:* Reprinted by permission of OSI Restaurant Partners, LLC)

					Affinity Club Report						
Report Date 12/31/09											
Customer #	Customer Name	Gender	Marital Status	DOB	Usage Dates	Reservation	# in Party	Promo Code Used	POS Account#	Food Subtotal	Beverage Subtotal
509029	Anderry	M	M	3/12/1952	Wednesday, November 05, 2008	20:30	2	Wine Harvest	42672	$131	$93
509029	Anderry	M	M	3/12/1952	Monday, December 15, 2008	20:00	12	Holiday Cheer	40353	$671	$356
509029	Anderry	M	M	3/12/1952	Wednesday, March 25, 2009	N	2	3-course Midweek	39636	$70	$41
509029	Anderry	M	M	3/12/1952	Wednesday, June 24, 2009	20:30	5	Birthday	42783	$289	$108
509029	Anderry	M	M	3/12/1952	Wednesday, July 15, 2009	N	2	Farmer's Market	40337	$68	$35
464830	Fostiz	F	S	11/27/1980	Monday, January 12, 2009	N	2	Comp Appetizer	36299	$48	$28
464830	Fostiz	F	S	11/27/1980	Monday, May 11, 2009	19:30	2	3-course Midweek	41386	$70	$29
464830	Fostiz	F	S	11/27/1980	Thursday, December 03, 2009	N	2	Club Rewards	36960	$68	$35
354837	Henstilly	M	S	6/23/1967	Tuesday, November 04, 2008	20:00	4	Wine Harvest	37810	$202	$199
292929	Garke	F	M	5/11/1980	Tuesday, June 02, 2009	20:00	16	Farmer's Market	41129	$515	$150
292929	Garke	F	M	5/11/1980	Wednesday, October 29, 2008	20:30	8	Wine Harvest	41550	$519	$254
292929	Garke	F	M	5/11/1980	Saturday, January 03, 2009	20:00	12	Club Rewards	43264	$693	$211
292929	Garke	F	M	5/11/1980	Monday, August 17, 2009	N	2	3-course Midweek	42681	$82	$58
501250	Rivan	M	S	9/30/1982	Monday, June 15, 2009	19:30	2	3-course Midweek	38428	$70	$26
501250	Rivan	M	S	9/30/1982	Wednesday, December 09, 2009	19:30	3	3-course Midweek	42795	$119	$38

Figure 4-3
Customer Database Report

EXERCISE 4-4
USING CUSTOMER DATA

Analyze the data in Figure 4-3 to discern as many patterns as possible among this small sample of customers.

Q1. What patterns can you use for future menu planning?

Q2. What are the limits of relying on data from a small sample?

Q3. What other data can realistically be solicited to enhance the value of this database?

---

your entire clientele. In return for providing personal data, customers belonging to loyalty clubs receive special offers through direct marketing, many of them tailored to their specific consumption preferences.

ASSESSING THE IMPACT OF COMPETITION

Your SWOT analysis likely touched on the opportunities for and threats to your business imposed by competitors. Your **competitive set** (also referred to as *peer set*) is the group of local businesses that you assume constitute the choices your market will select if they don't select your business. Whereas some particularly loyal customers will only eat or drink in one place of business, it is quite typical for customers to spread their business around. Your objective is to position yourself to obtain the largest fraction of

EXERCISE 4-5
CUSTOMER SURVEY

Develop a set of survey questions that can be administered for the purpose of collecting customer preference and competitor usage findings. (Two sample questions are included to begin the survey.)

Q1. "What is the number one reason you visit us?"

Q2. "What do our competitors offer that we don't?"

Q3.

Q4.

Q5.

Q6.

Q7.

Q8.

Q9.

Q10.

their dining dollar as possible. It is quite difficult to obtain hard and fast data on these competitive patterns; however, the focus group surveys and affinity club data can help you understand where customers dine when they are not with you.

As previously discussed, American Express provides market intelligence for a fee. American Express merchants are able to purchase quarterly *Competitive Focus Reports* that quantify market share and customer mix.[4]

Once you have identified your competitive set, you must decide whether to provide similar goods and services, or to differentiate your business. As discussed in Chapter 1, your vision statement should guide your business, including how you approach your competitors. One means to study the members of your competitive set is to identify several criteria and menu items that define each of you in the customer decision-making process. A simplified table for conducting this type of comparative research is illustrated in Figure 4-4. Whereas this example compares three competitors, you should construct your own table based on the actual number of competing businesses you identify within your own peer set.

Figure 4-4
Table for Comparing Competitive Set Attributes

	Competitor 1	Competitor 2	Competitor 3
Web site			
Reservations policy			
Lunch hours			
Dinner hours			
Parking			
Gratuity			
Appetizer			
Salad			
Entrée			
Entrée			
Entrée			
Side order			
Coffee			
Dessert			
Dessert			
House wine (glass)			

CASE STUDY 4-1 *COMPETITOR STUDY*

Key West, Florida, is a popular leisure destination. It possesses an open-minded, Bohe-mian vibe and may be described as "island casual." It is 129 miles from Miami, yet only 106 miles from Cuba. Consequently, Key West exhibits a wealth of Cuban culture and a significant population of Cuban-Americans. Cuban food and beverages are quite popu-lar, as are *Floribbean* and other tropical cuisines. Fine dining is available; however, most visitors enjoy informal meals in relaxed settings. Three competing Cuban restaurants are profiled in Figure 4-5, each of which is a family-run, independent business. Jose's Can-tina and El Siboney are low- to mid-price, providing a no-frills experience. El Meson de Pepe features a large dining room in a prime location. Entertainment and cocktail ser-vice feature prominently in its success, and there is also an atmospheric cigar shop where guests can purchase cigars hand-rolled to order. Figure 4-5 compares several criteria of the three restaurants. (Note that the competitors listed in this example are also included in the information dashboard in Figure 4-1. The convenience of the dash-board hyperlinks enables ease of updating the competitive set analysis on a periodic basis.) Whereas other criteria and menu items can be selected as benchmarks for com-parison, this example uses a few items that are relevant for simple menu analysis.

	El Siboney	El Meson de Pepe	Jose's Cantina
Web site	www.elsiboneyrestaurant.com/	www.elmesondepepe.com/	None
Reservations Policy	Not taken	Not taken	Not taken
Lunch Hours	11:00:00 AM till	11:00:00 AM till	11:00:00 AM till
Dinner Hours	9:30PM	11:00PM	9:30PM
Parking	Dedicated lot	On street	On street
Gratuity	Customer discretion	Automatic 18%	Customer discretion
Ropa Vieja	$10.40	$14.24	$9.99
Roast Pork Entrée	$9.40	$14.40	$9.99
Grilled Grouper Filet	$13.94	$19.94	$16.94
Paella Valenciana	$19.94	$29.99	$27.40
Tostones	$3.40	$4.94	$3.00
Moros	$2.40	$4.94	$1.94
Café Cubano	$0.814	$2.40	$0.94
Key Lime Pie	$3.24	$6.94	$2.94
Flan	$2.94	$6.24	$2.94
House Wine (glass)	$2.94	$4.24	Not available

Figure 4-5
Competitive Set
Comparative Study

EXERCISE 4-6
APPLYING COMPETITOR INFORMATION TO MENU PLANNING

Imagine that you have received startup financing to open a modest Cuban restaurant in Key West. The occupancy costs are minimal, and if prime costs can be maintained, then there is a high probability of long-term profitability and business success. With knowledge of the information in Figure 4-5, cre-ate a dinner menu that bears potential for market acceptance and competition. (You may need to research traditional Cuban recipes.)

Q1. Who will make up your intended market?

Q2. Who may make up your incidental market?

Q3. Research the three businesses listed in Figure 4-5. Create narrative statements that help explain the competitive reality they pose.

Q4. What was the reasoning for the particular menu selections you have chosen?

Q5. Who will be your closest competition? Why?

Q6. What is special about your menu that will attract suf-ficient business?

INGREDIENT AVAILABILITY, MARKET PRICES, VENDORS, AND DISTRIBUTION CHANNELS

When planning menu items, it is necessary to understand ingredient availability. As was illustrated in Exercise 1-2, a menu based on fleeting availability will present challenges, stock outages, price fluctuations, and the potential for customer dissatisfaction. Local produce and wild-caught fish/shellfish are just some of the ingredients that are prone to seasonality.

Modern distribution channels nearly assure that any product you seek is available from somewhere at some price, but the question that begs asking is, "How delicious is a perishable product that has been shipped from halfway across the globe?" Some of these products have been harvested or fished days ago and are "fresh" in the loosest possible use of the word. Some items are gassed, irradiated, or otherwise preserved to slow aging and degradation. In addition, the cost of packaging and transporting these items from afar must be factored into menu prices. A fairly recent backlash to this has emerged. The **locavore movement** is based on ingredients usually sourced within 100 miles of the kitchens they will be cooked in. These items are often grown and raised or processed without additives, growth hormones, and chemicals. There are several dimensions (e.g., sustainability, eco-consciousness) to the movement; however, when the ingredients reach the plate, they are likely to be as good, clean, and delicious as any product on the market. The locavore concept acknowledges seasonality and the subtle logic it imbues. Whereas you can buy Florida hothouse tomatoes year-round to serve in your Maine restaurant or Central American melons to serve in your Ohio dining rooms during winter, nothing will deliver the local flavor as an ingredient harvested in your own region during its typical growing season. New York State apples make the best apple pie served in New York. The same can be said for Maryland crabs served in Baltimore, and myriad other local ingredients served at or near the source.

Modern aquaculture, small-production farming, artisan brewing, craft beverage production, and a host of other emergent trends have changed the selection of ingredients available for our menus. Figure 4-6 lists some of the recent changes that have occurred.

Regarding Figure 4-6 and the preceding discussion, it is important to recognize that many established ingredients are appropriate for certain foodservice concepts. You

Figure 4-6
Changes in Ingredient Availability

Established Ingredients	Emergent Ingredients
Seasonally available wild-caught fish and seafood	Aquacultured fish and seafood
Livestock bred for intramuscular fat marbling	Reduced fat livestock breeds
Corn-fed and formula-fattened livestock	Grass-fed beef, veal, and lamb
Factory-farmed poultry	Free-range poultry
Pharmaceutically treated livestock	Antibiotic-free livestock
Produce shipped from all corners of the world; hothouse produce	Locally grown produce
Traditionally colored produce	Purple Peruvian potatoes, white eggplant, purple asparagus, blue corn, etc.
Scientifically enhanced growing procedures to maximize yield and shelf life	Heirloom produce
Chemically enhanced agricultural practices to maximize output	Certified organic produce
Wheat, oats, corn, and other popular cereals and grains	Ancient cereals and grains, including spelt, amaranth, and quinoa
High-volume mega breweries	Craft beers
Scientific vineyard practices to increase grape harvests	Organic and biodynamic wines
Cocktails mixed with convenience ingredients, including bottled sour mix and canned juices	Culinary cocktails made with fresh and creative ingredients
Large-production distilled spirits	Small-batch spirits

must make informed decisions to provide the menu and wine list options your target market seeks. For example, if you serve only biodynamic wines, you limit your customers to a mere fraction of the world's selections of fine wine. There are similar arguments for using mass-produced spirits rather than exclusive options. Quite frankly, when sweet components are mixed with spirits to produce cocktails, many of the nuances become combined into an acceptable—if not indistinguishable—drink. Similar decisions must be made regarding food ingredients. If you decide to offer grass-fed beef, you will be serving a product that many customers may be unaccustomed to. If they seek the typical unctuousness of grain-fed beef, the grass-fed product may not deliver what was anticipated. Likewise, strict adherence to seasonal produce means that you dramatically limit your recipes throughout most of the year. Your customers may not find it egregious to be served tomatoes in the winter or root vegetables in the summer. It is important that you base your product choices on sound, customer-centered rationale. Conversely, if your target market seeks innovation or novelty, then you might consider following emergent trends. If you cannot equate profit growth with new approaches to ingredients, then you may be better off following a conservative path.

During the past several decades, wholesale food distribution channels have consolidated and a few dominant broad line distributors lead the market. It is quite common for operators to purchase the majority of their food and supplies from Sysco, U.S. Foodservice, Performance Food Group, and other companies with a national presence, whereas in the past these restaurants may have spread their purchases across several vendors. These companies are reputable and carry a broad and deep catalog; however, their business models tend toward mass distribution and they may resist carrying low-demand items. If you choose to do business with these large distributors, you should also locate several specialty companies to round out your recipe needs.

Recipes must reflect current ingredient prices. Historically, vendor representatives would make personal sales calls on customers and provide lists of current prices or promotions. Now, many—if not most—vendors provide password-protected access to their online catalogs and current price lists. Figure 4-7 illustrates an example of an online catalog page from a broad line vendor.

In addition, vendors often provide their customers with commodity and market data to assist in menu development (Figure 4-8).

When vendors receive deals, they often pass them on to their customers. Your culinary team will be particularly interested in on-demand access to value-priced ingredients for daily and weekly specials. Profitable merchandising of these specials is enhanced when comparative price shopping can be facilitated. Ready access to vendor information enables immediate competitive shopping and potential for optimal ingredient costs.

Certain idiosyncrasies have a significant impact on the sourcing of alcoholic beverage ingredients. Spirits, malt beverage, and wine distribution is governed by state alcoholic beverage control regulations. In most states, this means that individual vendors hold exclusive distribution rights for particular products. Consequently, if you elect to serve Coors beers or Beringer wines for example, you will be required do business with vendors who possess exclusive rights to sell them in your area. In addition, certain rare products are allocated and a finite quantity is available in your market. Your ability to purchase allocated beverages often relies on your total purchase volume with respective vendors and perhaps the requirement to purchase allied products. For example, if you seek to purchase a case of a limited-release, vineyard-designated Cabernet Sauvignon, you might be required to also purchase several cases of mass-production red table wine. Spirits are most often purchased from state government stores ("ABC stores") and warehouses. States that sell spirits directly to restaurants and bars through government channels are referred to as **control states**. Other states allow spirits to be sold by private-sector vendors, as is typically the case for malt beverages and wines. In fact, some vendors in these states carry a full catalog of spirits, wine, malt beverages, and mixers.

Figure 4-7
Performance Food Group Online Catalog Page   (*Source:* Copyright © 2007, Performance Food Group. All Rights Reserved.)

U.S. Foodservice
Weekly market report update

Date: March 16, 2011

Poultry - Chicken	Overall category update	
Item	**Pricing situation**	**Comments**
Georgia Dock	steady	Higher on increased cost plus sales due to feed input costs. Some seasonal demand pick up.
NE Boneless Breast	price increase	Higher as seasonal demand usage picks up and retail features pick up in light of higher competing meat prices. Production is slowing down
NE Select Boneless Breast	gradual increase	Higher as seasonal demand usage picks up and retail features pick up in light of higher competing meat prices. Production is slowing down
NE Wings	steady	At the bottom for March
NE Jumbo Wings	price increase	Slight increases due to increased demand due to a low prices
NE Tenders	price increase	Following boneless breast upward so as to keep a reasonable gap to boneless.
NE Small Tenders	gradual increase	Following boneless breast upward so as to keep a reasonable gap to boneless.
NE Boneless Thigh Meat Special Trim	gradual increase	Seasonal increase, some pressure due to leg quarter exports taking bonless thighs off the market.
Fzn Turkeys 12-14	steady	A very high seasonal floor for whole bird turkeys.
Fzn Turkeys 20-22	steady	A very high seasonal floor for whole bird turkeys.
Fresh Tom Breast	steady	At or near seasonal low.
Boxed Beef	Overall category update	
Item	**Pricing situation**	**Comments**
Boxed Beef Cutout, Choice	gradual increase	Record high Live Cattle prices will force packers to cut harvest levels and push hard for across the board price increases. Prices must move higher.

Figure 4-8
Weekly Market Report Update   (*Source:* Reprinted by permission of U.S. Foodservice)

HARNESSING THE POWER OF INFORMATION TECHNOLOGY

Digital technology can be applied throughout the research and planning steps of the menu development process. The worksheets that accompany this textbook were created with Microsoft Excel and demonstrate how popular application software can readily be used for menu planning and management. Also, the worksheets can be linked so that as one sheet changes, all other linked sheets are updated, thus creating a dynamic set of solutions.

Exercise 4-7 illustrates how common application software can easily be used to update recipe costs as market prices of ingredients change. This level of technology permits even the smallest business to maintain a set of automated recipe management tools. Whereas Microsoft Excel does a fine job, you might elect to use Microsoft Access for larger databases or data that you will use for several applications.

EXERCISE 4-7
IMPACT OF INGREDIENT PRICE CHANGES ON MENU ITEMS

In Chapter 3, you were introduced to an innovative Bloody Mary recipe in text-only form. Figure 4-9 illustrates the same recipe in digital format as an Excel worksheet.

The following exercise illustrates what impact changes in ingredient prices have on recipe costs and cost percentages.

Step 1 Download bloody_mary.xls from http://pearson-highered.com/barrish and save the file to your hard drive or another storage device.

Step 2 Create another copy of the file and name it bloodymaryversion2.xls

Step 3 Replace the existing data with the following new data that resulted from price changes as a result of seasonality of produce:

- Cell F13 (tomatoes) $2.98
- Cell F14 (lemongrass) $0.35

- Cell F15 (Serrano chili) $0.05
- Cell F16 (Bermuda onion) $0.44

Q1. What is the portion cost of a Bloody Mary based on these new ingredient costs?

Step 4 Replace the data that you entered in Step 3, as follows:

- Tomatoes experience a seasonal price drop of 20%

- A premium vodka is selected to replace the current brand. The new vodka costs $33.50 per 25.4-ounce bottle.

Q2. What is the portion cost of a Bloody Mary based on these new ingredient costs?

Figure 4-9
Todd Thrasher's Tomato Water Bloody Mary (*Source: Reprinted by permission of EatGoodFood Group*)

	Inventory File #	Ingredient	Original Quantity	Amount	Recipe Unit	Unit Cost	Total Ingredient Cost
1	Item:	Todd Thrasher's Tomato Water Bloody Mary					
2							
3		Recipe File #		SP001			
4		Desired Yield (# of portions)		10			
5		Conversion Factor		1.00			
6		Batch Cost		$24.200			
7		Portion Cost		$2.420			
8		Sales Price		$7.50			
9		Cost %		32.27%			
10			10				
11	Inventory	Ingredient	Original	Amount	Recipe	Unit Cost	Total
12	File #		Quantity		Unit		Ingredient Cost
13	PR2654	Tomatoes, Fresh, Vine-On	5	5.00	pound	$2.490	$12.450
14	PR2387	Lemongrass	1	1.00	stalk	$0.120	$0.120
15	PR2328	Serrano Chile	2	2.00	each	$0.020	$0.040
16	PR2687	Bermuda Onion, small	1	1.00	each	$0.370	$0.370
17	SP7623	Vodka, Citrus-Flavored	15	15.00	ounce	$0.748	$11.220
18	SU8912	Salt	To taste		ounce		

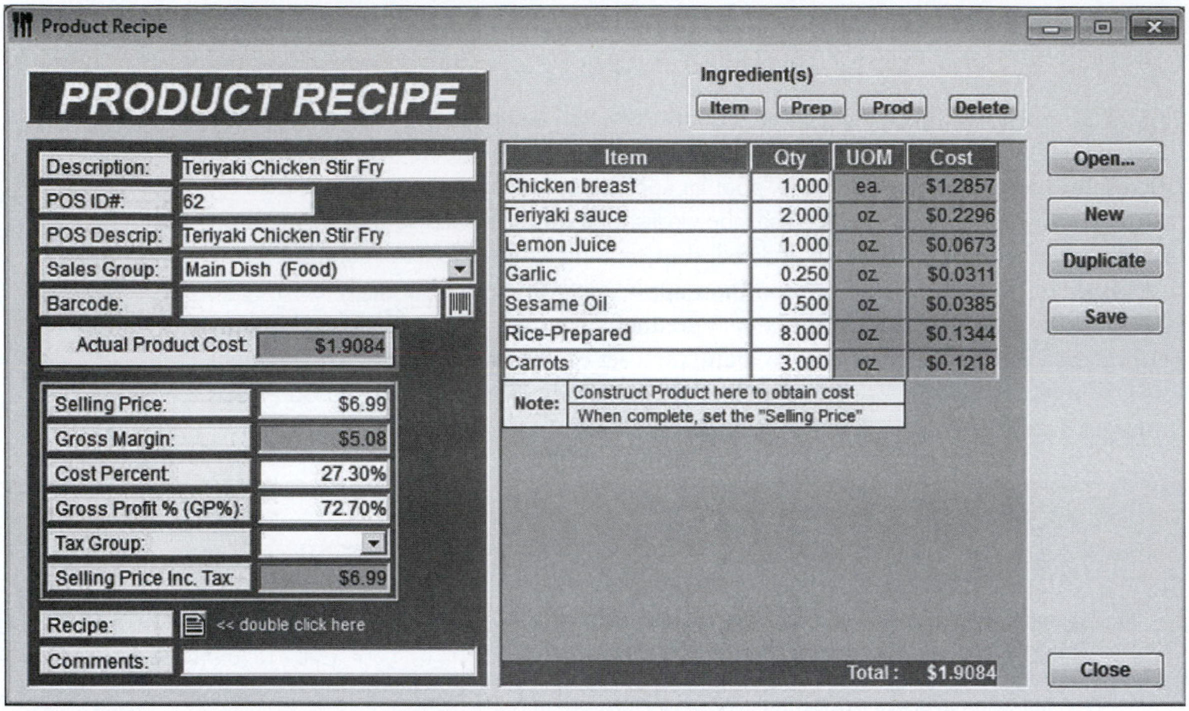

Figure 4-10
Digital Recipe Card from an Integrated Foodservice Management Software Suite   (*Source:* Reprinted by permission of Tracrite Software)

As businesses grow in volume and complexity, they benefit from task-specific application software. Figure 4-10 illustrates an example of a recipe card that is part of an **integrated foodservice management software suite**. This example shares similarities to the recipe cards discussed in Figure 4-9. The significant addition in Figure 4-10 is the criteria relating the recipe to the point-of-sale function. This level of integration enables tracking of **perpetual inventory**, which allows for advanced inventory control and comparison of **theoretical costs** versus actual costs. Each time a menu item (Teriyaki Chicken Stir Fry in this example) is sold, it is registered as a point-of-sale transaction. The ingredients listed on the recipe card are deducted from perpetual inventory during each transaction. For example, if 100 orders of Chicken Teriyaki Stir Fry were sold during a meal period, it would be safe to assume that the perpetual inventory is reduced by 100 chicken breasts (and other ingredients). If the perpetual inventory prior to the meal period equaled 600 chicken breasts, the following calculation applies:

$$\text{Ending Perpetual Inventory} = \text{Opening Perpetual Inventory} - \text{Items Sold}$$

$$500 \text{ chicken breasts} = 600 \text{ chicken breasts} - 100 \text{ chicken breasts}$$

The ending perpetual inventory anticipates what is actually in stock. You should be able to count the chicken breasts, and ideally, there should be 500 in stock at the end of the meal period. If that is true, then all chicken breasts are accounted for. If the count is less, then there are one or more control problems, or errors in your database. This level of control presents great potential and is one of the benefits of data integration. Another benefit involves calculation of ideal food and beverage costs. Using the example of 100 orders sold, and the recipe cost of $1.9084 illustrated on Figure 4-10, the following calculation can be performed:

$$100 \text{ orders sold} \times \$1.9084 = \$190.84 \text{ theoretical cost}$$

If similar calculations are performed for all food and beverage items sold and they are added to produce a composite, then a total theoretical ("ideal") cost can be predicted.

This total can then be compared to actual costs (confirmed by actual inventory consumption) to provide additional management control data. The predictive value of calculating theoretical costs enables a preemptive management posture and resultant profit enhancement. Figure 4-11 illustrates a worksheet comparing actual versus ideal (theoretical) costs based on items transacted through the integrated **point-of-sale system**.

Figure 4-12 illustrates an example of a menu engineering worksheet that is part of an integrated foodservice management software suite. (The mechanics of menu engineering are discussed in Chapter 10.)

The full extent of data integration is dictated by the information needs sought by management. The integrated software suites discussed in this section are typically sold as a core point-of-sale system, with optional software modules available as add-ons. These software solutions are scalable to fit single-unit businesses, multiunit enterprises, and complex combinations such as hotels, casinos, resorts, theme parks, and continuing care communities. The following list illustrates the spectrum of hardware/software functionality and options:

Point-of-Sale Features

- Multiple front-of-house and back-of-house client stations, with option for standalone integrity during network server downtime
- Various data entry methods, including keyboards, touch screen, and tableside handheld devices
- Preset keys or price lookup (PLU) numeric keys
- Seamless integration with back-office software, including recipe, forecasting, inventory, and financial modules
- Enterprise connectivity and real-time unit monitoring/polling
- Time and attendance functionality, including time clock and payroll
- Staff system access through unique alphanumeric accounts or swipe cards
- Perpetual inventory countdown to alert staff of item availability
- In-house email network and employee communications bulletin board
- Forced modifiers to customize guest preferences
- Automatic routing of work orders to printers, displays, and expeditor stations, including deferred work order communication
- Transaction tracking by employee, time increments, seats, tables, or user-defined menu categories
- Server or cashier banking
- Settlement to cash, credit cards, hotel folios, or club member/loyalty accounts
- Integration with credit card processing
- User-defined tip handling, including automatic gratuities
- Transfer of tabs between tables and accounts and check splitting

Credit Card Processing

- Preapprovals, real-time authorizations, deferred settlements, tip adjustments, and end-of-day batch calculations

Loyalty Club/Frequent Diner Features

- Integration between frequent customer databases, reservation modules, and point-of-sale prompts
- Management alerts of customer's presence in restaurant
- Reporting of visit frequency, expenditures, special occasion usage, and effectiveness of promotions

Remote Communications

- Secure internet-based system read/write access
- Integrated end-of-day polling capability and central site processing for multi-unit users

Usage Summary - by Count Amounts

From: Tuesday, March 10, 2009
To: Monday, April 06, 2009

Sales: $70,691.56

	Actual Cost of Sales:	$21,833.82	30.89%
	Ideal Cost of Sales:	$20,817.82	29.45%
	Variance:	$1,016.00	1.44%
	Waste:	$17.59	0.02%
	Net Variance:	$998.41	1.41%

Note: Inventory amounts that have been adjusted are marked with *, see the "Review Inventory Report".
Ideal amounts marked with * have been actualized. i.e. Ideal = Actual

Description	UOM	Opening Inventory	Period Purchases	Ending Inventory	Actual Usage Amount	Actual Usage Value	Ideal Usage Amount	Ideal Usage Value	Waste Amount	Waste Value	Difference Amount	Difference Value
Food Sales: Not Detailed												
Beverage												
Coffee	bag	319.450*	64.000	139.460	243.990	$152.31	236.153	$147.42	0.000	$0.00	7.837	$4.89
Coffee filters	bag	4.980*	0.000	4.800	0.180	$0.90	0.236	$1.18	0.000	$0.00	-0.056	-$0.28
Juice-Orange	pak.	36.320*	12.000	8.910	39.410	$103.73	39.059	$102.81	0.000	$0.00	0.351	$0.92
Pop syrup	bag	9.450*	8.000	2.527	14.923	$993.69	15.065	$1,003.14	0.000	$0.00	-0.142	-$9.46
Stir sticks	cs.	2.890*	0.000	3.000	-0.110	-$0.89	0.000	$0.00	0.000	$0.00	-0.110	-$0.89
Straws 8 "	box	44.900*	0.000	45.000	-0.100	-$0.12	0.000	$0.00	0.000	$0.00	-0.100	-$0.12
Sugar portion	cs.	2.980*	0.000	2.137	0.843	$14.74	0.841	$14.71	0.000	$0.00	0.002	$0.03
Sugar twin portion	bag	12.400*	0.000	11.746	0.654	$2.65	0.316	$1.28	0.000	$0.00	0.338	$1.37
Tea	box	2.900*	0.000	3.000	-0.100	-$0.81	0.000	$0.00	0.000	$0.00	-0.100	-$0.81
Beverage Totals					[1.79%	$1,266.21]|	1.80%	$1,270.54]|	0.00%	$0.00]|	-0.01%	-$4.34]
Bread												
Bread Crumbs	pak.	2.000	7.000	5.000	4.000	$37.36	3.990	$37.27	0.000	$0.00	0.010	$0.09
Bun-Beef dip	ea.	23.980*	864.000	308.000	579.980	$140.15	576.000	$139.19	0.000	$0.00	3.980	$0.96
Buns-Hamburger	ea.	54.000	2088.000	330.000	1812.000	$301.00	2336.000	$388.04	0.000	$0.00	-524.000	-$87.04
Buns-Kaiser	ea.	36.000*	0.000	36.000	0.000	$0.00	0.000	$0.00	0.000	$0.00	0.000	$0.00
Tortillas 10in	pak.	0.000	0.000	0.000	0.000	$0.00	0.000	$0.00	0.000	$0.00	0.000	$0.00
Bread Totals					[0.68%	$478.51]|	0.80%	$564.50]|	0.00%	$0.00]|	-0.12%	-$85.99]
Dairy												
Butter	lb.	2.000	90.000	3.500	88.500	$263.86	57.076	$170.17	0.000	$0.00	31.424	$93.69
Cheese-Feta	pail	2.000	5.000	0.633	6.367	$144.83	6.345	$144.32	0.000	$0.00	0.023	$0.51
Cheese-Monterey Jack	lb.	5.000	285.000	145.500	144.500	$318.19	168.029	$370.00	0.000	$0.00	-23.529	-$51.81
Cheese-Mozzarella	lb.	10.000	110.000	120.000	0.000	$0.00	0.000	$0.00	0.000	$0.00	0.000	$0.00
Cheese-Parmesan	lb.	10.000	0.000	10.000	0.000	$0.00	0.000	$0.00	0.000	$0.00	0.000	$0.00
Cheese-White cheddar	lb.	5.000	85.000	10.000	80.000	$344.20	74.875	$322.15	0.000	$0.00	5.125	$22.05
Cream 35%	ea.	2.000	16.000	4.750	13.250	$56.52	12.959	$55.27	0.000	$0.00	0.291	$1.24
Eggs, large	dz.	30.000	30.000	14.177	45.823	$74.30	45.418	$73.64	0.000	$0.00	0.405	$0.66
Ice Cream-Vanilla	pail	1.000	10.000	1.859	9.141	$140.50	9.122	$140.20	0.000	$0.00	0.019	$0.30
Milk	Liter	8.000	60.000	27.957	40.043	$40.12	40.000	$40.08	0.000	$0.00	0.043	$0.04
Milk 2% 250 ml.	ea.	1.000	570.000	8.280	562.720	$220.45	561.260	$219.88	0.000	$0.00	1.460	$0.57
Milk Chocolate 250 ml	ea.	1.000	0.000	2.000	-1.000	-$0.43	0.000	$0.00	0.000	$0.00	-1.000	-$0.43

Optimum Control Report

Page 1 of 6

Figure 4-11
Usage Summary Comparing Actual and Ideal Costs   (Source: Reprinted by permission of Tracrite Software)

88

Joes Fine Dining (JOES)

Menu Engineering Worksheet

9/28/2009
09:26:54

From: Sunday, March 01, 2009
To: Wednesday, September 30, 2009
Gross Sales for Period: $74,906.66

Note: This report calculates a menu product's Popularity (Menu Popularity Factor) and Profitability (Average Item Profit) within the group.

Sold	Popularity %	Selling Price	Current Cost	Margin	%	Totals Sales	Totals Cost	Profit	Analysis Profitability	Analysis Popularity	Menu Item Class
323.00	100.000%	$1.50	$0.47	$1.026	31.95%	$484.50	$154.78	$329.72	HIGH	HIGH	Star
323.00	Averages:	$1.50	$0.47	$1.021	31.95%	$484.50	$154.78	$329.72	**Based on averages**		
						Average Item Profit: $1.021			Menu Popularity Factor: 80.00%		
2.00	0.588%	$0.00	$1.52	$-1.524	0.00%	$0.00	$3.05	($3.05)	LOW	LOW	Dog
16.00	4.706%	$5.06	$0.89	$4.176	17.52%	$81.00	$14.19	$66.81	LOW	LOW	Dog
322.00	94.706%	$9.50	$3.10	$6.398	32.66%	$3,059.00	$998.97	$2,060.03	HIGH	HIGH	Star
340.00	Averages:	$4.85	$1.84	$6.246	32.36%	$3,140.00	$1,016.21	$2,123.79	**Based on averages**		
						Average Item Profit: $6.246			Menu Popularity Factor: 26.67%		
717.00	9.419%	$1.00	$0.16	$0.845	15.51%	$717.00	$111.21	$605.79	LOW	LOW	Dog
4.00	0.053%	$2.00	$0.57	$1.435	29.33%	$8.00	$2.35	$5.65	HIGH	LOW	Challenge
449.00	5.899%	$3.75	$0.39	$3.360	10.40%	$1,683.75	$175.11	$1,508.64	HIGH	LOW	Challenge
5481.00	72.005%	$1.25	$0.16	$1.086	13.12%	$6,851.25	$898.88	$5,952.37	LOW	HIGH	Workhorse
283.00	3.718%	$4.25	$2.07	$2.182	48.65%	$1,202.75	$585.13	$617.62	HIGH	LOW	Challenge
348.00	4.572%	$4.25	$0.88	$3.368	22.77%	$1,479.00	$336.72	$1,142.28	HIGH	LOW	Challenge

Figure 4-12

Menu Engineering Worksheet from an Integrated Foodservice Management Software Suite   (*Source:* Reprinted by permission of Tracrite Software)

Labor and Staffing Integration

- Relational databases for human resources management, scheduling, payroll benefit, and tax recordkeeping
- Integrated staff scheduling and labor forecasting, including overtime controls
- Multiple job classifications at different pay rates
- Tip reporting prompts at end-of-shift to promote IRS compliance
- Paycheck and W-2 printing

Banquets and Catering

- Comprehensive catering office function book
- Integrated banquet booking, arrangement, and menu databases
- Banquet menu, contract, function space setup sheet, and invoice printing

Cafeteria/University Board Plan Integration

- Prepaid, declining balance, or cash settlement accounts

Hotel Room Service Connectivity

- Hotel room caller ID
- Credit preapproval and posting to guest room folios or master folios

Delivery/Call-in Customer Data Integration

- Phone company caller ID for phone-in or delivery orders
- Tracks visit frequency, expenditures, and credit card numbers
- Promotional offer usage databases

Inventory Control

- Comprehensive perpetual inventory database
- Purchase order and receiving functionality
- Competitive bid evaluation functionality

(*Source:* Jupiterimages/Thinkstock)

- Physical inventory integration with perpetual inventory database
- Wireless technology physical inventory counting with uploading to inventory database
- Perpetual versus actual inventory deviation reporting

Menu Analysis

- Theoretical cost calculations based on transactional item sales
- Contribution margin analysis
- Menu engineering functionality

Accounting and Bookkeeping

- Compatibility with industry-standard uniform chart of accounts
- Integration with various financial accounting software packages
- Accounts payable integration with inventory control database
- Accounts receivable integration with point-of-sale database

As companies grow in number of units, it may be practical to commission development of custom-designed enterprise software. Large companies may employ sophisticated information technology departments that are skilled in applications development. Other options include outsourcing data development needs to software firms or using third-party menu purchasing integration applications.

ACTION TOOLKIT

American Express Business Insights provide detailed perspectives on consumer and business spending at the business, industry, and geographic levels, including Local IQ Reports and Competitive Focus Reports (businessinsights.americanexpress.com/).

There are a variety of points-of-sale systems designed for retail applications. The following list represents several solutions expressly designed for use in the foodservice industry:

- **Digital Dining POS**   www.digitaldining.com/
- **MICROS Systems Information Technology Solutions**   www.micros.com/

- **PAR PixelPoint Software Solutions** www.pixelpointpos.com/en/solutions/index.html
- **Radiant Systems Aloha Restaurant Point of Sale Software** www.radiantsystems.com/industries/hospitality/index.htm
- **Squirrel Systems** www.squirrelsystems.com/

In addition to the worksheets provided with this text, there are a variety of affordable software solutions for managing recipes and recipe costs including:

MasterCook CD, 11/E
Pearson Education
2011; Prentice Hall
ISBN-10: 0-13-255780-0
ISBN-13: 978-0-13-255780-1

As operational complexity increases, more robust information management systems are appropriate. The following vendors provide advanced integration and multiple control features:

- **CBORD Food Service Software Solutions for Restaurants** restaurants.cbord.com/solutions/solution.asp?id=28
- **Computrition Foodservice Software Solutions** www.computrition.com/
- **MenuMax** www.menumax.com/index.html
- **TracRite Optimum Control Restaurant Management Software** www.tracrite.net/index.htm

GLOSSARY

Competitive set—The group of local businesses that you assume constitutes the choices your market will select if they don't select your own business. Also referred to as a *peer set*.

Control states—Certain of the 50 United States that maintain a monopoly over the wholesaling or retailing of some or all spirits, wine, and malt beverages within their states. In control states, restaurant licensees must purchase alcoholic beverages from specific distributors as mandated by state alcoholic beverage (ABC) laws and regulations. In most of these states, distilled spirits must be purchased from state-operated stores or warehouses.

Integrated foodservice management software suite—Robust digital information systems that automate various operational, control, and reporting functions to provide enhanced management results.

Locavore movement—The interest among customers to consume locally produced food that supports a collaborative effort

between food producers and distributors and results in economic sustainability at the points of production.

Perpetual inventory—The estimated balance of inventory items calculated by the following formula: Ending Perpetual Inventory = Opening Perpetual Inventory – Items Sold.

Point-of-sale system—A combination of digital software and hardware that facilitates recording and communicating customer transactions by service personnel.

Theoretical costs—A calculation of what food and beverage costs should be, based on the recipe cost (standard cost) of one or more items multiplied by the actual number of those items sold to customers.

SWOT analysis—A management planning exercise used to identify Strengths, Weaknesses, Opportunities, and Threats to a business. The findings can be used to modify strategic plans or support tactical deployment to achieve enhanced business results.

ENDNOTES

1. thinkexist.com/quotation/the_difference_between_school_and_life-in_school/326386.html; retrieved May 1, 2011.
2. service-ability.com/?p=881; retrieved May 1, 2011.

3. The Action Toolkit provides a Web link to this resource.
4. The Action Toolkit provides a Web link to this resource.

5

Positioning Your Menus for Business Success

Key Terms

Conversion factor

Cost–benefit analysis

Daypart

Direct labor cost

Gross profit

Hospitality

Menu mix

Net income

Prime cost

Pro forma income
    statement

Revenue

Sub-recipes

(*Source:* Stockbyte/Thinkstock)

Objectives

Upon completion of this chapter, you should be able to:

5.1 Explain how menus are designed in relation to dayparts.

5.2 Discuss ways to optimize usage of space resources.

5.3 Perform calculations to evaluate daypart revenue.

5.4 Forecast food and beverage sales revenue using a variety of digital resources.

5.5 Forecast net income.

5.6 Calculate food and beverage costs by applying forecasts to standard recipes.

5.7 Analyze profit and loss forecasts to enable proactive decision making.

DAYPARTS

North American dining habits traditionally recognize breakfast, lunch, and dinner as food-service **dayparts** (Figure 5-1).

- Breakfast is characteristically consumed between 6:30 AM to 9:30 AM, depending on work, school, and other criteria (3 hours).
- Lunch is typically consumed between 11:30 AM and 1:30 PM, depending primarily on work-related criteria (2 hours).
- Dinner is usually consumed between 5:30 PM to 10:00 PM, depending on a greater variety of factors, including leisure considerations and the need for digestion prior to sleep (4.5 hours).

Based on typical consumer behavior and assuming the aforementioned hours are representative averages, only 9.5 hours of a 24-hour period are in demand for food service. This represents only about 40% of the 24-hour day. The problem is, you pay lease and other fixed costs for the entire day; therefore, it could be argued that your facilities are underutilized for nearly 60% of the day. Certain operators accept this reality and do not view it as a negative. You need to decide to what extent you will utilize your physical space assets. For example, if you are located in a suburb, for various reasons you may choose to serve dinner only. This strategy may suit a suburban market where businesspersons work downtown and return home in the evening. Conversely, your same suburban situation, if properly positioned and marketed, might appeal to those individuals not commuting downtown. This might consist of local merchants seeking lunch or spouses anchored to their immediate neighborhoods. The numerous possibilities point to the need for a well-researched, market-driven business vision. If your strategy involves maximum utilization of your physical space assets, then you should plan to capture existing demand for established dayparts (breakfast, lunch, and dinner, or any combination thereof) and create product and service offerings to generate **revenue** or reduce total cost during a percentage of the other hours between those established dayparts. Although certainly not an all-inclusive list, some strategies include

- using your dining room as rental space for meetings
- offering alternative food service, such as brunch, afternoon tea, or post-dinner late-night meals
- converting dining spaces to lounge or entertainment spaces after the dinner period
- using kitchen production facilities to prepare banquet food to be served off-premise
- using kitchen production facilities for scratch preparation cooking so as to reduce reliance on more expensive convenience ingredients
- renting by the hour or subleasing to others in need of kitchen space
- producing ingredients or recipes for other businesses
- producing ingredients or recipes for retail distribution on- and off-site

Figure 5-2 illustrates how an operation could potentially capitalize on creative opportunities for utilizing off-peak hours.

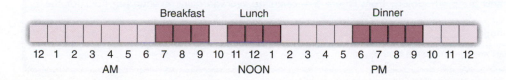

Figure 5-1
Typically Recognized North American Dayparts

Figure 5-2
Maximized Space Utilization

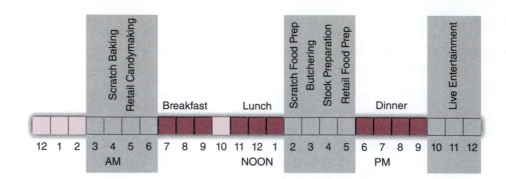

No matter how you envision the 24-hour period, you must develop menus to optimize seat turnover. This is not to suggest that impersonal, rapid seat turnover is an objective. Rather, your reputation must embody the spirit of **hospitality**. You must avoid nonproductive moments and align operational resources to parallel customer demand. You must be skillful and synchronized enough to delight as many customers that seek your services. You must have a keen understanding of preparation times and which menu items are suited for the combination of market preferences and production capabilities. In summary, strategic operators should use generally recognized dayparts solely as a guide, and conduct market research to identify opportunities to optimize utilization of their physical space. Then they should decide how these opportunities may fit with their existing business vision, or enact changes to create an enhanced vision better aligned with the market and their resources. There are various approaches for evaluating daypart utilization, including

- average total revenue per daypart
- average food only revenue per daypart
- average beverage only revenue per daypart

You can drill down even further within each daypart and calculate

- average total revenue per hour
- average food only revenue per hour
- average beverage only revenue per hour

Figure 5-3 illustrates a hypothetical scenario using average total revenue per daypart as the unit of analysis.

It must be noted that these data are neither "good" nor "bad." They gain meaning only when compared to expenses, planned goals, trends, or other benchmarks. For example, if the industry average for dinner daypart revenue exceeds your own results and you choose to benchmark against that industry data, then you have identified a strategic gap that you should work toward fixing with revenue enhancement strategies (these strategies are explained in Chapter 10).

EXERCISE 5-1
CALCULATING AVERAGE DAILY REVENUE PER HOUR

Using the data from Figure 5-3 and the methodology from Figure 5-4, calculate average daily revenue per hour for the remaining dayparts.

Lunch _____ Dinner _____

Note: Assume lunch is a 2-hour daypart and dinner is a 4.5-hour daypart.

JANUARY FOOD & BEVERAGE REVENUE

BREAKFAST	$35,000
LUNCH	$64,000
DINNER	$110,000
LATE NIGHT	$24,000

$$\frac{\text{TOTAL BREAKFAST REVENUE}}{\text{NUMBER OF DAYS IN PERIOD}} \quad \frac{\$35,000}{31 \text{ DAYS}} = \$ 1,129.03 \text{ AVERAGE REVENUE PER BREAKFAST DAYPART}$$

$$\frac{\text{TOTAL LUNCH REVENUE}}{\text{NUMBER OF DAYS IN PERIOD}} \quad \frac{\$64,000}{31 \text{ DAYS}} = \$ 2,064.52 \text{ AVERAGE REVENUE PER LUNCH DAYPART}$$

$$\frac{\text{TOTAL DINNER REVENUE}}{\text{NUMBER OF DAYS IN PERIOD}} \quad \frac{\$110,000}{31 \text{ DAYS}} = \$ 3,548.39 \text{ AVERAGE REVENUE PER DINNER DAYPART}$$

$$\frac{\text{TOTAL LATE-NIGHT REVENUE}}{\text{NUMBER OF DAYS IN PERIOD}} \quad \frac{\$ 24,000}{31 \text{ DAYS}} = \$ 774.19 \text{ AVERAGE REVENUE PER LATE-NIGHT DAYPART}$$

Figure 5-3
Calculation of Average Total Revenue per Daypart

A more sophisticated set of metrics can be derived from your initial computations. Using the data from Figure 5-3, you can refine your calculations to evaluate average revenue per hour for each of the dayparts. Figure 5-4 illustrates this type of calculation.

As you calculate operating data to obtain finer units of study, you can apply them effectively to analyze opportunities for financial improvement. For example, consider the hypothetical data table and trend line in Figure 5-5.

FOOD & BEVERAGE REVENUE

BREAKFAST	$35,000

$$\frac{\text{TOTAL BREAKFAST REVENUE}}{\text{NUMBER OF DAYS IN PERIOD}} \quad \frac{\$35,000}{31 \text{ DAYS}} = \$ 1,129.03 \text{ AVERAGE REVENUE PER BREAKFAST DAYPART}$$

DURATION OF BREAKFAST DAYPART	3 HOURS

$$\text{AVERAGE DAILY BREAKFAST REVENUE PER HOUR} = \frac{\$1,129.03}{3 \text{ HOURS}} = \$ 376.34$$

Figure 5-4
Calculation of Average Revenue per Hour in Breakfast Daypart

EXERCISE 5-2
ANALYZING AVERAGE REVENUE PER HOUR

Q1. What can you infer from the data trend in Figure 5-5?

Q2. What research might you undertake to explain data points on the trend line?

Q3. What planning and strategic actions might you implement based on your research? Why?

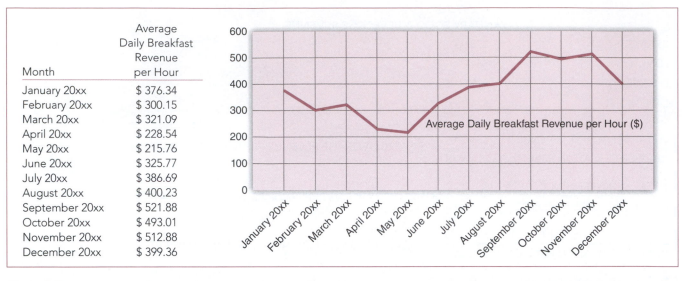

Month	Average Daily Breakfast Revenue per Hour
January 20xx	$ 376.34
February 20xx	$ 300.15
March 20xx	$ 321.09
April 20xx	$ 228.54
May 20xx	$ 215.76
June 20xx	$ 325.77
July 20xx	$ 386.69
August 20xx	$ 400.23
September 20xx	$ 521.88
October 20xx	$ 493.01
November 20xx	$ 512.88
December 20xx	$ 399.36

Figure 5-5
Trends—Average Revenue per Breakfast Daypart

	Average Hourly Breakfast Revenue
6:30 AM to 7:30 AM	$60.40
7:30 AM to 8:30 AM	638.75
8:30 AM to 9:30 AM	429.88
Total	**$1,129.03**

Figure 5-6
Hypothetical Average Hourly Breakfast Revenue

One immediate answer to studies such as those described in Exercise 5-2 relates to the length of the daypart. Trend analyses or other comparisons may indicate that you are serving a menu for too long a period of time. As discussed earlier in the chapter, you may not want to allow excessive non-revenue producing periods throughout the day. Figure 5-6 illustrates how hypothetical data from Figure 5-3 might be calculated on an hourly basis.

It is readily evident that the majority of revenue is generated between 7:30 AM and 8:30 AM. Research should be conducted to evaluate the **prime cost** of serving breakfast per hour. *Prime cost* is composed of food cost, beverage cost, and **direct labor cost**. If direct labor can be associated by the hour, then we can evaluate when it is best to begin and when it is best to end service of the various dayparts.

(*Source:* MNStudio/Shutterstock)

FORECASTING REVENUE

"Don't bother just to be better than your contemporaries or predecessors. Try to be better than yourself."

—WILLIAM FAULKNER[1]

Your menu is the planning and communication instrument that drives revenue and subsequent net income. An adequate revenue stream is necessary to ensure required cash flow as well as the base from which costs and expenses will be paid from. Insufficient revenue during the short term may be tolerable (business startups, seasonal resorts); however, a long-term trend of insufficient revenue is a business killer. Consequently, operators must be able to predict revenue by using forecasting tools. In its simplest form, a *forecast* is a gut feeling or subjective best guess. Once supported with data-modeling tools, a forecast can become a valuable predictive instrument.

Assuming that menu items and their prices have been established, a worksheet can be developed for forecasting revenue (Figure 5-7).[2]

Figure 5-7 forecasts bottled beer revenue; however, it can be used for any menu category. Column A lists the possible customer selections offered. Column B represents the forecasted sales of the items listed in column A. (This calculation represents numbers of items sold, rather than dollars.) Row 57 summarizes totals for the forecasted period. In this example, management anticipates 751 bottles of beer will be sold (cell B57). Each item adds to this total, and their relative popularity is listed in column C. The values calculated in column C are commonly referred to as **menu mix**. In essence, *menu mix* is the relative fraction or percentage of sales that each menu item contributes to the whole. Typically, menu mix is calculated on the basis of items sold; however, at certain times it will be calculated based upon dollar sales. The formula for menu mix (as a percentage) is:

Number forecasted of a particular item/the total number of items forecasted = menu mix % for an item

Menu Engineering Worksheet	# Sold	Menu Mix %	Item Bev Cost	Item Menu Price	Item Contribution Margin	Menu Bev Cost	Menu Sales	Menu Contribution Margin
Rolling Rock	78	10.4%	$0.420	$3.25	$2.83	$32.76	$253.50	$220.74
Pabst Blue Ribbon	93	12.4%	$0.360	$3.25	$2.89	$33.48	$302.25	$268.77
Blue Moon Belgian White	26	3.5%	$1.790	$4.75	$2.96	$46.54	$123.50	$76.96
Brooklyn Brown Ale	12	1.6%	$1.790	$4.75	$2.96	$21.48	$57.00	$35.52
Harpoon IPA	38	5.1%	$1.990	$4.75	$2.76	$75.62	$180.50	$104.88
Smuttynose IPA	36	4.8%	$1.990	$4.75	$2.76	$71.64	$171.00	$99.36
Victory Hop Devil Ale	55	7.3%	$1.990	$4.75	$2.76	$109.45	$261.25	$151.80
Yuengling Traditional Lager	70	9.3%	$1.190	$3.25	$2.06	$83.30	$227.50	$144.20
Abita Turbo Dog	26	3.5%	$1.970	$4.75	$2.78	$51.22	$123.50	$72.28
Pyramid Hefeweizen	31	4.1%	$1.790	$4.75	$2.96	$55.49	$147.25	$91.76
Pabst Blue Ribbon (Happy Hour)	286	38.1%	$0.360	$1.00	$0.64	$102.96	$286.00	$183.04
Totals	751	100.0%				$683.94	$2,133.25	$1,449.31

Figure 5-7
Malt Beverages Menu Engineering Worksheet

Menu Engineering Worksheet	# Sold	Menu Mix %	Item Food Cost	Item Menu Price	Item Contribution Margin	Menu Food Cost	Menu Sales	Menu Contribution Margin
Field Greens w/Cheese Tart	105	13.6%	$1.448	$5.00	$3.55	$152.00	$525.00	$373.00
Endive with Poached Quail Egg	87	11.3%	$0.215	$3.50	$3.29	$18.66	$304.50	$285.84
Marinated Vegetable Salad	54	7.0%	$0.858	$4.00	$3.14	$46.34	$216.00	$169.66
Cream of Parsnip Soup	85	11.0%	$0.996	$4.00	$3.00	$84.67	$340.00	$255.33
Autumn Bisque	94	12.2%	$0.408	$4.00	$3.59	$38.39	$376.00	$337.61
Crayfish Chowder	72	9.4%	$0.651	$4.00	$3.35	$46.85	$288.00	$241.15
Terrine Du Jourw/ Crusty Bread	44	5.7%	$0.775	$5.00	$4.23	$34.09	$220.00	$185.91
Wild Mushroom Strudel	102	13.2%	$0.982	$4.00	$3.02	$100.19	$408.00	$307.81
Leeks with Mustard Sauce	49	6.4%	$0.564	$4.00	$3.44	$27.61	$196.00	$168.39
Crab Supreme	78	10.1%	$2.311	$6.00	$3.69	$180.22	$468.00	$287.78
Totals	770	100.0%				$729.02	$3,341.50	$2,612.48

Figure 5-8
Appetizers Menu Engineering Worksheet

Example: Using the data in row 32, you can apply the formula as follows, and calculate the menu mix for Rolling Rock beer:

78 bottles of Rolling Rock/751 total bottles forecasted = 10.4% of total bottles sold

Column D lists the cost of preparing one portion of each menu item. Column E lists the current menu prices. Column F lists the difference between each item's menu price and portion cost. Column G lists the cost of serving the forecasted number of menu items (column B multiplied by column D). Column H equals the mathematical product resulting from multiplying columns B and E, and is of key importance because it forecasts menu category sales. Notice that in this example, rows 33 and 42 list the same menu item, but at different prices. As in this example, if you sell the same item at different prices, you must record sales differently as well. Marketing tactics such as "Happy Hour," "Early Bird," or couponing are some of the reasons for differential pricing. Cell H57 is the sum of all the cells in column H; thus, it indicates the total anticipated sales for the Malt Beverages (beer) menu category. Whereas this example is used to illustrate anticipated beer revenue, the same mechanics can be used for other food and beverage menu categories. Figure 5-8 illustrates revenue forecasts for the Appetizers category, and Figure 5-9 illustrates revenue forecasts for the Desserts category. For purposes of analysis and menu engineering, a separate worksheet should be prepared for each menu category. The level of menu categorization should be based on the perceived competition between menu items. The concepts of category competition and menu engineering is discussed in greater detail in Chapter 10.

As mentioned at the beginning of this chapter, the forecasted number of item sales may simply be a "guesstimate," or may be an objectively refined calculation. Some approaches include are discussed next.

(*Source:* Jupiterimages/Thinkstock)

Menu Engineering Worksheet	# Sold	Menu Mix %	Item Food Cost	Item Menu Price	Item Contribution Margin	Menu Food Cost	Menu Sales	Menu Contribution Margin
Spice Apple Cake w/ Custard	43	25.6%	$0.290	$4.00	$3.71	$12.47	$172.00	$159.53
Sabayon with Fruit	3	1.8%	$0.976	$4.00	$3.02	$2.93	$12.00	$9.07
Chocolate Mousse Cake	8	4.8%	$0.596	$4.00	$3.40	$4.77	$32.00	$27.23
Bread Pudding	6	3.6%	$0.190	$4.00	$3.81	$1.14	$24.00	$22.86
Profiteroles	27	16.1%	$1.444	$4.00	$2.56	$38.98	$108.00	$69.02
Pumpkin Cheesecake	45	26.8%	$0.428	$4.00	$3.57	$19.26	$180.00	$160.74
Pears in Port w/ Stilton	36	21.4%	$0.726	$4.00	$3.27	$26.12	$144.00	$117.88
Totals	168	100.0%				$105.67	$672.00	$566.33

Figure 5-9
Desserts Menu Engineering Worksheet

Historical Item Sales, with Adjustments

This method is based on historical records of actual sales. For example, using the data in Figure 5-9, you might see a pattern where approximately 45 slices of pumpkin cheesecake are sold during each period. Consequently, you might anticipate this level of sales in future periods. You might choose to modify the forecast based on intuition or other subjective means. Arguably, this method is prone to varying degrees of failure if guest traffic is substantially more or less than normal.

Percentage of Forecasted Customer Traffic

This objective approach is based on historical customer traffic data. Figure 5-10 is a useful format for displaying historical guest traffic.
This technique requires three distinct steps:

Step 1. Forecast total guest traffic for the period.

Step 2. Apply historical demand for individual menu categories to predict total category demand.

Step 3. Apply menu mix history to the predicted category demand.

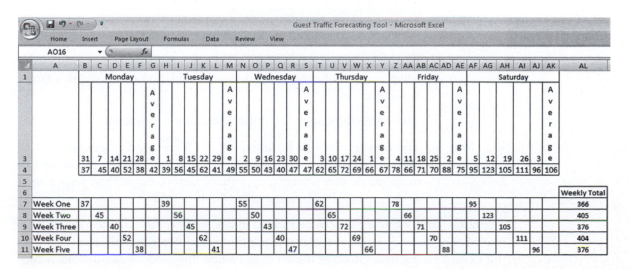

Figure 5-10
Guest Traffic Forecasting Tool

EXERCISE 5-3

FORECASTING GUEST TRAFFIC

Using the data in Figure 5-10, predict guest traffic (covers) for a future week. Explain your reasoning.

Monday ___ covers

Rationale _____

Tuesday ___ covers

Rationale _____

Wednesday ___ covers

Rationale _____

Thursday ___ covers

Rationale _____

Friday ___ covers

Rationale _____

Saturday ___ covers

Rationale _____

Total Week ___ covers

The following example uses previously introduced hypothetical data.

Step 1. Row 4 of Figure 5-10 lists *covers* (customer traffic) for each day in the study period. The values in row 4 are arrayed by day of the week (row 3 contains labels that indicate the dates within the month you are studying). This format enables the calculation of averages for the respective days of the week. For example, cells B4, C4, D4, E4, and F4 contain cover counts for Mondays within the study period. Cell G4 calculates the average of these five values. The following facts are observed:

- Minimum covers on Mondays = 37
- Maximum covers on Mondays = 52
- Average covers on Mondays = 42

The analysis can be continued for the other days of the week. This manner of analysis allows you to examine days of the week for the purpose of forecasting future periods.

Step 2. Once you have forecasted guest traffic for the period, you can use the forecast to predict menu category sales. The dessert sales listed in Figure 5-9 occurred as a result of 366 covers (refer to Figure 5-10, cell AL7). Note that not every cover purchased dessert that week. Approximately 46% of covers purchased dessert during week One.

168 desserts sold / 366 covers = 0.459 ~ 46%

This calculation can be applied to a future period. For example, if you forecast 400 covers for a future period, you could use this factor as follows:

400 covers forecasted × 0.459 = 184 desserts forecasted

Step 3. The next question to be answered is, "What specific desserts will be sold?" Using the values in column C of Figure 5-9, you can apply historical menu mix percentages (actually factors, rather than percentages) to the predicted 184 dessert sales (Table 5-1).

The results of this calculation can be entered into a menu engineering worksheet (Figure 5-11) to quantify forecasted sales revenue. The three-step calculation conducted in this example suggests $736.00 in dessert sales. When this series of calculations is conducted for all menu categories, a comprehensive revenue forecast is obtained.

TABLE 5-1
FORECASTED DESSERT SALES

Menu Item	Menu Mix	Forecasted Total Dessert Sales	Forecasted Menu Item Sales
Spice Apple Cake w/Custard	0.256	184	47
Sabayon with Fruit	0.018	184	3
Chocolate Mousse Cake	0.048	184	9
Bread Pudding	0.036	184	7
Profiteroles	0.161	184	30
Pumpkin Cheesecake	0.268	184	49
Pears in Port w/Stilton	0.214	184	39

It is important to assess the accuracy of your forecasts periodically. Figure 5-12 illustrates sample data for one week of bottled beer sales (the same data introduced in Figure 5-7).

Cells in each row of column B tally the menu items into a composite weekly forecast. Cells in column C list actual sales once they have occurred. Note that the forecast in row 9 was not realized. Cells in column D calculate the ratio of forecasted sales divided by actual sales. A factor of 1.00 or higher indicates the forecast was achieved or exceeded. A factor of less than 1.00 indicates that the forecast was not met. In retrospect, this operation seems to slightly underestimate bottled beer sales (with the exception of Yuengling Traditional Lager). Underestimates are problematic, in that sufficient inventory and operational resources may not be available. Customers do not respond well to advertised items that are not available, nor do they like waiting for excessive times to be served when demand exceeds production forecasts. Theoretically, you should strive for forecasts that are closely validated through actual sales results. Conversely, overestimates are tantamount to a flawed predictive process. Food spoilage and quality loss occurs when food is prepared in excess of demand. There may be other unnecessary expenses in addition to excessive food cost implications. If management

Menu Engineering Worksheet	# Sold	Menu Mix %	Item Food Cost	Item Menu Price	Item Contribution Margin	Menu Food Cost	Menu Sales	Menu Contribution Margin
Spice Apple Cake w/ Custard	47	25.5%	$0.290	$4.00	$3.71	$13.63	$188.00	$174.37
Sabayon with Fruit	3	1.6%	$0.976	$4.00	$3.02	$2.93	$12.00	$9.07
Chocolate Mousse Cake	9	4.9%	$0.596	$4.00	$3.40	$5.36	$36.00	$30.64
Bread Pudding	7	3.8%	$0.190	$4.00	$3.81	$1.33	$28.00	$26.67
Profiteroles	30	16.3%	$1.444	$4.00	$2.56	$43.31	$120.00	$76.69
Pumpkin Cheesecake	49	26.6%	$0.428	$4.00	$3.57	$20.97	$196.00	$175.03
Pears in Port w/ Stilton	39	21.2%	$0.726	$4.00	$3.27	$28.30	$156.00	$127.70
Totals	184	100.0%				$115.83	$736.00	$620.17

Figure 5-11
Dessert Forecasts Entered into a Menu Engineering Worksheet

	A	B	C	D
1	Menu Item	Forecasted Bottle Sales	Actual Bottle Sales	Ratio of Forecast to Actual
2	Rolling Rock	78	80	1.03
3	Pabst Blue Ribbon	93	101	1.09
4	Blue Moon Belgian White	26	28	1.08
5	Brooklyn Brown Ale	12	12	1.00
6	Harpoon IPA	38	45	1.18
7	Smuttynose IPA	36	44	1.22
8	Victory Hop Devil Ale	55	60	1.09
9	Yuengling Traditional Lager	70	52	0.74
10	Abita Turbo Dog	26	28	1.08
11	Pyramid Hefeweizen	31	33	1.06
12	Pabst Blue Ribbon (Happy Hour)	286	301	1.05

Figure 5-12
Comparison of Forecasted and Actual Bottled Beer Sales

	A	B	C	D
1	Menu Item	Forecasted Bottle Sales	Ratio of Forecast to Actual	Revised Forecast
2	Rolling Rock	78	1.03	80
3	Pabst Blue Ribbon	93	1.09	101
4	Blue Moon Belgian White	26	1.08	28
5	Brooklyn Brown Ale	12	1.00	12
6	Harpoon IPA	38	1.18	45
7	Smuttynose IPA	36	1.22	44
8	Victory Hop Devil Ale	55	1.09	60
9	Yuengling Traditional Lager	70	0.74	52
10	Abita Turbo Dog	26	1.08	28
11	Pyramid Hefeweizen	31	1.06	33
12	Pabst Blue Ribbon (Happy Hour)	286	1.05	301

Figure 5-13
Forecast Revisions Based on Historical Variances

anticipates forecasted revenue that subsequently is not realized, and schedules staff to support this level of sales, then excessive labor costs may result. In addition, if the unrealized revenue from this overestimate was needed for accounts payable or other cash requirements, there could be insufficient funds available. The most valuable use of the factors in Figure 5-12 column D is to fine-tune preliminary estimates (Figure 5-13).

In this example, column B lists preliminary forecasts obtained through the three-step process discussed preciously. Column C lists the historical factors by which forecasts vary from actual results. Column D calculates revised forecasts that may remove predictive bias and improve the quality of the forecasts.

It must be noted that the results of any forecasting process should be questioned prior to accepting them and mobilizing purchasing, recipe production, employee scheduling, and operational support. It is acceptable—if not appropriate—to modify

EXERCISE 5-4
DOCUMENTING THE IMPACT OF EXTERNAL VARIABLES ON CUSTOMER TRAFFIC

Q1. What specific regional events in your market area are likely to have an impact on your usual guest traffic? Create a calendar to illustrate these impacts. Can you discern any apparent trends for your market area?

Q2. Expand the calendar by including potential impacts arising from holidays, weather, and other specific regional idiosyncrasies.

AUTHOR'S INSIGHT

As a senior hotel manager, I was responsible for menu development for my various restaurants and other revenue outlets. I empowered my chefs to "own" the creative process and supported their work by providing information and staff resources. I believed (and still do) in hiring professionals and letting them do what they do best. I also believed (and still do) they needed a context to create within, so I compelled them to consider profit potential as they worked on their formative menus.

At the onset of the development process, I imposed only one condition that required the eventual answer to only one question: "How much profit will this menu generate over its lifespan? Give me a dollar figure." If they could not answer that question with a discrete number, then we could not precede. At that impasse, I would help them understand the mechanics of sales forecasting, costing, and the estimation of bottom-line profitability. Nobody could fail, but everybody had to understand the implications of their efforts.

To this day, I cannot imagine someone in research and development who is not held accountable for monetary results. Whether cocktails from the bar, meals from the kitchen, or wine from the cellar, it is imperative that we have a keen sense of where our menus may take us. Otherwise, the financial road we embark on may lead us into treacherous territory.

---

forecasts based on market volatility, extraneous factors, and subjective criteria, including but not limited to

- area or regional events
- holidays
- public works construction or other disruptions to convenient customer access
- actual or anticipated impact of weather
- managerial intuition ("Customers might be skittish due to an ingredient recall," or "I bet the new summer blockbuster movie might be good for rum sales," etc.)

Whatever combination of subjective and analytical forecasting methods you use, you can position yourself for success by calibrating your purchasing, preparation, and staffing based on historical guest traffic and menu-item sales predictions.

FORECASTING NET INCOME

Net income is the revenue remaining after all costs and expenses have been deducted. Most costs and expenses result from consumption of inventory (food, beverage, and supplies), labor costs, occupancy costs, taxes, insurance, and other operating costs. Nearly all industries ascribe to standard accounting formats and publish a uniform system of accounts that enable consistent categorization of revenues and expenses for their specific industry segments. Figure 5-14 is an example of a (partially populated) Statement of Income report that is compliant with the Uniform System of Accounts for Restaurants.[3] This is the primary accounting document used to depict operational success. Note that for illustrative purposes, forecasted revenue from beer sales has been entered into the report.

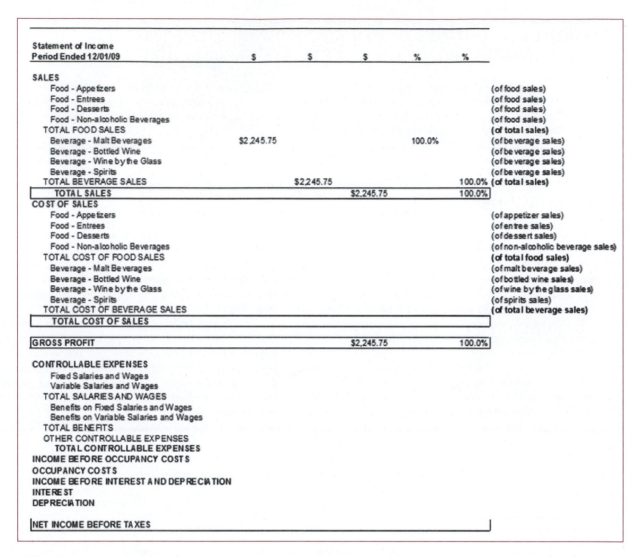

Figure 5-14
Statement of Income Report

The next element of forecasting involves costing the menu items anticipated being sold during the period. By adding all estimated food and beverage costs based on forecasted guest selections, you can better predict the net profitability for an upcoming period.

CALCULATING FOOD AND BEVERAGE COSTS

Food and beverage inventory valuation data are required to begin the calculation of estimated food and beverage costs. There are various valuation practices and these are governed by company policy as well as Internal Revenue Service (IRS) rules. The most logical valuation method is to use the actual purchase price for each item. This method is most useful when product prices are stable (minimal inflation/deflation). Operationally, there are certain difficulties when attempting to value items at actual purchase cost. Actual purchase costs may not be reflective of present value. Two examples illustrate this point. Certain primal beef cuts are sold to restaurants in wet-aged form. These packaged cuts are perfectly suitable; however, some operators elect to dry-age their beef to achieve greater tenderness and a more complex flavor profile. Alternatively, operators could simply purchase dry-aged beef rather than wet-aged beef; however,

(*Source:* PHB.cz (Richard Semik)/Shutterstock)

they pay a significantly higher price to their vendors. In essence, the dry-aging process is an in-house means of adding real monetary value. A fair question is, "Should inventory records document these meat products at their original purchase price (wet-aged) or at the comparable market value for dry-aged products?" This question is answered differently by individual operators; however, it should be applied uniformly over the long run and reported so as to comply with IRS rules. A second example involves bottled wine. Certain rare wines benefit from extended aging (cellaring). For instance, a 750-ml bottle of a particular Napa Valley cult cabernet sauvignon purchased by an operator at its release in 2004 was valued at $95.00. By 2011, the same bottle appreciated in value to $675.00. Similar patterns are shown with classified red Bordeaux, red Burgundy, Sauternes, and other wines. Once again, the question is raised as to the appropriate value (original purchase price versus current market price) assigned to these inventory items.

Another issue involves specific identification of inventory items relative to inventory costs. For example, if items are currently held in inventory and were purchased on different occasions at more than one price, how can an operator accurately identify the actual cost of these items? One method involves marking the price on the package/container upon receipt. This can be done with low-tech (handwritten prices) or high-tech (barcode labels) means. In essence, every ingredient in inventory is marked with its actual purchase price. It should be recognized that this is an additional and ongoing task, and has no direct impact on the customer dining experience. Consequently, a **cost–benefit analysis** should be conducted to determine the relative value of the additional work.

Certain inventory items are cooked or otherwise transformed to become ingredients in recipes. For example, you might purchase chicken frames to prepare chicken stock. You may keep several gallons of chicken stock as a par to use in various soup and sauce recipes. After preparing the stock, the frames (and other ingredients) are discarded, and all that remains is the finished stock. An appropriate question is, "What value do we assign to the gallons of chicken stock as we cost out the recipes it is used in?" This question involves the concept of **sub-recipes,** which are, in fact, quite common. Figure 5-15 illustrates several examples of sub-recipes and their applications in menu items.[4] It is useful to prepare recipe cards for these items and cost them out in

Figure 5-15
Sub-recipes and Applica-
tions in Menu Items

Inventory Item	Sub-recipe	Example of Menu Item Utilizing Sub-recipe
Whole butter	Clarified butter	Pan-fried entrees
Chicken frames	Chicken stock	*Veloute* sauce
Granulated sugar	Caramel sauce	Ice cream desserts
All-purpose flour	Roux	Thickened soups

units used in other recipes. Sub-recipes in Figure 5-15 are shown in italics.

Once the costs of inventory items and sub-recipes are established, the next step is to record and cost recipes for all menu items. In Chapter 4, you were introduced to a simple recipe-card format. Figure 5-16 illustrates the same recipe-card format (different recipe, however) with all features, including ingredients, quantities, the method of preparation (MOP), and costing information.

Key components of this recipe card include:

Cell B1	Recipe Name
Cell D2	Recipe File No.
Cell D3	(Desired) Yield (the number of portions produced by this recipe)
Cell D4	Conversion Factor (the factor that the original ingredient quantities are multiplied by to achieve a lesser or greater yield) *Conversion Factor = Desired Yield/Original Yield*
Cell D5	Batch Cost (the total cost to produce all portions) *Batch Cost = the Sum of Cells G12 through G28*
Cell D6	Portion Cost (the cost to produce one portion of the recipe) *Portion Cost = Batch Cost/(Desired) Yield*
Cell D7	Sales Price (the price a customer is charged for one portion)
Cell D8	Cost % (the relationship between Portion Cost and Sales Price) *Cost % = (Portion Cost/Sales Price) × 100*
Cells A12 through A28	Inventory File No. (a file designation assigned to every inventory item)
Cells E12 through E28	Recipe Unit (the volume, weight, or count that an ingredient is measured by)
Cells D12 through D28	Amount (the number of Recipe Units required to produce the desired recipe yield)
Cells F12 through F28	Unit Cost (the actual cost of one unit of an ingredient)
Cells G12 through G28	Total Ingredient Cost (the cost for the number of ingredients used in the recipe) *Total Ingredient Cost = Amount (of Ingredients) × Unit Cost (of Ingredients)*
Cells A29 through B41	Preparation Method (the steps required to prepare the recipe)

Figure 5-17 illustrates this recipe converted to yield four portions rather than the original yield of one portion illustrated in Figure 5-16. A **conversion factor** is useful to increase or decrease the original recipe yield and ingredient quantities to a desired yield.

$$\text{Desired Yield} = \text{Original Yield} \times \text{Conversion Factor}$$

Note that the amounts in column D and costs in column G have increased proportionately based on the conversion factor in cell D4. When comparing Figures 5-16 and 5-17,

	A	B	D	E	F	G	H
1	Item:	**Veal Medallions with Morels**					
2		Recipe File #	DinEnr201				
3		Desired Yield (# of portions)	1				
4		Conversion Factor	1.00				
5		Batch Cost	$9.965				
6		Portion Cost	$9.965				
7		Sales Price	$23.00				
8		Cost %	43.33%				
9							
10-11	Inventory File #	Ingredient	Amount	Recipe Unit	Unit Cost	Total Ingredient Cost	
12	PR022	morels, dried	0.25	ounce	$3.765	$0.941	
13		water	0.50	cup		$0.000	
14	MS008	veal butt tenderloin medallion, 3 ounce	2.00	each	$3.450	$6.900	
15	ST032	salt		TT			
16	SP012	black pepper		TT			
17	DA001	butter	1.00	teaspoon	$0.050	$0.050	
18	ST022	vegetable oil	0.50	tablespoon	$0.095	$0.047	
19	PR036	shallots	0.50	each	$0.235	$0.117	
20	ST055	wine, white	1.00	ounce	$0.200	$0.200	
21	ST033	chicken stock	2.00	ounce	$0.146	$0.291	
22	DA003	Crème fraiche	1.00	ounce	$0.329	$0.329	
23	PR020	lemon juice	0.25	teaspoon	$0.063	$0.022	
24	DinEnt1401	Baked Polenta	1.00	each	$0.254	$0.254	
25	DinEnt1501	Citrus Buttered Brussel Sprouts	3.00	each	$0.053	$0.160	
26	DinEnt1701	Fiddleheads	3.00	each	$0.129	$0.386	
27	DinApp	Sally Lunn Rolls	1.00	each	$0.180	$0.180	
28	DinApp	Grissini	1.00	each	$0.087	$0.087	

Preparation Method

1. Bring the water to a boil. In a heatproof bowl, soak the morels in the boiling water until softened, about 30 minutes.
2. Remove and rinse under running water, rubbing to loosen any grit. Let the soaking liquid stand.
3. Season the 3-ounce medallions (cut .5 inch thick) with salt and pepper. In a very large skillet, melt 1 Tablespoon of butter in the oil.
4. Add the veal and cook over high heat until browned on the bottom, 2 to 3 minutes. Turn and cook until browned on the bottom and the meat is just pink inside, about 3 minutes.
5. Transfer the veal to a warmed platter and cover loosely with foil.
6. Melt the remaining 1 Tablespoon of butter in the same skillet. Add minced shallots and cook over low heat, stirring until softened, about 5 minutes.
7. Add the wine and boil, scraping up any browned bits from the bottom until almost evaporated, about 4 minutes.
8. Add the morels and their liquid, leaving behind any grit. Cover and simmer over low heat until the morels are softened, about 5 minutes.
9. Add the chicken stock and any veal juices and simmer over moderately high heat until reduced by half, about 5 minutes.
10. Add the crème fraiche and simmer until thickened, about 4 minutes. Add the lemon juice and season with salt and pepper.
11. Return the veal medallions to the skillet and simmer for 1 minute, turning once.

Figure 5-16
Recipe Card

	A	B	D	E	F	G	H
1	Item:	**Veal Medallions with Morels**					
2		Recipe File # DinEnr201					
3		Desired Yield (# of portions)	4				
4		Conversion Factor	4.00				
5		Batch Cost	$39.860				
6		Portion Cost	$9.965				
7		Sales Price	$23.00				
8		Cost %	43.33%				
9							
10-11	Inventory File #	Ingredient	Amount	Recipe Unit	Unit Cost	Total Ingredient Cost	
12	PR022	morels, dried	1.00	ounce	$3.765	$3.765	
13		water	2.00	cup		$0.000	
14	MS008	veal butt tenderloin medallion, 3 ounce	8.00	each	$3.450	$27.600	
15	ST032	salt		TT			
16	SP012	black pepper		TT			
17	DA001	butter	4.00	teaspoon	$0.050	$0.200	
18	ST022	vegetable oil	2.00	tablespoon	$0.095	$0.189	
19	PR036	shallots	2.00	each	$0.235	$0.469	
20	ST055	wine, white	4.00	ounce	$0.200	$0.800	
21	ST033	chicken stock	8.00	ounce	$0.146	$1.165	
22	DA003	Crème fraiche	4.00	ounce	$0.329	$1.316	
23	PR020	lemon juice	1.00	teaspoon	$0.063	$0.087	
24	DinEnt1401	Baked Polenta	4.00	each	$0.254	$1.017	
25	DinEnt1501	Citrus Buttered Brussel Sprouts	12.00	each	$0.053	$0.641	
26	DinEnt1701	Fiddleheads	12.00	each	$0.129	$1.542	
27	DinApp	Sally Lunn Rolls	4.00	each	$0.180	$0.722	
28	DinApp	Grissini	4.00	each	$0.087	$0.347	

Preparation Method

30	1	Bring the water to a boil. In a heatproof bowl, soak the morels in the boiling water until softened, about 30 minutes.
31	2	Remove and rinse under running water, rubbing to loosen any grit. Let the soaking liquid stand.
32	3	Season the 3-ounce medallions (cut .5 inch thick) with salt and pepper. In a very large skillet, melt 1 Tablespoon of butter in the oil.
33	4	Add the veal and cook over high heat until browned on the bottom, 2 to 3 minutes. Turn and cook until browned on the bottom and the meat is just pink inside, about 3 minutes.
34	5	Transfer the veal to a warmed platter and cover loosely with foil.
35	6	Melt the remaining 1 Tablespoon of butter in the same skillet. Add minced shallots and cook over low heat, stirring until softened, about 5 minutes.
36	7	Add the wine and boil, scraping up any browned bits from the bottom until almost evaporated, about 4 minutes.
37	8	Add the morels and their liquid, leaving behind any grit. Cover and simmer over low heat until the morels are softened, about 5 minutes.
38	9	Add the chicken stock and any veal juices and simmer over moderately high heat until reduced by half, about 5 minutes.
39	10	Add the crème fraiche and simmer until thickened, about 4 minutes. Add the lemon juice and season with salt and pepper.
40	11	Return the veal medallions to the skillet and simmer for 1 minute, turning once.

Figure 5-17
Recipe Card—Converted to Yield Additional Portions

EXERCISE 5-5
MODIFYING RECIPE CARDS FOR INGREDIENT CHANGES

Visit http://www.pearsonhighered.com/barrish to obtain the Veal Medallions recipe card worksheet. Update the recipe as follows:

Q1. Replace the veal butt tenderloin medallions with veal leg slices. The cost per 3-ounce slice is $2.85. What is the new cost of the entrée?

Q2. Is the title of the recipe still correct? Is there a more apt name now that the ingredient change has been made?

note that the batch costs (cell D5) differ; however, the "Portion costs" (cell D6) and "Cost %" (cell D8) remain the same.[5]

Once recipe costs have been calculated, they should be updated on a continuous basis. This practice assures that recipe costs are reflective of the most current ingredient prices.

Figure 5-18 can be used to record current menu item cost, menu prices, and the number of items forecasted for sale.[6]

In this example, appetizer portion costs are entered into column C, menu prices are entered into column D, and the number of appetizers forecasted for sale in the upcoming period is listed in column E. Similar entries are made for the other menu categories. This software, by using linked cells, automatically posts these entries into the menu engineering worksheets, such as those previously studied in Figures 5-7, 5-8, 5-9, and 5-11. In essence, the software constitutes a series of linked worksheets that begin with recipes and culminate in a ***pro forma* income statement**.

Dinner Sales Forecast Worksheet

Period Start Date:	29-Apr-11		
Period End Date:	06-May-11		
Report Date:	29-Apr-11		

Appetizers

Menu ID	Menu Item Name	Food Cost	Menu Price	# Sold Forecast
DinApp1	Field Greens w/Cheese Tart	$1.448	$5.00	105
DinApp2	Endive with Poached Quail Egg	$0.215	$3.50	87
Din App3	Marinated Vegetable Salad	$0.858	$4.00	54
DinApp4	Cream of Parsnip Soup	$0.996	$4.00	85
DinApp5	Autumn Bisque	$0.408	$4.00	94
DinApp6	Crayfish Chowder	$0.651	$4.00	72
DinApp7	Terrine Du Jourw/ Crusty Bread	$0.775	$5.00	44
DinApp8	Wild Mushroom Strudel	$0.982	$4.00	102
DinApp9	Leeks with Mustard Sauce	$0.564	$4.00	49
DinApp10	Crab Supreme	$2.311	$6.00	78

Entrees

Menu ID	Menu Item Name	Food Cost	Menu Price	# Sold Forecast
DinEnt1	Rainbow Trout	$3.766	$19.00	42
DinEnt2	Veal Medallions w/ Morels	$2.846	$18.00	37
DinEnt3	Flatiron Steak	$3.276	$20.00	40
DinEnt4	Pork Tenderloin	$2.979	$18.00	39
DinEnt5	Filet Mignon	$5.974	$23.00	27
DinEnt6	Cassoulet	$3.484	$20.00	20
DinEnt7	Chicken Madeira	$2.210	$17.00	43
DinEnt8	Lamb Medallions	$2.708	$18.00	32
DinEnt9	Game Mixed Grill	$3.494	$18.00	31
DinEnt10	Stuffed Quail	$4.615	$21.00	9

Malt Beverages

Menu ID	Menu Item Name	Beverage Cost	Menu Price	# Sold Forecast
DinMalt1	Red Hook	$0.541	$4.00	38
DinMalt2	Brooklyn Brown Ale	$0.708	$4.00	41
DinMalt3	Starr Hill	$0.708	$4.00	15
DinMalt4	Anchor Steam	$0.708	$4.00	19
DinMalt5	Rogue Dead Guy	$0.708	$4.00	21
DinMalt6	Samuel Adams Winter Ale	$0.541	$3.00	39
DinMalt7				
DinMalt8				

Bottled Wines

Menu ID	Menu Item Name	Beverage Cost	Menu Price	# Sold Forecast
DinWine01	Duckhorn Merlot	$17.750	$40.00	4
DinWine02	Moet Chandon Brut	$30.750	$53.00	1
DinWine03	Pierrier Jouet Fleur	$93.000	$55.00	1
DinWine04	Andanne Brut	$28.560	$145.00	0
DinWine05	Bergerr kabinett Riesling	$12.510	$35.00	4
DinWine 06	Sobon Rockpile Zinfandel	$13.500	$36.00	3
DinWine07	Torcherre Cabernet	$11.650	$34.00	5
DinWine08	Clos du Bois Chardonnay	$10.190	$32.00	6

Figure 5-18
Forecast Worksheet

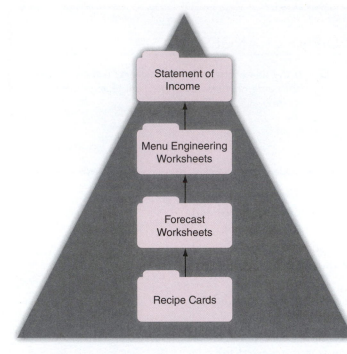

Figure 5-19
Hierarchical Linkage of Software

ANALYZING PROFIT AND LOSS

Figure 5-19 illustrates the hierarchical linkage of the software used throughout this textbook. It is important to remember that we seek to predict the magnitude of profit or loss prior to actual events occurring, and these linked tools support that objective.

Once (re)calculated, the menu engineering worksheets indicate the forecasted costs and sales for the various menu categories. The category totals should be entered into cells B6, B7, B8, and B9 (food sales); B11, B12, B13, and B14 (beverage sales); B18, B19, B20, and B21 (food costs); B23, B24, B25, and B26 (beverage costs) of the *pro forma* Statement of Income (Figure 5-20 illustrates a Statement of Income partially populated with sample data).

Cell D28 indicates total cost of sales as measured in dollars. Cell F28 indicates total cost of sales as a percentage of projected sales.[7] This percentage is often used as one measure of operational success. Table 5-2 lists examples of these percentages for various industry segments in 2009–2010.[8] If your total cost of sales appears excessive relative to industry medians, then your objective should be to reduce them without having a negative impact on sales. (Chapter 10 discusses tools and methods for conducting menu analyses and improving net profit.)

Cell D30 of Figure 5-20 indicates the dollar amount remaining after Total Cost of Sales have been subtracted from Total Sales. The difference of this equation is referred to as **gross profit**. Cell F30 indicates gross profit as a percentage of total sales. Table 5-3 lists examples of gross profit percentages for various industry segments in 2009–2010.[9]

In addition to cost of sales estimates, the Statement of Income must include forecasted data for non-food and beverage revenue (cover charges, tobacco, merchandise, etc.) and expenses (labor costs, operating expenses, occupancy costs, etc.) if it is to fully predict net income. The calculation of these line items is outside the scope of this textbook; however, sample data based on industry percentages has been entered into Figure 5-21. Row 47 indicates the net income remaining after food and beverage costs and other expenses have been subtracted. As in previous examples, this is reported in dollars and also as a percentage of total sales. It is valuable to compare your forecasted net income percentage to other industry data if only to obtain an initial measure of potential business success. Certainly, you should not overreact if your forecasted results are less than comparative industry averages; however, a brief study could identify areas for in-depth technical diagnosis and redesign. Whereas certain items (lease, property taxes, etc.) may not be subject to short-term cost reductions, your comparative studies might illustrate the need for enhanced labor controls or other operational modifications.

PUTTING IT ALL TOGETHER

The preceding discussion should impress on you the importance of positioning your menus within an informed context. You must understand the impacts of time (dayparts) and how menus function at different times of day. You must also understand the basics of revenue generation and how costs and expenses diminish revenue. If you are able to predict net income prior to each operating period, then the likelihood for suc-

	A	B	C	D	E	F	G
2	Statement of Income						
3	Period Ended 12/01/10	$	$	$	%	%	
4							
5	SALES						
6	Food – Appetizers	$15,985.75			23.1%		(of food sales)
7	Food – Entrees	$38,915.00			56.2%		(of food sales)
8	Food – Desserts	$7,389.25			10.7%		(of food sales)
9	Food – Non-alcoholic Beverages	$6,973.00			10.1%		(of food sales)
10	TOTAL FOOD SALES		$69,263.00			68.6%	(of total sales)
11	Beverage – Malt Beverages	$2,245.75			7.1%		(of beverage sales)
12	Beverage – Bottled Wine	$9,456.00			29.9%		(of beverage sales)
13	Beverage – Wine by the Glass	$7,310.00			23.1%		(of beverage sales)
14	Beverage – Spirits	$12,638.50			39.9%		(of beverage sales)
15	TOTAL BEVERAGE SALES		$31,650.25			31.4%	(of total sales)
16	TOTAL SALES			$100,913.25		100.0%	
17	COST OF SALES						
18	Food – Appetizers	$7,589.49			47.5%		(of appetizer sales)
19	Food – Entrees	$17,850.00			45.9%		(of entree sales)
20	Food – Desserts	$3,095.46			41.9%		(of dessert sales)
21	Food – Non-alcoholic Beverages	$1,958.31			28.1%		(of non-alcoholic beverage sales)
22	TOTAL COST OF FOOD SALES		$30,493.26			44.0%	(of total food sales)
23	Beverage – Malt Beverages	$587.49			26.2%		(of malt beverage sales)
24	Beverage – Bottled Wine	$4,761.00			50.3%		(of bottled wine sales)
25	Beverage – Wine by the Glass	$2,298.93			31.4%		(of wine by the glass sales)
26	Beverage – Spirits	$2,943.00			23.3%		(of spirits sales)
27	TOTAL COST OF BEVERAGE SALES		$10,590.42			33.5%	(of total beverage sales)
28	TOTAL COST OF SALES			$41,083.68		40.7%	
29							
30	GROSS PROFIT			$59,829.57		59.3%	
31							
32	CONTROLLABLE EXPENSES						
33	Fixed Salaries and Wages						
34	Variable Salaries and Wages						
35	TOTAL SALARIES AND WAGES		$0.00			0.0%	
36	Benefits on Fixed Salaries and Wages						
37	Benefits on Variable Salaries and Wages						
38	TOTAL BENEFITS		$0.00			0.0%	
39	OTHER CONTROLLABLE EXPENSES					0.0%	
40	TOTAL CONTROLLABLE EXPENSES			$0.00		0.0%	
41	INCOME BEFORE OCCUPANCY COSTS			$59,829.57		59.3%	
42	OCCUPANCY COSTS					0.0%	
43	INCOME BEFORE INTEREST AND DEPRECIATION			$59,829.57		59.3%	
44	INTEREST					0.0%	
45	DEPRECIATION					0.0%	
46							
47	NET INCOME BEFORE TAXES			$59,829.57		59.3%	

Figure 5-20
Pro Forma Statement of Income with Sample Data (Sales and Cost of Sales Only)

TABLE 5-2
RESTAURANT INDUSTRY COST OF SALES DATA, 2010

Limited Service Restaurants	Full Service Restaurants (average check per person <$15.00)	Full Service Restaurants (average check per person $15.00–$24.99)	Full Service Restaurants (average check per person ≥$25.00)
31.9%	32.2%	31.8%	31.9%

TABLE 5-3
RESTAURANT INDUSTRY GROSS PROFIT DATA, 2010

Limited Service Restaurants	Full Service Restaurants (average check per person <$15.00)	Full Service Restaurants (average check per person $15.00–$24.99)	Full Service Restaurants (average check per person ≥$25.00)
68.1%	67.8%	68.2%	68.1%

EXERCISE 5-6
ANALYZING STATEMENT OF INCOME STATISTICS

Compare the cost of sales percentage and the gross profit percentage from Figure 5-21 to the industry averages illustrated in Tables 5-2 and 5-3.

Q1. Do you find the cost of sales and gross profit results in Figure 5-21 acceptable? Why?

Q2. What industry segment (limited service, etc.) do you think this example is classified within? Why?

---

cess is enhanced and you will understand profit potential within a manageable framework. Whether you use the worksheets provided with this textbook or invest in technologies designed specifically for food service operations, you must discipline your actions by analyzing historical results and make future decisions based on facts and current data. Finally, as depicted in Figure 5-19, all components of your forecasting and cost-control system should synchronize so that your managerial workload is manageable and the use of data is approachable by all members of your team.

	A	B	C	D	E	F	G
2	Statement of Income						
3	Period Ended 12/01/09	$	$	$	%	%	
4							
5	SALES						
6	Food - Appetizers	$15,985.75			23.1%		(of food sales)
7	Food - Entrees	$38,915.00			56.2%		(of food sales)
8	Food - Desserts	$7,389.25			10.7%		(of food sales)
9	Food - Non-alcoholic Beverages	$6,973.00			10.1%		(of food sales)
10	TOTAL FOOD SALES		$69,263.00			68.6%	(of total sales)
11	Beverage - Malt Beverages	$2,245.75			7.1%		(of beverage sales)
12	Beverage - Bottled Wine	$9,456.00			29.9%		(of beverage sales)
13	Beverage - Wine by the Glass	$7,310.00			23.1%		(of beverage sales)
14	Beverage - Spirits	$12,638.50			39.9%		(of beverage sales)
15	TOTAL BEVERAGE SALES		$31,650.25			31.4%	(of total sales)
16	TOTAL SALES			$100,913.25		100.0%	
17	COST OF SALES						
18	Food - Appetizers	$5,083.47			31.8%		(of appetizer sales)
19	Food - Entrees	$13,192.19			33.9%		(of entree sales)
20	Food - Desserts	$2,364.56			32.0%		(of dessert sales)
21	Food - Non-alcoholic Beverages	$1,958.31			28.1%		(of non-alcoholic beverage sales)
22	TOTAL COST OF FOOD SALES		$22,598.52			32.6%	(of total food sales)
23	Beverage - Malt Beverages	$587.49			26.2%		(of malt beverage sales)
24	Beverage - Bottled Wine	$2,836.80			30.0%		(of bottled wine sales)
25	Beverage - Wine by the Glass	$2,193.00			30.0%		(of wine by the glass sales)
26	Beverage - Spirits	$3,298.65			26.1%		(of spirits sales)
27	TOTAL COST OF BEVERAGE SALES		$8,915.94			28.2%	(of total beverage sales)
28	TOTAL COST OF SALES			$31,514.46		31.2%	
29							
30	GROSS PROFIT			$69,398.79		68.8%	
31							
32	CONTROLLABLE EXPENSES						
33	Fixed Salaries and Wages						
34	Variable Salaries and Wages						
35	TOTAL SALARIES AND WAGES						
36	Benefits on Fixed Salaries and Wages						
37	Benefits on Variable Salaries and Wages						
38	TOTAL BENEFITS						
39	OTHER CONTROLLABLE EXPENSES						
40	TOTAL CONTROLLABLE EXPENSES			$56,915.07		56.4%	
41	INCOME BEFORE OCCUPANCY COSTS			$12,483.72		12.4%	
42	OCCUPANCY COSTS			$6,963.01		6.9%	
43	INCOME BEFORE INTEREST AND DEPRECIATION			$5,520.70		5.5%	
44	INTEREST			$1,110.05		1.1%	
45	DEPRECIATION			$2,018.27		2.0%	
46							
47	NET INCOME BEFORE TAXES			$2,392.39		2.4%	

Figure 5-21
Pro Forma Statement of Income with Sample Data (All Costs Included)

(*Source:* NAN/Fotolia)

ACTION TOOLKIT

You must make yourself aware of legalities if you intend to maximize your space by producing recipes for other businesses or for retail distribution. Depending on the scope of ingredients, preservation methods, and geographic range of distribution, you must be compliant with various federal, state, and local laws, codes, ordinances, and guidelines. The best place to gain an overview is with the United States Department of Agriculture. www.fsis.usda.gov/Home/index.asp

Restaurant SmartBrief is a free daily restaurant and foodservice e-mail newsletter that delivers news and features to help you stay informed of current events and industry research. www.smartbrief.com/news/restaurant/ index.jsp?categoryid=6A988DC8-E192-4503-8907-DE08D1DA8169

The following links provide information on food and beverage cost accounting and industry operating statistics:

- **Uniform System of Accounts for Restaurants** openlibrary.org/b/OL13254166M/Uniform_System_of_Accounts_for_Restaurants
- **National Restaurant Association Restaurant Industry Operations Report** www.restaurant.org/research/operations/index.cfm

GLOSSARY

Conversion factor—A multiplier used to increase or reduce the desired yield of a recipe.

Cost–benefit analysis—A study that catalogs the anticipated costs of implementing a particular decision versus the benefits from implementing that same decision. Managers and chefs are typically encouraged to act when the sum of benefits are believed to outweigh the sum of costs. The analysis can be based upon quantitative data (monetary, units of production, etc.), qualitative ("good," "bad") estimates, or a combination of the two.

Daypart—Functional division of the 24-hour time period. Typical dayparts in the foodservice industry are breakfast, lunch, and dinner.

Direct labor cost—The component of labor cost attributable to specific menu items. For example, the direct labor cost for a raw bar includes the wages of staff members that shuck the shellfish.

Gross profit—The difference between total revenue and cost of sales. In a foodservice operation, gross revenue remains after food cost and beverage cost is subtracted from food sales and beverage sales.

Hospitality—The practice of welcoming guests and providing goodwill and caring service.

Menu mix—The relative fraction or percentage of sales that each menu item contributes to the whole. Typically, menu mix is calculated on the basis of items sold; however, at certain times it will be calculated based upon dollar sales.

Net income—Income remaining after all costs and expenses, including taxes and depreciation have been subtracted from total revenue. Net income is also referred to as net profit, earnings, or "bottom line."

Prime cost—The combined cost of food, beverages, and the direct labor required to produce them.

***Pro forma* income statement**—An income statement based upon specific assumptions that anticipate the results of operations prior to their occurrence. A pro forma income statement is used as a tool to make management decisions that will improve financial outcomes.

Revenue—Business income derived from the sale of goods and services to customers.

Sub-recipes—Recipes that are components within other recipes.

ENDNOTES

1. www.quotationspage.com/quote/37783.html; retrieved May 1, 2011.

2. Most worksheets in this chapter can be used for the predictive task of forecasting or for recording actual results after sales have occurred. Consequently, certain data are listed as "No. Sold" (as in column B) or "Sales" (as in column H), and may depict forecasted sales targets or actual sales, depending on management's use of this instrument. Visit http://www.pearsonhighered.com/barrish for supplemental materials, including a digital version of this worksheet, as well as related files for other exercises in this textbook.

3. A source for the Uniform System of Accounts for Restaurants is listed in the Action Toolkit for this chapter.

4. Actual sub-recipes include multiple ingredients. The sub-recipes illustrated are titles only. For example, whereas chicken stock is made with chicken frames, it also requires various vegetables, aromatics, herbs, and water.

5. The recipe worksheet used in this textbook enables automated recalculation as you change desired yield. Visit http://www.pearsonhighered.com/barrish to obtain the files containing this and other worksheets.

6. As previously noted, the worksheet can also be used to record actual sales (rather than forecasts) based on management's desired use of the instrument.

7. Most operators correlate profitability with a low cost of sales; however, this assumption is explored in more depth in Chapters 8 and 10.

8. From the 2010 National Restaurant Association Restaurant Industry Operations Report.

9. From the 2010 National Restaurant Association Restaurant Industry Operations Report.

6

Operational Considerations

(*Source:* Bork/Shutterstock)

Key Terms

Convenience ingredients

Hazard Analysis Critical
    Control Point
    (HACCP)

Inventory turnover

Payback period analysis

Risk management

Workstations

Objectives

Upon completion of this chapter, you should be able to:

6.1 Manage risk by designing food menus that limit customer exposure to pathogenic organisms.

6.2 Manage risk by designing alcoholic beverage menus that balance marketability and moderation.

6.3 Discuss the need for consistent and reliable ingredient sources.

6.4 Explain the impact of menus on ingredient and equipment storage requirements.

6.5 Perform storage capacity calculations.

6.6 Explain how menus influence space division and workstations.

6.7 Apply analytic processes to identify equipment needs.

6.8 Conduct cost–benefit analyses to select appropriate equipment and supplies.

6.9 Perform payback period analyses on equipment purchase decisions.

6.10 Explain how menus influence serviceware decisions.

6.11 Discuss the relationship between menus and staffing.

MANAGING RISK IN FOOD MENUS

"Take calculated risks. That is quite different from being rash."

—GENERAL GEORGE S. PATTON[1]

When you develop a food menu, you create varying levels of risk for your clientele and exposure to varying levels of liability for your business. Recipe ingredients and their preparations may be or may become unsafe due to the presence of chemical, physical, or biological contaminants. Soil-grown vegetables may contain spores of potentially fatal *Clostridium botulinum* or other pathogens resulting from exposure to contaminated water. Seafood may contain viruses or high levels of toxic chemicals. Raw or undercooked ingredients can harbor hazardous bacteria or their toxic waste products. Moist, protein-rich foods held at improper temperatures provide excellent conditions for rapid growth of pathogenic bacteria. Complicating things further, multiple handling steps in a recipe (peeling, trimming, holding, stuffing, etc.) increase the likelihood that ingredients will become contaminated. The preceding list is but a fraction of the food-borne dangers you must guard against. The study of food safety deserves thorough treatment and is outside the scope of this textbook; however, a few principles merit discussion in this chapter.[2] Once informed, you can make appropriate decisions and manage the risk to your customers and your business. Figure 6-1 illustrates the spectrum of risk and shows where certain menu items fall within the continuum.

As you plan your menu, you must decide where on this continuum your selections will reside. The concept of **risk management**, as related to menu planning, involves

- identifying specific risks
- identifying and implementing controls to contain the risks
- obtaining regulatory approval of your risk management plans when high-risk ingredients and recipes are intended for inclusion on your menu
- systematizing your plans, documenting results, and modifying the system as appropriate

Nearly all health department jurisdictions promulgate strict regulatory codes to assure this manner of vigilance is in place when inherently unsafe foods are served. For

LOW RISK	MODERATE RISK	HIGH RISK
COMMERCIALLY SEALED SUGAR PACKETS	RECIPES COOKED AT LOW TEMPERATURES FOR EXTENDED PERIODS OF TIME	
FRESHLY PREPARED FOODS MAINTAINED AT APPROPRIATE TEMPERATURES FOR SHORT PERIODS OF TIME		UNCOOKED SHELLFISH
	RARE-COOKED STEAKS AND CHOPS OF MEAT	FORAGED MUSHROOMS
PACKAGED SNACKS (POTATO CHIPS, ETC.)		RARE-COOKED GROUND MEATS
UNPEELED FRUIT	RAW FISH PREPARATIONS (SUSHI, SASHIMI)	
		IN-HOUSE VACUUM PACKAGING

Figure 6-1
Risk Spectrum for Ingredients and Recipes

EXERCISE 6-1

IDENTIFYING FOOD-BORNE RISKS AND DEVELOPING RISK MANAGEMENT TACTICS

Q1. Research the Moderate Risk and High Risk items listed in Figure 6-1. How can you modify the purchasing, storage, or preparation to enhance the menu safety of these items?

Q2. Figure 6-1 lists 11 items/classes of ingredients. What other items might be added to Figure 6-1 under the classification of Moderate Risk or High Risk? What attributes prompted you to select these additional items?

example, in Virginia, operators must comply with the following sections of the Department of Health Food Regulations:[3]

12 VAC 5-421-700. Raw animal foods.*

A raw animal food such as raw egg, raw fish, raw-marinated fish, raw molluscan shellfish, or steak tartare, or a partially cooked food such as lightly cooked fish, soft cooked eggs, or rare meat other than whole-muscle, intact beef steaks as specified in subsection C of this section, may be served or offered for sale in a ready-to-eat form if:

The food establishment serves a population that is not a highly susceptible population; and

The regulatory authority grants a variance from subsection A or B of this section as specified in 12 VAC 5-421-3570 based on a HACCP plan that:

Is submitted by the permit holder and approved as specified under 12 VAC 5-421-3580,

Documents scientific data or other information that shows that a lesser time and temperature regimen results in a safe food, and

Verifies that equipment and procedures for food preparation and training of food employees at the food establishment meet the conditions.

There are various effective protocols for dealing with your internally conducted risk assessments that augment and enable you to comply with regulatory requirements. Perhaps the most systematic and comprehensive method is the **Hazard Analysis Critical Control Point (HACCP)** system of risk management, which was jointly developed by the federal government and the private sector and is widely used in food manufacturing and processing. It is readily adaptable by foodservice operators. The steps are as follows:

- Step 1: Conduct a Hazard Analysis
- Step 2: Identify Critical Control Points
- Step 3: Establish Critical Limits
- Step 4: Establish Monitoring Procedures
- Step 5: Establish Corrective Actions
- Step 6: Establish Verification Procedures
- Step 7: Record Keeping Procedure

For example, you might choose to serve *carpaccio,* an Italian appetizer composed of raw beef tenderloin served with garnishes.

- Step 1: A hazard analysis indicates that raw beef may contain pathogens that (as a result of the preparation method) will not benefit from the bactericidal effect of cooking. Customers can become ill if they consume these pathogens, or the toxins they can produce.
- Step 2: Several critical control points exist. As a result of the increased risk of this dish, special attention must be paid to purchase the beef in as fresh and wholesome

condition as possible. Whereas freezing does not kill all pathogens, it does inhibit growth. Frozen meat is seldom desirable over fresh meat, but this is a critical control worth considering. Once thawed, the meat must be served immediately.

- Step 3: You must adopt qualitative and quantitative standards for reference in the receiving process. You must also establish maximum times for holding the portioned beef prior to service.
- Step 4: You must assign monitoring responsibilities, including frequency of inspection.
- Step 5: You must decide what to do with product that fails to meet control standards at any point in the plan. You may decide that beef deemed unsuitable for *carpaccio* can be used in recipes calling for cooked beef tenderloin. These are decisions that are a foundation of the plan, rather than a consequential question should a breach occur. All parties must know what will be done with the product prior to a system failure.
- Step 6: Conceive a means for verifying the plan actually works. If you implement the first five steps of your risk management plan, then the next logical step should inform you of the plan's effectiveness. This may be achieved through periodic audits or other quality assurance means.
- Step 7: Establish a record-keeping system that can be studied in the future. This system also may be called for by your health inspector and can prove valuable as evidence should you have to defend yourself in court.

As previously mentioned, you should (or must, depending on your health department regulations) obtain approval of your HACCP plan for each recipe or process deemed inherently unsafe.

Another facet of risk management involves informing your clientele of specific risks. In Virginia, the following regulation applies:[4]

Consumer Advisory

3-603.11 Consumption of Animal Foods that are Raw, Undercooked, or Not Otherwise Processed to Eliminate Pathogens.*

(A) Except as specified in ¶ 3-401.11(C) and Subparagraph 3-401.11(D)(3) and under ¶ 3-801.11(D), if an animal FOOD such as beef, EGGS, FISH, lamb, milk, pork, POULTRY, or shellfish is served or sold raw, undercooked, or without otherwise being processed to eliminate pathogens, either in READY-TO-EAT form or as an ingredient in another READY-TO-EAT FOOD, the PERMIT HOLDER shall inform CONSUMERS of the significantly increased RISK of consuming such FOODS by way of a DISCLOSURE and REMINDER, as specified in ¶¶ (B) and (C) of this section using brochures, deli case or menu advisories, label statements, table tents, placards, or other effective written means.

(B) DISCLOSURE shall include:

(1) A description of the animal-derived FOODS, such as "oysters on the half shell (raw oysters)," "raw-EGG Caesar salad," and "hamburgers (can be cooked to order);" or

(2) Identification of the animal-derived FOODS by asterisking them to a footnote that states that the items are served raw or undercooked, or contain (or may contain) raw or undercooked ingredients.

(C) REMINDER shall include asterisking the animal-derived FOODS requiring DISCLOSURE to a footnote that states:

(1) Regarding the safety of these items, written information is available upon request;

(2) Consuming raw or undercooked MEATS, POULTRY, seafood, shellfish, or EGGS may increase your RISK of foodborne illness; or

(3) Consuming raw or undercooked MEATS, POULTRY, seafood, shellfish, or EGGS may increase your RISK of foodborne illness, especially if you have certain medical conditions.

By making informed menu development decisions, controlling risk, and informing your clientele of hazards, you will limit your liability should customers become injured from your food. It should be evident that risky ingredients and procedures require enhanced planning, but with forethought and diligence, you can serve the spectrum of menu items your clientele wants.

MANAGING THE RISK OF ALCOHOLIC BEVERAGE ITEMS

"Profit is the result of risks wisely selected."

—FREDERICK BARNARD HAWLEY[5]

In addition to risks presented from food ingredients, the service of alcoholic beverages is fraught with exposure to liability and potential litigation. Consider the following statistics:[6]

- In 2005, a New York state couple who had recently married was celebrating with another couple at a local restaurant. All of the individuals got into the same car and left the establishment, the driver later losing control of the vehicle and striking a telephone poll. The two women in the car were killed instantly, and one of the male passengers has since undergone multiple surgeries, in part to relieve pressure on his brain. The company that owned the restaurant was required to pay $900,000 to the survivors and the decedent's estate for over serving alcoholic beverages to the driver.
- In 2003, in a pretrial settlement, a California restaurant paid $1.5 million to a family of an underage child who died in a drunken driving accident after the driver of the car he was in crashed into a utility pole. The restaurant

(*Source:* Feverpitched/Dreamstime)

EXERCISE 6-2
DEFINING INTOXICATION AT THE SOURCE

Explain why the chart illustrated in Table 6-1 provides only limited guidance for menu planners and operators. What other factors must be considered when protecting your customers and business assets?

also agreed to contribute $50,000 toward alcohol awareness training at the victim's school.

- In 2006, a company hosted a Halloween party where alcohol was served. An intoxicated underage attendee assaulted another partygoer, resulting in a permanent injury to that individual. Both the company and the caterer were required to pay $450,000 in compensation, in part for serving alcohol to a minor.
- In 2006, an intoxicated Florida woman was killed when she was struck by a car after leaving a bar. The woman, a regular drinker at this establishment, had at one point passed out at the bar. When she later awoke, the bar continued to serve her alcohol. In the legal settlement, the bar was required to pay her surviving daughters $500,000.

Every state considers a 0.08 blood alcohol concentration (BAC) as the "*Per Se* driving while under the influence (DUI)" indicator. At this level, individuals are legally intoxicated and presumed unfit to drive, or carry on the same activities with appropriate focus and dexterity that a sober person can. In addition, many states use other measures such as "*Zero Tolerance*" BAC for sanctioning intoxicated minors and "*Enhanced Penalty*" BAC for penalizing extremely intoxicated individuals.[7] Table 6-1 relates BAC, the number of drinks, and weight of the individual.

TABLE 6-1
BLOOD ALCOHOL CONCENTRATION CHART
(NATIONAL HIGHWAY TRANSPORTATION SAFETY ADMINISTRATION)

Body Weight	1	2	3	4	5	6	7	8	9	10	11	12
100 lbs	0.038	0.075	0.113	0.150	0.188	0.225	0.263	0.300	0.338	0.375	0.413	0.450
110 lbs	0.034	0.066	0.103	0.137	0.172	0.207	0.241	0.275	0.309	0.344	0.379	0.412
120 lbs	0.031	0.063	0.094	0.125	0.156	0.188	0.219	0.25	0.281	0.313	0.344	0.375
130 lbs	0.029	0.058	0.087	0.116	0.145	0.174	0.203	0.232	0.261	0.290	0.320	0.348
140 lbs	0.027	0.054	0.080	0.107	0.134	0.161	0.188	0.214	0.241	0.268	0.295	0.321
150 lbs	0.025	0.050	0.075	0.100	0.125	0.151	0.176	0.201	0.226	0.251	0.276	0.301
160 lbs	0.023	0.047	0.070	0.094	0.117	0.141	0.164	0.188	0.211	0.234	0.258	0.281
170 lbs	0.022	0.045	0.066	0.088	0.110	0.132	0.155	0.178	0.200	0.221	0.244	0.265
180 lbs	0.021	0.042	0.063	0.083	0.104	0.125	0.146	0.167	0.188	0.208	0.229	0.250
190 lbs	0.020	0.040	0.059	0.079	0.099	0.119	0.138	0.158	0.179	0.198	0.217	0.237
200 lbs	0.019	0.038	0.056	0.075	0.094	0.113	0.131	0.150	0.169	0.188	0.206	0.225
210 lbs	0.018	0.036	0.053	0.071	0.090	0.107	0.125	0.143	0.161	0.179	0.197	0.215
220 lbs	0.017	0.034	0.051	0.068	0.085	0.102	0.119	0.136	0.153	0.170	0.188	0.205
230 lbs	0.016	0.032	0.049	0.065	0.081	0.098	0.115	0.130	0.147	0.163	0.180	0.196
240 lbs	0.016	0.031	0.047	0.063	0.078	0.094	0.109	0.125	0.141	0.156	0.172	0.188

Drinks

It should be readily evident that operators must manage the probability of alcohol-related incidents occurring. As with all management behaviors, there is a range of deliberateness demonstrated through policies and procedures. In its weakest manifestation, alcoholic beverage risk management involves restricting minors from service. The obvious flaw is that there might not be a concerted effort to control intoxication of adults being served. At the other end of the spectrum is aggressive management oversight that extends through the diligence of all staff. The perceived downside in an enlightened operation is that the spirit of hospitality may be overly moderated by an environment of "nannyism." This perception is harsh, and in all but the rarest cases a false argument. It is quite possible to succeed in business while offering a legally defensible, ethically grounded, and welcoming service environment. Whereas the following discussion focuses on restaurant/lounge menus, it is equally applicable to club, bar, and catering scenarios.

Vigilant, strategic service supervision and policies are the most common approaches to controlling alcohol-related liability. Nonetheless, thoughtful menu planning is a more subtle, yet important, risk-management practice. This is best illustrated by two extreme examples.

EXAMPLE ONE

Envision an operation that features Mexican-inspired cuisine. Their signature cocktail is a supersize Margarita made with four ounces of tequila, one ounce of triple sec, and appropriate mixers. After consuming only one drink, a 160-pound customer will be legally intoxicated. Imagine trying to defend your signature bar menu in a court of law if a customer was injured or injured a third party. This practice is not uncommon, and involves oversize portions of beer as well as cocktails. Figure 6-2 is an adaptation of an actual menu in use.

EXAMPLE TWO

Whereas some states and restaurants allow unfinished bottles of wine to be resealed and carried home by customers, this is not a universal practice.[8] Consequently, some guests may be compelled (after having spent money for a bottle marked up several times, and then not permitted to carry it home) to drink the entire bottle, if only to fully consummate the purchase. Thus, customers may be compelled to drink more than they might otherwise prefer, had they been given options.

In essence, practices related to alcoholic beverage recipes and portion sizes can promote risky customer decisions. The hard work and tight profit margins encountered in many foodservices cannot be compromised by an alcohol-related incident. Proactive menu planning is one component of an effective risk-management program. The major menu management principles include

- controlling drink portions and alcohol concentration
- developing signature drinks that support your concept yet do not promote intoxication

Pedro's Tequila Bar

Happy Hour

Monster Margarita . . . $ 7.77

16 ounces – always a deal –

made with Cuervo Gold (you know why)

Figure 6-2
Tequila Menu

AUTHOR'S INSIGHT

Several years ago, I was consulting for a lively restaurant that was the "It" place of the moment. Customers happily drove 1½ hours to a remote town to share in the buzz and savor the cuisine. By my estimates, less than half of the clientele were locals, so the remaining guests apparently were commuters. The perpetually filled parking lot confirmed my suspicions. The crowd enjoyed mingling at the bar while awaiting their dinner tables. The house specialty was oversize martinis of every sort. The 5-ounce glasses were generously filled with 4-ounce portions, guaranteeing a gaggle of intoxicated diners. I often scanned the dining room only to find several emptied cocktail glasses and a bottle or two of wine waiting to be tippled. I could not imagine how these well-lubricated guests could ferry themselves home on the dark country byways. On more

than one occasion, I engaged my client in frank conversations to address this issue, yet he was steadfast in his conviction to "give them what they want." I suggested that he negotiate rates with the local inn so that intoxicated guests could be given a room for the night—surely the cost would be offset by the reduced risk of not sending away drunken drivers. Regrettably, I was unsuccessful in my persuasive efforts, and the alcohol continued to flow freely. Despite my lucrative consulting agreement, I elected to sever ties with the business. As a consultant, my ethical and pecuniary interests were in jeopardy and I refused to let my professional reputation become tarnished. If there is a lesson here, it is that our moral duties trump any profit opportunities. Life and limb are ever more precious than a paycheck.

- offering alternatives to standard (750 ml) bottles of wine. Whereas a full bottle may be the standard purchase decision for a party of guests, it is wise to augment your wine list with a selection of half bottles, *quartinos*, and wines by the glass. As discussed in Chapter 3, a plan such as this allows guests to complement their meal without purchasing portions of wine in excess of their wishes or comfort level.

OPERATIONAL FEASIBILITY

"Out of intense complexities intense simplicities emerge."

—SIR WINSTON CHURCHILL[9]

Regardless of your team's marketing savvy and culinary creativity, you must possess the operational capability to consistently deliver quality results; otherwise, your menu is merely an exercise in futility. Some menu concepts are simply not suited for the business resources available to support them. An intelligent menu planner knows when to abandon a formative concept and redirect efforts that are grounded in knowledge of your organizational capabilities and space, human, and financial resources.

INGREDIENT SOURCES

As has been discussed throughout previous chapters, you must have a reliable source of the food and beverage ingredients you specify for your recipes. If the availability is unreliable, you run the risk of disappointing customers that have visited specifically

AUTHOR'S INSIGHT

I recall a hotel checkout where I was erroneously billed an additional $82.50 for in room items merchandised in the mini-bar. After respectfully requesting an explanation, I was told that the six items I handled were recorded by the technology as "purchased." In reality, I was reading the nutrition labels to see which products were fat-free (none were fat-free, so I bought nothing and my folio was adjusted accordingly).

Operators must be cautious when introducing food or beverage menus, particularly if transaction settlement involves supplementary departments or staff linked by technologies. Operational feasibility involves well-conceived processes, dependable system integration, as well as adequate resources. If any of these elements are missing, customer satisfaction and profit generation may be compromised.

(*Source:* © Tim Pannell/Corbis)

for certain items. Customers are prone to generalization, and all it takes is one item on one visit for their confidence in your menu to come into question. In addition, when affected by product outages, the menu mix used to forecast purchasing, production, and income becomes a less reliable tool for predicting sales revenue and associated profit. When ingredient sources are unreliable, some operators retreat to inferior products. For example, if certain fish species are listed on the menu and their availability is spotty, you might feel compelled to procure frozen or lesser-quality ingredients just to produce the item. In doing so, you sacrifice the quality standards that win customers and convert them into repeat visitors. A better strategy is to identify, during the conceptual stages, those ingredients prone to seasonality and occasional unavailability, and relegate those items to the fresh sheet/*du jour* menu.

STORAGE

Your menu decisions have an impact on the types and size of ingredient, cookware, utensil, and serviceware storage that your facility must accommodate. Exercise 1-2 illustrated, among other problems, that insufficient storage has a negative impact on quality,

---

EXERCISE 6-3
CALCULATING STORAGE CAPACITIES

Step 1   Select a size for a walk-in refrigerator from Figure 6-3.

Step 2   Noting the actual floor size for the refrigerator you selected, outfit the interior with shelving (use options from Figure 6-4).

Step 3   Specify the shelving options and quantities you selected to use in your refrigerator.

   Q1.   Why did you select these dimensions and quantities?

Step 4   Noting the shelving sizes and configurations you selected, outfit the shelves with food storage boxes (Figure 6-5).

   Q2.   Why did you select these dimensions and quantities?

   Q3.   What specific foods will you be using them for?

Sizing Guidelines

Figure 6-3
Walk-in Refrigerator Size
Options   (*Source:* Reprinted
by permission of Manitowoc
Foodservice)

Actual Floor Size	OD Floor Area Sq. Ft.	7'-6" Height Gross CU. FT. Capacity	8'-6" Height Gross CU. FT. Capacity
3' 11" x 5' 10"	23	114	130
5' 10" x 5' 10"	34	182	209
5' 10" x 7' 9"	45	250	287
5' 10" x 9' 8"	56	318	364
5' 10" x 11' 7"	68	385	442
5' 10" x 13' 6"	79	453	520
5' 10" x 15' 5"	91	531	609
6' 9.5" x 7' 9"	53	296	340
6' 9.5" x 9' 8"	67	377	432
6' 9.5" x 11' 7"	79	457	524
6' 9.5" x 13' 6"	92	528	616
6' 9.5" x 15' 5"	105	621	708
6' 9.5" x 15' 5"	105	714	800
7' 9" x 8' 8.5"	67	390	448
7' 9" x 10' 7.5"	83	482	553
7' 9" x 12' 6.5"	97	575	660
7' 9" x 14' 5.5"	113	668	765
7' 9" x 16' 4.5"	127	761	872
7' 9" x 18' 3.5"	142	853	978
7' 9" x 20' 2.5"	156	946	1084
7' 9" x 22' 1.5"	172	1039	1191
8' 8.5" x 8' 8.5"	76	442	508
8' 8.5" x 10' 7.5"	93	548	627
8' 8.5" x 12' 6.5"	110	653	748
8' 8.5" x 14' 5.5"	126	757	868
8' 8.5" x 16' 4.5"	143	863	990
9' 8" x 9' 8"	93	554	635
9' 8" x 11' 7"	112	671	770
9' 8" x 13' 6"	131	789	905
9' 8" x 15' 5"	149	907	1040
9' 8" x 17' 4"	160	1025	1175
9' 8" x 19' 3"	186	1143	1310
9' 8" x 21' 2"	205	1261	1445
10' 7.5" x 10' 7.5"	107	678	777
10' 7.5" x 12' 6.5"	130	808	927
10' 7.5" x 14' 5.5"	154	938	1076
10' 7.5" x 16' 4.5"	174	1069	1226
10' 7.5" x 18' 3.5"	195	1199	1375
10' 7.5" x 20' 2.5"	216	1330	1525
10' 7.5" x 22' 1.5"	235	1460	1674
10' 7.5" x 24' 0.5"	266	1655	1824
11' 7.5" x 12' 6.5"	145	886	1016
11' 7" x 12' 6.5"	168	1029	1179
11' 7" x 14' 5.5"	190	1172	1343
11' 7" x 18' 3.5"	212	1315	1507
11' 7" x 20' 2.5"	234	1458	1671
11' 7" x 22' 1.5"	256	1600	1835
12' 6.5" x 14' 5.5"	278	1742	1999
12' 6.5" x 14' 5.5"	182	1119	1283
12' 6.5" x 16' 4.5"	206	1275	1461
12' 6.5" x 18' 3.5"	230	1430	1639
12' 6.5" x 20' 2.5"	254	1586	1818
12' 6.5" x 22' 1.5"	278	1741	1996
12' 6.5" x 24' 0.5"	302	1897	2174
12' 6.5" x 25' 11.5"	328	2052	2353
13' 6" x 16' 4.5"	221	1378	1579
13' 6" x 18' 3.5"	247	1546	1772
13' 6" x 20' 2.5"	274	1714	1964
13' 6" x 22' 1.5"	297	1882	2157
13' 6" x 24' 0.5"	324	2050	2350
13' 6" x 25' 11.5"	351	2218	2543
13' 6" x 25' 11.5"	376	2386	2735
13' 6" x 28' 10"	390	2470	2832

Item # _____

Job _____

HD SUPER™
SOLID SHELVING

- **Extra Strong:** HD Super™ shelving employs the patented, proven Super Erecta Shelf® principle with large diameter posts and heavy gauge shelves.

- **Easy to Assemble:** Units can be put together in minutes without special tools. Tapered plastic sleeves lock into position on grooved posts and fit into the matching taper in the cast corners of the shelf, providing a positive lock. Shelves are adjustable in 2" (51mm) intervals and can be repositioned if use changes.

- **Several Shelf Options:** Heavy-duty solid shelves are available in flat or louvered/embossed styles in galvanized or stainless steel. Choose from 18" or 24" (457 or 610mm) widths and lengths ranging from 36" to 60" (914 to 1524mm). Shelves are made of heavy-duty 16-gauge steel.

- **Posts Provide Greater Rigidity:** HD Super™ posts have an outside diameter of $1^5/_8$" (42mm) providing 28% to 128% greater rigidity than posts of lesser diameter on other makes of modular shelving. Posts are available in chrome-plated or stainless steel.

- **Stationary or Mobile:** Standard units are stationary with leveling foot on each post. Posts are also available fitted with 5" (127mm) polyurethane swivel or brake casters. (Recommended load capacity for mobile units is 1,000 lbs. [454kg] gross cart weight.)

HD Super™ Solid Shelving

10.65

InterMetro Industries Corporation
North Washington Street
Wilkes-Barre, PA 18705
www.metro.com

EMERSON™

Figure 6-4

Shelving Options   (*Source:* Reprinted by permission of InterMetro Industries Corporation)

10.65

Job _____

HD SUPER™
SOLID SHELVING

METRO®

Specifications

- Shelves: Shelves are 16-gauge galvanized or T-304 stainless steel. Louvered/embossed is available in stainless steel.

- Posts: Steel posts have an outside diameter of $1\frac{5}{8}$" (42mm), with rolled grooves in 2" (51mm) increments along entire height. Available in chrome-plated or stainless steel.

- Posts with Casters: Special posts are available

fitted with 5" (127mm) donut bumpers and 5" (127mm) polyurethane swivel (5HHP) or swivel/brake (5HHPB) casters if desired.

- Load Rating:

  Shelf: 1,000 lbs. (454kg) evenly distributed per shelf, not to exceed unit load rating.

  Stationary - 3,000 lbs. (1363 kg.) evenly distributed.

  Mobile - 1,000 lbs. (454 kg) with casters.

Dimensions

Shelves — 16 gauge

FLAT

Cat. No. Galvanized	Cat. No. Stainless	Width/Length (in.)	(mm)	Approx. Pkd. Wt. (lbs.)	(kg)
1836HFG	1836HFS	18x36	457x914	21	9.5
1842HFG	1842HFS	18x42	457x1066	23	10.4
1848HFG	1848HFS	18x48	457x1219	26	11.7
1854HFG	1854HFS	18x54	457x1370	28	12.7
1860HFG	1860HFS	18x60	457x1524	31	14.0
2436HFG	2436HFS	24x36	610x914	25	11.3
2442HFG	2442HFS	24x42	610x1066	29	13.1
2448HFG	2448HFS	24x48	610x1219	32	14.4
2454HFG	2454HFS	24x54	610x1370	35	15.8
2460HFG	2460HFS	24x60	610x1524	38	17.1

LOUVERED/EMBOSSED*

Cat. No. Stainless	Width/Length (in.)	(mm)	Approx. Pkd. Wt. (lbs.)	(kg)
1836HLS	18x36	457x914	21	9.5
1842HLS	18x42	457x1066	23	10.4
1848HLS	18x48	457x1219	26	11.7
1854HLS	18x54	457x1370	28	12.7
1860HLS	18x60	457x1524	31	14.0
2436HLS	24x36	610x914	25	11.3
2442HLS	24x42	610x1066	29	13.1
2448HLS	24x48	610x1219	32	14.4
2454HLS	24x54	610x1370	35	15.8
2460HLS	24x60	610x1524	38	17.1

*On special order only.

HD Super™ Posts for Stationary Units

Cat. No. Chrome	Cat. No. Stainless	Height* (in.)	(mm)	Approx. Pkd. Wt. (lbs.)	(kg)
54HPC	54HPS	54	1421	5.8	2.6
63HPC	63HPS	64	1624	6.3	2.9
74HPC	74HPS	76	1929	7.5	3.4

All Metro Catalog Sheets are available on our Web Site: www.metro.com

HD Super™ Solid Shelving (vertical side text)

InterMetro Industries Corporation
North Washington Street, Wilkes-Barre, PA 18705
Phone: 570-825-2741 • Fax: 570-825-2852

For Product Information Call: 1-800-433-2232

L02-030
Printed in U.S.A. Rev. 4/09
Information and specifications are subject to change without notice. Please confirm at time of order.
Copyright © 2007 InterMetro Industries Corp.

Figure 6-4
Continued

Camwear® Food Boxes

Camwear® Polycarbonate

CODE	18263CW	● 18266CW	18269CW
DIMENSIONS	18" x 26" x 3½"	18" x 26" x 6"	18" x 26" x 9"
APPROX. CAPACITY	5.0 gal.	8.75 gal.	13.0 gal.
CASE PACK	6	6	4
CASE LBS. (CUBE)	21.93 (2.14)	30.05 (4.61)	27.03 (4.45)
LIST PRICE EACH	$ 40.75	$ 52.80	$ 69.45

CODE	182612CW	182615CW	12183CW	● 12186CW	12189CW
DIMENSIONS	18" x 26" x 12"	18" x 26" x 15"	12" x 18" x 3½"	12" x 18" x 6"	12" x 18" x 9"
APPROX. CAPACITY	17.0 gal.	22.0 gal.	1.75 gal.	3.0 gal.	4.75 gal.
CASE PACK	4	3	6	6	6
CASE LBS. (CUBE)	34.4 (5.56)	31.68 (6.56)	12.15 (1.01)	16.02 (2.13)	20.45 (2.70)
LIST PRICE EACH	$ 84.60	$ 99.80	$ 22.30	$ 28.25	$ 37.95

Color/InStock Color: Clear (135).   18266CW & 12186CW are available in Clear & Red.
● Safety Red (467).

Camwear® Covers

CODE	● 1826CCW FLAT LID	1826SCCW SLIDINGLID™	● 1218CCW FLAT LID	1218SCCW SLIDINGLID™
DIMENSIONS	18" x 26"	18" x 26"	12" x 18"	12" x 18"
CASE LBS. (CUBE)	16.01 (0.92)	19.03 (1.72)	7.88 (0.49)	9.50 (0.72)
LIST PRICE EACH	$ 27.65	$ 49.50	$ 13.80	$ 29.45

Case Pack: 6   **Color/InStock Color:** Clear (135).   1826CCW & 1218CCW are available in Clear & Red.
● Safety Red (467).

Figure 6-5
Cambro Camwear® Food Boxes   (*Source:* Reprinted by permission of Cambro Manufacturing Company)

food safety, and business success. Whereas the desire for ample storage is understandable, real estate is leased by the square foot and space carries a recurring cost. Some degree of correlation between space needs and space availability must be established.

Ingredient storage is optimized with a limited menu where ingredients are used in various items across the menu over multiple dayparts. Conversely, a menu with broad scope or frequent changes (*du jour* items, cycle menus, etc.) requires significant ingredient storage. Beware of selecting too many items used in only one or two recipes. If the menu items prove unpopular, these ingredients occupy space with limited turnover opportunities. In a perfect world, you set par stock values that enable rapid **inventory turnover** so that ingredients do not set idle on shelves. More typically, operators set overstated par stock values to avoid run outs, and as they later gain experience, they refine the quantities downward so as to reduce storage space consumed, dollars tied up in inventory, and to move product so it is used at its peak freshness. Setting up a par stock list to support the planned menus allows you to conceptualize required ingredient storage and derive storage requirements. Depending on the items, you can aggregate the space needed as measured by area or volume. Ideally, in the initial facility design stages, you conduct a comprehensive set of these calculations to properly match your anticipated chilled, frozen, and other ingredient storage needs to sufficient shelving and refrigeration. Similar types of calculations can also be conducted for utensil, cookware, serviceware, and equipment storage.

Whereas Exercise 6-3 involves only a few storage products and an oversimplified set of decisions to make, it points to the logical approach you can and should use as you analyze the relationship between menus and physical design/equipment features.

SPACE DIVISION/CONSERVATION

As discussed previously, space must be matched to needs. The situation becomes even more complex as you conceive and formalize **workstations**.

Some operators lease or purchase food services that already are designed and equipped. In cases such as these, the decision might be made to undertake minimal if any space renovations, thus accepting the workstation implications, be they positive or negative. Other operators possess investment resources and the will to modify spaces for optimal task efficiency, food safety, and work flow. Although not an entirely objective exercise, a cost–benefit analysis should be conducted to decide what level of capital investment and improvements are appropriate. For example, a kitchen with very high ambient temperatures may be unsuitable for dessert preparation. Managers might desire a dedicated space where heat and other negative factors cannot compromise the dessert output. A pastry workstation or even a full pastry kitchen might be a possible solution. The first step is to analyze and identify the costs versus the benefits of action (or inaction). Table 6-2 illustrates a cost–benefit model used to evaluate this example.

EXERCISE 6-4
SPACE-RELATED COST–BENEFIT ANALYSES

(Refer to Table 6-2.)

Q1. Which benefits and costs can actually be quantified in monetary terms?

Q2. Using the example of a dedicated pastry workstation, expand the list of costs and benefits begun on Table 6-2.

Q3. Based on the costs and benefits identified, at what point does a dedicated workstation become appropriate?

Q4. Based on the costs and benefits identified, at what point does a dedicated pastry kitchen become appropriate?

TABLE 6-2
COST–BENEFIT MODEL

Benefits		Costs	
Non-recurring Benefits	Reduced sharing of equipment with savory kitchen operations	Non-recurring Costs	Design, construction, and equipping of pastry workstation with its own dedicated equipment
Recurring Benefits	Longer product shelf-life as a result of enhanced temperature control; increased dessert sales as a result of higher-quality production environment	Recurring Costs	Opportunity cost of capital investment; the monies spent to build a dedicated pastry workstation could be invested elsewhere
			Occupancy costs (lease per square foot, utility costs)
Non-quantifiable Benefits	Higher-quality product; reduced odor contamination (onions, fish, etc.) and purer pastry results	Non-quantifiable Costs	Potential for employee isolation if workstation is too distant from center of activity

Unless the scale of operations is substantial, wherever possible, it is wise to design generalized space and divide it into as few specialized workstations as possible. If too intricate a space division is developed and the menu mix changes significantly, you may end up with some spaces underutilized and other spaces inadequate for the current demand. Flexible design facilitates changes in menus over time. Nonetheless, there will be times when you decide to outfit workstations for dedicated tasks. More important, you should consider the potential for retrofitting the workstations should their intended use no longer be justified. Needless to say, decisions of this nature should be approached with a commitment to long-term investment recovery, as any capital outlay is costly at the front end, and generally will not pay for itself in the short term.

AUTHOR'S INSIGHT

I was a member of the preopening management team for a large, full-service conference hotel. The property featured generous function space, including four ballrooms, numerous boardrooms and flexible meeting spaces, as well as two restaurants, in-room dining, and a deli-market serving the attached office towers. As is often the case in new ventures, traffic and revenue projections were unrealistically optimistic. My team soon realized that our signature restaurant was unable to compete with the bevy of restaurants throughout the neighboring retail corridor. Despite the exorbitant interior design investment, the signature dining room was begrudgingly converted to banquet space. Regrettably, the banquettes and other restaurant-specific features rendered the room less than effective in its new role.

The outsize kitchen was designed with an eye to the past rather than the future. Within a month of opening, the satellite banquet kitchen proved needless and was all but abandoned. In addition, a 5,000-square-foot glass-windowed, fully refrigerated butchering room dominated the central production kitchen. With this space, our chefs possessed a top-notch room to fabricate meat, seafood, and poultry while preserving quality and minimizing cross-contamination of work surfaces. Unfortunately, the industry had changed and our preopening facilities design team failed to take notice. The relatively low cost of fabricated portion cuts reduced our reliance on whole poultry or primal cuts of meat. Soon the space was underutilized to the point that it became remarkable to see the room ever in use. The last time I visited the property, the refrigeration was no longer functioning and the room was converted to store paper goods, china, silver, and glassware.

PRODUCTION EQUIPMENT REQUIREMENTS

Every piece of equipment you select must support the preparation or service of one or more menu items. Ideally, each piece of equipment will serve multiple needs. With menus and daily forecasts in hand, complete Table 6-3.

Once the equipment requirements are identified, they must be specified in sufficient quantities to meet peak forecasts. Certain items (cutting boards, serviceware, etc.) are quantified by numbers needed. Other items are quantified by production capacity. For example, Figure 6-6 illustrates specifications for a counter griddle. Whereas it is likely to be used for a variety of foods, it indicates typical production capacities for hamburgers, pancakes, steaks, and fried eggs.

Figure 6-7 illustrates another example—specifications for a stone hearth oven. Whereas it is likely to be used for a variety of foods, it indicates typical production capacities for pizzas.

In addition to supporting preparation and service of multiple menu items, each piece should be safe and easily cleanable (NSF and UL approved).[10] Wherever possible, automated or self-cleaning equipment should be considered, because it provides ongoing labor savings.

For years and still to this day, the workhorse of the kitchen has been the open-burner range. Each of the gas "eyes" can be used to heat a variety of cooking vessels. Under the burners are one or more oven compartments. A salamander is often located above the burners, or a griddle is partnered with the range top. This one piece of equipment can accomplish nearly any moist- or dry-heat cookery. Moving beyond ranges into specialized equipment, the choices appear endless, with new variations introduced regularly. Items such as *panini* grills, rotisseries, wood-fired ovens, and so on are tempting, if not expensive. As illustrated in Exercise 6-4, you must conduct a cost–benefit analysis for each piece of equipment to decide its true value.

For certain items, it is quite easy to conduct a simplified **payback period analysis** to discern if the contribution from the items produced justifies the purchase of the equipment. For example, a commercial ice-cream maker costing $2,600.00 can be used to produce gelato, sorbet, and other frozen confections. If the average food cost for items produced in this machine equals $0.50 per portion, each portion is sold for

---

TABLE 6-3
EQUIPMENT NEEDS TABLE

Menu-Driven Need		Equipment/Supply Requirements				
Menu Item	Forecasted Quantity at Peak	Ingredient Holding	Prep	Production	Holding	Service
Meatball sub	15	Walk-in refrigerator	Cutting boards	Convection oven	Half-size steam table well	Faux-wicker basket
		Bread rack	Slicer	Open-burner range	*Bain marie* well	
		Storage racks (for No. 10 cans)			Under-counter refrigerator	

HOBART

701 S Ridge Avenue, Troy, OH 45374
1-888-4HOBART • www.hobartcorp.com

Item # _____

Quantity _____

C.S.I. Section 11400

CG SERIES ELECTRIC COUNTER GRIDDLES

STANDARD FEATURES

■ Stainless steel front, sides and 4" adjustable legs.

■ ½" thick polished steel griddle plate.

■ 13" cooking height on 4" adjustable legs.

■ Two solid sheathed tubular incoloy heating elements, one snap action thermostat and cycling light per each 12" griddle width. Thermostats adjust from 200° to 450°F.

■ Stainless steel 3" back and tapered side splashes.

■ 3⅛" wide front grease trough and a large capacity grease drawer.

■ Available in 208V or 240V, 50/60 Hz, 1 or 3 phase power supply. 480V, 50/60 Hz, 3 phase power supply.

■ One year limited parts and labor warranty.

MODEL

❑ **CG24** 24" wide x 24" deep griddle plate
❑ **CG58** 36" wide x 24" deep griddle plate
❑ **CG41** 48" wide x 24" deep griddle plate
❑ **CG50** 60" wide x 24" deep griddle plate
❑ **CG59** 72" wide x 24" deep griddle plate

Specifications, Details and Dimensions on Inside and Back.

NSF **UL LISTED** **c UL LISTED**

CG41

Figure 6-6
Specifications for a Counter Griddle, Including Typical Production Capacity   (*Source:* Reprinted by permission of Hobart)

CG SERIES ELECTRIC COUNTER GRIDDLES

701 S Ridge Avenue, Troy, OH 45374
1-888-4HOBART • www.hobartcorp.com

SPECIFICATIONS

CONSTRUCTION: Stainless steel free-standing counter-style griddle. Stainless steel heating units with a ½" thick polished steel griddle plate. Cold-rolled steel 3" high splatter guard welded to griddle plate bottom. 4" legs with adjustable feet. A full-width front and rear grease trough directs grease to a removal chute. Full depth grease drawer with weep hole is front removable. (Model CG59 has two grease removal chutes and drawers.) Wrap-around grease guard protects wall and equipment from splatter.

HEATING: Uniform pattern of enclosed tubular stainless steel heating units eliminates hot and cold spots. Perimeter is heated and units are attached

to grid bottom. Extra heat-retaining baffle reduces watts to hold. Preheats to 350°F in just 7 minutes.

CONTROLS: A thermostat provides independent controls of each 12" wide area of grid. Temperature range is 200-450°F. A signal light for each thermostat indicates whether or not that it is operating and when preset temperature is reached.

ELECTRICAL: See Electrical Characteristics chart below. Left rear terminal box. (CG59 power terminal box are at left rear and center rear.) Knockouts in back and bottom permit connections to suit varied conditions.

ELECTRICAL CHARACTERISTICS

MODEL NO.	TOTAL CONN. KW	TOTAL KW PER CONN	3 PHASE LOADING KW PER PHASE PER CONN.*			NOMINAL AMPS PER LINE WIRE CONN.*										
						3 PHASE									1 PHASE	
						208 VOLT			240 VOLT			480 VOLT			208 VOLT	240 VOLT
			X-Y	Y-Z	X-Z	X	Y	Z	X	Y	Z	X	Y	Z		
CG24	10.8	10.8	5.4	5.4	0.0	22.5	45.0	22.5	19.5	39.0	19.5	9.7	19.5	9.7	51.9	45.0
CG58	16.2	16.2	5.4	5.4	5.4	45.0	45.0	45.0	39.0	39.0	39.0	19.5	19.5	19.5	77.9	67.5
CG41	21.6	21.6	10.8	5.4	5.4	67.4	67.4	45.0	58.5	58.5	39.0	29.2	29.2	19.5	103.8	90.0
CG50*	27.0	16.2	5.4	5.4	5.4	45.0	45.0	45.0	39.0	39.0	39.0	19.5	19.5	19.5	77.9	67.5
		10.8	5.4	0.0	5.4	45.0	22.5	22.5	39.0	19.5	19.5	19.5	9.7	9.7	51.9	45.0
CG59*	32.4	16.2	5.4	5.4	5.4	45.0	45.0	45.0	39.0	39.0	39.0	19.5	19.5	19.5	77.9	67.5
		16.2	5.4	5.4	5.4	45.0	45.0	45.0	39.0	39.0	39.0	19.5	19.5	19.5	77.9	67.5

STANDARD VOLTAGES – 208 VOLTS OR 240 VOLTS 60 Hz. – SINGLE OR THREE PHASE
480 VOLTS 60 Hz. – THREE PHASE ONLY

*Model CG50 and CG59 require two separate electrical connections and services.

DATA CHART

MODEL NO.	OVERALL DIMENSIONS			GRIDDLE SURFACE DIMENSIONS		SHIP WT. lbs/kg
	WIDTH	DEPTH	HEIGHT	WIDTH	DEPTH	
CG24	24" (610)	27⅝" (702)	16⅜" (415)	24" (610)	24" (610)	200/91
CG58	36" (914)	27⅝" (702)	16⅜" (415)	36" (914)	24" (610)	275/125
CG41	48" (1219)	27⅝" (702)	16⅜" (415)	48" (1219)	24" (610)	360/163
CG50	60" (1524)	27⅝" (702)	16⅜" (415)	60" (1524)	24" (610)	485/220
CG59	72" (1821)	27⅝" (702)	16⅜" (415)	72" (1821)	24" (610)	560/254

(Dimension in parenthesis are in millimeters)
Installation clearances: Sides and rear must be 1" from the nearest combustible construction and 0" from noncombustible construction. Bottom must be 4" from combustible or non-combustible construction.

As continued product improvement is a policy of Hobart, specifications are subject to change without notice.

Figure 6-6
Continued

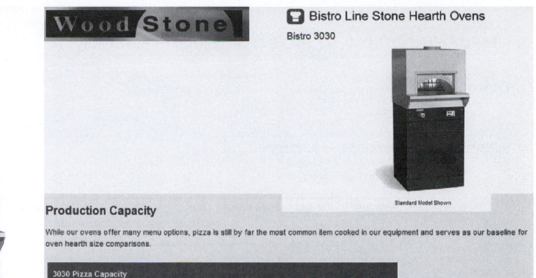

Wood Stone

Bistro Line Stone Hearth Ovens
Bistro 3030

Standard Model Shown

Production Capacity

While our ovens offer many menu options, pizza is still by far the most common item cooked in our equipment and serves as our baseline for oven hearth size comparisons.

3030 Pizza Capacity	
8" pizzas	4
10" pizzas	2-3
12" pizzas	1
16" pizzas	1

Figure 6-7
Specifications for a Stone Hearth Oven, Including Typical Production Capacity   (*Source:* Reprinted by permission of Wood Stone Corporation)

$4.50, and 50 portions are sold per week, then the payback period can be calculated as follows:

$$\text{Payback Period} = \text{Investment in Asset}/\text{Contribution per Item} \times \text{Number of Items Sold per Week}$$

$$13 \text{ weeks} = \$2,600.00/\$4.00 \times 50$$

Thus, management must decide if that is an acceptable length of time to recover the capital outlay, and convert the investment into a stream of profit.

It must be noted that this simplified calculation does not account for the fact that overhead is not offset until the equipment is paid for. Every asset used must contribute to profit objectives, so capital investments of this nature must be approached with care and consideration.

There is a normal tension between the square footage you seek to lease or own versus the combined footprint required by the equipment to produce your menus. As with the open-burner

Figure 6-8
Decorative Espresso Maker   (*Source:* Reprinted by permission of Nuova Simonelli)

EXERCISE 6-5
SIMPLIFIED EQUIPMENT PAYBACK PERIOD ANALYSIS

A high-quality, decorative espresso maker (Figure 6-8) can be purchased for $7,299.00 and installed for an additional $200.00. Weekly sales forecasts for espresso-based drinks are as follows:

	A	B	C	D	E	F	G	H	I
1	Dinner Non-Alcoholic Beverages Menu Analysis Report								
3	Period Start Date:	01-Mar-10							
4	Period End Date:	08-Mar-10							
27									
28	Menu Engineering Worksheet	# Sold	Menu Mix %	Item Food Cost	Item Menu Price	Item Contribution Margin	Menu Food Cost	Menu Sales	Menu Contribution Margin
31									
32	Espresso	20	23.5%	$0.250	$2.50	$2.25	$5.00	$50.00	$45.00
33	Cappucino	30	35.3%	$0.420	$3.00	$2.58	$12.60	$90.00	$77.40
34	Latte	35	41.2%	$0.400	$3.00	$2.60	$14.00	$105.00	$91.00
56									
57	Totals	85	100.0%				$31.60	$245.00	$213.40

Figure 6-9
Weekly sales forecasts for espresso-based beverages

Considering only the capital investment, how long will it take to pay for the equipment and installation (Figure 6-9)?

Figure 6-10
Combi oven   (*Source:* Reprinted by permission of Blodgett Corporation)

range, there are space-saving pieces of equipment that can be used for a variety of tasks. The following are but a few examples of equipment that are intelligently engineered to provide multiple solutions while conserving valuable space:

Combi oven—a specialized convection oven with which heat and moisture can be programmed by users to enable poaching, broiling, roasting, baking, oven-drying, and rethermalizing. This one piece can effectively replace a steamer, oven, and warming cabinet (Figure 6-10).

Food processing attachments for motorized hubs—Food cutters, mixers, and power-drive units provide a motorized hub that enables auxiliary slicers, shredders, and grinder attachments to be swapped as needed (Figure 6-11).

Item # _____

Quantity _____

C.S.I. Section 11400

HOBART
701 S Ridge Avenue, Troy, OH 45374
1-888-4HOBART • www.hobartcorp.com

VS9 VEGETABLE SLICER, MEAT CHOPPER ATTACHMENT AND MIXER ACCESSORIES

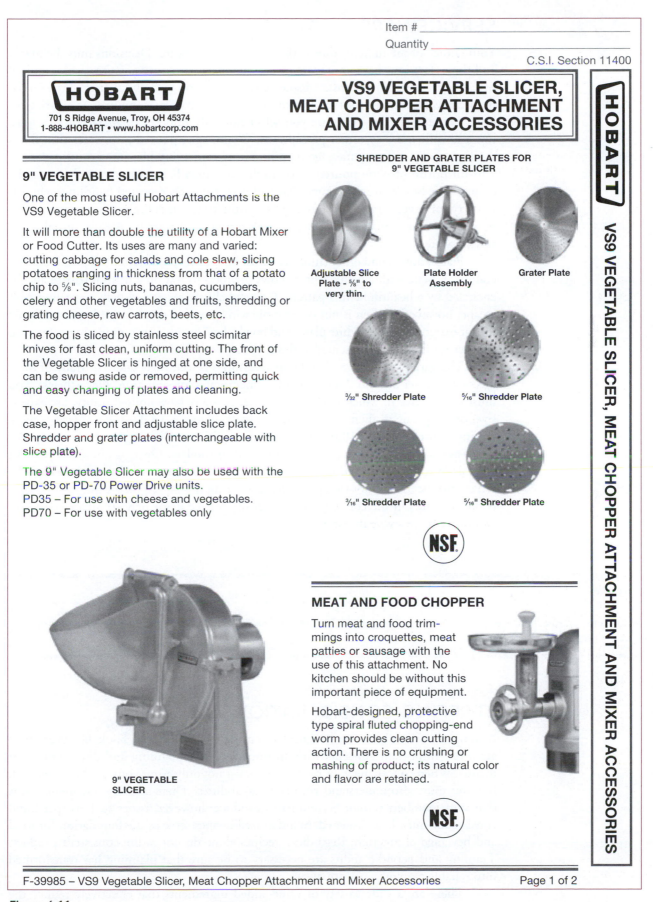

9" VEGETABLE SLICER

One of the most useful Hobart Attachments is the VS9 Vegetable Slicer.

It will more than double the utility of a Hobart Mixer or Food Cutter. Its uses are many and varied: cutting cabbage for salads and cole slaw, slicing potatoes ranging in thickness from that of a potato chip to ⅝". Slicing nuts, bananas, cucumbers, celery and other vegetables and fruits, shredding or grating cheese, raw carrots, beets, etc.

The food is sliced by stainless steel scimitar knives for fast clean, uniform cutting. The front of the Vegetable Slicer is hinged at one side, and can be swung aside or removed, permitting quick and easy changing of plates and cleaning.

The Vegetable Slicer Attachment includes back case, hopper front and adjustable slice plate. Shredder and grater plates (interchangeable with slice plate).

The 9" Vegetable Slicer may also be used with the PD-35 or PD-70 Power Drive units.
PD35 – For use with cheese and vegetables.
PD70 – For use with vegetables only

SHREDDER AND GRATER PLATES FOR 9" VEGETABLE SLICER

Adjustable Slice Plate - ⅝" to very thin.

Plate Holder Assembly

Grater Plate

³⁄₃₂" Shredder Plate

⁵⁄₁₆" Shredder Plate

³⁄₁₆" Shredder Plate

⁵⁄₁₆" Shredder Plate

NSF

9" VEGETABLE SLICER

MEAT AND FOOD CHOPPER

Turn meat and food trimmings into croquettes, meat patties or sausage with the use of this attachment. No kitchen should be without this important piece of equipment.

Hobart-designed, protective type spiral fluted chopping-end worm provides clean cutting action. There is no crushing or mashing of product; its natural color and flavor are retained.

NSF

F-39985 – VS9 Vegetable Slicer, Meat Chopper Attachment and Mixer Accessories   Page 1 of 2

HOBART VS9 VEGETABLE SLICER, MEAT CHOPPER ATTACHMENT AND MIXER ACCESSORIES

Figure 6-11
Attachments for motorized hub   (*Source*: Reprinted by permission of Hobart)

SERVICEWARE

Your choice of menu items directs the need for serviceware. Decisions must be made, and these decisions have an impact on storage space, intensity of warewashing, initial investment, replacement costs, obsolescence cycles, and overall esthetics of the served items. Beverages can be served in tumblers, footed glasses, stemware, or a variety of other containers. The glassware you select not only imposes financial implications, but also influences customer perceptions. Champagne poured into wafer-thin flutes sends a wholly different message than if poured into a durable rimmed tulip glass. A 750-ml bottle of wine poured into ample 20-ounce balloons, although dramatic, empties the bottle in record time. Faceted glass tolerates repeated handling, whereas lead crystal is very fragile. Colored glass is attractive, but is limited in use because of its visual impact on natural beverage coloration, and frankly, is most suitable for serving water.

Plates, bowls, and other china also must be specified only after thoughtful consideration. A plate with a blank center allows the food to rest on a neutral palette and be encircled by a beautiful china pattern. Colorful china creates a visually appealing tablescape; however, it often is not compatible with the food that is served on or in it. At the far extreme are pure white plates and bowls that introduce no competing coloration and permit food to be presented without visual distraction.

The variety of china and tabletop accessories is seemingly endless. Many of these pieces are clever and no doubt provide a memorable presentation. Nevertheless, you must be selective in which items you choose, as many have limited utility, are expensive, or are prone to theft by customers or staff. Figure 6-13 illustrates a service piece costing approximately $10.00. The cost of acquiring sufficient par stock to support forecasted sales can easily spiral into hundreds of dollars. Once again, a cost–benefit analysis must be conducted for each piece to ascertain the true value of these types of service pieces. This is not to suggest that procuring specialized pieces such as this item is imprudent. On the contrary, the cachet of creative items may stimulate purchases and prove to be a wise investment.

EXERCISE 6-6

Compare and contrast the three glasses illustrated in Figure 6-12 for serving martinis. Consider portion sizes, handling, storage, and other criteria as appropriate.

STAFFING CONSIDERATIONS

A comprehensive discussion of staffing is outside the scope of this book; however, there are a few important concepts with an impact on the planning and development of menus. When conceiving your menus, you must not only assess your market's demand, but you must also understand your staff capabilities. There are very few menu items that staff members cannot be trained to produce; however, issues such as speed and consistency must be considered. Standardized recipes serve as the foundation for food and beverage production. Regardless, recipes alone do not assure consistent product. Training and periodic audits are necessary to be sure that planning has transformed into reliable employee performance.

There are a wide variety of value-added ingredients that effectively reduce the amount of preparation and production labor your staff must provide. Cost analyses

SPECIALTY

new martinis

Omega Martini
No. 8883 ●
6¾ oz./20.0 cl./200 ml.
H6½ T4⅞ B3¼ D4⅞
1 doz./8# • 1.35 cu.ft.
SCC 319739
TRAEX TR-18JJ □

Bravura Martini
No. 7700 ●
6¾ oz./20.0 cl./200 ml.
H6⅜ T4⅞ B3¼ D4⅞
1 doz./8# • 1.28 cu.ft.
SCC 315229
TRAEX TR-18JJ □

Bravura Martini
Cobalt Stem
No. 7700BS ●
6¾ oz./20.0 cl./200 ml.
H6⅜ T4⅞ B3¼ D4⅞
1 doz./8# • 1.28 cu.ft.
SCC 318107
TRAEX TR-18JJ □

Metropolis Cocktail
No. 3649 ●
9¾ oz./28.8 cl./288 ml.
H7 T4⅞ B3¼ D4⅞
1 doz./9# • 1.39 cu.ft.
SCC 234933
TRAEX TR-18JJJ □

Metropolis Cocktail
Mediterranean Blue Stem
No. 3649LS ●
9¾ oz./28.8 cl./288 ml.
H7 T4⅞ B3¼ D4⅞
1 doz./9# • 1.39 cu.ft.
SCC 234940
TRAEX TR-18JJJ □

Z-Stem Martini
No. 37719 ■
5 oz./14.8 cl./148 ml.
H5⅝ T3⅞ B2¾ D3⅞
1 doz./5# • .71 cu.ft.
SCC 018007
TRAEX TR-11GG □

Z-Stem Martini
No. 37339 ■
7½ oz./22.2 cl./222 ml.
H6⅜ T4¼ B3 D4¼
1 doz./7# • .99 cu.ft.
SCC 315243
TRAEX TR-8DD □

Z-Stem Martini
No. 37799 ■
9¼ oz./27.4 cl./274 ml.
H6½ T4⅜ B3 D4⅜
1 doz./7# • 1.13 cu.ft.
SCC 019585
TRAEX TR-8DDD □

Cocktail
No. 8882 ●
4½ oz./13.3 cl./133 ml.
H5⅞ T3⅝ B3 D3⅝
3 doz./14# • 2.09 cu.ft.
SCC 309948
TRAEX TR-11GG □

Cocktail
No. 8876 ●
6½ oz./19.2 cl./192 ml.
H6 T4¼ B3 D4¼
3 doz./18# • 2.87 cu.ft.
SCC 312528
TRAEX TR-8DD □

Citation Cocktail
No. 8454 ●
4½ oz./13.3 cl./133 ml.
H5⅝ T3½ B2⅞ D3½
3 doz./15# • 2.01 cu.ft.
SCC 093854
TRAEX TR-11GG □

Citation Cocktail
No. 8455 ●
6 oz./17.7 cl./177 ml.
H5⅞ T4¼ B2⅞ D4¼
3 doz./17# • 2.68 cu.ft.
SCC 093847
TRAEX TR-8DD □

Salud Grande
No. 8485 ●
8½ oz./25.1 cl./251 ml.
H6¾ T4½ B3 D4½
1 doz./8# • 1.18 cu.ft.
SCC 350374
TRAEX TR-18JJJ □

Salud Grande
No. 8480 ●
10 oz./29.6 cl./296 ml.
H6⅞ T4¾ B3 D4¾
1 doz./8# • 1.71 cu.ft.
SCC 669479
TRAEX TR-18JJJ □

Domaine Martini
No. 8978 ●
8 oz./23.7 cl./237 ml.
H7 T4½ B3 D4½
1 doz./7# • 1.23 cu.ft.
SCC 027993
TRAEX TR-18JJJ □

▲ Finedge ● Safedge Rim Guarantee ■ Safedge Rim and Foot Guarantee ✖ Sheer Rim/D.T.E.
□ Recommended Traex Glass Rack See pages 114-116 for details.

Figure 6-12
Martini glasses (*Source:* Reprinted by permission of Libbey Glass, Inc)

new martinis (continued)

Bristol Valley Cocktail
No. 8555SR ✕
7½ oz./22.2 cl./222 ml.
H6¼ T4¼ B3¼ D4¼
2 doz./14# ▪ 1.74 cu.ft.
SCC 496013
TRAEX TR-8DD □

Vina Martini
No. 7512 ▲●
8 oz./23.7 cl./237 ml.
H6⅞ T4⅞ B3¼ D4⅞
1 doz./6# ▪ 1.42 cu.ft.
SCC 308269
TRAEX TR-10FFF □

Vina Martini
No. 7518 ▲●
10 oz./29.6 cl./296 ml.
H7¼ T4⅝ B3¼ D4⅝
1 doz./7# ▪ 1.38 cu.ft.
SCC 376619
TRAEX TR-18JJJ □

Midtown Martini
No. 7507 ▲●
12 oz./35.5 cl./355 ml.
H7⅜ T4⅞ B3¼ D4⅞
1 doz./7# ▪ 1.50 cu.ft.
SCC 084347
TRAEX TR-18JJJ □

Embassy Mini-Martini
No. 3701 ■
3 oz./8.9 cl./89 ml.
H3¾ T3⅛ B2⅛ D3⅛
1 doz./4# ▪ .37 cu.ft.
SCC 351548
TRAEX TR-12H □

Embassy Cocktail
No. 3771 ■
5 oz./14.8 cl./148 ml.
H5¼ T3¾ B2¾ D3¾
3 doz./16# ▪ 1.96 cu.ft.
SCC 147991
TRAEX TR-11GG □

Embassy Cocktail
No. 3733 ■
7½ oz./22.2 cl./222 ml.
H6⅜ T4¼ B3 D4¼
1 doz./7# ▪ .99 cu.ft.
SCC 317575
TRAEX TR-8DDD □

Embassy Martini
No. 3779 ■
9¼ oz./27.4 cl./274 ml.
H6½ T4⅜ B3 D4⅜
1 doz./8# ▪ 1.13 cu.ft.
SCC 019578
TRAEX TR-8DDD □

Stemless Martini
No. 224 ●
13½ oz./39.9 cl./399 ml.
H3½ T4½ B1⅝ D4½
1 doz./5# ▪ .70 cu.ft.
SCC 291455
TRAEX TR-18J □

Cosmopolitan
No. 400 ●
8¼ oz./24.4 cl./244 ml.
H3⅞ T4 B2¼ D4
1 doz./8# ▪ .60 cu.ft.
SCC 364098
TRAEX TR-8D □

NOT SOLD SEPARATELY

Martini Chiller
No. 70855 ●
5¾ oz./17.0 cl./170 ml.
H3½ T4¼ B2½ D4⅜
1 doz./8# ▪ .90 cu.ft.
SCC 330109
TRAEX TR-8D □

Shaker 500 w/black lid
No. 13230520
19¾ oz./58.5 cl./585 ml.
H6⅞ T2½ B2⅝ D3⅜
1 doz./14# ▪ .44 cu.ft.
SCC 08002713098949
TRAEX TR-6BBB □

SPECIALTY

H=Height, T=Top Diameter, B=Bottom Diameter, D=Maximum Diameter (see pages 114-116; voir pages 114-116; vea las páginas 114-116)

43

Figure 6-12
Continued

Figure 6-13
Table service accessory
(*Source:* Reprinted by permission of American Metalcraft)

Stainless Steel Fry Baskets

Just like their kitchen counterparts but a fraction of the size. Definite conversation pieces.

Item #	Description	Pack	Cu. Ft.	Wt.	List Price
FRYR375	Round, 3-3/4" Dia. x 2-7/8" H	48			$12.80 EA
FRYS443	Square, 4" L x 4" W x 3" H		1.134	13	$10.60 EA
FRYT433	Rectangular, 4" L x 3" W x 3" H		1.649	22	$9.60 EA

should be conducted to arrive at "make-or-buy" decisions. Many highly trained chefs view these **convenience ingredients** with disdain; however, you can realize savings in the form of reduced space and equipment needs as well as a simplified staffing model by incorporating certain items.

In addition to being able to produce and serve your menu items, your staff should possess a sensory knowledge acquired by tasting all items on the menu. A universal maxim instructs cooks to taste their dishes regularly as they evolve toward completion. It is necessary, however, to provide staff with a benchmark to conduct their tastings. Staff must know what properly prepared/plated items smell, taste, and look like. This should be viewed as a necessary training expense for culinary staff as well as service staff.

AUTHOR'S INSIGHT

Early in my career, I worked as an assistant general manager for a national restaurant chain. The company prided itself on consistent results and above-average guest satisfaction. Recipes were developed in corporate kitchens and were conveyed to units in the form of a corporate recipe manual. Behind the bar and in the kitchen, no variations were tolerated. In fact, cooks were required to have recipe cards in front of them at all times during their work. Regardless of how many times they prepared the items, if they were caught preparing recipes without the cards, they were terminated on the spot. The prevailing managerial logic was that memories and routines were never so perfect as to be trusted without the standardized recipes at hand. Many good employees suffered the hatchet as a result of their deliberate or inadvertent lapses from the policy. A survival response emerged whereby employees deceptively displayed the recipes at their workstations, yet intentionally ignored them, thus creating occasional variations and vanquished good intent.

EXERCISE 6-7
STANDARDIZED FOOD PRODUCTION

(Refer to the Author's Insight.)

Q1. What other means can managers use to achieve standard results?

Q2. Does a termination policy of this nature have any defense?

ACTION TOOLKIT

The following links provide current information of food and recipe ingredient safety:

- **Federal Food Safety Information** www.foodsafety.gov/index.html

- **Food and Drug Administration Product-specific Information** www.fda.gov/Food/FoodSafety/Product-SpecificInformation/default.htm

- **Food and Drug Administration Retail Food Protection (for retail and foodservice operations)** www.fda.gov/Food/FoodSafety/RetailFoodProtection/default.htm

- **USDA National Agricultural Library Food Safety Research Information Center** www.foodsafety.nal.usda.gov/nal_web/fsic/Contact_Us.php

- **ServSafe Food Safety** www.servsafe.com/foodsafety/

- **ServSafe Coursebook** www.pearsonhighered.com/educator/product/ServSafe-Course-Book-Fifth-Edition-Updated-with-2009-FDA-Food-Code-5E/9780135107324.page.html

The following link provides information on Hazard Analysis Critical Control Point (HACCP) that can be used by restaurant operators to manage the risk of food-borne illness:

- **Managing Food Safety: A Manual for the Voluntary Use of HACCP Principles for Operators of Food Service and Retail Establishments** www.fda.gov/Food/FoodSafety/RetailFoodProtection/ManagingFoodSafetyHACCPPrinciples/Operators/default.htm

The following links provide current information on regulatory oversight of restaurant food safety and sanitation:

- **Food and Drug Administration 2009 Food Code** www.fda.gov/Food/FoodSafety/RetailFoodProtection/FoodCode/FoodCode2009/default.htm

- **State Retail and Food Service Codes and Regulations by State** www.fda.gov/Food/FoodSafety/RetailFoodProtection/FederalStateCooperativePrograms/ucm122814.htm

The following links provide current information on alcoholic beverage liability:

- **ServSafe Alcohol** www.servsafe.com/Alcohol/

- **HospitalityLawyer.com** www.hospitalitylawyer.com/

- **State Driving While Under the Influence (DUI) Laws** www.dui.findlaw.com/dui/state-dui-law/

- **U.S. National Law Library readings on food & beverage law** www.hospitalitylawyer.com/national_listings.php?industry=1&topic=8

A resource to check seasonal availability of produce:

- **Field to Plate** www.fieldtoplate.com/guide.php

A resource to help assure future availability of fish and seafood:

- **Seafood Watch Information for Restaurants and Retailers** www.montereybayaquarium.org/cr/cr_seafoodwatch/sfw_restaurants.aspx

The North American Association of Food Equipment Manufacturers (NAFEM) is a trade association of more than 625 foodservice equipment and supplies manufacturers that provide products for food preparation, cooking, storage, and table service. www.nafem.org

GLOSSARY

Convenience ingredients—food and beverages purchased with various levels of preparation or value addition. Peeled vegetables, portion-cut meats, par-baked breads, and frozen desserts are common examples.

Hazard Analysis Critical Control Point (HACCP)—A systematic risk-management process that focuses on prevention rather than remediation. Potential hazards are identified and controls are instituted to reduce or eliminate the risk of these hazards occurring.

Inventory turnover—the rate at which your food and beverage purchases are consumed as prepared menu items sold to customers. A high inventory turnover rate is desirable and indicates that purchases are moved quickly in and out of your business.

Payback period analysis—a study that quantifies the length of time it takes for menu item sales to offset investment in the asset used to produce the menu items.

Risk management—Assessment of potential risks that includes impact analysis and process modifications to mitigate the occurrence of unwanted events.

Workstations—areas of the front- and back-of-the-house that are equipped for specific sets of tasks. Common examples of foodservice workstations include host stands, server stations, dish rooms, hot lines, and prep kitchens.

ENDNOTES

1. www.quotationspage.com/quote/2905.html; retrieved May 1, 2011.

2. The Action Toolkit directs you to several food-safety information resources.

3. Food Regulations, Virginia Department of Health; www.healthspace.ca/vdh.

4. Food Regulations, Virginia Department of Health; www.healthspace.ca/vdh.

5. www.dictionaryofeconomics.com/article?id=pde2008_H000172; retrieved May 1, 2011.

6. National Restaurant Association; www.restaurant.org/legal/law_alcohol.cfm.

7. The Action Toolkit contains a Web address for researching each state's specific classifications of intoxication.

8. Check specific state and local laws, as they vary.

9. www.thinkexist.com/quotation/out_of_intense_complexities_intense_simplicities/15826.html; retrieved May 1, 2010.

10. Originally, NSF stood for National Sanitation Foundation; currently, it's NSF International, which provides testing and certification of equipment to assure safe construction, durability, and easy cleanability. UL refers to Underwriters Laboratories, which evaluates products for standards compliance.

7
Conceiving Menus that Respond to Your Market

(*Source:* Blaz Kure/Shutterstock)

Objectives

Upon completion of this chapter, you should be able to:

7.1   Develop food and beverage menus that respond to shifting market opportunities

7.2   Discuss the importance of sustainability and American Regional cuisine in the hospitality marketplace

7.3   Discuss the strategic implications of nutrition on contemporary menus

7.4   Conduct nutritional analyses on menu items

7.5   Modify recipes to improve their nutritional value

7.6   Address the special dietary needs of individuals

7.7   Respond to challenging economic conditions with strategic concepts and creative tactics

7.8   Understand that customer preferences are dynamic and can be better understood through industry research

RESPONDING TO SHIFTING MARKET OPPORTUNITIES

"When one door closes another opens but we often look so long and so regretfully upon the closed door that we do not see the one which has opened."

—ALEXANDER GRAHAM BELL[1]

As was previously discussed in Chapter 1, you must continuously align your menus with prevailing customer demand. Furthermore, every menu has a life cycle, after which time it should be modified, retired, or replaced. The speed at which the menu life cycle matures is subject to societal and economic forces external to your control, culinary trends falling out of fashion, and eventual customer disinterest over time.

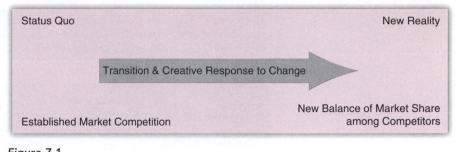

Figure 7-1
Change Continuum

As external forces influence consumer behavior, you must confirm the current strategic value of your menus and modify them as appropriate. Collection of survey data, focus-group findings, and anecdotal feedback helps you better understand your local market, as do public domain resources and industry publications. Previously in this text, you studied the value of a strengths, weaknesses, opportunities, and threats (SWOT) analysis as it relates to menus (and organizational change). One of the action-based SWOT components involves capitalizing on market opportunities. Conventional management treatises urge students to discern and understand the psychological motivations of their clientele. These textbooks often talk of customers' perceived needs and wants; however, most restaurateurs lack the formal training to study the underlying nuances of market psychology effectively. A more practical approach is to harness the intuitive nature of foodservice managers and combine it with the power of **trendspotting**. By continuously scanning patterns within the environment, it is possible to predict future consumption preferences of your own target market. As also discussed in Chapter 1, market opportunities are often associated with societal paradigm shifts. Observant operators that are first to sense these transitions can respond prior to their competitors and capture a disproportionately high percentage of the dynamic market.

The following discussion explores several market conditions that have provided opportunities and may be significant in the future.

A Multiplicity of Concepts

Dining preferences of today's consumers are as difficult to categorize as ever. Certainly, individuals can be clustered into general consumption–based niches, but the hospitality marketplace is rife with experimentation and change, and in some cases philosophical retrenchment by customers as well as operators. The overlapping spheres of socioeconomic events and emergent trends are dizzying. For example, national chains develop calendars for rolling out new menu items, product promotions, and other initiatives to avert customer fatigue and defection. Many of these promotions meld genres in illogical fashion, yet yield successful results. In the 1970s **fusion cuisine** emerged, combining disparate ingredients and gastronomic techniques from different locales, seasons, and eras. Fusion cuisine was a high-minded concept whereby chefs attempted to demonstrate their inventiveness and culinary acumen in the name of adventure. Dishes such as *beef liver avec cinnamon jelly et wasabi* caused most diners to just scratch their heads, although to this day, some vestiges of fusion cuisine still lurk. Soon after, attentive culinarians quickly learned that adventure has its place, but palatability should never be compromised. Over the long run, substance always trumps style. Nonetheless, there are customers who welcome (or are oblivious to) the marriage of disparate foodways. In fact, there are several operators who analyzed their clientele's interests correctly and responded with successful menu offerings that defy genres yet find acceptance by their markets. These leaders should be commended for challenging convention and succeeding in their risk-taking. Figure 7-2 illustrates menu items that defy strict culinary pedigree.

Figure 7-2

Selection of Menu Items from National Chain Restaurants   (*Source* for top: Reprinted by permission of Claddagh Irish Pub)   (*Source* for bottom: Reprinted by permission of OSI Restaurant Partners, LLC)

At the same time, there are enclaves of operators who cling desperately to time-tested customer favorites such as ("old school") burgers, beer, and onion rings and seek the stability that inertial guidance might provide. Not surprisingly, "mom and pop" operations often find longevity as a result of their formulaic nature and the public's desire to connect with simplicity and freedom from pretense. Furthermore, in bold contrast across town, fervent molecular gastronomists experiment with laboratory paraphernalia in place of traditional cooking equipment, and are divining recipes with calcium chloride, glycerol monostearate, transglutaminase, and other powders. Molecular gastronomists embrace the science of *modernist cuisine* in an effort to manipulate food chemistry for their guests' amazement.

Down the street are the eco-friendly chefs who have pledged allegiance to minimizing their carbon footprint and fostering sustainable foodways. For example, *Slow Food USA* exists in sharp contrast to the fusionists, the molecular school of cooking, or the heavily invested research-and-development departments of chain restaurants. In 2009, *Slow Food* celebrated the first 20 years of its existence as an international association. Since its beginnings in Italy in the mid 1980s, *Slow Food* has developed into a vast network in 150 countries and with more than 100,000 members. Among other initiatives, *Slow Food* proponents are committed to defense of biodiversity and reawakening and training the senses of diners. Their approach to food harkens back to simpler times when producers, chefs, and consumers understood their shared stakes in the global food web.

Lesson Learned

Recognizing the range of customer preferences, it will be increasingly difficult for restaurants to succeed at mass-appeal concepts. Customers expect there will be a restaurant that "has what they want" and know they will be successful in finding one or more that are closely aligned to their specific desires. You must research your target market and identify the most valued attributes they desire, and deliver them with clarity and consistency.

EXERCISE 7-1
FUSION MENU ITEMS

Scan a series of local and national restaurant menus to identify 10 menu items that combine divergent ingredients, locales, or preparation methods. Interview the culinary team leaders to better understand how these items were developed and to what extent the markets accept the items.

Q1. Do customers really care if cuisines are fused? Is fusion a wise approach toward menu development in these markets?

Q2. Create three fusion menu items for your own market. Create a menu listing and appropriate descriptions. Why will your items work? What customer demographics are most likely to find interest in these three items?

Understanding What Children Want to Eat

According to a Y-Pulse 2007 study,[2] the most significant criterion influencing the choice of a restaurant for children in grades 3 through 5 (ages 8–11) is "good food" (71%). This might be treated as an overly simplified perspective without digging deeper; however, these consumers have articulated well-defined expectations. In this study, children making up the focus group stated "great taste," "fun packaging," "quick-service restaurant or local restaurant," "branding," "convenient," and "made for me" as key selection criteria. Of key importance is that food "tastes good" and "tastes fresh." The majority of children responding to the study (60%) reported that parental influence and peer pressure had little impact on their preference for restaurants. In fact, the majority (75%) make their own choices rather than deferring to suggestions from adults. Approximately two-thirds of respondents prefer the choices on adult menus to those on kid's menus. In rank order, respondents identified the local diner as their favorite restaurant (23%), followed by Mexican restaurants (11%) and McDonald's (10%). Older children were more likely to prefer the diners, and as children grow older, they are less interested in McDonalds. Subway (4%) and Olive Garden (4%) were also cited as favorites. Children in this age group prefer to order pizza (11%), chicken (9%), and hamburgers (9%), although hamburgers become less desirable as children age. Mexican food and seafood each ranked at 8% popularity. Pasta (7%) and chicken tenders/strips/fingers (6%) rounded out top preferences.

Generally speaking, the range of dietary likes and dislikes for children is considerably more compact than that of adults. Children enjoy chicken, turkey, beef, shrimp, and other familiar animal protein foods. Vivid colors are tolerated. Sauces are not popular among children, but ketchup and other condiments are generally well liked. Children enjoy familiar fruit, particularly when bite-size and ready to eat. Despite youthful independence in the selection process, parents and restaurateurs still believe there is a place for children's menus. It could be argued that parents have a duty to make informed decisions for their children when dining out. Parents regularly attempt to influence the menu selections that their younger children make, and parents should be able to choose among nutritious alternatives developed especially for these young diners. Whereas adult menus may contain selections accepted by children, often the portions and prices are not ideally suited for youthful diners. For that reason, many restaurants (mostly in the family-friendly category) offer "Kid's Menus." It isn't surprising that many children's menus fail to offer the scope of choices and preparations that facilitate both appealing and nourishing meals. Recently, several chains and independent restaurants acted to improve this situation by practicing healthier cooking methods and including low-fat and whole-grain children's entrées.

Not only have menu planners taken action to support the objective of healthier children, but local government has also exerted its will. During 2010, the San Francisco Board of Supervisors passed an ordinance banning the inclusion of toys or similar incentives with children's' meals unless the meals complied with specific nutritional requirements. The attraction of popularly themed gift items and promotional tie-ins was (and still is) believed to be a potent factor in motivating purchases of "Happy Meals" and similar menu selections, and legislators believed that operators shouldered a social responsibility to respond by reducing sugar, fat, sodium, and total calories in those menu items. The mayor of San Francisco countered the board's action by declaring, "Parents, not politicians, should decide what their children eat . . . ." The message here is that menu planners must navigate the ever-changing currents of governmental regulations and parental influence as it effects the decisions that young customers make.

EXERCISE 7-2

ASSESSING CHILDREN'S RESTAURANT PREFERENCES

Q1. Create an interview script for collecting market information on youthful diners. Develop your questions with an action orientation so that the results can be used for menu development.

Q2. Field test the interview questions on a group of local children. How many respondents are necessary to assume a valid sample? How can you structure the interviews to enhance candor and filter out bias or other distortions?

Lesson Learned

The forgoing observations are generalizations and may be further influenced by ethnicity or upbringing. Nonetheless, if you craft children's menus from fresh and natural ingredients and provide whole-grain options and use cooking techniques that preserve nutrients while controlling fat, you can still offer menus that appeal to a wide range of children (and their parents). Perhaps the most successful approach is for you to conduct market research on children's menus using focus groups and other techniques much as you would for an adult population. In the end, you will most likely possess a menu that is acceptable to children, supported by their parents, and complimentary to your overall strategic concept.

Connecting with the Next Generation of Clientele

Teenagers have always been viewed as a desirable market segment because of their highly social nature and relative freedom from debt. If teenagers become indoctrinated to a brand or adopt a particular foodservice as their own, then the likelihood for loyalty and repeat business is particularly high. Teenagers seek an environment that welcomes extended visits and dining parties that expand or contract at a moment's notice. Taste and menu choices are essential, and value is a primary decision criterion for young customers. One commonality among brands attracting youthful clientele is a modestly priced menu. Starbucks and other cafés enable patrons to purchase items for a few dollars. Chili's successfully introduced a "THREE COURSES—TWO PEOPLE—$20" promotion, whereby two diners can share an appetizer, enjoy two entrées, and share a dessert for $10.00 per person (beverages, tax, and tip are additional). Wi-Fi availability is also important, as is networking via Facebook, Twitter, and other social media. McDonald's hamburger chain, recognizing the affinity of their youth market and digital connectedness, began offering free Internet access at its 11,000 domestic stores in 2010, making it the largest supplier of free Wi-Fi hot spots in the United States. Observant operators have established social networking strategies to leverage the power of Foursquare, YouTube, Facebook, and other media. For example, several companies send tweets to their Twitter followers describing daily specials or when items will be emerging fresh from the oven. This just-in-time strategy fits well with the active lifestyle of youthful clientele. Companies such as Starbucks, Chili's Grill & Bar, Panera Bread, Qdoba, and Olive Garden are examples of brands that are accessible and desirable to the youth market.

Lesson Learned:

When young diners believe they are valued, their unique interests are addressed, and have received a fair deal, they tell their friends and they certainly return. It is reasonable to expect these customers to patronize these brands well into their young adult lives and beyond.

Supermarkets Reinvent Themselves

As discussed in Chapter 2, grocery stores have taken advantage of shifting customer shopping and lifestyle patterns and have begun to compete with restaurants by providing well-executed on-premise dining. What began as an additional revenue outlet for ready-to-serve foods prepared at the supermarkets (or their commissaries) has been dramatically transformed. Several chains have dedicated seating areas that serve as stylish dining rooms. Astute operators understand that many Americans find utility in combining their periodic grocery excursions with a convenient meal at the local supermarket. Many of these stores include floral departments, dry cleaners, pharmacies, and auto fuel. As such, the stores fill the niche of customers seeking one-stop shopping and dining. Certain of these chains have invested serious research, development and resources to deliver in-store dining that rivals the experience of a true restaurant. Figure 7-3 illustrates an extract from The Pub at Wegmans menu.

Whole Foods Market has presented a whole other set of competitive challenges for traditional restaurants. Just like many other supermarkets, they provide inviting dining areas and a lively atmosphere; however, the chain amplifies the experience with an astounding selection of menu options. Customers can select made-to-order sandwiches, vegan and vegetarian entrées, soups, barbecue and smoked meats, wood-baked pizzas, and a myriad of salads, sides, desserts, and gelati. At some of the locations, customers can pluck hand-rolled sushi from conveyer belts or browse among several branded "restaurants" in a food court setting. Not content to succeed on the allure of delicious food alone, Whole Foods Market employs strategic practices that position it as a "third place,"[3] ranked by customers in psychological import alongside their homes and workplaces. The company's blend of community-mindedness, food-centrism, and an eye toward healthy eating has won the hearts and minds of well-heeled customers. In the context of dining, a third place distinguishes itself from strictly defined competition as a result of the multiple meanings (and value) it represents to its users. By adding lifestyle experiences to the dining options, the stores are not easily engaged by competing restaurants. Whole Foods Market customers can mingle in the handsome wine bars and serve themselves flights of fine wines in various portion sizes. There are Riedel wine glass seminars, cooking classes, and in-store entertainment. On Friday evenings, several locations provide a progressive series of food and wine tastings ("Five After Five") in their stores for a nominal fee. The proceeds go to local charities, and the convivial events amount to a modest dinner substitute while navigating customers through the various aisles of retail products.

Across the country, the introduction of live bands and dancing, overstuffed chairs and plasma screen lounges, complementary Wi-Fi, charging stations for electric cars, celebrity chef demonstrations, beauty makeover events, and Zumba exercise classes dramatically redefines the supermarket segment's competition for customer attention. Once within the store, prepared meals become a logical element to round out the guest's visit.

Lesson Learned

The market has been lucrative for grocery stores seeking to compete in the arena traditionally dominated by restaurants. Restaurants that narrowly define their competitive set may be ignoring significant threats that merit analysis and potential defensive maneuvers.

Beef for Tomorrow's Plate

America loves beef at the center of the plate. Large-scale stockyard production, grain-fattening, and focus on the most precious fraction of the steer (rib and loin) have defined our most popular steakhouse and fine-dining offerings. These primal cuts

Sandwiches

All sandwiches served with fresh daily vegetable, dill pickle spear, and Super Soft Vienna Roll

Corned Beef on Rye . . . . 8.
Six ounces thinly sliced corned beef piled high, Thousand Island dressing, seeded Caraway Rye (510 calories)

The Cheese Burger* 8.5
Eight ounce hand-formed, irradiated (so we can grill to your liking) beef patty, Adams Reserve Cheddar, Thousand Island dressing, leaf lettuce, vine-ripened tomato (900 calories)

Pan-Seared Mahi Mahi . . . . 8.
Barbecue spice seasoning, Remoulade Sauce, leaf lettuce, vine-ripened tomato (620 calories)

***Italian Classics* Chicken Sandwich** 8.5
Lemon-garlic marinated chicken grilled & topped with Wegmans *Italian Classics* Bruschetta, fresh mozzarella, and basil, served on a ciabatta baguette

Signature Crab Cake . . . . 11.
Remoulade Sauce, leaf lettuce, vine-ripened tomato (760 calories)

Pub Steak Sandwich . . . . 10.
Mushrooms, caramelized onions, Adams Reserve Cheddar & savory sauce (990 calories)

The Langer . . . . 9.
Roasted eggplant, zucchini, soy protein & oatmeal formed into burger topped with fresh mozzarella, and our Seasoned Tomato Sauce served on a ciabatta baguette

Naan Pizzas

Our tasty Indian-style flatbread makes great, crispy crusted pizza

Cheese and Mini-Cup Pepperoni . . . . 6.
Hand-sliced pepperoni that cups and crisps (640 calories)

San Marzano Margherita 6.5
San Marzano tomatoes, mozzarella, olive oil and basil (670 calories)

Fig, Gorgonzola, and Prosciutto . . . . 7.
A combination of sweet and savory from our market (500 calories)

Cheese . . . . 6.
Savory vine-ripened, fresh tomato sauce topped with a blend of mozzarella and provolone (490 calories)

Pan-Seared Meals

All pan-seared meals served with: Fresh daily vegetable, and one of our great finishing sauces or over field greens, romaine lettuce, Kalamata olives, roasted red peppers, crumbled feta cheese, red onion, herb vinaigrette (add 280 calories to entrée)

Signature Crab Cake . . . . 11.
(510 calories) Remoulade Sauce

Atlantic Farm-Raised Salmon 10.25
(470 calories) Horseradish Cream Sauce

All-Natural Day-Boat Sea Scallops 12.25
(440 calories) Citrus Soy Sauce

Black Tiger Shrimp 10.25
(330 calories) Bouillabaisse Sauce

Farm-Raised Tilapia 9.75
(380 calories) Lemon Butter Sauce

Baked Herb-Marinated Tofu . . . . 8.
(280 calories) Citrus Soy Sauce

Grilled Meals

Australian Lamb Chops* . . . . 12.
(490 calories) Chimichurri Sauce or Demi Glace

New York Strip Steak* 16.5
10 oz cooked to your specification topped with Wegmans Garlic Cheese Finishing Butter & served with Demi Glace (750 calories)

Lemon Garlic Marinated Chicken Breast 9.25
(390 calories) Chimichurri Sauce

Sauce Choices

These delicious Wegmans chef-developed finishing sauces (1½ oz portions) are also available in our Prepared Foods Department in convenient recipe-size pouches.

Remoulade: Spicy New Orleans classic (290 calories)

Lemon Butter: Slightly tangy, rich and creamy (40 calories)

Citrus Soy: Asian-inspired, mellow blend of flavors (45 calories)

Demi Glace: Rich, meaty, concentrated flavor (25 calories)

Chimichurri: Refreshing, brisk herbal notes (180 calories)

Bouillabaisse: Intense, slightly spicy, and briny (15 calories)

Horseradish Cream: A bit of a kick; thick and creamy (150 calories)

*Consumer Advisory: Consuming raw, rare or uncooked foods of animal origin may increase your risk of foodborne illness, especially if you have certain medical conditions

Figure 7-3
Extract from The Pub at Wegmans Menu, Collegeville, Pennsylvania   (*Source:* Reprinted with permission from Wegmans Food Markets)

Beverages

2.
(Free refills)

Wegmans "Just Tea"
Pepsi
Diet Pepsi
Sierra Mist
Pink Lemonade
"Brisk" Tea
Ginger Ale
Mountain Dew
Wild Cherry Pepsi

Desserts

Wegmans Ultimate White Cake . . . . 3.
Vanilla cake with vanilla butter cream icing

Wegmans Ultimate Chocolate Cake . . . . 3.
Chocolate cake with chocolate icing

Seasonal Scratch Pie. . . . . 3.
Fresh seasonal peak-of-perfection pie selection

Cheesecake Selection . . . . 4.

Collegeville
600 Commerce Dr.
1-484-902-1560

Follow the pub at twitter.com/wegmanspub

Items and prices are subject to change.

58268AL 1/11 Collegeville 500

Snacks, Sharings, & Pairings

Shrimp & Crab Cocktail Cup. . . . . 8.
Court bouillon shrimp, lump crab meat salad, lemon
(190 calories)

Steamed Chesapeake Clams . . . . 7.
One dozen in garlic cheese butter broth (240 calories)

Australian Lamb Lollipops* . . . . 7.
Two grilled chops, roasted eggplant caponata (320 calories)

Parmesan-Crusted Chicken Strips 6.5
Lemon garlic marinated chicken with a crispy Parmesan
crust, Seasoned Tomato Sauce (360 calories)

Pork and Shrimp Won Tons 5.25
Topped with Spicy Orange Sauce with garlic, chilies and
scallions (560 calories)

Crispy Mozzarella. . . . . 6.
Fresh Mozzarella from our Cheese Shop coated in panko
bread crumbs, cracked black pepper & herbs, then deep fried;
served on top of Wegmans Tomato Basil Sauce (610 calories)

Fried Calamari. . . . . 6.
Crispy calamari deep fried & then lightly tossed with yellow
peppers, olives & herbs

Buffalo Shrimp . . . . 7.
Crispy shrimp tossed in Wegmans Buffalo Wing Sauce
(520 calories)

Tuscan Fries 3.5
Fresh cut, blanched, and fried russets, with fresh herbs,
garlic & Wegmans Savory Finishing Sauce (550 calories)

Zucchini Fries 3.5
Served with Horseradish Cream Sauce for dipping (340
calories)

Side Salad . . . . 3.
Field greens and romaine lettuces, Kalamata olives, roasted
red peppers, crumbled feta cheese, red onion with tarragon
vinaigrette (90 calories)

Soup

Cream of Crab . . . . 6.
Twelve ounces of rich crab soup with a hint of classic
Old Bay (380 calories)

Soup of the Day . . . . 6.

Figure 7-3b
Continued

EXERCISE 7-3

COMPARING DINING IN SUPERMARKETS VERSUS RESTAURANTS

Identify a local supermarket that provides in-store dining. Benchmark the supermarket against a comparable restaurant.

Q1. Create a list comparing the competitive advantages unique to each business. Consider depth of talent, dining room aesthetics, etc.

Q2. Seek out common menu items between the two entities. Compare and contrast ingredients, preparation techniques, plate presentation, menu price, and other relevant criteria. What is most significant about your findings?

represent only slightly more than 25% of the carcass. A few other cuts, including flank steak and skirt steak have found their way to the char grill and broiler, but beef costs continue to increase, and foodservice operators seek ways to manage tight contribution margins. Savvy menu planners and chefs have recently learned of novel ways to offer tender steaks by better utilizing cuts from the chuck and the round. After five years of research, the National Cattlemen's Beef Association introduced a variety of new cuts suitable for dry-heat cooking and status as a premium entrée. Diners have already learned to enjoy the toothsome and flavorful qualities of char-grilled Flatiron Steaks. These popular items are fabricated from the shoulder clod, as are Petite Tender and Ranch Steaks. Also new to the market are Denver Cut Steaks, Sierra Cut Steaks, Delmonico Steaks, and Boneless Country-style Beef Chuck Ribs fabricated from the chuck roll. The knuckle of the primal round yields the Sirloin Tip Center Steak and the Sirloin Tip Side Steaks. The bottom round yields the Western Tip Steak and the Western Griller Steak.

Lesson Learned

In addition to continuously scanning other information sources, it is critical that you remain current on new products entering the market. You may only find interest in some of these items; however, those you do select may create significant cost savings and profit improvement.

The Power of Nonconformity

The whole concept of foodservice menus is subject to dramatic, if not defiant, paradigm shifts.

- Whereas the concept of a conventional dining room for restaurant meals still prevails, a variety of hybrids is emerging. Pok Pok Restaurant serves Thai cuisine in what was once an old house in a residential Portland, Oregon, neighborhood. When in operation, the driveway is lined with outdoor grills overflowing with textbook renditions of Southeast Asian specialties. The decidedly homespun concept succeeds because of its respect for authentic ingredients and observance of time-honored Thai cooking methods.
- Further down the coast in San Francisco (and beyond), renowned chefs are serving stellar cuisine to small crowds in dives, warehouses, an old Greyhound bus, and from pushcarts. The chef, in all his/her celebrity, is the attraction, and a restaurant is not necessary for crowds to assemble. Foodies flock to the art galleries, makeshift kitchens, and outdoor venues where notable chefs work their magic for limited-time engagements (often a one-night stand), or guest with the resident staff in an established kitchen. Long a tradition in Cuba and other foreign nations, underground "supper clubs" have emerged in the United States, fueled by word-of-mouth and the allure of something very personal and apart from established commercial enterprises. Some of these are held in

residences[4]; others are held in existing restaurants or retail spaces with excess capacity at certain times of the day or week.[5] The universal intent is to gain exposure with minimal investment in overhead. An approach such as this is a creative means of testing the market for a possible new venture. These "pop-up restaurants" are defined by an intentionally short life span, often less than one month and with no fixed location. For "the followers of hip," uncovering the newest dining option can become a passionate pursuit, thus establishing a personal connection between business and customer. Few if any of these "restaurants" utilize traditional advertising or even any physical signage. Clientele never stumble upon them; they either know about them or they don't. Social media, such as Twitter and Facebook, are used to post last-minute announcements and openings.

- Lounges such as the Blue Owl Cocktail Room in New York City or the Downtown Cocktail Room in Las Vegas operate as speakeasies with a minimum (or total absence) of wayfinding signage and a secret password for entrance into the inner sanctum of the barroom. These swank, retro concepts appeal to an urbane clientele who are not interested in blended frou-frou drinks, but are serious about artisan highballs and honest-to-goodness cocktails.

- Not only is there a renaissance in *cocktail culture,* but there are emerging tavern concepts that feature high-quality food to accompany the variety of beer, wine, and spirits. In the United Kingdom, a public house (*pub*) that elevates its culinary standards by serving superior food to accompany its beverages is referred to as a **gastropub.** In the United States, we have seen an adaptation of the British version, whereby sturdy food and beverages are served in a highly social and casual atmosphere. An example of a menu from an American gastropub is illustrated in Figure 7-4.

Figure 7-4
Extract from the Publican Dinner Menu, Chicago, Illinois   (*Source:* Reprinted by permission of The Publican)

Lesson Learned

Creativity knows no bounds. Throughout this textbook, we focus on addressing marketplace needs and matching your operational capabilities with a willing target market. The departure from tradition that characterizes today's trends speaks to an abandonment of doctrine and openness to dramatic new dining approaches. Maverick entrepreneurs glean the best of traditional food and beverage concepts, but orchestrate a radically different hospitality experience. Delicious and profitable meals and drinks are central to the new ventures, and this speaks to the need for navigating menu management fundamentals into novel directions.

Emerging Beverage Trends

Restaurant & Institutions (R&I) 2009 Beverage Census Study[6] identified several interesting beverage trends, including the following:

- Customers order nonalcoholic beverages 72% of the time on average when dining out. Restaurant operators must be realistic, if not conservative, when forecasting sales and anticipated profit from beer, wine, and mixed-drink sales.
- Whereas colas hold a dominant position in the carbonated beverage market, an increasing number of customers seek root beer. In fact, whereas 20% of Americans dining out have ordered root beer in a six-month period, 34% of Generation Y youth have chosen root beer.
- The success of canned energy drinks opens the door to positive modifications of other foods. For example, entrenched products such as iced tea can be further endeared to consumers. In 2009, Subway Restaurants introduced vitamin-enhanced iced tea in its nearly 22,500 stores.
- Novel beverages should be considered for inclusion on menus. Survey respondents say they would order more flavored coffees, green tea, branded specialty sodas, and flavored water if offered.
- When drinking alcoholic beverages, **Generation Y** customers like to order cocktails. It is also important to note that females order cocktails nearly three times as much as their male counterparts.

Organic and **fair trade** coffee is increasingly popular with contemporary clientele. In addition, white tea (from the bud, rather than the leaf) has found favor alongside more traditional black and oolong tea leaves. Green tea (unfermented leaves) is served hot or iced and viewed as a healthy alternative to other beverages because of its high antioxidant value. Alternatively, some diners have become enamored with the exceptionally sweet tea popularized in the southern United States. In fact, several sweet tea vodkas have entered the market with signs of widespread acceptance.

As discussed in previous chapters, there is a revival in handcrafted cocktails. Pioneering mixologists are distilling their own bitters, creating tinctures and extracts, building drinks from produce and herbal ingredients, and gilding the proverbial lily with edible silver and gold, or aromatic vapors wisped from atomizers. The interest in **molecular gastronomy** has spilled over to the bar, and the level of adventure seems boundless. Old-fashioned cocktails are now being flavored with smoke and tobacco essences. Encapsulated liquids (spherified "caviars") are floated in drinks to provide extra dimensions of texture and flavor. These molecular mixology trends must be approached intellectually, and within a historical perspective. For example, the use of herbs and vegetables in cocktails is actually more common than might be realized. Celery (Bloody Mary), cucumber (Pimm's Cup), and olives (Martini) are entrenched old-school garnishes. In fact, many spirits succeed as a result of the aromas and flavors imparted by the vegetal and herbal components used during distillation. What has changed is the palette of flavors that bartenders are choosing from, and the drama with which they design their bar menus.

In 2010, Wyndham Hotels and Resorts introduced an eco-friendly beverage menu in their North American and Caribbean properties. The menu features organic beers and wines, and specialty cocktails, including the *TRU Blue Signature Organic Cocktail.* This special martini is the hallmark of their "Ecology Mixology—Have a Drink, Plant a Tree" initiative that melds beverage marketing with the company's commitment to global environmental stewardship.

At Frances restaurant in San Francisco, boundaries are tested even further. Diners may choose from the concise wine list, and are also offered a unique twist on house wines. With a craftsman's enthusiasm, the restaurant's beverage director purchases kegs directly from a local winery, and blends them in-house to create food-centric, proprietary signature wines. The wines are tapped directly from the kegs (no bottles involved) and served in graduated carafes. The carafes are set on the tables and guests are charged $1.00 per ounce for whatever they pour themselves. This creative approach eschews the pomp of traditional wine list protocol in favor of evolving cuvees that change along with seasonal food menus. The tap-to-table concept serves as a unique signature item, assures freshness, and reduces landfill waste associated with traditional bottle-based wine lists. In addition to their inventive house wine program, Frances offers "Market Shots," made from a bevy of freshly juiced ingredients that are mixed with spirits and also sold for $1.00 per ounce, and a host of other imaginative beverages.

Lesson Learned

As is the case with food menus, your customers have drink preferences that change over time. Regardless of whether these beverages contain alcohol, you should approach them with the same profit generation tactics as all other menu items. Gender and generational favorites should be provided as appropriate to the market you serve. With creative planning, you can instill underlying themes of comfort, global influences, sophistication, or a multitude of other subtle contexts.

SUSTAINABLE FOOD AND REGIONAL AMERICAN CUISINE

Today's consumers are increasingly committed to conserving the world's limited resources, including those that affect our food supply. **Sustainability** is an overarching concept that involves management of the harvest of a resource so that is not depleted, thus conserving its availability for the future.

Sustainability focuses on the seas, the soil, and the atmospheric impacts of food production.

It must be noted that the world's inland and marine waterways have suffered the effects of industrial waste, overfishing, and violations of seasonal harvest regulations. Many waters no longer yield traditional species or viable catches. Concerted efforts to manage the supply of seafood are of critical importance. Sustainable seafood includes species that reproduce quickly and breed young, and if aquacultured, are produced locally, including those shown next:

Anchovies	Catfish	Clams
Cod	Crab	Dover Sole
Flounder	Haddock	Halibut
Herring	Mackerel	Perch
Pollack	Salmon	Sardines
Scallops	Sea bass	Tilapia

Even more insightful is the Monterey Bay Aquarium's "Super Green" list of seafood that is 1) good for human health and 2) conservative of the world's oceans. To be included on the "Super Green" list, seafood must meet all three of the following conditions[7]:

- Low levels of contaminants (>216 parts per billion [ppb] mercury and >11 ppb PCBs)
- The daily minimum of omega-3 oils (at least 250 milligrams per day [mg/d])
- Classified as a Seafood Watch "Best Choice" (green)

Currently, the "Super Green" list includes:

- Albacore Tuna (troll- or pole-caught, from the United States or British Columbia)
- Freshwater Coho Salmon (farmed in tank systems, from the United States)
- Oysters (farmed)
- Pacific Sardines (wild caught)
- Rainbow Trout (farmed)
- Salmon (wild caught, from Alaska)

While not strictly "Super Green," the following items are classified by the Aquarium as "Other Healthy Best Choices"[8]:

- Arctic Char (farmed)
- Barramundi (farmed, from the United States)
- Dungeness Crab (wild caught, from California, Oregon, or Washington)
- Longfin Squid (wild caught, from the U.S. Atlantic)
- Mussels (farmed)

Sustainability is a multifaceted concept that demands response on many levels. It encompasses a supply chain of food that has been grown, raised, and harvested using additive and chemical-free processes on sustainable farms or ranches transported over short distances and served in its freshest state by culinarians respectful of the inherent product attributes. Sustainable food lends itself to simple preparations, yet also supports more complex recipes in world-class establishments. In 1990, the U.S. government defined *sustainable agriculture* in Public Law 101-624, Title XVI, Subtitle A, Section 1603 as follows:

> [A]n integrated system of plant and animal production practices having a site-specific application that will, over the long term, satisfy human food and fiber needs; enhance environmental quality and the natural resource base upon which the agricultural economy depends; make the most efficient use of nonrenewable resources and on-farm resources and integrate, where appropriate, natural biological cycles and controls; sustain the economic viability of farm operations; and enhance the quality of life for farmers and society as a whole.[9]

Despite the legal definition, the path from philosophy to action is evolving. As stated by the United States Department of Agriculture (USDA), "Economic and social concerns present significant challenges to sustainable agriculture. Specific issues include farm profitability, economic comparisons among conventional and non-conventional farming components, viability of rural communities, fair trade and agricultural labor."[10]

Perhaps the central concern lies in how customers view and comprehend the realm of sustainability. Concepts such as fair trade, carbon footprint, and solar/wind energy use are novel to many individuals and have varying cachet and marketing value. Reasons for seeking sustainable products vary across demographic lines. Some segments prefer these products because they infer high quality. For other consumers, these issues are intertwined with a sense of ethical duty, and these same individuals may favor restaurants that share in their support of sustainable practices. Finally, there is a sizeable group that opts for these products and believes they are less prone to contamination and safer as a result.

Lesson Learned

The choice to serve sustainably produced ingredients bears implications both on the plate and on the bottom line. Arguably, it is the right thing to do for multiple reasons. As discussed in Chapter 4, locally produced foods with minimally invasive processing are likely to be flavorful and delicious. Regarding financial impacts, the expense of obtaining sustainable products may or may not increase food cost percentages. Family-run small production farms are returning to the American supply chain and are worth seeking out (Figure 7-5). In fact, some farms and ranches, such as Chino Farms, Meadow Creek Dairy, and Niman Ranch, are widely acknowledged as purveyors of top-quality products, and menu planners use their cachet as a marketing asset by citing their names in menu item descriptions. Some pundits also envision the ascendency of artisan farmers much in the same way that chefs have earned celebrity over the years. The extra research to source these products can result in competitively priced ingredients, and also educate you on the care and use of the ingredients. Other solutions are extraordinary in their elemental appeal. Several enterprising chefs have assumed the role of farmer and have established vegetable gardens on their restaurant rooftops or on plots of earth adjacent to their businesses. The allure of cooking with produce still warm from the sun strikes a chord with culinarians desiring to serve the finest recipes possible. Some of these chefs are also amateur beekeepers, using the ultra-fresh honey at the bar, in the kitchens, and at the table.[11]

Figure 7-5
Screen Shot from The Chef's Garden Web Site, Huron, Ohio
(*Source:* Reprinted by permission of The Chef's Garden)

(*Source:* Mneale/Dreamstime)

Another bottom-line impact involves how the market may be attracted to your ingredient choices. The 2010 Zagat survey of U.S. restaurants reports that 61% of diners are willing to pay more for green products and menu items, up 5% from the previous year despite the tough economy. Whereas not all clientele are attenuated to the issues of sustainability, a growing segment of the population "vote with their feet" and spend their dining and entertainment budget with those businesses that share in their values on sustainable agriculture and the environment. Restaurant operators in tune with their markets are aware of this, and make efforts to support sustainability initiatives and environmental stewardship. Sush-iSamba, a multiunit fusion cuisine destination with restaurants in Miami, Las Vegas, Chicago, and New York, committed to banning the sale of bluefin tuna, an endangered species, in all of its units. The company's "No Blue" campaign supports worldwide efforts to protect this species, which faces extinction within the next 10 years unless fishing practices are modified significantly. In addition, Sush-iSamba intends to eliminate all non-sustainable seafood from its menus and rally customers to sign petitions in support of sustainable sourcing practices. Following in the footsteps of the pioneering Fairmont Hotels & Resorts, in 2010, Marriott International introduced a system-wide sustainable seafood program, aptly named "FutureFish," and in doing so became the largest hotel chain to use strategically conceived seafood menus as a vehicle for company stewardship of marine conservation. Components of the program include specific selection and procurement guidance for each of Marriott's four major regions (the Americas, Europe, Asia Pacific, and Middle East/Africa), as well sales preferences and solutions to sustainability concerns influencing the company as well as the global community.

Capitalizing on Your Own Address

For decades, menu planners and *haute* restaurant operators embraced escapism as a *modus operandi*. Chefs emulated European recipes and tableside techniques to whisk their clientele along gastronomic journeys to faraway places. High prices for imported ingredients were tolerated as a cost of facilitating the approach. Chefs from Germany, France, Austria, and Switzerland were deified and welcomed into America's kitchens, along with their foodways and table-service traditions. In recent years, however, we have reflected on and celebrated our own national culinary heritage. Notwithstanding the notable cuisines of the world, there is a movement afoot to feature food and beverages from our own shores, skies, and local soil. Locavores have shifted their focus to foods produced in nearby farms and ranches, fish caught in local waterways, and craft beverages created in regional breweries, wineries, and distilleries. Many chefs have taken this message to heart, and fabricate all their own meats and sausages, cure all their own seafood, make all pasta in house, and prepare cheeses from scratch with locally sourced milk. Some food services have established cooperative partnerships with regional farmers, and contract plots of land, with harvests reserved especially for their kitchens. Similar arrangements involve livestock or dairy animals raised exclusively by ranchers for ultimate use by the restaurant.

When you combine these products in a holistic manner, the potential for marketing **regional American cuisine** emerges. To the astute menu planner, regional character is a marketable asset. For New Orleans diners, Louisiana oysters make more sense than those flown in from Canada and elsewhere. Prosciutto can be luscious, but Smithfield ham imbues a sense of place to Virginia menus. Australian and New Zealand lamb is delicious and readily available, but consumer demand for fresh American lamb is increasing. Visitors and leisure travelers enjoy being able to sample regional food and beverage, and when satisfied with the results, become emissaries to expand your out-of-market messaging. Table 7-1 represents a partial list of foods and cuisines that are unique to regions throughout the United States. Certainly, the list is incomplete, if not arguable, because local pride and geographic diffusion of culture is normal over time.

TABLE 7-1
SAMPLE OF TRADITIONAL U.S. FOODWAYS AND INGREDIENTS

New England and Northeastern	Cod, haddock, halibut, scrod
	Maine lobster, scallops, clams, quahogs, mussels, steamers
	Lobster rolls
	New England clam bake
	Fried clams
	Maple syrup
	Vermont Cheddar
	Cape Cod cocktail
	Manhattan cocktail
	Beef on Weck Sandwiches
	Buffalo wings
	Philly cheese steak sandwiches
	New York delicatessen specialties
	Apple cider
	Boston baked beans
	Brown bread
	Clam chowder, corn chowder, fish chowder
	Cranberries
	Indian pudding
	Johnny cakes

TABLE 7-1
CONTINUED

Midwestern	Midwest grain-fed beef and pork
	Freshwater fish, including lake perch, walleye, smelt, and trout
	Michigan cherries
	Wisconsin cheeses
	Swedish pancakes
	Polish sausages and pierogi
	Cincinnati chili
	Goetta
	Chicago hot dogs, deep-dish pizza, and italian beef
	Kansas City–style barbecue
	St. Louis–style barbecue
	Indiana sugar cream pies
	Michigan Upper Peninsula pasties
	Minnesota lefse and lutefisk
	Sauerkraut balls
	Wisconsin Danish Kringle
	Summer sausage and assorted wursts
	Bread-and-butter pickles
	Frozen custard
	Morel mushrooms
	Wild rice
Southern	Mint juleps
	Muscadine grapes, jelly, and wine
	Sazerac cocktails
	Pit-cooked barbecue
	Chitlins
	Blue crabs, crab cakes, she-crab soup
	Crawfish (crawdads)
	Alligator
	Cast iron skillet–fried chicken
	Fried catfish
	Grits, red-eye gravy
	Country ham, most notably Smithfield ham
	Creole cuisine
	Cajun cuisine
	Floribbean cuisine
	Lowcountry cuisine
	Old Bay seasoning
	Brunswick stew
	Kentucky burgoo
	Conch chowder
	Butter beans
	Slow-cooked greens, pot liquor
	Black-eyed peas
	Fried green tomatoes
	Vidalia onions

TABLE 7-1
CONTINUED

	Hush puppies, cornbread, corn pone, corn pudding, spoonbread
	Biscuits and sausage gravy
	Pralines
	Chess pies
	Key lime pies
	Bread pudding
Southwestern	Tortillas
	Jalapeño peppers, Serrano peppers
	New Mexico chilies
	Tex-mex cuisine
	Huevos rancheros
	Salsa, pico de gallo
	Guacamole
	Frijoles
	Chili con carne
	Chili con queso
	Tacos, nachos, burritos, chimichangas, tostadas
	Fajitas
Hawaiian	Kona coffee
	Tiki cocktails
	Taro, poi
	Breadfruit
	Tuna
	Spam
	Poke
	Lu'au
	Kalua pig
	Lomi salmon
	Laulau
	Pineapples
Western	Fiddlehead ferns
	Freshwater trout
	Gilroy garlic
	Fish tacos
	Dungeness crabs
	Rex sole, petrale sole, sandabs
	Pacific salmon
	Cedar-planked fish
	Moose, elk, caribou

In addition to the spectrum of American ingredients, recipes, and foodways, it notable that wine is produced in more than 3,000 commercial wineries across all 50 states. The federal government approves **American Viticultural Areas (AVA)** that permit winemakers to market the unique regional character (***terroir***) of their grapes.

TABLE 7-2
EXAMPLES OF REGIONAL AMERICAN DISTILLED SPIRITS

Alabama Conecuh Ridge Whiskey	Kentucky Maker's Mark Bourbon	Oregon Clear Creek *Eaux De Vie*
California Old Potrero Single Malt Rye	Michigan True North Vodka	Tennessee Gentleman Jack
Colorado Stranahan's Colorado Whiskey	Massachusetts Triple Eight Vodka	Texas Tito's Handmade Vodka
Kansas Most Wanted Pioneer Whiskey	Minnesota Phillips Union Whiskey	Virginia Wasmund's Single Malt Whisky
Illinois Lion's Pride Whiskey	Missouri Platte Valley Corn Whiskey	Washington Gold Buckle Club Whisky
Indiana Cougar Bourbon	New York Hudson New York Corn Whiskey	West Virginia Mountain Moonshine
Iowa Templeton Rye Whiskey	Ohio Wild Scotsman Whisky	Wisconsin Death's Door Gin
Idaho Teton Glacier Potato Vodka	Louisiana Old New Orleans Rum	South Carolina Firefly Vodka

Breweries of varying size are located in all 50 states as well, and distilled spirits are produced in more than 40 states (Table 7-2). Whereas many of these distilleries offer ambitious product lines, certain of them craft spirits with a decidedly historical pedigree (Figure 7-6).

Lesson Learned

Just like Dorothy acknowledged in The Wizard of Oz, "There's no place like home," there are a plethora of reasons for marketing local food and beverage, including heritage, freshness, appeal to visitors, community stewardship, and bottom-line finances. International cuisines certainly have a place on menus and may fit well with customer expectations, but you should always keep a trained eye toward possibilities offered by regional ingredients and preparations. Figure 7-7 illustrates a menu extract from an operation that capitalizes on the power of local food and beverage traditions.

EXERCISE 7-4
CREATING REGIONAL MENUS

Research the local foodways of your region. Identify specific ingredients, beverages, recipes, and preparations that distinguish your regional cuisine.

Q1. Develop five menu items that deliver a sense of place and have the potential to serve as signatures for your restaurant. What makes them memorable? What words will out-of-market visitors use to describe these items?

Q2. Why will your items work better in your area than if transported to a menu across the country?

Figure 7-6

Example of Historical American Spirits   (*Source*: Reprinted by permission of Buffalo Trace Distillery)

Figure 7-7

Extract from Chez Panisse Dinner Menu, Berkeley, California   (*Source*: Reprinted by permission of Chez Panisse)

THE INTERSECTION OF NUTRITION AND CONTEMPORARY MENUS

As a group, Americans exhibit an ambivalent attitude to healthy restaurant dining. Nearly 9 out of 10 Americans believe that eating healthy is important. However, findings from *Mintel Menu Insights* suggest that healthy menu options at restaurants are not particularly well accepted relative to traditional menu selections.[12] Of American diners surveyed in 2009, only one in five respondents (20%) ranked healthy food as an important factor when ordering dinner. The most frequent response was "taste" (77%), followed by "hunger satisfaction" (44%). Although greater than three-quarters of adults stated that they would like to find more healthy items on menus, only 51% said they usually select them. Also of note is the majority opinion (75%) that restaurants should become more transparent on the matter of food health. Complicating matters even further is the fact that many lower-priced menu items are less healthy. This need not be the case, yet it represents the reality that has developed. According to *Mintel* research, the majority of adults (54%) believe that it is more costly to eat healthy at restaurants as opposed to not eating healthy.

In 1992, the USDA introduced the *Food Guide Pyramid*, and then *MyPyramid* (2005) as educational dietary guides for Americans. The models considered food groups, portion sizes, variety, activity levels, and recommendations for consumption of fats, sugars, and salt. In 2011, the USDA replaced the *MyPyramid* guidance system with *MyPlate*. The new model uses a different (non-pyramid) shape to command consumer attention with a contemporary visual cue mirroring a meal place setting. In essence, the plate icon serves as a reminder for healthy eating (Figure 7-8). Most important, *MyPlate* intersects with information in a more

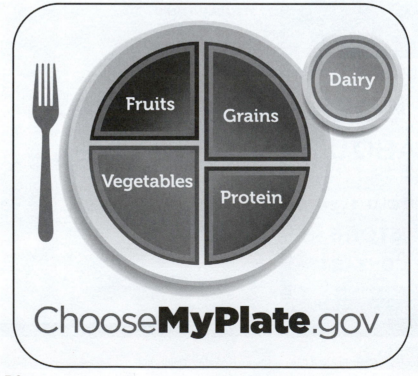

Figure 7-8
MyPlate Icon

(*Source:* www.mypyramid.gov/downloads/resource/MyPyramidGraphicStandards.pdf; accessed May 1, 2011)

Figure 7-9
Dietary Guidelines for Americans 2010
(*Source:* http://www.cnpp.usda.gov/Publications/DietaryGuidelines/2010/PolicyDoc/InsideFrontCover.pdf; accessed May 1, 2011)

detailed format provided by the *USDA Dietary Guidelines for Americans 2010* (Figure 7-9).

When menu items from certain popular restaurants are evaluated in comparison to these guidelines, the results raise poignant questions (Figure 7-10).

Lesson Learned

What diners say they want and how they act are often very different when it comes to healthful dining. Customers understand the importance of nutrition; yet when dining out, they opt for taste, texture, and the overall experience. Many chain restaurants sell hamburgers, bagels, steaks, and pasta that are at least twice the size of portions recommended by nutritionists. This should not be overly surprising, as restaurant operators have worked hard to develop tempting foods with an ever-focused eye on expanding market share and profitability. The science of nutrition has often taken a back seat to the artistry of cuisine and the pecuniary desire to generate market share and profit. In a 2008 survey by Pennsylvania State University researchers, 432 culinary and foodservice professionals were questioned concerning their perceptions of serving healthy foods in their restaurants. Many of the respondents expressed aversion to modifying their existing recipes to reduce fats and calories, suggesting that promotion of healthy dishes is the "kiss of death" for business. These same operators conceded that introduction of low-calorie foods in addition to their existing menus might be something they would consider. The majority of survey respondents also believed that reducing portion sizes was an acceptable tactic, yet they did not generally embrace the reduction of "calories per bite" as a strategy. Consequently, if operators are committed to serving the best interests of their clientele, they must develop menu offerings that

Figure 7-10

Sample Comparison of Nationally Branded Menu Items and Recommended Daily Intake

Popular Nationally Branded Menu Item	Recommendations for a Daily 2,000 Calories Diet	Analysis
Quesadilla Burger (1 portion)		
• 1,820 calories	• 2,000 calories per day	• This item represents 91% of daily calories
• 46 g saturated fat	• 20 g or less saturated fat	• This item exceeds the recommended daily maximum for saturated fat by 130%
• 4,410 mg sodium	• Consume less than 2,300 mg sodium per day	• This item exceeds the recommended daily maximum for sodium by 91%
White Chocolate Raspberry Cheesecake (1 portion)		
• 900 calories	• 2,000 calories per day	• This item represents 45% of daily calories
• 62 grams total fat	• Keep total fat intake between 20% and 35% of calories	• One gram of fat equals 9 calories; this menu item contains 558 calories from fat. According to USDA guidelines for a 2,000-calorie diet, the range of daily calories from fat should not exceed 700 calories, yet this item equals 80% of the recommended daily intake.
• 35 g saturated fat	• 20 g or less of saturated fat	• This item exceeds the recommended daily maximum for saturated fat by 75%

Note:
• These are only two illustrative menu items that might represent a portion of an individual's daily intake. It is probable that other food and beverages must be added to the analysis for a more complete snapshot of the total daily intake and its correspondence to guidelines.
• Other items on the source restaurants' menus are lower or higher in calories, fat, and sodium. These sample items are intended to illustrate extreme cases.

meld a marketable balance of flavor, satiety, and nutrition. Menu planners intent on providing nutritious food should focus on fresh, natural, quality ingredients. Certainly, there is no stigma to these items, and they fit customers' definitions of healthy dining. More so, operators must educate themselves and their clientele on the nutrition facts behind their menu offerings if customers are to become confident in making the right choices.

The appropriate actions to provide healthy menus are not formulaic. Every situation must be evaluated on its own merit. To start, you should conduct a nutritional analysis of your recipes to discern what items are appropriate for modification, if any. As discussed in Chapter 4, there are software packages that enable you to manage recipes, including nutrient analysis (Figure 7-11). Also, there are free resources for analyzing recipes provided via the Internet. The USDA, through its Agricultural Service Nutrient Data Laboratory, provides a public nutrient database of thousands of food and beverage items (Figures 7-12 and 7-13). This resource can be used to analyze individual ingredients, after

Figure 7-11
"Cost Genie" Recipe Card with Nutritional Analysis (*Source:* Reprinted by permission of Cost Genie)

which their values can be combined to provide a comprehensive analysis for an entire recipe.

Figures 7-14 and 7-15 illustrate features of the public domain USDA *MyPyramid Tracker* tool, which enables you to enter multiple ingredients, resulting—among other information—with an analysis for an entire recipe.

Once you obtain nutritional analysis data, you must decide if it is appropriate to modify the recipes and menu items. The most common tactics are as follows:

- Eliminate, reduce, or replace ingredients. For example, adding smoked paprika rather than bacon or ham imparts the desired smoke flavor and

Figure 7-12
USDA Nutrient Analysis Database Search Screen for Raw Arugula
(*Source:* http://www.ars.usda.gov/Services/docs.htm?docid=8964)

Figure 7-13
USDA Nutrient Analysis
Database Record for Raw
Arugula

(*Source:* http://www.ars.usda.gov/

Services/docs.htm?docid=8964)

Arugula, raw

Refuse: 40% (Roots, stems and yellowed leaves)
Scientific Name: *Eruca sativa*
NDB No: 11959 (Nutrient values and weights are for edible portion)

Nutrient	Units	0.25 × 0.5 cup 2.5g
Proximates		
Water	g	2.29
Energy	kcal	1
Energy	kJ	3
Protein	g	0.06
Total lipid (fat)	g	0.02
Ash	g	0.04
Carbohydrate, by difference	g	0.09
Fiber, total dietary	g	0.0
Sugars, total	g	0.05
Minerals		
Calcium, Ca	mg	4
Iron, Fe	mg	0.04
Magnesium, Mg	mg	1
Phosphorus, P	mg	1
Potassium, K	mg	9
Sodium, Na	mg	1
Zinc, Zn	mg	0.01
Copper, Cu	mg	0.002
Manganese, Mn	mg	0.008
Selenium, Se	mcg	0.0
Vitamins		
Vitamin C, total ascorbic acid	mg	0.4
Thiamin	mg	0.001
Riboflavin	mg	0.002
Niacin	mg	0.008
Pantothenic acid	mg	0.011
Vitamin B-6	mg	0.002
Folate, total	mcg	2
Folic acid	mcg	0
Folate, food	mcg	2
Folate, DFE	mcg_DFE	2
Choline, total	mg	0.4
Betaine	mg	0.0
Vitamin B-12	mcg	0.00
Vitamin B-12, added	mcg	0.00
Vitamin A, RAE	mcg_RAE	3
Retinol	mcg	0
Carotene, beta	mcg	36
Carotene, alpha	mcg	0
Cryptoxanthin, beta	mcg	0
Vitamin A, IU	IU	59
Lycopene	mcg	0
Lutein + zeaxanthin	mcg	89
Vitamin E (alpha-tocopherol)	mg	0.01
Vitamin E, added	mg	0.00
Vitamin D (D2 + D3)	mcg	0.0
Vitamin D	IU	0
Vitamin K (phylloquinone)	mcg	2.7
Lipids		
Fatty acids, total saturated	g	0.002
4:0	g	0.000

Figure 7-13
Continued

6:0	g	0.000
8:0	g	0.000
10:0	g	0.000
12:0	g	0.000
14:0	g	0.000
16:0	g	0.002
18:0	g	0.000
Fatty acids, total monounsaturated	g	0.001
16:1 undifferentiated	g	0.000
18:1 undifferentiated	g	0.001
20:1	g	0.000
22:1 undifferentiated	g	0.000
Fatty acids, total polyunsaturated	g	0.008
18:2 undifferentiated	g	0.003
18:3 undifferentiated	g	0.004
18:4	g	0.000
20:4 undifferentiated	g	0.000
20:5 n-3 (EPA)	g	0.000
22:5 n-3 (DPA)	g	0.000
22:6 n-3 (DHA)	g	0.000
Cholesterol	mg	0
Other		
Alcohol, ethyl	g	0.0
Caffeine	mg	0
Theobromine	mg	

Foods Consumed	Select Serving Size	Number of Servings (Enter a number (e.g. 1.5))
LETTUCE, ARUGULA, RAW	1 cup	0.25
MOZZARELLA, PART SKIM LOWFAT CHEESE	1 slice (1 oz)	2
OLIVE OIL	1 tablespoon	0.5
TOMATOES (TOMATO), RAW	1 thin/small slice	2
VINEGAR	1 cup	0.05

Figure 7-14
USDA MyPyramid Tracker
Data Entry Screen
(*Source:* www.mypyramid.
gov/downloads/resource/
MyPyramidGraphicStandards.pdf)

reduces the fat within the dish (and also may transform it into a vegan dish). Replacing soup/sauce bases with freshly made stock is an effective means of reducing sodium in recipes. Condiments such as reduced-fat mayonnaise are examples of ingredients that can be used to reduce fat yet maintain palatability.

- Discontinue the use of trans fats. Trans fats are engineered products and not essential in human diets. Consumption of trans fats increases the risk of coronary heart disease by lowering high-density lipoprotein (HDL) cholesterol and increasing low-density lipoproteins (LDL) cholesterol levels in humans.
- Add a new ingredient. For example, extending quiche or other egg dishes with vegetables reduces the volume of eggs required for a portion.
- Utilize strong flavors as appropriate so that you can use less of an ingredient. For example, dark meat poultry is more flavorful and requires smaller portions to deliver the same amount of taste as white meat poultry.
- Preserve inherent nutrients by handling ingredients minimally and using them at peak freshness. Procure items so that they are processed and stored for the briefest time possible.

=	
Food Energy/Total Calories (kcals)	239
Protein (gm)	15
Carbohydrate (gm)	4
Total Fiber (gm)	0
Total Fat (gm)	18.2
Saturated Fat (gm)	8.1
Monounsaturated Fat (gm)	8
Polyunsaturated Fat (gm)	1
Linoleic (omega 6) (gm)	0.9
Alpha Linolenic (omega 3) (gm)	0.2
Cholesterol (mg)	31
Vitamin A (mcg RAE)	96.2
Vitamin C (mg)	4.6
Vitamin E (mg α-TE)	1.4
Thiamin (mg)	0.1
Riboflavin (mg)	0.2
Niacin (mg)	0.3
Folate (mcg, DFE)	15
Vitamin B6 (mg)	0.1
Vitamin B12 (mcg)	1.3
Calcium (mg)	426.3
Phosphorus (mg)	308
Magnesium (mg)	23
Iron (mg)	0.4
Zinc (mg)	1.8
Selenium (mcg)	9.3
Potassium (mg)	155
Sodium (mg)	302

Figure 7-15
USDA MyPyramid Nutritional Analysis for Arugula Salad (*Source:* www.mypyramid.gov/downloads/resource/MyPyramidGraphicStandards.pdf)

- Steam and then blanch foods to preserve flavor, nutrients, and color.
- Braise less tender cuts of meat as a lower-fat alternative. Combination-cooking methods, such as stewing and braising, permit flavorful ingredients to marry over time, thus amplifying taste and aroma.
- Modify recipes by altering preparation. For example, high-heat roasting in the oven causes Maillard reactions and caramelization, thus providing attractive colors. This no-added-fat technique can substitute for frying and sautéing, each of which involves the use of oil or fat.
- Modify recipes by altering other cooking techniques. Moist-heat cooking with steam is feasible for certain items, as are other healthy methods.
- Use dry heat cooking methods to allow rendered fats to drip away.
- Utilize multistage roasting in the oven. An initial high heat stage (400° Fahrenheit or higher) creates a cuticle or crust. Then, lowering the temperature permits the food to cook gently, causing the finished product to remain juicy within the protective exterior.
- Deglaze cooking vessels to capture flavor and color. The caramelized bits remaining after cooking an item are packed with flavor and can impart a savory finish to a dish.
- Puree ingredients to add texture without adding starch thickeners.
- Thicken sauces by reducing them, rather than adding starch thickeners. Driving off moisture through the evaporative process of reduction concentrates flavors, thus creating depth and viscosity.
- Skim fat from moist-cooked protein dishes. Skimming is an important step that removes an undesirable layer of grease, leaving natural water-based liquids.
- Consider the use of customer-controlled salt addition at the table whenever possible. Diners have varying preference for saltiness, and may appreciate the option of adding more or less salt then your cooks may choose to.
- Perhaps the most immediate and effective means for providing healthier meals is to reduce portion sizes. For years, restaurants have equated generous portions as a measure of product quality. Whereas some customers enjoy the ample quantities, other diners have come to question the desirability and benefit of outsize portions. In fact, many customers elect not to consume their entire

EXERCISE 7-5
CONDUCTING NUTRITION ANALYSIS

Q1. Use a resource of your choice to analyze the recipe in Figure 7-11.

Q2. What difficulties did you encounter? Did your nutritional values equal those listed on Figure 7-11? If not, what might be the problem?

Q3. Why might nutritional analysis outside of a laboratory setting be subject to inaccuracies?

meal selection (or choose to split items) because the portions are larger than they are accustomed to. In such cases, there is obviously a disconnect between what diners seek and what operators provide to them. When this occurs, a negative gap affects value decisions (refer to Chapter 1) and may result in customer defection. One approach, although not universally feasible, is to offer multiple or customized portion sizes.

Other businesses that have responded with smaller or variable portion sizes include:

- The Cheesecake Factory, long known for its grand portions and blithe approach to nutritional moderation, has introduced a line of "Small Plates & Snacks," at lower price points.
- Chili's Grill & Bar debuted 10 menu items for under $7.00 including, a pair of mini burgers, Honey-Chipotle Chicken Crispers, a half order of quesadillas, and its "Bites" line of miniature sandwiches.
- Chipotle Mexican Grill is testing a line of smaller items entitled "Low Rollers," including a taco and soup combination, a vegetarian soup, and a small salad with chicken.
- Miniature desserts have been introduced at TGI Fridays, P.F. Changs, and a host of independent restaurants.

Major hotel chains have also responded to guest surveys with a variety of healthier options and nutrition disclosures. Courtyard by Marriott began posting calorie counts in its hotel bistros, and provides handouts listing comprehensive nutrient information on request. Sofitel introduced their De-Light menu in several North American cities. The menus enable diners to order three-course meals prepared without flour, butter, oil, or cream, totaling less than 500 calories.

Effective menu items, in addition to supporting profitability objectives may be thought of as an aggregate of sensory attributes (Figure 7-16). These attributes combine to form a matrix of satisfaction for diners.

Certain recipe development and menu design philosophies focus on all elements, other approaches emphasize a few. For example, the somewhat tired practice of architectural plating often stresses the vertical dimension with stacking of components. Whereas this may magnify the visual appeal of the dish, it can also jeopardize temperature. The lesson here is that modifications to one sensory component can diminish the

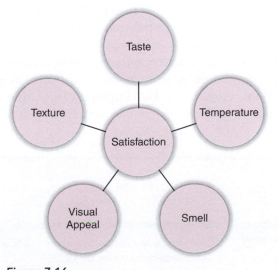

Figure 7-16
Relationship of Sensory Attributes

AUTHOR'S INSIGHT

Over the many years of my careers as hospitality professional and college educator, I observed a dynamic that you could safely bet on. Whenever I gathered several dietitians in a room with a like number of chefs, the individuals would migrate into discrete groups. Chefs would chat with other chefs and dietitians would converse with other dietitians. Certainly there was mutual respect for each other's talents and professionalism, yet a rift seemed to be assured. Underlying all this, the chefs seemed to view food as an outlet for art and drama, and the dietitians recognized the duty to provide healthful meals as a primary calling. Ingredients and recipes were the common denominator, yet the approaches varied wildly. Lest you think this tendency occurred only in industry, it was also quite prevalent in academic settings. Over time, I discovered that *the sharing of knowledge* was essential to uniting the divergent mindsets. Whether in task groups, team meetings, or in lesson planning, I arranged for the various individuals to apply their respective lenses and provide professional insights. It was apparent that the "what" (importance of nourishing meals) was commonly understood, but the "how" (can we convince guests to eat healthy and still grow a profitable business) eluded the group. As trust among group members evolved, the debates tended toward portion sizes, nutrient-dense recipes, and how to retain unctuousness while reducing fat. Ultimately, the discussions became more technical and less defensive, and eventually the parties succeeded in educating each other.

"Coming together is a beginning. Keeping together is progress. Working together is success."

—Henry Ford[13]

overall aggregate of satisfaction. For example, when fat or sodium is reduced to create a more healthful recipe, you must consider if compensation with another sensory component is appropriate. Rapidly cooking vegetables to *al dente* can preserve nutrients and preserve natural colors. As such, visual appeal is enhanced. Use of nutritious whole grains provides a toothsome mouth feel, thus focusing on the textural sensation. In summary, any time you modify recipes and menu items, particularly in the case of improving nutritional value, you should reflect on the interplay between all sensations and arrive at a combination that delivers what customers want, as well as what they benefit from receiving.

Addressing the Special Needs of a Broader Clientele

Americans with special needs have progressively enjoyed greater opportunities to share in the enjoyment of goods and services provided by the public sector and the private sector. Title III of the Americans with Disabilities Act requires that public accommodations must comply with basic nondiscrimination requirements that prohibit exclusion, segregation, and unequal treatment. They also must comply with specific requirements related to architectural standards for new and altered buildings; reasonable modifications to policies, practices, and procedures; effective communication with people with hearing, vision, or speech disabilities; and other access requirements. Also, public accommodations must remove barriers in existing buildings where it is easy to do so without much difficulty or expense, given the public accommodation's resources.[14] This important legislation enhances access to restaurants, but once seated, customers may be faced with a dearth of choices

EXERCISE 7-6
MODIFYING RECIPES TO REDUCE FAT

Q1. Use a resource of your choice to analyze the recipe in Figure 4-10. Assume the chicken breast is trimmed of skin and bones and weighs 4 ounces.

Q2. What difficulties did you encounter?

Q3. Modify the recipe to reduce the total grams of fat in the original recipe by 20%.

because of their particular dietary needs. Compounding this situation is the fact that Americans are living longer and participating in social activities such as restaurant dining as older seniors. Not surprisingly, foodservice operators are faced with the question of how to provide for special requests and acute dietary needs of their clientele.

- **Food sensitivities**   These are physical reactions to foods that cause allergic responses or intolerances. Lactose intolerance and allergies to a variety of nuts are increasingly common. Certain individuals experience allergic reactions to soy, finfish, shellfish, or chicken eggs. Intake of foods containing the amino acid tyramine can prompt migraines and other agonizing reactions. Additives and preservatives including benzoates, sulfites, BHT, and food dyes are not tolerated by many individuals. It is believed that 1 in 100 Americans carries the genetic code that causes celiac sprue disease, a serious disorder that causes damage to the small intestine. Symptoms are triggered when individuals consume gluten-containing foods, including wheat, rye, barley, and oats.

- **Carbohydrate restrictions**   There are increasing numbers of customers seeking to lose weight by reducing carbohydrate intake. More important, an increasing number of Americans suffer from type 2 diabetes. Individuals with diabetes must pay ongoing daily attention to their dietary intake, portion sizes, and frequency of meals. These individuals must control the glucose in their blood, and one strategy involves controlling carbohydrate intake. Sugar, starchy foods like potatoes and pasta, and grain-based foods like breads and cereals are carbohydrates. Carbohydrates are also found in dairy products and certain fruits and vegetables, as well as many beverages such as beer.

- **Sodium restrictions**   Hypertension (high blood pressure) affects 25% of the adult population in America. Another 25% of adults have blood pressure readings considered to be on the high end of normal. In some individuals, there is a causal relationship between sodium intake and hypertension.

- **Vegetarian and vegan preferences**   A variety of reasons influence the decision to pursue a *vegetarian* (plant-based foods including vegetables, fruit, cereal grains, nuts, and seeds, possibly excluding dairy products and eggs) or *vegan* (no animal products of any kind) dietary regimen.

Lesson Learned

If you choose not to address the special dietary needs and preferences of the broader population, you automatically deter if not exclude an increasing percentage of the market from your business. Although certainly an option, it is not necessary to present your fundamental concept as one dedicated to dietary restrictions. Rather, you should explore operational approaches and affordable alternatives to your core menu items. Your first step requires disclosure and consumer advisories. If recipes don't evidently imply their presence, you should alert customers to the inclusion of soy, gluten, groundnuts, and other ingredients that are frequently involved in food allergies and sensitivities. The next step requires your decisions for recipe modification and/or operational adjustments. Preparation of an entrée that is glazed with tamari (soy) or an appetizer usually served with a peanut dipping sauce can readily be modified to suit customer requests. Segregated storage of allergy-related ingredients is

Figure 7-17
Daily Menus at Shaw's
Crab House, Chicago,
Illinois (*Source:* Reprinted by
permission of Shaw's Crab House)

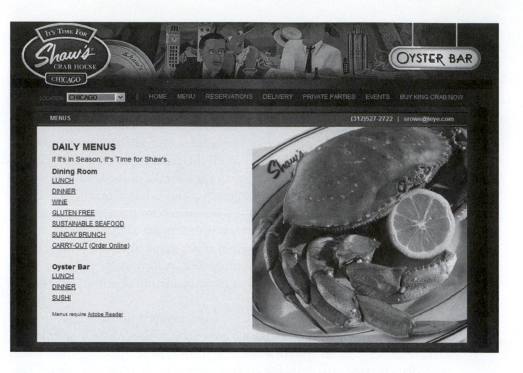

also a possibility. Some operators have made commitments to maintaining "gluten-free zones" in their kitchens. A practice of this nature enables operators to offer a safe option for a segment of the population that otherwise struggle for worry-free restaurant dining (Figures 7-17 and 7-18). Chains such as Uno, Chipotle Mexican Grill, and P.F. Chang's China Bistro have committed to gluten-free programs for portions of their menus. Another noteworthy and perhaps more difficult step involves offering recipes expressly developed for modified diets. Fairmont Hotels is a notable leader in the field of high-concept menus for dietary restrictions. Their Lifestyle Cuisine and Lifestyle Cuisine Plus menus are designed to satisfy diners seeking raw, macrobiotic, and vegan diets, and needs of guests with diet-dependent conditions such as heart disease, diabetes, and gluten intolerance.

Vegan and vegetarian items are an example of choices that may appeal to omnivores and vegans alike. Gluten-free breads can be purchased in par-baked form and finished to order. Cornstarch, arrowroot, and other natural ingredients can be used as alternatives to wheat-based roux. When accommodations for your clientele are easily obtained, the positive word spreads quickly, and you may find your market reach expands with little effort.

EXERCISE 7-7
IDENTIFYING CHALLENGES FOR MODIFIED DIETS

Q1. Why are printed menu descriptions insufficient to safeguard diners effectively from all hazards they may encounter at a banquet reception?

Q2. Scan the menu illustrated in Figure 2-9. What menu items on this menu merit a customer advisory for

guests suffering from food sensitivities or other special dietary concerns? Why is this question not easily answered?

Q3. What corrective actions can you suggest to better protect guests in these situations?

OYSTERS ON THE HALF SHELL

Cocktail Sauce, Horseradish, Champagne Mignonette

1 Dozen... 26.99   ½ Dozen... 13.99

ASK YOUR SERVER FOR TODAY'S SELECTION

SUSHI

Nigiri & Sashimi

Shrimp (Ebi)	2.5
Salmon (Sake)	2.5
Tuna (Maguro)	3.5
Yellowtail (Hamachi)	3.5
King Crab (Kani)	4

Maki

Yellowtail & Scallion	10
Tuna & Avocado	10
King Crab California	12
Rainbow Roll	15
Spicy Yellowtail	15

GLUTEN-FREE SOY SAUCE IS AVAILABLE

APPETIZERS

Jumbo Shrimp Cocktail (6pcs)	11.99
Oysters Rockefeller	12.99
Blue Crab Fingers	13.99
Cold Appetizer Combo	14.99
Oysters, Shrimp, Blue Crab Fingers, King Crab Bites	
Chilled Alaskan King Crab Bites	24.99

SALADS

Organic Mixed Greens Herb Vinaigrette	6.99
Shaw's Caesar Salad Marinated White Anchovy	6.99
Chopped Salad Italian Vinaigrette	7.99
Chopped Seafood Salad	18.99
King Crab, Shrimp, Dungeness Crab, Lobster, Italian & Louis Dressing	

GLUTEN-FREE SALAD DRESSINGS AVAILABLE:

Oil & Vinegar, Herb Vinaigrette, Louis Dressing, Italian, Caesar & Ranch

PLEASE NOTIFY YOUR SERVER ANY ALLERGIES OR INTOLERANCES

FRESH FISH & SEAFOOD

Griddled Garlic Shrimp Shaw's Seafood Rice, Garlic Butter	21.99
Sautéed George's Bank Sea Scallops	26.99
Lemon or Garlic Butter, Sautéed Spinach, Shaw's Seafood Rice	
Grilled Yellowfin Tuna Green Beans	31.99
Wild Pacific Salmon Seasonal Garnish	MARKET

GLUTEN FREE SAUCES AVAILABLE:

Lemon Butter, Garlic Butter, Tomato Herb Butter, Cocktail Sauce, Mustard Mayonnaise, Salsa Verde & Tartar Sauce

CRAB & LOBSTER

STEAMED ALASKAN RED KING CRAB LEGS	42.99
Our Specialty 1lb. – Drawn Butter	
Live Maine Lobsters – 1lb.	MARKET
Steamed or Broiled Maine Lobster – Drawn Butter	
Twin Western Australian Lobster Tails	MARKET
Two 6oz. Tails - Drawn Butter	

SHAW'S COMBINATIONS

The Club Room Combination	39.99
6 oz. Filet Mignon, Garlic Shrimp, Bay of Fundy Maine Sea Scallops	
Shaw's Surf & Surf 6 oz. Tail & ¾ lb. Alaskan Red King Crab Legs	54.99
The Signature	55.99
6 oz. Filet & ¾ lb. Steamed Alaskan Red King Crab Legs	
Shaw's Surf & Turf	58.99
6 oz. Filet & 6 oz. Western Australian Lobster Tail	

PRIME STEAKS

Filet Mignon Bearnaise Sauce	(12oz.) 44.99 (8oz) 34.99
Oscar Style Filet Mignon 8 oz., King Crab, Asparagus, Bearnaise	42.99
Premium Cut New York Strip 14 oz. Bearnaise Sauce	44.99

PRICES AND AVAILABILITY ARE SUBJECT TO CHANGE

4/2011

Figure 7-18
Gluten-free Menu Items at Shaw's Crab House, Chicago, Illinois   (Source: Reprinted by permission of Shaw's Crab House)

173

RESPONDING TO CHALLENGING ECONOMIC TIMES

Recessionary economic pressures characteristically compel customers to rethink their normal dining practices. In 2008, conservative spending replaced conspicuous consumption and became the "new normal." Nearly all socioeconomic strata were affected by challenges in the financial, housing, and employment sectors. Research indicated that among consumers earning more than $75,000 per year, nearly three-quarters of the individuals within this segment significantly modified their food and beverage purchases[15]:

- nearly half of these individuals now spend less on entertainment
- nearly 60% of survey respondents reported eating out at fast-food restaurants less
- 89% are eating out at full-service restaurants less
- nearly 25% are attempting to eat less food or fewer meals

Restaurants responded by trimming frills, stripping away table linens and focusing on the plate, as opposed to relying on ancillary elements. Regrettably, actions such as these, although reducing expenses, do not drive sales in a down market. When pinched by contracting budgets, customers often seek value pricing. Discounting is one approach; however, it has seldom proved to build customer loyalty. Discount pricing, whether in the form of coupons or other promotions, is more likely to prompt an initial visit, but without an ongoing cycle of discounts, customers may fail to revisit. A more enduring approach is to develop lower-cost menu options that appeal to budget-minded customers while continuing to offer higher-priced selections for the rest of the clientele. Brand extension, downscaling, and offering lower-priced (non-discount) options are all effective means of addressing an economizing customer base. Deep in Sonoma wine country in Healdsburg, California, Chef Charlie Palmer operates Dry Creek Kitchen. This world-class venue caters to well-heeled locals and visitors. In 2008, the restaurant began offering an "End of the Work Week" lunch special (Figure 7-19), whereby a three-course meal could be enjoyed for $25.00 (with an optional $7.00 surcharge if wine is desired). Chef Palmer also introduced the "Sonoma Neighbor" *prix fixe* dinner menu whereby a three-course dinner could be enjoyed for $36.00 (a $15.00 surcharge pairs wine with the meal). The cost of the meal includes a $2.00 donation to Healdsburg Education Foundation, benefiting Healdsburg area schools. Whereas both

Figure 7-19
Dry Creek Kitchen "End of the Work Week" Lunch Menu, Healdsburg, California   (*Source:* Courtesy of Charlie Palmer Group)

of these menus make Chef Palmer's outstanding cuisine a bit more accessible to the throngs of wine-country visitors, an appeal to the local market is obvious. Menu development that expressly speaks to neighbors reaffirms a restaurant's vision and communicates their recognition of the community.

Lesson Learned

Negative external forces such as national and global economic downturns can be expected to influence the use of and spending at restaurants. This results in revenues no longer covering costs and expenses, and subsequent diminished profits. Operators in this situation are forced to act, but discounting may not be a wise response. Rather, the nexus of consumer interest in simplicity and "living smaller" opens the door for lower prices and the improved likelihood of customer retention and sustained repeat visitation.

PREDICTIONS OF THE FUTURE

Researchers and futurists provide the foodservice industry with a seemingly endless stream of prophecies and predictions for upcoming periods. Whereas these forecasts are based on consumer research and macroeconomic trend analyses, they must be accepted as time-sensitive and relatively generalized. *Mintel International* provides a context for understanding the global marketplace by suggesting the following consumer trends:

1. **Resilience**   People have developed strengthened resolve and consumers have become increasingly conditioned to recover from and adjust to hardships brought on by the recession.
2. **Reviewing and re-evaluating**   Consumers have learned to hunt for the best deals and accept compromises. Value initiatives are important to consumers; however, they will purchase more expensive products if they are convinced of the cost–benefit relationship.
3. **Accountability**   Failed promises and questionable business practices have eroded consumer confidence. Customers now demand evidence of results and proof of claims.
4. **Escapism**   The self-imposed discipline of economizing reaches a point where people feel the need to splurge on big-ticket items or occasional indulgences that reenergize the spirit and validate the otherwise normal frugality.
5. **Media evolution**   As social media technology evolves and accelerates, companies must work harder to engage, attract, and interact with consumers.
6. **Ethical responsibility**   For businesses to rebuild brands through ethical efforts, they must connect with consumers, giving them an emotional reason to buy. As consumers demand more from the companies they do business with, they want ethical responsibility to be a chief concern, creating more scrutiny on ethical claims than ever before.
7. **Stability**   Balance, moderation, and preparation for the future replace unbridled spending and overt pursuit of luxury.

More specifically, *Mintel* suggests the following trends will affect America's foodservices over the long term:

- Customer demand for healthier menu choices
- Automated menu and digital order takers that allow guests to order foods the way they prefer them
- Operator-provided nutrient information on menus and posting of health department inspection scores/grades
- More traditional and authentic ingredients used in ethnic and globally themed dishes

• Exemptions to nutrition labeling by providing "limited time offers" that are not required to communicate nutrition information to customers

The National Restaurant association is perhaps the most robust and accessible source of culinary trend research. Their "Chef Survey: What's Hot in 2011" used an Internet survey of 1,527 professional chefs (members of the American Culinary Federation) during October 2010 to predict top trends by rank and category.[16] Respondents ranked their responses as "Hot Trend," "Yesterday's News," or "Perennial Favorites." Major findings from the survey are as follows:

Top 20 Trends

Locally sourced meats and seafood

Locally grown produce

Sustainability

Nutritionally balanced children's dishes

Hyper-local (e.g., restaurant gardens, do-your-own butchering)

Children's nutrition

Sustainable seafood

Gluten-free/food allergy conscious

Simplicity/back to basics

Farm/estate-branded ingredients

Micro-distilled/artisan liquor

Locally produced wine and beer

Half-portions/smaller portion for a smaller price

Organic produce

Nutrition/health

Culinary cocktails (e.g., savory, fresh ingredients)

Newly fabricated cuts of meat (e.g. Denver steak, pork flat iron, Petite Tender)

Fruit/vegetable children's side items

Ethnic-inspired breakfast items (e.g., Asian-flavored syrups, chorizo scrambled eggs, coconut milk pancakes)

Artisan cheeses

Category	Top Ranked Trend
Appetizers/starters	Ethnic/street food-inspired appetizers (e.g., tempura, taquitos, kabobs, hummus)
Main dishes/center of the plate	Locally sourced meats and seafood
Sides/Starches	Black/forbidden rice
Desserts	Artisan/house-made ice cream
Breakfast/brunch	Ethnic-inspired breakfast items (e.g., Asian-flavored syrups, chorizo scrambled eggs, coconut milk pancakes)
Kid's meals	Nutritionally balanced children's dishes
Produce	Locally grown produce
Ethnic cuisines and flavors	Regional ethnic cuisine
Other food items/ingredients	Artisan cheeses
Preparation methods	Sous vide
Culinary themes	Sustainability
Nonalcoholic beverages	Specialty iced tea (e.g., Thai-style, Southern/sweet, flavored)
Alcohol and cocktails	Micro-distilled/artisan liquor

In addition to ranking the survey items, the respondents weighed in on three other menu-related questions:

Q1. What has been the most successful strategy for maintaining and building business during the recession?

A1: Offering value specials (e.g., discounts, coupons, *prix fixe* menus)

Q2. What will be the hottest restaurant operational trend in 2011?

A2: Mobile food trucks and pop-up restaurants

Q3. How can chefs/restaurateurs best promote health and nutrition?

A3: Create diet-conscious menu sections (e.g., lower sodium, lower calorie, lower fat)

Whereas all responses may direct you to better serve your market's interests, perhaps these last three questions are most enlightening. The answer to Q1 acknowledges the need to be responsive to the changing desires of the market as economic pressures become the new reality. The answer to Q2 points to pioneer spirit of entrepreneurs and reinvention of foodservice concepts. Finally, their answer to Q3 illustrates an enhanced understanding of customer preferences for healthy options.

Time will tell if these predictions are accurate, yet they point to a transformed consumer and new economic reality that deserves monitoring and attendant menu solutions. Today's customers are increasingly interested in sustainability, healthy dining, and value, and this translates to the plate. Based on this survey, chefs and foodservice operators seem to be less focused on immoderation and are willing to provide value, balance, and authenticity on the menu.

ACTION TOOLKIT

The National Cattlemen's Beef Association is the information center for the U.S. beef industry, and provides resources for product procurement and handling, and beef recipe development www.beef.org/

Slow Food USA is a grassroots movement that links the pleasure of food with a commitment to community and the environment. www.slowfoodusa.org/index.php

The following Web sites connect you to organizations promoting vegetarian and vegan dietary practices:

- Vegan Action—www.vegan.org
- Vegetarian Resource Group—www.vrg.org

The following Web sites connect you to resources and information on sustainable food:

- Chefs Collaborative—www.chefscollaborative.org
- Global Aquaculture Alliance—www.gaalliance.org
- Ocean Stewards Institute—www.oceanstewards.org
- Blue Ocean Institute—www.blueocean.org/home
- Marine Stewardship Council—www.msc.org

- FishWatch U.S. Seafood Facts—www.nmfs.noaa.gov/fishwatch
- Seafood Watch Restaurant Program—www.montereybayaquarium.org
- Sustainable Table—www.sustainabletable.org/intro/whatis
- USDA National Agricultural Library—Sustainability in Agriculture—afsic.nal.usda.gov/nal_display/index.php?info_center=2&tax_level=2&tax_subject=292&topic_id=1398&&placement_default=0

This textbook serves as a core reference for menu planners seeking information on applied nutrition:

Nutrition: An Applied Approach, 3/E
Janice Thompson, Melinda Manore
2012
ISBN-10: 0321696646 ISBN-13: 9780321696649
Publisher: Benjamin Cummings

The United States Department of Agriculture (USDA) provides resources and guidelines for supporting healthy human nutrition:

- Dietary Guidelines for Americans—www.cnpp.usda.gov/DGAs2010-PolicyDocument.htm
- MyPlate—www.choosemyplate.gov
- MyPyramid Tracker (for nutrient analysis)—www.mypyramidtracker.gov
- Agricultural Research Service Nutrient Data Laboratory National Nutrient Database—www.nal.usda.gov/fnic/foodcomp/search

Healthy Dining maintains a robust Web site and a variety of resources for operators interested in providing nutritious meals for their customers.

- www.restaurantnutrition.com

Nutritional analysis of menu items can be achieved through the use of registered dietitians and consultants, software and Web-based applications, and laboratory analysis of your recipes. The National Restaurant Association provides valuable information on products, research, and best practices in healthy menu development. Association members enjoy discounts on tools and services at this site: www.restaurant.org/tools/nutrition.

The following Web sites connect you to resources and information on special dietary needs:

- American Dietetic Association—www.eatright.org
- American Diabetes Association—www.diabetes.org
- Food Allergy and Anaphylaxis Network—www.foodallergy.org

Ypulse specializes in youth marketing to teens, tweens, and Generation Y, and provides valuable market research for understanding youthful consumption preferences: www.ypulse.com.

The following Web sites connect you to restaurant industry trend research:

- Mintel Menu Insights—www.mintel.com/menu-insights
- National Restaurant Association "Restaurant Trendmapper"—www.restaurant.org/trendmapper/index.cfm
- National Restaurant Association Research & Insights—www.restaurant.org/research
- National Restaurant Association Chef Survey: What's Hot in 2011—www.restaurant.org/pressroom/social-media-releases/release/?page=social_media_whats_hot_2011.cfm

GLOSSARY

American Viticultural Area (AVA) A designated wine grape–growing region in the United States defined by the United States Department of the Treasury. AVA designations infer winemaking characteristics and quality potential arising from specific geography, soil attributes, and climactic conditions.

Fair trade An organized global socioeconomic movement that promotes sustainability of resources and welfare for producers.

Fusion cuisine A gastronomic culinary movement begun in the 1970s whereby ingredients and cooking methods were freely merged in an attempt to create novel recipes that were free from boundaries of culinary tradition.

Gastropub In the United Kingdom, a public house (pub) that, elevates its culinary standards by serving superior food to accompany its beverages. In the United States, it is a hybrid adaptation of the British version, whereby affordably priced sturdy food and beverages are served in a highly social and casual atmosphere.

Generation Y Individuals born between the mid 1970s and the late 1990s that are thought to share in generational attitudes and behaviors, including propensity to use digital media and strive for a highly social and connected lifestyle. Also referred to as the *Millennial generation*.

Molecular gastronomy A hypercreative approach to cooking that uses the application and manipulation of food science and chemistry to pioneer dramatically new sensations and presentations of menu items.

Regional American cuisine The study and practice of food, beverage, and cooking that recognizes the unique heritage and distinct foodways of geographic regions throughout the United States.

Sustainability The sum of agricultural, breeding, and fishing practices that promote the long-term viability of natural resources. In practice, sustainability involves low-impact farming, fishing, and stockyard practices that respect biodiversity and the interconnectedness of ecological systems.

Terroir The distinguishing nature that wine and foods exhibit as a result of where they are grown or harvested.

Trendspotting Environmental scanning that enables intuitive speculation and deductive reasoning to identify emerging trends in a marketplace.

ENDNOTES

1. See thinkexist.com/quotation/when_one_door_closes-another_opens-but_we_often/12671.html; accessed May 1, 2011.

2. See research.ypulse.com; accessed May 1, 2011.

3. The *third place* refers to social environments distinct yet compatible with the two usual social environments of home and the workplace. In his prescient book *The Great Good Place*, Ray Oldenburg (1989, 1991) suggests that third places provide, among other things, a sense of personal identity. Third places serve as oases of community life and nurture broader and more creative social interaction.

4. An "underground" foodservice operating without a permit from the local health department may very likely be operating illegally. Operators should always maintain appropriate permits and licenses to assure they conform to all legal requirements.

5. As discussed in Chapter 5, underutilized space can be creatively re-tasked or sublet to create a synergistic relationship with other parties in need of space.

6. See www.rimag.com/article/CA6704143.html; accessed May 1, 2011.

7. See www.montereybayaquarium.org/cr/cr_seafood-watch/sfw_health.aspx; accessed May 1, 2011.

8. "Other Healthy Best Choices" are seafood low in contaminants, providing a lesser amount of omega-3 oils (between 100 and 250 mg/d, assuming 8 ounces of fish per week) than "Super Green" items.

9. See www.nal.usda.gov/afsic/pubs/agnic/susag.shtml; accessed May 1, 2011.

10. See afsic.nal.usda.gov/nal_display/index.php?info_center=2&tax_level=2&tax_subject=292&level3_id=0&level4_id=0&level5_id=0&topic_id=1398&&placement_default=0; accessed May 1, 2011.

11. Operators should check local health department regulations prior to serving self-farmed ingredients and site-harvested honey.

12. See www.mintel.com/press-release/On-restaurant-menu-light-items-struggle-against-heavyweight-norms?id=365; accessed May 1, 2011.

13. See thinkexist.com/quotation/coming_together_is_a_beginning-keeping_together/146314.html; accessed May 1, 2011.

14. See www.ada.gov/cguide.htm#anchor62335; accessed May 1, 2011.

15. See www.rimag.com/article/CA6708875. html?nid=3458&rid=13949616; accessed May 1, 2011.

16. See the National Restaurant Association Chef Survey: What's Hot in 2011 at www.restaurant.org/pressroom/social-media-releases/release/?page=social_media_whats_hot_2011.cfm; accessed May 1, 2011.

8

Menu Pricing

(*Source:* Enrico Carlone/Shutterstock)

Objectives

Upon completion of this chapter, you should be able to:

8.1   Discuss the relationships between menu prices, menu costs, and profit.

8.2   Explain key features involving the psychology of menu pricing.

8.3   Identify means to add value to transactions.

8.4   Guide customer purchase decisions.

8.5   Explain appropriate means for incorporating add-ons, surcharges, and supplements.

8.6   Discuss value decisions made by customers when selecting beverages.

8.7   Discuss how customers quantify value, including price elasticity of demand.

8.8   Apply marginal pricing analysis to identify optimal price points.

8.9   Identify techniques for increasing perceived value.

8.10 Explain and apply mechanics of menu pricing, including the factored markup method, cost-volume-profit analysis, and LogicPath™ pricing.

8.11 Discuss other pricing approaches.

8.12 Identify acceptable tactics for changing prices over time.

RELATIONSHIPS AMONG MENU PRICES, MENU COSTS, AND PROFIT

"If more of us valued food and cheer and song above hoarded gold, it would be a merrier world."

J. R. R. TOLKIEN[1]

Pricing strategy is likely the most pivotal decision process you will be involved in. Even if you develop a sound marketable menu, an improperly conceived pricing strategy will deter customer traffic or navigate purchase decisions to the wrong items. Consequently, menu pricing is a combination of psychology and mechanics. As implied throughout this book, most operators are novice psychologists at best, so a healthy dose of common sense and intuition must be judiciously applied. Although this textbook intentionally avoids prescriptions, two facts are undeniable:

Truism 1 *The consequences of pricing are many times more important than the consequences of cost control.*
Envision a menu where a seafood mixed grill is the house specialty. The ingredients include fish and shellfish accompanied by appropriate garnishes. The ingredient cost (food cost) equals $7.00. The dish sells for $26.00 In this case, $1.00 in sales is worth nearly four times each dollar of food cost ($26.00/$7.00 = 3.71). This same relationship bears importance when costs and menu prices change. For example, if food cost is improved by 10%, then $0.70 is saved (10% × $7.00 = $0.70). If pricing (revenue) is improved by 10%, the impact is $2.60 (10% × $26.00 = $2.60). Once again, in this example, the magnitude of sales is 3.71 times that of food cost ($2.60/$0.70 = 3.71). If management focuses solely on cost control (purchasing, portioning, waste reduction, etc.) and fails to focus adequately on strategic pricing, potential sales could ultimately be driven away, or opportunities for additional revenue could be missed, diminishing, or making the need for cost control meaningless. You *should* save pennies (food and beverage costs), but you *must* earn dollars (food and beverage revenues).

Truism 2 *The contribution margin from a sale is more important than the food or beverage cost percentage of the sale.*
In Chapter 2, you were introduced to the concept of *marginal revenue,* the sales revenue that remains after the direct variable cost of goods is subtracted. **Variable costs** are any costs that increase or decrease proportionately as sales volume increases or decreases. When sales increase (or decrease) by 3%, 8%, or any other amount, then directly variable costs increase (or decrease) at the same rate. For example, if a department's labor cost doubles when sales volume doubles, then that department's labor cost is considered directly variable. In reality, there are economies of scale in food production and service staffing, where an increase in volume does not create an exactly mathematical increase in variable labor. The labor cost for producing 10 gallons of soup is not typically twice the cost of producing 5 gallons of soup. As opposed to labor costs, there is a directly variable relationship between recipe ingredients and sales volume. The ingredient cost to produce 10 gallons of soup is twice the cost of producing 5 gallons of soup. There are very, very few exceptions to this rule.

One mathematical relationship between food cost and food sales is referred to as *contribution margin:*

$$\text{Contribution Margin (\$)} = \text{Menu Price (\$)} - \text{Direct Variable Costs (\$)}$$

In an ideal world, you could isolate all variable costs associated with each particular menu item. There are certain preparation tasks required of every menu item and it behooves you to identify them. For example, to prepare house-made sorbet, you must extract flavoring bases, prepare the syrup, freeze the mixture, and scrape or scoop portions at service time. In the pursuit of identifying direct variable costs, it may be possible to conduct a task analysis that catalogs and monetizes each step in preparing sorbet or other menu items, but the time studies involved may be of limited accuracy and of insufficient benefit relative to the cost of the research. In reality, the majority of foodservices employ staff who conduct multiple tasks to produce multiple menu-item revenues during the course of their daily work shifts. It is difficult (but not impossible) to match every task to specific revenues. Consequently, labor costs are seldom allocated to specific menu items, unless the labor is especially impactful and clearly related (for example, the direct labor to shuck oysters at a raw bar, or pastry chef labor to produce a wedding cake). For the remainder of this discussion, the aggregate of labor costs is treated as a variable cost, but is not assigned to specific menu items. (In Chapter 10, several models for analyzing direct labor costs and their relationship to menu items are studied.) By filtering labor costs from the immediate discussion of variable costs, we are left with food and beverage (i.e., recipe) costs. Our formula for calculating contribution margin for menu items is thus simplified as follows:

$$\text{Contribution Margin (\$)} = \text{Menu Price (\$)} - \text{Recipe Costs (\$)}$$

Continuing to use the data from the seafood mixed grill entrée example, contribution margin for this item is calculated as follows:

$$\$19.00 = \$26.00 - \$7.00$$

In Chapter 6, you learned about the relationship of costs, expenses, and sales. Another mathematical relationship between food cost and food sales is referred to as **food-cost percentage**:

$$\textbf{Food-Cost Percentage (\%)} = \left[\textbf{Food Cost (\$)/Menu Price (\$)}\right] \times \textbf{100}$$

Similar calculations can be conducted for beverage items:

$$\textbf{Beverage-Cost Percentage (\%)} = \left[\textbf{Beverage Cost (\$)/Menu Price (\$)}\right] \times \textbf{100}$$

Returning to the previous example, food-cost percentage for the seafood mixed grill example is calculated as follows:

$$26.92\% = (\$7.00/\$26.00) \times 100$$

Contribution margin ($19.00) offsets non-food and beverage expenses and ultimately provides profit. In fact, without contribution margin, there is no profit. The same cannot be said for food-cost percentage (or beverage-cost percentage). By understanding these formulas for calculating contribution margin and cost percentages, you can now understand their relative value and limitations. Cost percentages are useful management tools for planning and monitoring operational results, but they are not the primary objective of the financial plan. The truly informed business owner does not strive for a cost percentage objective exclusively; rather, he or she seeks a target net income (bottom-line profit) measured in dollars. Cost percentages are merely a measure of relationship. Contribution margins are what matter.

THE PSYCHOLOGY OF MENU PRICING

"What is a cynic? A man who knows the price of everything and the value of nothing."

OSCAR WILDE[2]

Your menu pricing approach speaks volumes to your customers. With the rise in recreational cooking and the growth of cook-at-home enthusiasts, there are fewer trade secrets within our professional toolkit. More than ever before, customers understand the expense of scratch cooking, preparing stocks, artisan baking, and the general cost of ingredients. There was a time when we could sell certain ingredients at almost any price because they were available only to the trade and their true cost was mostly unknown to customers. Now there is widespread availability of truffle oil, game birds, dry-aged beef, and other exotica, and customers can prepare sophisticated dishes at home, and possess firsthand knowledge of ingredient prices. When we establish menu prices in our operations, we send messages to our clientele. If a potential customer knows they can obtain veal sweetbreads at their grocer for $12.00 and you are selling a sweetbreads entrée for $25.00, it is likely they will sense the value in your gentle markups. Conversely, if that same person knows they can buy mesclun at the local market and plate a salad at home for $0.90, your $8.00 *salade au mesclun* may cause your entire menu to be viewed as overpriced, even if the conclusion is based on that one item. Every menu item, bottle, or glass can attract or repel potential visitation.

There are two pricing realities that your clientele judge and respond to. The first reality is a *prima facie* assessment of your published prices. This is the price your customers see prior to addition of add-ons, surcharges, gratuities, and taxes. The second reality is the **inclusive price** that is paid. This is best illustrated by studying banquet menus. When a client enters into a banquet contract to feed their invited guests, there are several charges that combine to yield the total price of the meal. Using a hypothetical three-course lunch selection, the ultimate price is derived as follows:

Three-course lunch (per person)		$48.00
7.5% tax on lunch	7.5% × $48.00	$3.60
21% service charge	21% × $48.00	$10.08
7.5% tax on service charge	7.5% × $10.08	$0.756
Inclusive price per person		**$62.436**

In this example, when all is said and done, customers will have spent 30% more than the published menu price itself ($62.436/$48.00 = 1.30075). As such, the $48.00 price tag takes on a new meaning. There is nothing particularly insidious about this example; rather, it is meant to illustrate how final prices increase when all components of the sale are aggregated. You must recognize the consequences this can create if the inclusive price varies too dramatically from the published price. There are fine nuances between *prima facie* prices and inclusive prices in restaurants as well. Most customers filter value decisions based on entrée pricing. For example, a restaurant with an average entrée price of $23.00 is initially judged less expensive than a restaurant with an average entrée price of $31.00. Customers typically reserve this type of analysis to entrées and do not usually compare soup, dessert, or other prices for the purpose of categorizing and selecting restaurants for visitation. Many operators understand this, and set their *prima facie* entrée prices to capture customers. When the inclusive prices (entrée, plus salads, appetizers, desserts, beverages, surcharges, taxes, gratuities, and service charges) disproportionately exceed the *prima facie* prices, customers question the wisdom of their purchase decisions and may feel misled. You do not want a customer to have selected your business for a certain value decision, only to receive an unexpectedly less-valuable exchange. The lesson here is to temper (where possible) and communicate your pricing so that guests are not surprised by the final bill.

The preceding discussion recognizes the relationship between pricing and value. When a customer receives value in excess of what they anticipated, then they believe they have received a good deal. There are various means to create a value-added transaction of this nature. Some chefs provide an *amuse bouche* at the start of or a *mignardise* at the end of the meal. These are not advertised courses; rather they are "gifts" provided without asking. Other approaches involve providing intangibles in the form of services. For example, a $50.00 wine that is decanted by the server is viewed as more valuable than the same $50.00 bottle poured directly into goblets. The same can be said for

(*Source:* Chubykin Arkady/Shutterstock)

other service flourishes. Salads tossed in the presence of the diners or *en papillote* items presented tableside are examples of value addition without increasing food cost. As discussed in Chapter 1, you should never assume that these flourishes are what your guests necessarily equate with value. If diners seek speedy service and you choose to conduct fancy tableside histrionics, then you have misread your market and there is a disconnect. You must understand what your customers desire from your business and provide value and value addition within the scope of their needs and wants.

It is nearly impossible to identify incontrovertible rules to govern your menu prices; however, there are certain logical relationships and practices that are generally held to be true.

- Regarding food items, customers expect to pay the highest increment of their meal for the entrée. Consequently, appetizers, soups, salads, and desserts are typically priced lower than the entrée. The closer these other items are priced to the entrée, the more likely they are to deemed to be too expensive, and be passed over. Exceptions include seafood towers, or appetizer platters that are intended for sharing (although if divided by the number of diners within the party, they are still likely to equal less than an entrée).

- *Mezze, tapas, sushi,* and other small plates can add up quickly. In fact, diners may find their total check exceeds a normal entrée-based dining experience. If this is how you have set your prices, then you must be careful not to create an expectation of low-price dining. Charge what you must, but subtly inform your customers that small plates don't necessarily equate with small prices.

- Carryout prices are sometimes lower than prices charged for on-premise consumption of the same items. Customers who don't occupy your dining room don't expect to pay for its use.

- Half-portions are typically not half-priced. For example, a full rack of barbeque ribs might sell for $14.00, whereas as a half rack might sell for $10.00 (rather than one half of $14.00).

- Prices ending with "9," such as $2.99, $15.99, and so on, may connote value, but not necessarily quality. Most customers are savvy enough to realize how

Overstuffed Deli Sandwiches	
Roasted Turkey Breast	$ 9.95
Tongue	$ 10.95
Pastrami	$ 10.95
Brisket of Beef	$ 10.95
Chopped Liver	$ 8.95
Corned Beef	$ 10.95
Bologna	$ 7.95
Hard Salami	$ 8.95
Chicken Salad	$ 8.95
Tuna Salad	$ 7.95
Smoked Whitefish	$ 10.95
Extras: on Kaiser Roll or Pretzel Roll $ .50	
Tomato & Lettuce $ .50	
Extra Lean $ 1.00	

Figure 8-1
Menu Preceding Prices with Dollar Signs

Overstuffed Deli Sandwiches	
Roasted Turkey Breast	9.95
Tongue	10.95
Pastrami	10.95
Brisket of Beef	10.95
Chopped Liver	8.95
Corned Beef	10.95
Bologna	7.95
Hard Salami	8.95
Chicken Salad	8.95
Tuna Salad	7.95
Smoked Whitefish	10.95
Extras: on Kaiser Roll or Pretzel Roll .50	
Tomato & Lettuce .50	
Extra Lean 1.00	

Figure 8-2
Menu Not Using Dollar Signs

close these are to whole dollars, and the preliminary (*prima facie*) appeal is overshadowed by the contrived nature of the approach.

- At prices less than $10.00, increments of $1.00 have a moderate impact on customer decisions. For example, a $6.00 item is viewed as a slightly better value than a $7.00 item. Above a certain price, incremental changes do not influence value decisions. For example, an entrée priced at $22.50 is not perceived as significantly less expensive than the same entrée priced at $23.50.

With few exceptions, customers weigh personal financial decisions as an ongoing practice. Do I have enough coins for this parking meter? Did my deposit make it into my bank yet? Did I budget for this repair? None of these questions are unusual or particularly ominous. Nonetheless, as much as possible, your restaurant should be a respite from personal financial decisions. Certainly, you are in business to earn a respectable profit, so commerce underpins your *raison d'être*. Nonetheless, it helps if you "cleanse" monetary symbols from the guest experience as much as possible. Whereas this is most appropriate for upscale establishments, it may also have merit in other settings as well. (Exceptions might include menus where dollar-based promotions benefit from calling attention to the monetary savings.) You should make dining pleasant and shield customers from commercial symbolism. As related to menu pricing, it makes sense not to list dollar signs on your menus. The numerals themselves will get the point across. Compare Figures 8-1 and 8-2 to appreciate the subtle, yet significant difference between the two approaches.

GUIDING YOUR CUSTOMERS' PURCHASE DECISIONS

"The true way to gain much, is never to desire to gain too much."

—FRANCIS BEAUMONT[3]

You must approach your role as menu planner with integrity. It should never be your

intent to deceive your customers. That being said, you should not hesitate to maximize revenue, particularly if you are delivering consistently high-quality food, beverage and service. In addition to serving as a communication tool, your menu should navigate customer decisions in a strategic manner. Customers who are prepared to spend freely

EXERCISE 8-1

GUIDANCE, MANIPULATION, AND ABUSIVE PRACTICES

As related to menu pricing, discuss the nuances that distinguish guiding customers, manipulating customers, and abusive pricing practices. Cite examples of each. At what point does profit seeking compromise your clientele's perceptions of your business?

in your business should not be inhibited because of your menu's conceptual, structural, or design errors.

Figure 8-3 illustrates a *prix fixe* dinner menu set at $29.00 for food only. The menu also lists the *à la carte* prices for each course. Thus, customers are able to conduct simple calculations and compare relative value of the *prix fixe* menu and its components. One combination of the three *à la carte* courses would equal $31.00. Does this

Figure 8-3
Williamsburg Lodge Restaurant January 2010 "Wine and Dine" Dinner Menu, Williamsburg, Virginia *(Source:* The Colonial Williamsburg Foundation.)

Lodge Restaurant
Wine and Dine Dinner Menu

Each month we explore the joys of food and wines from around the world.
Our Wine and Dine prix fixe menu,
carefully prepared by Chef Keith Nickerson and Sommelier Charles Birr,
features timeless food and wine parings from some of the world's greatest culinary regions. Enjoy!

January 2010: Virginia

Three-course Prix Fixe Menu
Select one item per course
without wine $29
with two glasses of wine $39
(one glass of selected wine for the first and second courses)
Tax and gratuity not included.

A la carte pricing listed with each item.

First Course
Baked Pepper Creek Oysters $8
Champagne-Oyster Crema

Port-poached Pear Salad $7
Baby Greens, Virginia Goat Cheese Cake, Poached Pear, Port Wine Vinaigrette

Entrée Course
Virginia Ham–crusted Black Cod Loin $20
Rock Shrimp Stew, Yukon Gold Potatoes, Charred Leeks, Herb Nage

Flash-grilled Pork Tenderloin $18
Heyman Sweet Potato Hash Browns, Farmers Market Vegetables, Bourbon Pork Jus

Dessert Course
Classic Blueberry Crisp $6
Red Wine Caramel, Vanilla Bean Ice Cream

Individual Apple Almond Tart $6
Vanilla Bean Ice Cream, Riesling Wine–Caramel Sauce

Figure 8-4
Extract from Bistrot Lepic
& Wine Bar Prix Fixe Lunch
Menu, Washington, DC
(*Source:* Reprinted by permission of
Bistrot Lepic.)

Bistrot Lepic & Wine Bar

Upper Georgetown's favorite restaurant and bar

" It is a refreshing spot in which to relax, sip some wine, have a good meal… " *Bon Appetit*

The Place | Cuisine | Wines | Holiday Specials | Vos festivités | What they say | About us | Contact | Make a Reservation | Gift Certifica

Lunch | Dinner | Wine Bar | Les Formules Déjeuner | Les Desserts

La formule Déjeuner

Available Monday through Thursday only

Power Lunch

Plat du Jour

Glass of Wine (3oz pour)

$17.95

Or

3 Course Prix-Fixe Menu

$24.95

Appeteasers

Week starting Monday, April the 25th, 2011
Soupe du Jour

Salade de crevettes grillées
Grilled shrimp served with frisee salad

Salade d'avocat, tomates confites et roquette
Baby arugula salad served with avocado and confit tomato

· Entrees

Monday
Saumon poché, ratatouille, coulis de coriandre
Poached filet of salmon served with ratatouille and cilantro coulis

Tuesday
Blanquette de veau
Veal stew served with mushroom, navel, carrot and rice Pilaf

knowledge cast the *prix fixe* menu as a particularly good value? Is it worth purchasing, or are separate courses a better value option? The lesson here is that in many cases, less information is preferable. Alternatively, Figure 8-4 illustrates an extract from a *prix fixe* luncheon menu. Note that it is impossible for customers to assign incremental value to the various components of the menu. Of the $24.95 (lunch) price tag, how much is the *soupe* or *salade* worth? What is the fair price of the veal entrée (by itself)? As long as your customers believe the *prix fixe* is a good value, they really don't need to know anything else about prices of the items that make up the *prix fixe* selection. It does not benefit you to prompt needless analytical dissection of your menus.

In most instances, customers like choices. Even with a *prix fixe* or degustation menu, there are usually one or two choices, so that likes and dislikes can be accommodated. This philosophy also applies to menu pricing. It is typical and appropriate to provide a range of prices within each menu category. As a rule, customers scan each category and filter out items that they dislike or otherwise don't want. What remains are possible selections. From this list, your diners must decide if they will order the least expensive item, the most expensive item, or something in between. Customers usually gravitate toward central prices unless you provide compelling alternatives. Generally, they decide on a mid-price option. As is the case with most rules, there are some creative exceptions. For example, Bistro Twenty Seven in the arts district of downtown Richmond, Virginia, embraces an imaginative food and beverage program. The address of the restaurant is 27 West Broad Street. Twenty-seven is a meaningful number to this business and is used for creative merchandising. In addition to a full *à la carte* dinner menu there is also a $27.00, four-course dinner menu. They also offer a varied list of wines by the glass and thoughtfully selected bottles. Notably, the bistro promotes their unique "27 List," which contains 27 wines priced at $27.00 or less. This list does not ascribe to the theory of price ranges; however, its value positioning and creative synergy with the overall concept makes it a success.

Some operators use a pricing practice of questionable value by including an artificially high-price item at the top of the range. Compare the following examples:

	Menu A	Menu B
Low price	$16.00	$16.00
High price	28.00	42.00
Mean price	22.00	29.00
Range	12.00	26.00

The arithmetic mean of the low price and high price on menu A equals $22.00. Customers will likely make purchase decisions clustered around this point. The mean of the low and high items on menu B equals $29.00. As long as customers do not see the high price ($42.00) as out of place, then the strategy may be effective and purchases may cluster around the $29.00 price point. If the high-price item appears out of character from the rest of the selection prices, it will be ignored—or even worse, deemed a ploy.

A corollary to the price range recommendations involves sequencing of the list. Prices within a menu category should not be listed in ascending order. In fact, pricing patterns should not be obvious and should be avoided. If the first selection is the least expensive, and a customer stops scanning shortly thereafter, he or she will never see nor consider the higher-price options. Do not focus the organization or sequence on price. Rather, if you are intent on organizing within a category, use other criteria, such as preparation method ("From the Smokehouse") or flavor profile ("Hot & Spicy"). The best practice is to list items using a logical approach that randomizes the sequence of prices (Figure 8-5).

ADD-ONS AND SURCHARGES

Many operators ascribe to the theory, "If customers want something extra, then they should pay for it. Those who don't want extra should not have to pay for something they don't order." On the face of it, this makes sense; however, relatively small surcharges that plague the menu may result. Figure 8-6 illustrates an example of add-on and surcharge pricing. In this example, customers who prefer an egg-white omelet are required to pay a $1.00 surcharge in addition to the approximately $10.00 base price of an omelet. A similar approach is shown in Figures 8-1 and 8-2, where customers are asked to pay surcharges for add-ons such as tomato or a bread selection on their deli sandwich.

The use of add-ons and surcharges may not be the wisest tactic. In many instances, they are perceived as "nuisance fees" and cast your pricing minutiae as opportunistic. An alternative to surcharges involves building the additional food cost of add-ons into the overall menu structure and raising the prices across the board. Table 8-1 applies hypothetical sales data to the omelet menu from Figure 8-6.

Based on this hypothetical data, total sales equal $9,165.50. This is achieved by selling 1,000 omelets, and surcharges for 60 orders prepared with egg whites only, and 45 orders of salsa.

Table 8-2 illustrates an alternative pricing method, where the revenue previously obtained from surcharges ($60.00 + $22.50 = $82.50, as illustrated in Table 8-1) is equally distributed throughout the entire menu mix. The calculation is

$82.50 Surcharge Revenue/1000 Omelets Sold = $0.0825 Average
Surcharge to Be Distributed

This average ($0.0825) is added to the current menu prices to create revised prices for each item. Once you have distributed the total surcharges, there is no longer

Soup & Salad

Exhibition-tossed salads – with today's freshest ingredients	market price
Greengrocer vegetable soup au pistou	3.25
Seasonal soup du jour	2.25
House salad of limestone lettuce & watercress with toasted hazelnuts & lavender-peppercream dressing	4.25
Salad Nicoise - all-white tuna, cooked egg, crisp green beans, anchovies potatoes, Nicoise olives & ripe tomatoes with caper-balsamic vinaigrette	8.50
European farmer's market salad of baby greens & roasted pears, served with aged sherry vinegar, walnut oil & a miniature chevre soufflé	7.50

Panini & Artisan Sandwiches

Croque Monsieur – country ham, Gruyere cheese & a dab of Dijon crème toasted between two slices of brioche bread	6.00
Tamari-glazed grilled tuna with daikon, cucumber, and black sesame seeds served open-faced on multigrain bread	8.50
Wood-smoked turkey breast with Tillamook cheddar cheese, oakleaf lettuce & freshly grated horseradish on brown bread	5.50
Shrimp, artichoke & crayfish salad with golden tomatoes & baby spinach on toasted brioche bread	7.50
Panini of marinated flank steak, pan-grilled red onions and smoked provolone cheese on sourdough bread	6.50
Panini of grilled seasonal vegetables with fresh mozzarella cheese & roasted garlic oil on sourdough bread	5.50
Panini of marinated and chargrilled chicken breast with arugula & roasted red peppers on sourdough bread	7.50

Companions

Market vegetable du jour	2.50
Whole baked sweet potato	2.50

House Specialties

Greengrocer quiche, made fresh daily	6.00
Pasta du Jour	market price
Sea salt baked potato filled with roasted lobster, sugar snaps, wild mushrooms and a white wine-chive beurre blanc	8.50
Vegan Mixed Grille – sautéed portabella mushrooms, roasted beets & chargrilled Japanese eggplant with a savory white bean coulis	6.50
Seafood Pan Roast – today's market selection of seafood finished with a complimentary seasoning & garnish	market price
Charcuterie Platter – homemade sausages & country-style pâté, cornichons, whole-grain mustard & a pain-batard	9.50

From Our Wood Grill

Fresh Fish of the Day	market price
½ Game Hen marinated in Herbs du Provence, served with a saffron aioli	9.00
Dry-rubbed Angus flank steak, served with 3-onion marmalade	8.50
Boneless chicken breast served with a wildflower honey & Dijon mustard sauce	6.25

Sweets

European pastries – a daily selection of tarts, beignets and more	5.50
Homemade ice creams and sorbets	4.25

Beverages

Our featured wines	glass 5.50 / bottle 21.00
Freshly squeezed fruit juices	2.75
Our Signature cranberry lemonade	2.25
Hot or cold Virginia apple cider with mulling spices	2.50
Assorted regional spring & mineral waters	1.50/2.50
Arabica coffee or Espresso	1.50
Café latte	2.50
Looseleaf teas and herbal teas	1.50

Figure 8-5
Menu with Randomized Price Sequence

Figure 8-6
Omelet Menu with Add-ons

Fluffy Omelets

All omelets are served with grilled 8-grain toast.

Albuquerque
> Red onions, cilantro, ripe tomatoes, pepper jack cheese and New Mexico green peppers. 9.75

Western with Cheese
> Finely diced sugar-cured ham with green & red bell peppers, onions and your Colby or Swiss cheese 9.50

Greek Isles
> Crumbled Feta cheese, fresh spinach, ripe tomatoes, grilled onions, oregano & sliced Kalamata olives 9.75

Cheesy Vegetarian
> Broccoli, red onions, ripe tomatoes and shitake mushrooms with your choice of Wisconsin Cheddar or Gouda cheese 9.75

Stockyard
> Crumbles of pepper-cured bacon and country sausage with your choice of Swiss, Cheddar or pepper jack cheese 9.25

Forest Mushroom
> Sautéed assorted mushrooms and Swiss cheese with bubbling sherry-mushroom sauce on the side 8.95

Spinach and Cheese
> Fresh spinach, Brie and fondue tomato sauce 9.25

Build Your Own Cheese Omelet
> 3 eggs with your choice of Swiss, Colby, Wisconsin Cheddar, pepper jack, Feta, Brie or Gouda 7.95
> Egg white omelets 1.00 additional   Homemade Salsa .50 additional

reason to charge individually for them. You still receive the same total sales, and each of the omelets has barely increased in price. Hence, you have removed a "nuisance fee."

This same method can be used in almost any pricing scenario with miniscule impact on the menu items. By using this approach, you avoid the "litter" of add-ons and other surcharges. If there is a shift in the volume of add-ons, then you should revisit the distribution and verify your calculations are still appropriate for this sales mix. You may find it appropriate to modify your prices during the next scheduled revision cycle.

TABLE 8-1
OMELET MENU WITH HYPOTHETICAL DATA

Menu Item	Number Sold	Menu Price	Total Sales
Albuquerque omelet	70	$9.75	$682.50
Western with cheese omelet	80	9.50	760.00
Greek Isles omelet	70	9.75	682.50
Cheesy vegetarian omelet	175	9.75	1,706.25
Stockyard omelet	145	9.25	1,341.25
Forest mushroom omelet	130	8.95	1,163.50
Spinach and cheese omelet	95	9.25	878.75
Build your own cheese omelet	235	7.95	1,868.25
Omelet subtotal	**1000**		**$9,083.00**
Egg white surcharge	60	1.00	60.00
Homemade salsa surcharge	45	0.50	22.50
Surcharge subtotal	**105**		**$82.50**
		Total	$9,165.50

TABLE 8-2
OMELET MENU WITH REVISED HYPOTHETICAL DATA

Menu Item	Number Sold	Menu Price	Distributed Surcharge	Revised Menu Price	Total Sales
Albuquerque omelet	70	$9.75	$0.0825	$9.83	$688.28
Western with cheese omelet	80	9.50	0.0825	9.58	766.60
Greek Isles omelet	70	9.75	0.0825	9.83	688.28
Cheesy vegetarian omelet	175	9.75	0.0825	9.83	1,720.69
Stockyard omelet	145	9.25	0.0825	9.33	1,353.21
Forest mushroom omelet	130	8.95	0.0825	9.03	1,174.23
Spinach and cheese omelet	95	9.25	0.0825	9.33	886.59
Build your own cheese omelet	235	7.95	0.0825	8.03	
Omelet subtotal					$9,165.52
Egg white surcharge	60	—			0.00
Homemade salsa surcharge	45	—			0.00
Surcharge subtotal					$0.00
				Total	$9,165.52

Despite the goodwill obtained by distributing these charges and rendering them invisible, there are certain situations when surcharges are appropriate (Figure 8-7), because they are inherently pricy or they substantially change the dish. In cases when add-ons are appropriate, the term **supplement** is often used, because it sounds less commercial than the term *surcharge*.

BEVERAGE VALUE DECISIONS

Chapter 3 discusses the sales potential of house-made artisan soft drinks. Whereas national brands (Pepsi, Coca-Cola, etc.) can be marked up only to a certain point, house-made beverages open a host of enhanced revenue possibilities. Also, you can take advantage of seasonal cost savings to create syrup ingredients. When produce is in peak supply, or if you can obtain surplus-priced herbs in season, the possibility of producing inexpensive yet profitable signature drinks is improved even further. This is only one example of an intelligent approach to beverage menus, yet it points to the importance of assessing the profit potential of beverages and exploring what can be done to enhance their appeal in the eyes of your customers. As also discussed in Chapter 3, there is a range of value additions you can apply to beverages. Adding next to nothing limits your ability to mark up your menu items. For example, you barely add any value to an order of milk, other than providing a glass to pour it in and conveying it to the table. Brewed iced tea requires tea leaves and hot water, and involves a bit more work for your staff. Alternatively, when you use creative ingredients, skilled preparations, boutique ice cubes, or unique service presentations, you can justify higher prices and command attractive contribution to net income.

The value you add directly influences the level of markups your customers will tolerate. Too opportunistic a markup deters sales and results in customers choosing a beverage-free, food-only experience. You want to sell alcoholic beverages if only to

First Course Selections

♦ *A Mélange of Spicy Big Eye Tuna
with Avocado, Crispy Shallots and Sake-Yuzu Sorbet

♦ Carpaccio of Herb Crusted Baby Lamb with Caesar Salad Ice Cream

♦A Quartet of Maine Oyster Slurpees

V Beet Fantasia: Three Varieties of Roasted Beets, Beet Mousse and Citrus Salsa

Chilled Maine Lobster with Root Vegetables, Braised Celery Hearts
and Citrus Vinaigrette

A Tin of Sin: American Ossetra Caviar with a Crab and Cucumber Rillette
($24 Supplement)

V Indicates Vegetarian Selection   * Indicates Vegetarian Option Available
♦ Indicates Uncooked Preparation

Figure 8-7
Menu with Supplemental Charges for Caviar, The Inn at Little Washington, Washington, Virginia   (*Source:* Reprinted by permission of
The Inn at Little Washington)

enrobe the dining visit within a rosy glow. Just as important, you want thoughtfully paired beverages to transform good food into a delicious dining experience.

Your beer menu, and especially your wine list, must address multiple dimensions. Your **wine program** involves the scope and character of your wines, the pricing scheme you develop, the glassware you use, and the protocol your staff uses to serve their customers. Some wine programs are simple and do not merit high markups. These operations provide a few wines by the glass and perhaps a half-dozen bottled wines. Bottles that cost you no more than $10.00 fit this type of program. The majority of wine programs typically range between 28% and 35% of the cost of sales; however, this is not a hard and fast rule. Many authorities believe that to entice customer purchases, the lowest priced bottle of wine should not exceed the price of the lowest entrée. As such, a menu with a $24.00 food entrée as the least expensive selection should include a $24.00 bottle of wine on the wine list. When it comes to wine by the glass, many operators price the glass to cover the wholesale price of the wine. Under this arrangement, a bottle costing you $15.00 would sell for $15.00 by the glass, and so forth. There is a downside to this practice. If customers are familiar with the price of these wines from their retail experiences, they may view your pricing as predatory. You must be careful not to derail your sales efforts because wine-by-the-glass revenues are the key profit generator for most wine lists. Nonetheless, as is the case throughout this textbook, you should not rely on old saws or prescriptions, but rely on what your clientele seek. Your market may be more or less tolerant of a variety of beverage markups, and it is critical that you understand how they define value.

Some states permit restaurant operators to invite diners to bring their own bottles as an accompaniment to their meals. A *Wine Spectator* survey indicates that more than half of the states in the United States allow some form of corkage in restaurants. Some diners invest in personal wine collections and choose to enjoy their bottles alongside foods prepared by skilled restaurant chefs. Restaurants typically charge **corkage fees** ranging between $10.00 and $30.00 per bottle to customers who bring in their own wine. Some exclusive operations charge as much as $75.00 per bottle. These fees replace the contribution margin that would otherwise be earned from a typical bottle sale. The logic behind imposition of these fees is that operators shoulder the expense of beverage licenses, operating expenses, and fixed costs, and the potential for defense of an alcoholic beverage liability lawsuit if injuries are caused by the consumption. Why would operators even consider forgoing the profitable sale of their own wine simply to collect a fee? The answer can be explained within the context of market competition. If you are one of the few select operators who allows guests to bring in their own wine, and the majority of your competitors do not, then you possess a competitive advantage. You may elicit customer visits that generate food sales, even if they do not generated wine sales. This arrangement is best conceived as a marketing effort. Depending on the overall concept, some operators even provide personal wine lockers to loyal guests. These lockers may be filled with personal wines, but more frequently are stocked with age-worthy wines purchased from the restaurant after consultation with the restaurant's sommelier. It is easy to see the powerful loyalty connection this can create. The lines become blurred between "my cellar" and "my regular restaurant." Either way, there are food sales just waiting to accompany the wine.

In fact, some restaurants offer corkage-free days when customers may bring in their own wines and enjoy them at no additional cost when purchasing meals. Some operators waive corkage fees for large dinner parties, or to acknowledge guests bringing in rare wines with substantial cellar age. Kimpton Hotels offers "Let the Corks Fly" at their portfolio of hotels to stimulate summer traffic. Bayona in New Orleans hosts "Let Them Drink Wine," a corkage-free promotion that fills seats during the typically slower mid-July period.

HOW CUSTOMERS MEASURE VALUE

Determination of value is as varied as the spectrum of foodservice customers. One diner may refuse to pay more than $4.00 for a pint of beer. Another customer won't blink at a $9.00 tipple. The consequences of price resistance are introduced in Chapter 3. The following discussion expands on that concept. In a competitive market, menu prices that are too high diminish customer motivation to spend.[4] Economists refer to this relationship between the demand for a good and the price it is offered for, as **price elasticity of demand**. In the previous example, if the price for a pint of beer increases and the demand for it (as measured in customer purchase decisions) decreases, then beer can be said to have an **elastic demand**. Conversely, some products have a relatively **inelastic demand**. For example, coffee served at breakfast can be sold over a wide range of prices with little effect on demand. It can be said that coffee has a relatively inelastic demand. Nonetheless, there are price points above which customers simply choose not to spend. Whereas generally used as a concept within a broader context, the **market-clearing price** is the menu price at which quantity demanded is equal to quantity supplied. It is also referred to as the **equilibrium price**. For example, if customers accept a *prix fixe* menu of $39.00 but sales dramatically diminish at higher prices, it can be assumed that $39.00 is the equilibrium price for *prix fixe* dining in this market. The concept of equilibrium infers that over time, forces tend to create supply, demand, and prices that have incrementally moved to a point of balance and sustainable competition. There is a regional influence that defines most markets. Metropolitan areas such as Los Angeles, Chicago, New York, San Francisco, Boston, and Washington DC exhibit a relatively high cost of living, and this is seen in menu prices as well as other consumer goods and services.

Over time, a local market tends to move toward competitive pricing, whereby the capacity to serve meals (supply) is utilized if customers are satisfied with the overall value they receive. If pricing is too high, then seats are underused, restaurants are partially empty, and there is surplus capacity. Understanding elasticity helps you identify ideal prices for menu items.

Marginal Analysis Pricing

The following example illustrates a **marginal analysis pricing**[5] model for menu items, and shows the impact on sales (demand) and **marginal profit** (the difference between

Selling Price	Number Sold
$ 3.50	180
$ 3.75	170
$ 4.00	160
$ 4.25	150
$ 4.50	140
$ 4.75	130
$ 5.00	120
$ 5.25	110
$ 5.50	100
$ 5.75	90
$ 6.00	80
$ 6.25	70
$ 6.50	60
$ 6.75	50
$ 7.00	40
$ 7.25	30
$ 7.50	20
$ 7.75	10

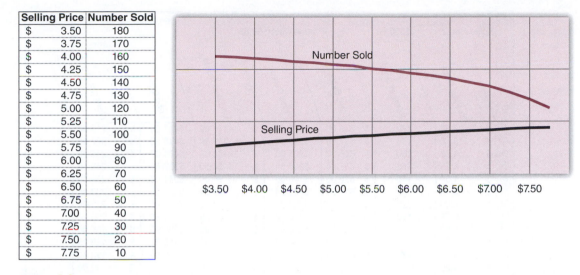

Figure 8-8
Relationship of Beer Pricing and Number of Units Sold

total sales and total costs) as price varies. This example examines a 12-ounce glass of draft beer that is test marketed within the price range of $3.50 and $7.75. As the graph illustrates, the *demand* (number sold) decreases as the price is increased (Figure 8-8). This behavior is typical of a basic supply and demand curve within an elastic market.

Selling items for barely any profit is seldom a goal. Nonetheless, marginal analysis illustrates how increased price (and accompanying contribution margin, measured as the difference between sales and direct costs) drives down volume. The tactical question you must answer is this: What combination of menu price and sales volume is most desirable to your customers and your business interests? To answer that question, you must know two additional pieces of data. The variable cost in this example is the beverage cost for 12 ounces of beer, for which we assign a hypothetical cost of $0.65. The other data you must identify involves the **fixed cost** of serving draft beer, which is the cost that exists whether you sell zero portions or many portions. In this example, we classify the $300.00 beer-refrigerator/tap-rental fees as fixed costs. Once you engage in the rental contract, these expenses must be paid whether you succeed at selling beer or not. Consequently, you must sell enough draft beer to cover the fixed costs of the equipment rental. As you do this, you also incur variable costs, because each portion of beer costs $0.65. The relationships among pricing, fixed costs, variable costs, the number of glasses sold, and marginal profit is illustrated in Figure 8-9.

The data in column A represents the menu prices (selling price) you are testing. The data in column B represents the number of glasses sold at these various price points. Note that an elastic relationship is assumed, because increased selling prices cause the number of portions sold to decrease. The data in column C (total sales) is the product of data in column A multiplied by the data in column B. The data in column D represent the fixed cost of selling draft beer; notice that it is constant (fixed) and does not change, even as the level of sales change. Column E represents the total variable beverage costs for the respective sales, which in this example is the beverage cost of the draft beer. For example, cell B4 indicates 180 glasses of beer were sold. The beverage cost per portion (cell E1) times the value in cell B4 equals $117.00. Adding the fixed cost from cell D4, a sum of total costs is calculated in cell F4. Thus, column F lists the sum of variable and fixed costs associated with this volume of sales. If total costs (cell F4) are subtracted from total sales (cell C4), the difference (cell G4), referred to as *marginal profit*, results. Column G lists marginal profit for each price–volume point. Using this method and set of data, the highest marginal profit can be found in cell G7; thus, the ideal selling price is

Figure 8-9
Relationship among Pricing,
Fixed Costs, Variable Costs,
Number of Units Sold, and
Marginal Profit

	A	B	C	D	E	F	G	H
1	Fixed Costs=	$300.00		Portion Cost= $0.65				
2								
3	Selling Price	Number Sold	Total Sales	Fixed Costs	Variable Costs	Total Costs	Marginal Profit	
4	$ 3.50	180	$ 630.00	$300.00	$ 117.00	$417.00	$ 213.00	
5	$ 3.75	170	$ 637.50	$300.00	$ 110.50	$410.50	$ 227.00	
6	$ 4.00	160	$ 640.00	$300.00	$ 104.00	$404.00	$ 236.00	
7	$ 4.25	150	$ 637.50	$300.00	$ 97.50	$397.50	$ 240.00	
8	$ 4.50	140	$ 630.00	$300.00	$ 91.00	$391.00	$ 239.00	
9	$ 4.75	130	$ 617.50	$300.00	$ 84.50	$384.50	$ 233.00	
10	$ 5.00	120	$ 600.00	$300.00	$ 78.00	$378.00	$ 222.00	
11	$ 5.25	110	$ 577.50	$300.00	$ 71.50	$371.50	$ 206.00	
12	$ 5.50	100	$ 550.00	$300.00	$ 65.00	$365.00	$ 185.00	
13	$ 5.75	90	$ 517.50	$300.00	$ 58.50	$358.50	$ 159.00	
14	$ 6.00	80	$ 480.00	$300.00	$ 52.00	$352.00	$ 128.00	
15	$ 6.25	70	$ 437.50	$300.00	$ 45.50	$345.50	$ 92.00	
16	$ 6.50	60	$ 390.00	$300.00	$ 39.00	$339.00	$ 51.00	
17	$ 6.75	50	$ 337.50	$300.00	$ 32.50	$332.50	$ 5.00	
18	$ 7.00	40	$ 280.00	$300.00	$ 26.00	$326.00	$ (46.00)	
19	$ 7.25	30	$ 217.50	$300.00	$ 19.50	$319.50	$ (102.00)	
20	$ 7.50	20	$ 150.00	$300.00	$ 13.00	$313.00	$ (163.00)	
21	$ 7.75	10	$ 77.50	$300.00	$ 6.50	$306.50	$ (229.00)	

$4.25. Sales levels below $4.25 rely on a price point that is too low to generate sufficient revenue. Prices above that point begin to drive away demand, resulting in insufficient sales. You should also note that as demand significantly decreases, there is insufficient sales volume to cover the combination of variable and (particularly) fixed costs.

The intrinsic problem with this model involves knowing exactly how elastic the demand truly is. (Just how much demand will change as you vary prices.) One method to measure this can be conducted by multi-unit foodservice operators. If most other criteria are equivalent (customer demographics, overall menu, level of market competition), then the same menu item can be tested in various stores at various price points to provide a rough measure of elasticity. It is difficult for independents with one location to measure elasticity and price resistance. Customers will be confused if the same product is offered at different prices without a logical explanation. Nonetheless, there are some opportunities to test different prices. For example, you can test demand at different prices during various dayparts (happy hour, regular meal periods, late night) to measure customer sensitivity and "sweet spots" for pricing.

EXERCISE 8-2
APPLYING MARGINAL ANALYSIS PRINCIPLES

Download *Marginal Analysis Pricing.xls* from http://www. pearsonhighered.com/barrish. Use the file to calculate the most profitable price points for the following menu item:

Fresh Shellfish Appetizer

Fixed Cost = $160.00

Food cost per portion = $3.65

Selling Price	Number Sold
$ 8.50	200
9.00	185
9.50	160
10.00	150
10.50	145
11.00	100
11.50	90
12.00	85
12.50	70

TECHNIQUES FOR INCREASING PERCEIVED VALUE

As discussed previously, restaurateurs often equate value with quantity and provide oversize portions. This resonates with some clientele; however, for those individuals managing their dietary intake, this approach is contrary to their definition of value. Of late, there has been a fundamental shift that focuses on quality rather than quantity. Some of the more common techniques for increasing perceived value include

(*Source:* Comstock/Thinkstock)

- list and describe origin of ingredients if they exhibit praiseworthy qualities
- finish dishes and drinks with creative edible garnishes
- train and develop knowledgeable service staff members who are conversant on menu specifics
- create visual aesthetics with artistic plate presentation
- use serviceware that is sized strategically for the standard portions served
- use creative plates and serviceware that depart from the norm
- use heated or chilled serviceware as appropriate
- serve condiments as personal portions rather than from a bottle or jar
- filter your tap water for beverage service
- use quality ice cubes for beverages
- finish dishes tableside (tossing salads, removing casserole lids, etc.) as appropriate
- provide cocktails in personal decanters
- decant wine tableside
- generate goodwill by providing accompaniments or other items not expressly requested
- other pleasant surprises—personalized reservation place cards at each seat, scented hot towels accompanying shellfish courses, creative carryout wrapping/containers, and so on

Regarding listing and describing the origin of ingredients, one study indicates compelling opportunities for merchandizing local ingredients. A 2010 study conducted by Pennsylvania State University researchers and the Leopold Centre for Sustainable Agriculture at Iowa State University indicated that when presented a recipe prepared from non-local ingredients and the same recipe prepared from local ingredients but sold for a higher menu price, customers actually were willing to pay a premium for the local option.[6] Based on this study, the provenance of ingredients may, within limits, trump the rules of price sensitivity.

The preceding list is not a substitute for the basics. Service should be professional and caring. Hot food should always be served hot; cold food should always be served cold. Beverages should be served prior to or along with the food so that each course is complete. Glasses should be refilled without asking. The entire order as agreed on is what should be delivered. Timing of service should be efficient and in keeping with the nature of the restaurant's theme. Diners should never be kept waiting. That being said, the combined delivery of hospitality basics plus value additions can effectively increase perceived value with little or no expense to your customers or your business.

MECHANICS OF MENU PRICING

There are many approaches to pricing, each with proponents and detractors. Rather than cover every model, this textbook compares two methods that range from simple to highly structured.

The **factored markup pricing method** is a simple pricing method that does not require extensive calculations. To apply this method, you begin by deciding on a target cost percentage that you aim to achieve for each food and beverage category:

$$\text{Markup Factor for } X\% \text{ Food or Beverage Cost } = 100/X$$

$$(\text{where } X \text{ equals the Desired Cost \%})$$

As is evidenced in the formula, divide 100 by the number representing the desired cost percentage, thus resulting in a factor. For example, you might seek a 30% food cost for your entrées or a 25% beverage cost for cocktails. **Markup factors** for these examples are calculated as follows:

$$\text{Markup Factor for 30\% Food Cost } = 100/30 = 3.33$$

$$\text{Markup Factor for 25\% Beverage Cost } = 100/25 = 4.0$$

The markup factors can be used to calculate prices by multiplying the food or beverage costs times the respective markup factor. For example, if seeking a 30% food cost, the following entrées would be marked up as illustrated in Table 8-3.

If you were interested in targeting a different food cost percentage—for instance, 40%—the markup factor would be calculated as follows:

$$\text{Markup Factor for 40\% Food Cost } = 100/40 = 2.5$$

TABLE 8-3
MARKUP FACTOR APPLIED TO ENTRÉES TO ACHIEVE 30% FOOD COST PERCENTAGE

Entrée	Food Cost	Markup Factor	Menu Price
Dungeness crab cakes	$8.53	3.33	$28.40
Grilled tuna steak	7.47	3.33	24.88
Catch of the day	6.56	3.33	21.84
Cioppino	6.93	3.33	23.08
Steak *frites*	7.45	3.33	24.81
Grilled veal loin chop	9.21	3.33	30.67
Free-range roast chicken	4.16	3.33	13.85
Cassoulet	4.78	3.33	15.92
Roasted vegetable risotto	3.43	3.33	11.42

TABLE 8-4
MARKUP FACTOR APPLIED TO ENTRÉES TO ACHIEVE 40% FOOD COST PERCENTAGE

Entrée	Food Cost	Markup Factor	Menu Price
Dungeness crab cakes	$8.53	2.5	$21.33
Grilled tuna steak	7.47	2.5	18.68
Catch of the day	6.56	2.5	16.40
Cioppino	6.93	2.5	17.33
Steak frites	7.45	2.5	18.63
Grilled veal loin chop	9.21	2.5	23.03
Free-range roast chicken	4.16	2.5	10.40
Cassoulet	4.78	2.5	11.95
Roasted vegetable risotto	3.43	2.5	8.58

The resulting factor can then be applied as illustrated in Table 8-4.

Similarly, the markup factor for cocktails can be calculated as follows:

$$\text{Markup Factor for 25\% Beverage Cost} = 100/25 = 4.0$$

The resulting factor can then be applied as illustrated in Table 8-5.

For the sake of convenience, a table of markup factors can be calculated for future reference, as partially illustrated in Table 8-6.

TABLE 8-5
MARKUP FACTOR APPLIED TO COCKTAILS TO ACHIEVE 30% BEVERAGE COST

Cocktail	Beverage Cost	Markup Factor	Menu Price
Grey Goose martini	$2.15	4.0	$ 8.60
Hendrick's gin & tonic	2.96	4.0	11.84
Bacardi 8 Mojito	1.75	4.0	7.00
Woodford Reserve on the rocks	2.00	4.0	8.00
Rusty Nail	3.01	4.0	12.04
Caipirinha	1.97	4.0	7.88
Appletini	1.48	4.0	5.92
Absinthe	2.78	4.0	11.12
Amaretto di Saronno on the rocks	1.53	4.0	6.12

TABLE 8-6
TABLE OF MARKUP FACTORS

Target Cost (%)	Calculation	Markup Factor
20	100/20	5.0
25	100/25	4.0
30	100/30	3.33
35	100/35	2.86
40	100/40	2.5
45	100/45	2.22
50	100/50	2.0

EXERCISE 8-4
CALCULATING MARKUP FACTORS

Calculate markup factors for the following target cost percentages.

Target Cost (%)	Calculation	Markup Factor
22		
31		
34		
37		
42		
46		
55		

EXERCISE 8-5
USING MARKUP FACTORS

Apply markup factors to identify menu prices at various cost percentage targets.

Menu Item and Food Cost	25%	30%	35%	40%	45%
Guacamole appetizer ($2.58)					
Menudo ($1.19)					
Pozole ($0.89)					
Carnitas ($2.47)					
Tacos al Pastor ($2.11)					
Tamales ($1.83)					
Pastel de Tres Leches ($.94)					

There are two significant shortcomings to this pricing method:

- Whereas the method allows quick calculations, the results are not necessarily suitable for use. Closer examination of Table 8-4 indicates several entrees that are priced lower than what the market will bear. The calculation of the markups is mathematical, but not necessarily functional.
- Whereas the method accurately relates menu prices to the target food cost percentage, it fails to consider the contribution margins. As previously stated, it is aggregate of contribution margins that represent profit, not the targeted food cost percentage.

The second pricing method does not base final menu prices solely on target cost percentages. Rather, you first set a target profit objective and then use averaged markups to set appropriate prices. The method is sequential and based on the discipline of **cost-volume-profit analysis**. It is aptly referred to as **LogicPath™ pricing**.

LOGICPATH™ PRICING

LogicPath™ pricing begins with calculation of required sales to produce desired profit (DP) before income taxes and is achieved by applying cost-volume-profit analysis. Once the estimated target sales figure is calculated, average markups (AMU) are identified and used to suggest menu prices. The final step refines these suggestions into usable selling prices.

Cost-volume-profit (CVP) analysis recognizes the relationships among sales, variable and fixed cost behaviors, and varying levels of profit. It can be used for calculating breakeven point of a business, as well as sales volume required to produce various profit targets. The relevant basic assumptions when applying CVP to LogicPath™ pricing include

- the behavior of costs and revenues is linear and does not address discounts or economies of scale in production
- units sold equal units produced; there is no surplus production returned to inventory

To begin the study of LogicPath™ pricing, a series of new formulas is introduced. The first relevant CVP formulas are as follows:

$$\text{Contribution Rate (CR)} = 1 - \text{Variable Rate (VR)}$$

$$\text{Target sales} = [\text{Fixed Costs (FC)} + \text{Desired Profit (DP)}]/\text{Contribution Rate (CR)}$$

The steps to calculate sales required for desired profit are as follows:

DP Step 1: Specify desired profit (in dollars). This figure does not include the cost of income taxes, which are typically evaluated as a component of the owner's or shareholders' overall tax indebtedness.

DP Step 2: Set initial assumptions for check averages. These assumptions reflect the average amount you would like each customer to spend on food and beverages.

DP Step 3: Forecast guest traffic levels.

DP Step 4: Calculate variable rate. The *variable rate* is dependent on the sum of variable costs. Variable costs typically include cost of food and beverages, hourly wages, benefits and payroll taxes on hourly wages, certain direct operating expenses, a portion of general and administrative expenses, and utility costs related to guest traffic. The more accurate the classification of variable costs, the higher quality the overall projection of variable rate will be. Variable rate can be calculated by adding the rates of all variable cost components.

DP Step 5: Calculate contribution rate.

DP Step 6: Total all fixed costs. *Fixed costs* typically include certain direct operating expenses, music and licensing fees, corporate overhead, marketing expenses, the major fraction of utility costs, repairs and maintenance, depreciation, a portion of general and administrative expenses, interest on loans, and possible other expenses. The more accurate the classification of fixed costs, the higher quality the overall projection will be.

DP Step 7: Calculate annual sales required to produce desired profit.

DP Step 8: Reconcile initial assumptions and requirements, and revise plans if the variance is excessive.

This eight-step process is best understood by a hypothetical example, as illustrated in Case Study 8-1.

Once you have identified target sales to achieve desired profit, you can calculate the total **average markup (AMU)** required from menu item sales and use the calculations to set menu prices.

AMU Step 1: Calculate the sum of all variable costs other than food and beverage costs, plus fixed costs, plus desired profit.

CASE STUDY 8-1A *APPLYING COST-VOLUME-PROFIT ANALYSIS TO CALCULATE REQUIRED SALES*

The *Urban Vineyard Café* is a 40-seat restaurant startup. The owner realistically seeks a modest return on sales and does not intend to extract a salary during the first 18 months of operations. The business serves dinner only, and operates 6 days per week, each week of the year. Every night, the menu feature five *prix fixe* meal selections and a value-priced rotating wine list of five wines by the glass and five bottle choices.

DP Step 1: Specify desired profit (in dollars).
The owner seeks Year 1 desired profit (DP) equal to or in excess of $65,000 prior to income taxes.

DP Step 2: Set initial assumptions for check averages.
The owner believes she can obtain an average of $25.00 in food sales and $15.00 in beverage sales per cover.

DP Step 3: Forecast guest traffic levels.
The owner forecasts 1.5 turns of the dining room, generating 60 covers per day. If this occurs, daily sales volume can be calculated as follows:

$$\text{Daily Sales} = 60 \text{ covers} \times (\$25.00 \text{ average food sales} + \$15.00 \text{ average beverage sales})$$
$$= \$2,400.00$$

DP Step 4: Calculate variable rate.
For this study, the only costs/expenses considered to be variable are food cost, beverage cost, payroll, benefits, and payroll taxes.
The owner believes she can achieve a 32.4% (0.324) combined cost of food and beverage sales.
To service the anticipated guest traffic levels, the owner plans the following staffing model:

Staff Position	Hours per Daily Shift	Hourly Wage	Shift Payroll Cost
Chef d'Cuisine	8	$23.00	$184.00
Line cook	8	16.00	128.00
Prep cook	8	14.00	112.00
Warewasher	8	9.00	72.00
Dining room supervisor	6	12.00	72.00
Bartender	6	12.00	72.00
Server	6	2.25	13.50
Server	6	2.25	13.50
Server	6	2.25	13.50
Total Daily Payroll			**$680.50**

In addition to payroll, the owner must account for benefits and payroll taxes. Based on prevailing tax rates and the benefits she offers, this equals an additional 29% of payroll, calculated as follows:

$$\text{Daily Benefits and Payroll Taxes} = 0.29 \times \$680.50 = \$197.35$$

Total daily payroll cost and total daily benefits and payroll taxes can be calculated by adding $680.50 and $197.35, which equal $877.85. This sum, if divided by the anticipated daily sales, provides the forecasted labor cost percentage, as follows[7]:

$$\text{Labor Cost Percentage (stated as a decimal)} = \$877.85/\$2,400 = 0.36577$$

Variable rate can be calculated by adding together the rates of all variable cost components, in this case, combined food and beverage cost percentages and labor cost percentage, as follows:

$$\text{Variable rate (VR)} = 0.324 + 0.36577 = 0.68977$$

CASE STUDY 8-1A *CONTINUED*

DP Step 5: Calculate contribution rate.
As discussed previously,

$$\text{Contribution Rate} = 1 - \text{Variable Rate}$$

and for this example is calculated as follows:

$$\text{Contribution Rate (CR)} = 1 - 0.68977 = 0.31023$$

DP Step 6: Total all fixed costs.
The owner identified the following annualized costs that do not vary even when sales increase or decrease:

Direct operating expenses	$33,696.00
Music licensing and royalties	1,497.60
Marketing expenses	11,232.00
Utilities	20,966.40
Occupancy cost	44,179.20
Repairs and maintenance	11,980.80
Depreciation	14,976.00
General and administrative expenses	19,468.80
Interest on loans	8,236.80
Other expenses	6,739.20
Total Fixed Costs	**$172,972.80**

In reality, portions of Direct Operating Expenses and Utilities vary as customer traffic increases or decreases. The ability to isolate and allocate these expenses involves sub-metering water flow, counting non-edible consumables per cover, and other minute calculations that may be beneficial, but are outside of the scope of this example.

DP Step 7: Calculate annual sales required to produce desired profit.
As previously explained:

$$\text{Target sales} = [\text{Fixed Costs (FC)} + \text{Desired Profit (DP)}]/\text{Contribution Rate (CR)}$$

Applying the formula to this example:

$$\text{Target Sales} = (\$172,972.80 + \$65,000)/0.31023 = \$767,085.06$$

DP Step 8: Reconcile initial assumptions and requirements, and revise plans if the variance is excessive.
Sales required to generate the desired annual profit for Year 1 ($65,000) equal $767,085.06, or $2,458.61 per day for each of the 312 days the restaurant operates. A variance of 2.44% ($58.61 per day) exists between the initial assumptions (DP Step 3) and the required sales (DP Step 7). The owner believes her assumptions were sufficiently modest and the variance will not actually occur. As such, she elects to proceed with her plan to generate $767,085.06 in combined food and beverage sales.

AMU Step 2: Divide the sum obtained in AMU Step 1 by the number of operating days per year.

AMU Step 3: Allocate required gross profit across menu categories as an average markup.

AMU Step 4: Refine calculations into usable selling prices.

This four-step process is best understood as a continuation (Case Study 8-1b) of the hypothetical example illustrated in Case Study 8-1a.

CASE STUDY 8-1B *APPLYING AVERAGE MARKUP TO ACHIEVE*

DESIRED PROFIT

Using a set of assumptions, the owner of the *Urban Vineyard Café* estimated that she must sell $767,085.06 in her first year to obtain desired Year 1 profit of $65,000.00. She wants to price her food and beverage menus so that forecasted traffic produces the contribution to cover all costs and provide desired profit.

AMU Step 1: Calculate the sum of all variable costs other than food and beverage costs, plus fixed costs, plus desired profit.

Annual payroll (from DP Step 4)	$273,889.20
$877.85 daily payroll × 312 days	
Annual fixed costs (from DP Step 6)	172,972.80
Desired profit	65,000.00
Total	**$511,862.00**

AMU Step 2: Divide the sum obtained in AMU Step 1 by the number of operating days per year.

$$\$511,862.00/312 = \$1,640.58$$

This is the total daily gross profit that must be generated by all items combined.

AMU Step 3: Allocate required gross profit across menu categories as an average markup.

For this simplified example, the owner has identified three menu categories. She forecasts menu mix and costs for each category. The calculations for *prix fixe* food are as follows:

	Unit/Recipe Cost	Daily Menu Mix Forecast	Total Daily Cost
Prix fixe meal 1	$7.00	11	$77.00
Prix fixe meal 2	8.00	13	104.00
Prix fixe meal 3	5.00	7	35.00
Prix fixe meal 4	9.00	23	207.00
Prix fixe meal 5	10.00	6	60.00
Total		**60**	**$483.00**

The food cost percentage used for planning during cost-volume-profit (CVP) calculations equaled 32.4% (0.324). Possessing the forecasted menu mix and accompanying theoretical food cost ($483.00), the following calculations are enabled:

$$\text{Required Food Sales} = \text{Food Cost/Food Cost \% (expressed as a decimal)}$$
$$\$1490.74 = \$483.00/0.324$$

If $1490.74 in food sales is sought and theoretical food cost for the menu mix ($483.00) is known, then the following calculation is enabled:

Sales	$1,490.47
−Cost	483.00
Gross Profit	$1,007.74

The *gross profit* is the difference between total sales and total cost of sales. In this instance and at this menu mix, it equals the difference between anticipated daily food sales minus the theoretical food cost. By allocating this difference among the menu items as markups, each item contributes to paying expenses, and (one hopes) leaving a remainder as profit. **The key to the LogicPath™ pricing method is the averaging of markups and distributing them equally within respective categories.** In this example, the following calculation is used for *prix fixe* meals:

$$\text{Average Markup} = \frac{\text{Gross Profit}}{\text{Units Sold}} = \frac{\$1,007.74}{60} = \$16.80$$

CASE STUDY 8-1B *CONTINUED*

	Unit/Recipe Cost	Average Markup	Menu Price	Total Sales	Cost (%)
Prix fixe meal 1	$7.00	$16.80	$23.80	$261.75	29.4
Prix fixe meal 2	8.00	16.80	24.80	322.34	32.3
Prix fixe meal 3	5.00	16.80	21.80	152.57	22.9
Prix fixe meal 4	9.00	16.80	25.80	593.30	34.9
Prix fixe meal 5	10.00	16.80	26.80	160.77	37.3
Total				$1,490.74	

The average markup is added to each item's food cost to suggest a menu price. It is important to note that although this is only a forecast, no matter what items are eventually selected by diners, the same markup results and contributes to paying expense and profit. It should also be noted that whereas 32.4% was used for overall planning, no single item equals that particular percentage. Had this percentage been applied uniformly to each menu item (using the factored markup method), the following results would have occurred:

	Unit/ Recipe Cost	Factored Markup Method	Factored Markup Method Cost (%)	Daily Menu Mix Forecast	Total Sales	Gross Profit
Prix fixe meal 1	$7.00	$21.60	32.4	11	$237.65	$160.65
Prix fixe meal 2	8.00	24.69	32.4	13	320.99	216.99
Prix fixe meal 3	5.00	15.43	32.4	7	108.02	73.02
Prix fixe meal 4	9.00	27.78	32.4	23	638.89	431.89
Prix fixe meal 5	10.00	30.86	32.4	6	185.19	125.19
Total				60	$1,490.74	$1,007.74

Using the factored markup method, the same total cost and sales would result, but individual menu prices would be different. The inherent power of the LogicPath™ pricing method is in its guarantee of planned contribution margins per item regardless of the actual menu mix For example, if the following menu mix happened, the results would be as follows:

	Unit/Recipe Cost	Daily Menu Mix Forecast	Total Daily Cost
Prix fixe meal 1	$7.00	25	$175.00
Prix fixe meal 2	8.00	10	80.00
Prix fixe meal 3	5.00	17	85.00
Prix fixe meal 4	9.00	4	36.00
Prix fixe meal 5	10.00	4	40.00
Total		60	$416.00

	Unit/ Recipe Cost	Factored Markup Method	Factored Markup Method Cost (%)	Daily Menu Mix Forecast	Total Sales	Gross Profit
Prix fixe meal 1	$7.00	$21.60	32.4	25	$540.12	$365.12
Prix fixe meal 2	8.00	24.69	32.4	10	246.91	166.91
Prix fixe meal 3	5.00	15.43	32.4	17	262.35	177.35
Prix fixe meal 4	9.00	27.78	32.4	4	111.11	75.11
Prix fixe meal 5	10.00	30.86	32.4	4	123.46	83.46
Total				60	$1,283.95	$867.95

Note that although 60 meals are sold, the gross profit is nowhere near that achieved with the average markup calculations. If there is concern that a menu mix may result in diminished gross profit, the LogicPath™ pricing method can buffer the impact. Every

CASE STUDY 8-1B *CONTINUED*

item sold within a category is equally profitable, and the same financial impact results regardless of the diners' selections. The converse is also true. By natural selection, certain menu mixes could result in gross profit that is higher than might be achieved with the LogicPath™ pricing method. You must decide what level of risk and uncertainty you are willing to accept, and adopt a pricing method that supports your perspective.

Another consideration is the impact this pricing method has on price ranges. Using the LogicPath™ pricing method, you compress price ranges, as compared to other pricing methods. Using the data set from this case study, the following data ranges can be observed for:

	Factored Markup Method	Average Markup Method
High price	$30.86	$24.47
Low price	15.43	19.47
Range	15.43	5.00

Each menu category should be priced according to a target cost percentage, which when paired with respective unit/recipe costs provides an average markup to be added to the costs. It is typical, although not necessary, to select differing cost percentages for each category to guide pricing. In this example, the following costs percentages are used:

	Guide Cost (%)
Prix fixe meals	32.4
Bottled wines	40.0
Wines by the glass	31.0

Calculations for bottled wines in this case study are as follows:

	Unit/Recipe Cost	Daily Menu Mix Forecast	Total Daily Cost
Bottled wine 1	$7.00	4	$28.00
Bottled wine 2	11.00	3	33.00
Bottled wine 3	15.00	2	30.00
Bottled wine 4	7.00	5	35.00
Bottled wine 5	22.00	1	22.00
Total		15	$148.00

	Unit/ Recipe Cost	Average Markup	Menu Price	Total Sales	Cost (%)	Factored Markup Method	Factored Markup Method Cost (%)	Factored Markup Method Daily Menu Mix Forecast	Factored Markup Method Total Sales	Factored Markup Method Gross Profit
Bottled wine 1	$7.00	$14.80	$21.80	$87.20	32.1	$17.50	40.0	4	$70.00	$42.00
Bottled wine 2	11.00	14.80	25.80	77.40	42.6	27.50	40.0	3	82.50	49.50
Bottled wine 3	15.00	14.80	29.80	59.60	50.3	37.50	40.0	2	$75.00	45.00
Bottled wine 4	7.00	14.80	21.80	109.00	32.1	17.50	40.0	5	87.50	52.50
Bottled wine 5	22.00	14.80	36.80	36.80	59.8	55.00	40.0	1	55.00	33.00
Total				$370.00				15	$370.00	$222.00

	Comparative Analysis	
	Factored Markup Method	Average Markup Method
High price	$55.00	$36.80
Low price	17.50	21.80
Range	37.50	15.00

CASE STUDY 8-1B *CONTINUED*

Calculations for wines by the glass in this case study are as follows:

	Unit/Recipe Cost	Daily Menu Mix Forecast	Total Daily Cost
Wine by the glass 1	$1.25	26	$32.50
Wine by the glass 2	2.00	15	30.00
Wine by the glass 3	3.75	17	63.75
Wine by the glass 4	3.00	10	30.00
Wine by the glass 5	1.55	22	34.10
Total		90	$190.35

								Factored Markup Method		
	Unit/ Recipe Cost	Average Markup	Menu Price	Total Sales	Cost (%)	Factored Markup Method	Factored Markup Method Cost (%)	Daily Menu Mix Forecast	Total Sales	Gross Profit
Wine by the modifyglass 1	1.25	4.71	5.96	154.90	21.0	4.03	31.0	26	104.84	72.34
Wine by the glass 2	2.00	4.71	6.71	100.61	29.8	6.45	31.0	15	96.77	66.77
Wine by the glass 3	3.75	4.71	8.46	143.78	44.3	12.10	31.0	17	205.65	141.90
Wine by the glass 4	3.00	4.71	7.71	77.08	38.9	9.68	31.0	10	96.77	66.77
Wine by the glass 5	1.55	4.71	6.26	137.67	24.8	5.00	31.0	22	110.00	75.90
Total				$614.03				90	$614.03	$423.68

Comparative Analysis

	Factored Markup Method	Average Markup Method
High price	$12.10	$8.46
Low price	4.03	5.96
Range	8.06	2.50

Totals from all categories are as follows:

	Sales	Cost	Gross Profit	Cost (%)
Food	$1,490.74	$483.00	$1,007.74	32.4
Bottled wine	370.00	148.00	222.00	40.0
Wine by the glass	614.03	190.35	423.68	31.0
Total	$2,474.77	$821.35	$1,653.42	33.2

The results of this step (AMU Step 3) are as follows:

- Prices have now been calculated for each menu item within the three categories.

- Total daily food and beverage sales ($2,474.77) have now been forecasted for the anticipated 60 daily covers.

- Total daily gross profit ($1,653.42) has been calculated. This compares favorably with the goal set in AMU Step 2, and if achieved will result in desired profit as calculated with cost-volume-profit (CVP) analysis.

AMU Step 4: Refine calculations into usable selling prices.
After completing AMU Step 3, you will have obtained suggested prices in raw form. You should evaluate the results and modify them into usable prices. You may choose to raise certain or all prices with the knowledge that your desired profit (refer to DP Step 1)

CASE STUDY 8-1B *CONTINUED*

will be preserved (and enhanced). You might selectively raise certain prices based on your intuition and knowledge of the market. Cents should be rounded upward to increments you have already settled on ($0.05; $0.25; whole dollars). For example, the prices calculated for the *prix fixe* meals might be modified as follows:

	Menu Price from AMU Step 4	Menu Price from AMU Step 5
Prix fixe meal 1	$23.80	$24.00
Prix fixe meal 2	24.80	25.00
Prix fixe meal 3	21.80	22.00
Prix fixe meal 4	25.80	26.00
Prix fixe meal 5	26.80	27.00

Most important, you should now possess a set of prices that make sense to your intended market, and support your overall theme and concept.

EXERCISE 8-6
APPLYING CVP ANALYSIS TO IDENTIFY REQUIRED SALES

The *Burger Shack* is a beachside carryout restaurant with no indoor seating or table service. The owner seeks a modest return on sales and does not intend to extract a salary during the first 12 months of operations. The business provides walkup service from noon until 9:00 PM, and operates 6 days per week, 50 weeks of the year. The menu features burgers, hand-cut french fries, and onion rings. The price of each burger includes a side of fries, an onion ring, and a medium-size beverage.

Owner's Assumptions:

- Year 1 desired profit (DP) ≥ $55,000.

- The owner believes he can obtain an average cover of $8.00 in food and soft-drink sales (no alcohol will be sold, so no beverage revenue is forecasted).

- The owner forecasts 300 covers per day.

- For this exercise, the only costs/expenses considered to be variable are food cost, payroll, benefits, and payroll taxes. The owner believes he can achieve a 36.0% (0.36) food cost.

- The following staffing model will be used each day the *Burger Shack* is open:

Staff Position	Hours per Daily Shift	Hourly Wage	Shift Payroll Cost
Grill cook 1	8	$10.00	$80.00
Grill cook 2	8	10.00	80.00
Grill cook 3	8	10.00	80.00
Prep cook 1	8	10.00	80.00
Prep cook 2	8	10.00	80.00
Cashier 1	8	10.00	80.00
Cashier 2	8	10.00	80.00

- Benefits and payroll taxes equal an additional 24% of payroll.

- Fixed costs for Year 1 equal as follows:

Direct operating	$61,000.00
Music	—
Marketing	$15,000.00
Utilities	19,000.00
Occupancy cost	35,000.00
Repairs and maintenance	8,800.00
Depreciation	16,000.00
Other expenses/income	—
General and administrative	19,000.00
Corporate overhead	—
Interest	8,200.00
Other expenses	18,000.00

Q1   Based on the owner's assumptions, calculate the sales required to generate his desired profit for Year 1.

Q2   How does this figure compare with initial assumptions? What impact will this have on the proposed average check?

EXERCISE 8-7
USING LOGICPATH™ PRICING TO DETERMINE MENU PRICES

The Bubble Bar forecasts the following daily sales of champagne by the glass. Use LogicPath™ pricing to calculate menu prices, assuming a 30% beverage cost and at least $1,000 daily gross profit from this menu category.

Menu Item	Unit/Recipe Cost (per glass)	Daily Menu Mix Forecast
NV *Gruet Brut* New Mexico	$2.40	40
Santa Margherita Prosecco Brut Valdobbiadene	4.40	15
NV Roederer Estate *Brut* Estate Anderson Valley	3.60	30
Brice *Brut Tradition*	6.00	25
NV *Domaine Chandon Blanc de Noirs Carneros*	3.00	20

OTHER PRICING APPROACHES

Rather than using cost-based or profit-based calculations as a foundation for pricing, many operators set their prices in relation to their competitors. Certainly, there is logic to knowing the prices your competitors charge; however, their expense structure and business objectives may allow them to set prices lower than you. For example, they may own their property, whereas you lease yours. They may employ family members within a unique payroll scheme, whereas you may have a more typical labor/payroll structure. It is understandable to seek a pricing advantage within your competitive set; however, you should not succumb to this intent unless it covers all costs and desired profit. You may be attempting to compete in a market where you will not succeed, or more optimistically, your quality and consistency will transform you into a market favorite regardless of price competition.

ACCEPTABLE TACTICS FOR CHANGING PRICES OVER TIME

Inflation is a cyclical tendency of markets. When your costs of ingredients, labor, operations, occupancy, and taxes increase, you must decide if raising prices is appropriate.

(*Source:* Fotolia)

If this becomes the action you choose to take, then you must decide how to present it to your customers. Some customers are prone to defect when prices for the same items appear to have increased overnight. Perhaps the best approach to raising prices involves framing the changes within the context of a new menu deployment. Daily menus, weekly menus, and seasonal menus all provide the vehicle for price changes without raising too many eyebrows.

It is not recommended that you diminish portion sizes as an alternative to raising prices. In doing so, you run the risk of customers leaving hungry, or at least watching established favorites shrink before their own eyes. If you decide your portions are too large, then that is one reason to modify them, but do not do so as a response to pricing issues.

ACTION TOOLKIT

Food service operators must continuously scan the spectrum of menus inside and outside their market. The following links allow you to peruse and analyze hundreds of menus as well as the contexts they are offered within:

- Distinguished Restaurants of North America
  www.dirona.com/
- menupix.com
  www.menupix.com/dc/index.php
- OpenTable
  www.opentable.com/home.aspx

The following publications present additional scholarly perspectives on menu pricing:

- Barrows, C. W. (1993). "Marketing for Maximization." *Journal of Restaurant & Foodservice Marketing, 1052–214X, 1*(1):75–88.
- Carmen, J., and Norkus, G. (1990). "Pricing Strategies for Menus: Magic or Myth?" *Cornell Hotel and Restaurant Administration Quarterly 31*(3):44–50.
- Frode A., and Sharma, A. (2010). "Locally Produced Food in Restaurants: Are the Customers Willing to Pay a Premium and Why?" *International Journal of Revenue Management 4*(3/4):238–258.
- Mooney, S. (1994). "Planning and Designing the Menu." In Jones, P., and Merricks, P. (Eds.), *The Management of Foodservice Operations*. London: Cassell, pp. 45–58.
- Pavesic, D. (1989). "Psychological Aspects of Menu Pricing." *International Journal of Hospitality Management 8*(1):43–49.
- ———. (1983). "Cost-Margin Analysis: A Third Approach to Menu Pricing and Design." *International Journal of Hospitality Management 2*(3):127–134.

GLOSSARY

Corkage fees   fees charged to customers by restaurants for service of wine that customers have been permitted to bring into the restaurant to accompany their meal.

Cost-volume-profit analysis   a cost accounting model that recognizes the relationships among sales, variable and fixed cost behaviors, and varying levels of profit. It can be used for calculating breakeven point of a business, as well as sales volume required to produce various profit targets.

Elastic demand   demand for a good or service that changes when prices charged for those goods or services changes.

Equilibrium price   the price at which the supply of an item equals the quantity demanded by the market. Also referred to as *market-clearing price.*

Factored markup pricing method   a pricing method that multiplies factors by food cost to determine menu prices.

Fixed cost   a cost that does not change, even as sales volume increase or decreases.

Food-cost percentage   a mathematical relationship between food cost and food sales calculated as follows:

$$\text{Food-Cost Percentage (\%)}$$
$$= [\text{Food Cost (\$)}/\text{Menu Price (\$)}] \times 100$$

Inclusive price   the amount charged to customers that includes the menu price and all surcharges, supplements, taxes, and gratuities.

Inelastic demand   demand for a good or service that does not change when prices charged for those goods or services changes.

LogicPath™ pricing   a sequential pricing method based on cost-volume-profit analysis that identifies a target profit objective and then use averaged markups to set appropriate prices.

Marginal analysis pricing   a pricing model that relates the impact on sales and marginal profit as price varies. If elasticity of demand can be predicted accurately, then the model will identify the optimum price point for a menu item.

Marginal profit   in the marginal analysis pricing model, the remainder after variable costs and fixed costs have been subtracted from sales.

Market-clearing price   the price at which the supply of an item equals the quantity demanded by the market. Also referred to as *equilibrium price.*

Markup factor   used to calculate prices by multiplying the food or beverage costs times the respective markup factor.

Price elasticity of demand   the degree that the quantity demanded for a good or service changes in relation to changes in its price.

Supplement   an upcharge added to a menu price as the result of the customer's selection of one or more additional ingredients. Also referred to as an *add-on* or *surcharge.*

Variable costs   those costs that increase or decrease proportionately as sales volume increases or decreases.

Wine program   the dimensions that characterize how you approach wine sales, including the scope and character of your wines, the pricing scheme you develop, the glassware you use, and the protocol your staff uses to serve their customers.

ENDNOTES

1. See thinkexist.com/quotation/if_more_of_us_valued_food_and_cheer_and_song/212634.html; accessed May 1, 2011.

2. See thinkexist.com/search/searchquotation.asp?search=What+is+a+cynic%3F+A+man+who+knows+the+price+of+everything+and+the+value+of+nothing; accessed May 1, 2011.

3. See thinkexist.com/search/searchquotation.asp?search=%93The+true+way+to+gain+much%2C+is+never+to+desire+to+gain+too+much.%94; accessed May 1, 2011.

4. An example of a *competitive market* is an urban or suburban commercial corridor with a variety of dining options within close proximity. An example of a *non-competitive market* is in an airline cabin. Those passengers who want to drink alcoholic beverages have only one choice—to purchase from the flight attendant.

5. The only variable costs this model considers are food or beverage costs, and the only fixed costs this model considers are those directly necessary to produce/sell/serve this item.

6. Frode A., and Sharma, A. (2010). "Locally Produced Food in Restaurants: Are the Customers Willing to Pay a Premium and Why?" *International Journal of Revenue Management* 4(3/4):238–258.

7. In actual practice, where the staffing model varies throughout the year, the calculation of labor cost percentage should be based on the annual sum of each day's labor-related costs and that year's sales forecast.

9
Communicating with Menus

(*Source:* Fotolia)

Objectives

Upon completion of this chapter, you should be able to:

9.1 Evaluate menus for effective communications.

9.2 Explain how standards of identity and truth-in-menu legislation provide guidance for factual menu communications.

9.3 Author consumer advisories to caution guests against menu item hazards.

9.4 Explain conditions under which nutrition labeling must be provided on menus.

9.5 Apply nutrition labeling guidelines and rules to list menu item nutrient content claims and health claims appropriately.

9.6 Discuss and apply key principles of descriptive menu content and imagery.

9.7 Discuss and apply key principles of menu organization.

9.8 Identify principles of menu layout and design, and the impact on customer purchase decisions.

9.9 Discuss best practices in the structure and design of wine lists.

9.10 Discuss the scope and merchandizing features of menu communications media.

EFFECTIVE COMMUNICATIONS

"Effective communication is 20% what you know and 80% how you feel about what you know."

—JIM ROHN[1]

(*Source:* Thinglass/Shutterstock)

The primary objective of your menus is to clearly communicate intended visual and narrative messages to customers. In addition, your menus should stimulate imagination and provide sufficient information for your customers to make purchase decisions. Every menu should be designed so diners are enticed to order those particular items you specifically want them to purchase. Most important, once you have determined your prices, you must use menus to transform your strategic objectives and marketing plan into a vehicle for realizing optimal revenue streams.

If customers are able to envision each menu selection's characteristics during the selection process, then they can quickly filter out those items that do not appeal to them, and are thus left with potential choices. It is important to customers (and therefore to you) that decision making is supported with sufficient information so that ultimate selections meet or exceed expectations. You must use language, graphics, and menu design in a calculated and thoughtful manner. Consider the description from a successful chain restaurant menu shown in Figure 9-1.

Several expectations are likely to have been created by the language used in this menu. Every word has the power to conjure sensory images in your customers' minds.

Asiago Crusted Chicken

Tender breasts of chicken seasoned with Italian herbs and freshly shredded Asiago cheese. Flash-fried to crispy perfection in olive oil and served over a steaming portion of vermicelli pasta and our homestyle pomodoro sauce.

Figure 9-1

Example of Menu Item Description

Asiago-crusted . . .	A savory flavor evocative of asiago cheese should be noticeable in a crust that is discernable by sight (color) or crisp texture.
Tender breasts . . .	The meat should not be tough or chewy, and there should be more than one breast portion.
. . . flash-fried to crispy perfection . . .	Infers that a high level of culinary attention is lavished in the preparation, yielding a superior cooked product.
. . . steaming portion of vermicelli pasta . . .	Customers who are familiar with this ingredient anticipate a portion of pasta that is thinner than typical spaghetti noodles.

Not every customer will envision these attributes, but the example highlights the need for you to deliver what you imply. In addition, you should be careful not to present surprises that weren't expressly communicated. In this example, customers expect olive oil to be used. In addition, you should be careful not to present surprises that are not expressly communicated. Do not substitute ingredients, because your diners may have food allergies, sensitivities, or specific reasons for their selections. Although it is difficult to define a universal list, there are certain ingredients that should be listed expressly in print, or otherwise not included in the recipe:

Highly seasoned or heavily spiced ingredients	Certain diners seek out highly flavored dishes, yet others cannot tolerate them. For many customers, this would be an unwelcome surprise if not forewarned through menu language.
Ingredients generally recognized as allergens	As discussed later in this chapter, you should disclose the presence of those ingredients that may prompt allergic reactions, and you should request that diners inform your staff of their specific food allergies.
Other ingredients that are generally unexpected based on the menu description	Example: Most customers do not expect a menu item listed as *Traditional Chicken Paella* to contain shellfish stock.

Certainly, there are exceptions to this rule. In some cases, intentionally vague descriptions are used to create intrigue and (one hopes) delight. As emphasized throughout this textbook, you must align your merchandizing concept with your target market. If, in the case of Figure 9-2, the operator has been successful in this alignment, then he or she will attract diners who are eager for surprises and find the menu language alluring rather than obscure. The wrong match of communications strategy and clientele, however, could be disastrous when unconventional communication approaches such as this are employed.

You must refrain from such negative language or admonishments as *We are not responsible for fish cooked beyond medium doneness* or *No substitutions*. Humor can be a wonderful thing; however, you must be careful not to offend when you are attempting to titillate. (I recall eating in a chain restaurant whose menu stated: "If you want yer steak cooked Well Done, then you came to the wrong place.") If customers want ketchup on their hot dogs, or their steaks cooked well done, then they should not be made to feel churlish. Printed words can be potent and should be used selectively. Certain disclosures are important, but they should be framed in a positive manner or reserved for verbal communication. As much as possible, dining should be a respite for your guests from the realities of the day.

You should avoid the use of dollar signs ($) if possible. In fact, you should consider avoiding the use of the words *dollar* and *dollars*. Customers understand what *twenty-one fifty* or *6* refers to without monetary descriptors or symbols. Also, any price listing, although kept easily visible, should not be overemphasized or otherwise highlighted.

In summary, your menus enliven the relationship building that began with your advertising, continue when your guests walked through the door, and culminate with the decision whether to return. Your menus should reinforce your guests' visitation decisions and build confidence and comfort, rather than uncertainty. A well-communicated menu transitions your clientele onto the threshold of positive expectations, ready for the arrival of food and beverage.

10 Course	GTM

GTM

gtm 195
MARGARITA ceviche
CO2 grapefruit
CHICKENnoodle
GOLDEN twist ale
CLAM bake
YELLOW snow
NUAC man
BASEBALL snacks
ASTRONAUT tartare
CUBAN cigar
FOREST roll
SHABU shabuccino
VENISON & alium
CREPES that are cheese
FRITES frozen and fried
CURRY lime
BANANA split
ACME bombs
COOKIE crumbs
SODA float

Figure 9-2
10 *course grand tasting menu from Moto, Chicago, Illinois* (Source: Reprinted by permission of Homaro Cantu.)

TRUTH-IN-MENU

Providing accurate information is not only a strategic objective, but is also a legal requirement.

The typical complexity of commercial foodservice supply chains creates difficulty in identifying certain items. Food items that originate at farms, feedlots, or marine/inland fisheries and then travel through a maze of processing and packaging en route to the consumer may have their true identity confused or obscured. At any of these junctures, unscrupulous or uninformed actions can cause misrepresentation of products (for example: frozen, yet portrayed as fresh; mislabeled origin or species). To illustrate this point, in 2010, the Florida Department of Business and Professional Regulation cited 186 restaurants for mislabeling their fish. Certainly not all operators intentionally misrepresent their products; however, you as the final seller are required to advertise your menu factually, and you are subject to strict liability should you breach your responsibilities. A logical approach (where possible) is to shorten the supply chain by removing steps in the process. For example, if you purchase whole fish directly from commercially licensed fishermen (without intermediaries), it is more likely that the true species and waters where the fish were caught can be identified than if shipped across a variety of circuits. Conversely, if you are buying chilled fillets from a broad-line distributor, it is much more difficult to identify species, origin, and freshness. Most distributors provide reasonable assurance that your ingredients are exactly as portrayed; however, when you buy direct from local producers, you reduce the likelihood that intermediaries have obfuscated the provenance of your purchases.

(*Source:* Michael Blann/Thinkstock)

The Food Safety and Inspection Service (FSIS) of the U.S. Department of Agriculture (USDA) has developed standards of identity for dozens of food products; you can access them at www.access.gpo.gov/nara/cfr/waisidx_03/9cfr319_03.html. Figure 9-3 is an example of a federal standard of identity.

[Code of Federal Regulations]
[Title 9, Volume 2]
[Revised as of January 1, 2003]
From the U.S. Government Printing Office via GPO Access
[CITE: 9CFR319.80]

[Page 299]

TITLE 9—ANIMALS AND ANIMAL PRODUCTS
CHAPTER III   FOOD SAFETY AND INSPECTION SERVICE, DEPARTMENT OF AGRICULTURE
PART 319—DEFINITIONS AND STANDARDS OF IDENTITY OR COMPOSITION—
Table of Contents

Subpart C—Cooked Meats

Sec. 319.80 Barbecued meats.

Barbecued meats, such as product labeled "Beef Barbecue" or "Barbecued Pork," shall be cooked by the direct action of dry heat resulting from the burning of hard wood or the hot coals therefrom for a sufficient period to assume the usual characteristics of a barbecued article, which include the formation of a brown crust on the surface and the rendering of surface fat. The product may be basted with a sauce during the cooking process. The weight of barbecued meat shall not exceed 70 percent of the weight of the fresh uncooked meat.

Figure 9-3
Federal Standard of Identity for Barbequed meats

Figure 9-4
Federal Standard of Identity for Raisin bread, rolls, and buns

[Code of Federal Regulations]
[Title 21, Volume 2]
[Revised as of April 1, 2002]
From the U.S. Government Printing Office via GPO Access
[CITE: 21CFR136.160]

[Page 369]

TITLE 21—FOOD AND DRUGS
CHAPTER I—FOOD AND DRUG ADMINISTRATION, DEPARTMENT OF HEALTH
AND HUMAN SERVICES (CONTINUED)
PART 136—BAKERY PRODUCTS—Table of Contents

Subpart B—Requirements for Specific Standardized Bakery Products

Sec. 136.160 Raisin bread, rolls, and buns.

(a) Each of the foods raisin bread, raisin rolls, and raisin buns conforms to the definition and standard of identity and is subject to the requirements for label statement of ingredients prescribed for bread, rolls or buns by Sec. 136.110, except that:

(1) Not less than 50 parts by weight of seeded or seedless raisins are used for each 100 parts by weight of flour used.
(2) Water extract of raisins may be used, but not to replace raisins.
(3) The baked units may bear icing or frosting.
(4) The limitation prescribed by Sec. 136.110(c)(6) on the quantity and composition of milk and/or other dairy products does not apply.
(5) The total solids are determined by the method prescribed in Sec. 136.110(d), except that section 14.091(b) of "Official Methods of Analysis of the Association of Official Analytical Chemists," 13th Ed. (1980), which is incorporated by reference, will apply. Copies may be obtained from the Association of Official Analytical Chemists International, 481 North Frederick Ave., suite 500, Gaithersburg, MD 20877-2504, or may be examined at the Office of the Federal Register, 800 North Capitol Street, NW., suite 700, Washington, DC.

(b) The name of the food is "raisin bread", "raisin rolls", "raisin buns", as applicable. When the food contains not less than 2.56 percent by weight of whole egg solids, the name of the food may be "raisin and egg bread", "raisin and egg rolls", or "raisin and egg buns", as applicable, accompanied by the statement "Contains __ medium-sized egg(s) per pound" in the manner prescribed by Sec. 102.5(c)(3) of this chapter, the blank to be filled in with the number which represents the whole egg content of the food expressed to the nearest one-fifth egg but not greater than the amount actually present. For purposes of this regulation, whole egg solids are the edible contents of eggs calculated on a moisture-free basis and exclusive of any nonegg solids which may be present in standardized and other commercial egg products. One medium-sized egg is equivalent to 0.41 ounce of whole egg solids.

[42 FR 14400, Mar. 15, 1977, as amended at 47 FR 11826, Mar. 19, 1982; 49 FR 10096, Mar. 19, 1984; 54 FR 24894, June 12, 1989; 63 FR 14035, Mar. 24, 1998]

[[Page 370]]

The Food and Drug Administration (FDA) of the Department of Health and Human Services (DHHS) has also developed standards of identity for foods; you can access them at www.access.gpo.gov/nara/cfr/waisidx_02/21cfrv2_02.html. Figure 9-4 is an example of a federal standard of identity.

These definitions are used primarily by food manufacturers, but it is also prudent to verify that your own items are compliant, if there are standards for your ingredients and menu items. Perhaps a more valuable set of guidance involves **truth-in-menu** legislation, which require that any expressed or implied claims be substantiated with facts. Truth-in-menu legislation involves a mosaic of rules, laws, and statutes that collectively protect consumers against false advertising and breach of warranty. Violations are subject to civil and criminal penalties depending on the jurisdiction. For example, in Florida, the Department of Business and Professional Regulations imposes a $1,000 per incident fine for providing "false/misleading statements published or advertised relating to food/beverage."[2] In addition, some states allow for treble damages so as to punish those who break the law in excess of the actual damage to the plaintiff. Of greater concern is the increasing incidence of serial plaintiffs, whose legal counsel initially secures judgment for *breach of statutory law* (breach of warranty), then secures other individuals with similar claims to injury and files a class action suit on behalf of these individuals. The results can be devastating, and you must protect yourself by avoiding unsubstantiated claims.

Menu claims involving portion size (weight, volume, and count), place of origin, preparation methods, qualitative attributes ("homemade," fresh," "aged," etc.), and health-related benefits must not mislead customer-purchase decisions.

- Ingredient identity claims are strict expressions. For example, "Pure vanilla extract" is not the same as a blend of natural and artificial vanilla.
- You must be clear when communicating the primary means of cooking. For example, "grilled" items must receive significant cooking on a grill, rather than simply receiving grill marks to be finished in an oven. (This technique is actually a practical means for handling volume production, but the term *grilled* should not be used.)
- A commercial establishment is very seldom a residence, so the term homemade is not appropriate; a more accurate term would be *homestyle, house-made,* or *made in-house.*
- Customers often equate place of origin with quality and are willing to pay a premium for it. For example, "Smoked Wild Scottish Salmon" is a very definitive description. Most customers expect the fish to have been caught and smoked in Scotland.
- Some claims, such as "World's Finest," are viewed as puffery, and no reasonable person would believe the claim as stated. Other claims, such as "Award Winning," are more closely scrutinized, and an award of some recognizable import should be available as proof.
- Some descriptors are loosely defined. "Dijon mustard," if produced anywhere besides Dijon, France, is not intentionally deceptive, as the name typically implies a style rather than place of origin.
- Weight of ingredients that you buy pre-portioned is particularly contentious. For example, you might purchase trimmed and ready-to-use "12-ounce strip steaks" delivered at refrigeration temperature in individual vacuum-sealed bags. Through natural wet-aging processes, the meat weeps and purges itself of blood and juices over time. Although the meat is not flawed, it has lost weight per portion. You would be mistaken to list the item as a 12-ounce portion if it really is lighter when it hits the grill. Your customers rely on the information you provide them (expressed on your menu), rather than specifications on vendor purchase orders or invoices they will never see.

CONSUMER ADVISORIES

You must accept the duty to provide disclosures, reminders, and advisories when food items may present a health risk because of food-borne pathogens. If meat, fish, poultry, shellfish, or eggs are served raw, undercooked, or cooked to order (e.g., customer specifications), a disclosure identifying the foods and a reminder must appear on the menu or in a written statement declaring that "consuming [the specified types of animal products] raw or undercooked may increase your risk of food-borne illness." You

EXERCISE 9-1
LISTING CONSUMER ADVISORIES

1. Scan the menu exhibits throughout this chapter. Based on your review, what menu items merit increased staff awareness and a printed or verbal advisory? Why?

2. Based on your assessment, develop appropriate consumer advisory language as needed.

should also consider providing cautionary statements for other foods on your menu. Some foods, although not inherently unsafe, are routinely identified as risks for specific populations. A partial list of cautionary statements to consider includes:

- "We use peanut and soybean oil in our kitchens."
- "Small bones are natural to this item and may be present."
- "Wines have been treated with sulfates."
- "Dishes with an * contain small amounts of added MSG."

It also is wise to put your customers on notice that information and answers are available and it their responsibility to ask if they have questions about preparations. One of several appropriate statements might include:

"Guests should alert their server to any food allergies prior to ordering."

Some jurisdictions have legislated the inclusion of cautionary statements. In 2009, St. Paul, Minnesota, took this decision away from operators by making it law that allergen information must be provided to restaurant diners, and that employees must be trained to prevent cross contact between allergenic and non-allergenic foods. Massachusetts followed suit in 2010.

Some companies, such as Panera Bread and Darden Restaurants, have elected to provide enhanced disclosures for a wide array of allergens, including wheat, peanuts, dairy products, eggs, and shellfish. Printed information is distributed on demand in several of their restaurants, and the information warns of allergens included in recipes as well as those that may be conveyed through cross-contamination from other foods on grill surfaces or in deep fryers.

NUTRITION LABELING

Research indicates that customers make healthier choices when nutritional information is included on menus. A 2010 study published in the *American Journal of Public Health* provides evidence that diners consume significantly fewer calories at dinner and afterward when the caloric value of entrees is listed on menus in tandem with information on how many calories they should consume.[3] Primary researcher Christina Roberto explained, "The reason menu labeling is so important is decisions in restaurants are not intuitive. At a lot of chain restaurants, some of the salads have more calories than the burgers." Roberto's research emphasizes the need for a reference (2,000 daily calorie intake for adults) so that restaurant diners can make decisions within a factual context. In another study, Stanford University Graduate School of Business researchers used Starbucks stores in New York City, Boston, and Philadelphia as data sources, and found that when calorie counts were posted for viewing by customers, there was a 14% reduction in calories of foods selected.[4] In addition, they found that there may be a competitive advantage to providing nutrition facts—Starbucks stores in close proximity (50 meters) of a competitor enjoyed increases in revenue as a result of their posting nutrition information.

Despite the consumer health benefits of nutrition labeling, many foodservices are resistant. The question bears asking, "Why don't operators take the initiative and disclose nutrition information rather than wait for a regulatory mandate?" Certainly, the question of where to begin and the fear of unknown territory inhibits some operators; however, others have chosen to move forward. Standardized system-wide menus enable chains and multiunit food service operators to channel corporate resources, and most casual, fast-casual, and quick-service chains have developed components for their Web sites whereby nutrition information helps customers make informed decisions prior to visiting the stores. Operators are increasingly electing to provide comprehensive nutrition in their stores (i.e., on site), even if they are not compelled by scale or immediate legislative requirements. McDonald's offers eight separate ways for customers to obtain nutrient information, including tray liners, a voice-activated toll-free phone number, as well as their Web site. In 2010, in advance of regulatory mandates, Panera Bread Company chose to post calorie counts voluntarily for its entire menu in all company-owned Panera Bread and St. Louis Bread Company stores nationwide. Burgerville, a quick-service chain located in the Pacific Northwest, recently adopted a novel means of disclosing nutrition information by printing calorie, protein, fat, carbohydrate counts, and recommended daily values on point-of-sale receipts. The receipts then guide customers to informed decisions on their future visits. Other companies, including Red Lobster, Olive Garden, Romano's Macaroni Grill, and Chili's, elected to deploy voluntary disclosure programs in advance of government mandates.

The reluctance on the part of many operators to communicate nutrition information is rooted in tradition of sorts. Restaurants in particular have been a bastion for iconoclasts and a place where moderation often defers to culinary indulgence. Some operators believe that printing words such as *cholesterol* or *calories* is antithetical to the aesthetic they are attempting to create. They believe that scientifically rooted measurements such as nutritional analyses run counter to the dining experiences they provide. Other operators merely have yet to learn how to analyze their menus or don't know where to begin.

Complicating matters, some food-service concepts feature dynamic menus that advertise items conceived within hours or minutes of service, and the calculation of nutrition information in those environments is a formidable challenge. More typical is a core menu planned in advance and used for several months to allow utility and "reuse" of the recipes and nutrient calculations, Daily menu changes create a daunting (yet achievable) task, but the cost (in both time and money) of conducting analyses

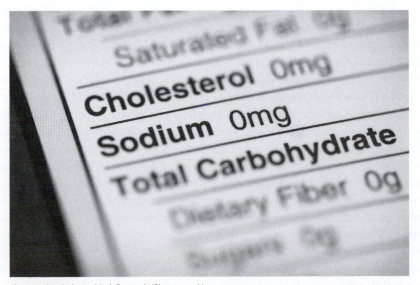

(*Source:* iStockphoto, Mark Poprocki/Shutterstock)

or contracting obtain this information may be prohibitive for small businesses. Conversely, multiunit operations benefit from the utility of using nutritional analyses in more than one location. Economies of scale are enjoyed by chains and they realize a more feasible cost–benefit ratio and competitive advantage than does an independent, single-location business. Government efforts to require nutrition labeling recognize this fact, and nearly all government mandates thus far are aimed at multiunit operators.

Several jurisdictions were pioneers in advancing the communication of nutrition information to customers. In 2008, New York City enacted a law requiring all restaurants with 15 or more units to post calorie information as prominently as the prices listed on their menus and menu boards. New Jersey enforces a similar law for companies with 20 or more units nationwide, whereby stores in that state must post calorie counts on menus and menu boards, with daily specials, temporary menu items, customized orders or food or beverage items from the salad bar as the only exceptions. These locations joined other jurisdictions including the states of Vermont, California, Maine, Oregon, and Massachusetts, and the localities of Nashville, Tennessee; Philadelphia; the counties of Albany, Schenectady, Nassau, Westchester, Suffolk, and Ulster in New York; King County in Washington; and Montgomery, Maryland, in the patchwork of governmental mandates to provide nutrition information to customers under various conditions. This has been particularly challenging for multiunit chains operating in different jurisdictions, each imposing a different labeling requirement.

Nationwide standardization to alleviate the local variation emerged as a solution. In 2010, public interest and the political will of federal legislators prompted sweeping and comprehensive changes to labeling laws. The Federal Patient Protection and Affordable Care Act contains a nutrition-disclosure provision[5] that amends the Food, Drug and Cosmetic Act by requiring the nation's 278,000 chain restaurants,[6] similar retail food establishments, and vending machines with 20 or more locations to provide evidence-based nutrition labeling information. The rule is broad in scope, and includes cafeteria-service, quick-service, full-service, coffee shops, snack bars, ice cream shops, pastry and confectionary stores, grocery stores, convenience stores, and food services within larger establishments (i.e., chain restaurants inside a big-box retail store). Exempted businesses include those whose primary business is not food service, including airlines, trains, hotels, amusement parks, and movie theaters.

Calories must be posted alongside corresponding menu items, on menus, menu boards, drive-through boards, and Web sites. Calories must be posted so as to be "clear and conspicuous." The color and size of the text and numerals as well as the background must mirror that of the item listing so as to facilitate readability. Also, salad bars, buffets, and other self-service items are required to provide caloric information. In addition to mandatory posting of total calories per portion, operations covered by this legislation must also provide evidence-based printed information on demand, including calories from fat, total fat, saturated fat, cholesterol, sodium, carbohydrates, sugars, dietary fiber, and total protein. Finally, as a benchmark to guide customer decision making, operations must post a succinct statement communicating recommended daily caloric intake. Some items, including alcoholic beverages, condiments on tables, custom orders (based on customer specifications), test items on the menu for less than 90 days during their market research period, and specials offered for less than 60 days (daily/weekly specials and "limited time offers") are exempted from the revised legislation. This federal act supersedes existing local and state laws that are less strenuous in their consumer protection. Industry leaders, including the National Restaurant Association, acknowledge that the revised legislation replaces the hodgepodge of regulations with one uniform standard that will be of particular value to businesses operating in multiple jurisdictions.

There are already concerns of untoward affects arising from the Federal Patient Protection and Affordable Care Act. Exemption for limited time offers (LTOs) may in fact motivate operators to augment their core menus more aggressively with *du jour* offerings that—absent of nutrient or health claims—do not require nutrition labeling. In fact, there is consumer and industry concern that this exemption serves as a loophole for operators desiring to offer high-calorie items for two-month cycles, and ostensibly fly under the regulatory radar screen. Other operator responses to mandatory labeling include "disassembly" of recipe items, where the central item is merchandized and nutritionally labeled on its own, and condiments and side dishes are merchandized as auxiliary add-ons. A strategy of this nature presents a superficially lower calorie count at first blush, although astute customers will understand that as ingredients are added to build their selections, nutritional totals also increase.

The provision of accurate nutrition information on restaurant menus is not without other problems. As opposed to manufacturing plants where process controls are more readily standardized, restaurants are prone to deviation in ingredient composition, inconsistency of portioning, and variation in recipe testing for nutritional analyses. In fact, many chain restaurants provide erroneous information and understated calorie counts in their menu postings. A 2009 research study of 10 chain restaurants indicated that, on average, the number of calories in 29 meals or other menu items was 18% higher than listed.[7] The federal government does not verify nor does it police nutritional claims provided by restaurants. Consequently, mistakes are made and they go unchallenged. Chapter 7 discusses solutions for conducting nutritional analyses. Also, several companies specialize in assisting restaurants in their quest to provide accurate nutrition information by providing user-friendly Web-based resources partnered with the services of registered dietitians (Figure 9-5).

Preliminary research, although not conclusive or comprehensive, indicates that many customers, once made aware of the nutritional value of their menu options, select healthier items even if they are priced higher. Consequently, despite the regulatory obligations, food-labeling requirements may actually be a revenue driver for businesses.

Nutrient content and health benefit claims are subject to federal law. Under the Federal Nutrition Labeling and Education Act (NLEA) of 1990 and the final regulations to implement the NLEA (1993), nutrient claims on restaurant menus are highly regulated. If a restaurant makes a claim regarding nutrient content ("fat free," etc.), relative amounts of a nutrient ("low fat," etc.), or health claims ("heart healthy," etc.), they automatically invoke the labeling and notification requirements of the Act. This involves conducting a "reasonable basis determination" that the nutrition information it provides is accurate, and then making the nutrient information available to customers on request. The FDA is responsible for reviewing the accuracy of the content and whether the intent of the Act is being met by the restaurant, and may demand evidence from you if a complaint is filed.

Appendix A includes an extract from a compliance and reference guide prepared especially for restaurants and retail establishments.

EXERCISE 9-2
ADVERTISING HEALTH BENEFIT AND NUTRIENT CONTENT CLAIMS

Q1 Review the following recipes. Using Appendix A, identify if any nutrient content claims or health claims (light, heart healthy, low fat, etc.) can be published on the menu for these items. If so, use appropriate language for your descriptions.

Q2 Do portion sizes conform with RACC (**reference amounts customarily consumed**) standard reference amounts? If not, what impact does this have on your ability to advertise nutrition claims?

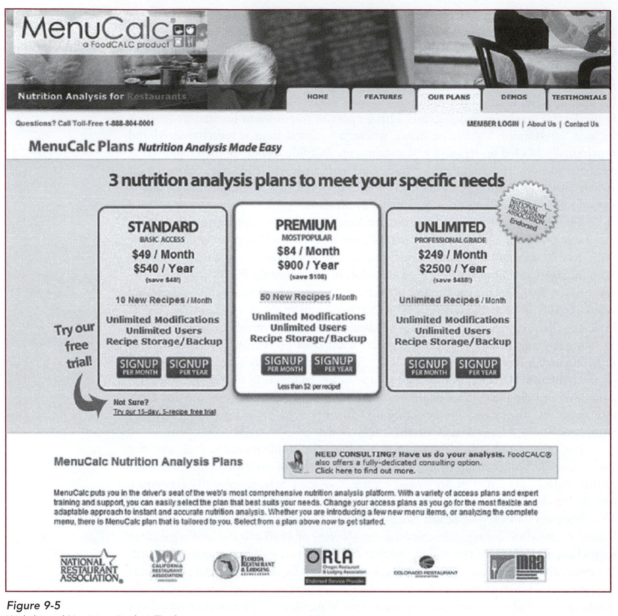

Figure 9-5
Web-based Nutrition AnalysisTool   (*Source*: Reprinted by permission of FoodCALC.)

Cobb Salad

- 3 extra-large hard-boiled eggs, peeled and chopped
- 8 slices bacon
- 1 head romaine lettuce, torn into bite-size pieces
- 4 cups cooked chicken, diced
- 2 avocados, peeled and diced
- 2 tomatoes, chopped
- 4 ounces blue-veined (Roquefort, etc.) cheese, crumbled

Dressing

- ½ teaspoon Dijon mustard
- ¼ cup red wine vinegar
- 1 teaspoon Worcestershire sauce
- 1 clove garlic, crushed
- ¼ teaspoon salt
- ½ teaspoon fresh-ground black pepper
- ½ cup olive oil

Yield = 4 entrée portions

Italian Wedding Soup
- 1 stewing chicken
- ½ cup celery, chopped
- ½ cup carrots, chopped
- ½ cup onion, chopped
- 1 tablespoon parsley, chopped
- 4 quarts water
- salt and pepper (to taste)
- 1 head escarole
- 1 cup pastina, uncooked

Meatballs
- 1 pound ground meat
- ½ cup Parmesan cheese, grated
- 3 extra-large eggs
- 3 tablespoons parsley
- ½ pound Italian-style pork sausage
- salt and pepper (to taste)
- 1 cup dry bread crumbs

Yield = 15 entrée portions

DESCRIPTIVE MENU CONTENT AND IMAGERY

The preceding discussion has focused on insightful and disciplined practices to prevent misinformation and limit your liability. The next step in menu development is to create narrative content, graphics, organization, and design to prompt strategic customer purchases. Your objective at this stage is to create descriptive and visual imagery to "excite the imagination," or at the very least, stimulate confident purchase decisions.

Menu copy includes information about your business, the list of food items, headings, descriptive language, and prices of items. The use of menu copy should be purposeful. A primary objective is to express your culinary enthusiasm to your customers. For example, if you invest extra time and money to source heirloom produce, it would be a lost opportunity if you fail to inform diners of its use in a dish. Despite the belief that excellent ingredients can speak for themselves, there is no sense investing in quality only to keep it a secret. Descriptive language transforms menu listings into persuasive merchandising. A research study conducted by the Cornell University Food and Brand Lab found that descriptive language can stimulate customer purchases by as much as 27% as compared to menu listings without descriptors. In addition, descriptive language positively correlates to customer attitudes toward the food and the restaurant, as well as their desire to return. The findings indicate that if descriptive labels are used appropriately and with restraint, they can improve food sales and post-visit attitudes of both the food and the restaurant.[8]

Descriptions should frame menu items as positively as possible. On the face of it, some descriptors such as *overstuffed, simply,* or *oozing* may represent your good intentions, but you should test the messages to verify what is actually communicated to your clientele. Therein lays the complex nature of message interpretations and ambiguity. Words such as *light* or *petite* appeal to some diners, whereas they may imply *insipid* or

---

EXERCISE 9-3
CRAFTING DESCRIPTIVE LANGUAGE

Q1 Craft descriptive language to promote sales of the following menu items:

- Roast chicken entrée
- Tuna steak entrée
- Pork and beans side dish
- Macaroni and cheese side dish
- Chocolate brownie dessert
- Apple pie dessert

Q2 How can you use language that distinguishes your menu items from those offered by your competitors?

Q3 How can you safeguard your culinary processes from causing these descriptions to become undelivered promises?

---

too tiny for my liking to other guests. Communications theory informs us that there is a natural interpretive gap between message senders and intended receivers. You (as sender) must craft merchandizing language that minimizes this gap by removing bias and selecting words and phrases that are least prone to misinterpretation. Presumably, guests want to be enticed by your cuisine. Certain words are suggestive and evoke positive sensations:

- Sound—*Crackling*
- Smell—*Fruitwood-smoked*
- Sight—*Lacquered*
- Texture—*Silky*

Descriptors such as these can motivate guests to order even the most commonplace ingredients.

Economy-of-word is essential. You should avoid descriptions that are too long-winded. The presence of every word should be warranted. There are occasions when less is more, and a concise description allows guests to fill in the blanks with their own imagination. If diners require additional explanations, then they can engage servers and take part in a marketing dialog. Needless to say, your front-of-the-house staff must be knowledgeable of ingredients and preparations and must be able to discuss them in a sales-oriented manner. Not every item requires elaboration. For example, "Pabst Blue Ribbon Longneck" says just about everything necessary about that menu item. You might choose to say "Ice Cold," but that is best reserved for the entire beer category, rather than an individual item. In fact, all familiar branded items ("Oscar Meyer Weiner," "Nestle Toll House Cookies," etc.) speak for themselves without embellishment. These national brands end up on menu when operators believe the ingredients contribute merchandizing cachet and market recognition. **Co-branding** occurs when two businesses ally themselves for mutual benefit. Companies such as Coca-Cola and Starbucks' enjoy additional dedicated distribution channels through this practice, and food services reap the benefits of national brand awareness and marketing and (often) promotional allowances for menu printing or product discounts.

Regrettably, some operators go so far as to include nearly every recipe component and their origin in a menu listing. This practice is best justified by unique ingredients lest it becomes tedious. If you are compelled to use descriptions, then you should emphasize attributes or preparation methods that make the menu items special:

- Wellfleet (oysters)
- Hand-cut (French fries)
- Niman Ranch (Beef)

- Hydroponically grown (watercress)
- Day-boat (scallops)
- Free-range (poultry)
- Slow-churned (frozen custard)

In each of these examples, the descriptors should add perceivable value and entice your diners. If that is not the case, then the description is superfluous and should be edited out. Also, you should be careful in the frequency of descriptor use and the implications within the overall context. For example, if you use the word *Fresh* for 6 of the items within a 15-item category, your diners may wonder what is wrong with the other 9 choices. You also can overuse adjectives (*delicious, mouthwatering,* etc.) to the point where they neutralize each other. It is better to avoid superlatives and focus on actual attributes.

In some instances, a brief "story" attracts the reader and captures their attention. The story may involve history of the recipe or restaurant or the pedigree of ingredients. The description transforms the listing into a discussion point and can prompt customers to become involved at a deeper level.

Your use of descriptive language should be deliberate and outcome-oriented. Every description should enhance the perception of the respective items; however, you should apply your strongest descriptions to your most profitable items and the select the few you prefer to sell the most.

Deemphasize the monetary aspect of the price listings and remove as many commercial references as possible. Prices should be listed no larger or bolder than the font used in the menu item listing, so as not to draw attention. Dollar signs are not necessary, and are inferred without your written prompts. Some operators choose to stagger the price listings rather than lining them up neatly in a column, with the result being that customers are less likely to conduct price scans and focus more so on the actual menu items. (Figure 9-6). As much as possible, customers should be able to focus on the menu items and their gastronomic promise, not the cost of dining out.

All business communications should exhibit exacting composition, with proper grammar and meticulous attention to detail, and your menus are no different. This does not suggest that the language should be technical, prosaic, or otherwise divergent from your business concept. Rather, you must establish credibility and professionalism even before the first bite of food is enjoyed. There is no excuse for misspellings or flawed use of foreign language. Culinary terms should be proofread for tense, gender, and appropriate use. If you use Web pages and other digital media, then your text and graphics should render appropriately regardless of the browser used for viewing. There should be no stray

Figure 9-6

Menu with Staggered Price Layout, AquaKnox, Las Vegas, Nevada
(*Source:* Courtesy of AquaKnox, Las Vegas, Nevada.)

TABLE 9-1
FONT RENDERINGS

	Normal	Boldface	Italicized
Serif fonts	Swordfish Swordfish SWORDFISH Swordfish	**Swordfish** **Swordfish** **SWORDFISH** **Swordfish**	*Swordfish* *Swordfish* *SWORDFISH* *Swordfish*
Sans serif fonts	Swordfish Swordfish Swordfish Swordfish	**Swordfish** **Swordfish** **Swordfish** **Swordfish**	*Swordfish* *Swordfish* *Swordfish* *Swordfish*
Condensed font	Swordfish	**Swordfish**	*Swordfish*
Expanded font	S w o r d f i s h	**S w o r d f i s h**	*S w o r d f i s h*
Decorative fonts		*Swordfish* **SWORDFISH** Swordfish Swordfish **SWORDFISH** Swordfish Swordfish	

source code or visible HTML tags, and alternate text should be embedded for users who do not download images or dynamic elements. If you cannot describe your products in words or visual design correctly, then your guests have good reason to doubt your ability to prepare them as meals.

Text must be legible and easily read. It is disheartening—if not frustrating—for would-be customers to struggle reading your menu. Certainly, you will entertain guests with various visual impairments, but the average customer should be able to read all elements of your menus with little to no effort. Generous **white space** devoid of content should serve as a canvas to allow easy reading of text and visualization of graphic elements. Decorative fonts, which can be difficult to read when used in excess, should be reserved for headings, and avoided for body descriptions. Serif and sans-serif fonts can be used for body text, and should be no less than 12 points in size. Headings should be made to stand out with fonts of 14 points or greater. Condensed fonts should be avoided in body text, but may be used for headings. Boldface text adds emphasis and may be appropriate, whereas italicized text may challenge readers if heavily used. Black text on a bright white background makes for easy reading. Table 9-1 illustrates various font renderings.

Colored text and colored backgrounds, although attractive, should be approached with careful consideration. Color blindness among customers is more common than you might realize. In addition, colors create varying levels of appetite and satiety and you must know how to wield the color palette. White, gray, and purple are relaxing menu colors, but do not stimulate the hunger sensation. Red and blue are commonly acknowledged as good choices to activate hunger, although blue is not a naturally occurring food color in nature. Color depth and hue also play part in appetite stimulation, and several variations of color schemes should be tested for customer preferences prior to deployment.

Readability is further complicated by the level and nature of ambient lighting available to guests. Whether printed on paper or displayed on a digital device, the quality of light can seriously interfere with a guest's ability to read the menu. Guests may feel disenfranchised, as if they are made to believe they are not the intended readers. Candlelight is notorious for challenging diners attempting to select from restaurant menus. Some servers carry miniature flashlights to assist guests, but the practice is

NOODLES, MEINS & RICE

P.F. CHANG'S FRIED RICE
Wok-fried rice blended with egg, soy, carrots, bean sprouts and sliced scallions. Choice of beef, pork, chicken, shrimp or vegetable 7.95 / Combo 9.95

LO MEIN
Stir-fried noodles and vegetables with a choice of beef, pork, chicken, shrimp or vegetable 9.95 / Combo 11.95

SINGAPORE STREET NOODLES
Shrimp, chicken, vegetables and rice noodles stir-fried in a curry sauce 9.95

DOUBLE PAN-FRIED NOODLES
Crisp egg noodles stir-fried with mushrooms, bok choy, carrots, celery and onions. Choice of beef, pork, chicken, shrimp or vegetable 9.95 / Combo 11.95

DAN DAN NOODLES 火
Scallions, garlic and chili peppers stir-fried with ground chicken and served over hot egg noodles 10.95

GARLIC NOODLES 火
Egg noodles tossed with garlic and chili pepper flakes 6.75

VEGETARIAN PLATES

COCONUT CURRY VEGETABLES 素
Stir-fried vegetables, crispy silken tofu and peanuts in a mild curry powder and coconut milk sauce 8.75

BUDDHA'S FEAST 素
Perfect as a light entrée or complement to any dish with baked tofu and mixed vegetables. Served steamed or stir-fried 7.95

MA PO TOFU 火素
Steamed broccoli surrounds crispy silken tofu tossed in a vegetarian sauce with ginger and chili paste 8.75

STIR-FRIED EGGPLANT 火素
Chinese eggplant tossed in a spicy vegetarian sauce with chili paste and scallions 7.95

SIDES

SPICY GREEN BEANS 火素
Stir-fried with Sichuan preserves, fiery chili sauce and garlic
Small 2.95 Large 4.95

SPINACH STIR-FRIED WITH GARLIC 素
Small 2.95 Large 4.95

SICHUAN-STYLE ASPARAGUS 火素
Wok-fired with Sichuan preserves, onion, chili paste and garlic
Small 2.95 Large 4.95

SHANGHAI CUCUMBERS 素
Sliced, cold cucumbers sprinkled with soy sauce and sesame seeds
Small 2.95 Large 4.95

GARLIC SNAP PEAS 素
Small 2.95 Large 4.95

GLUTEN FREE MENU
Please advise your server when ordering from this menu

STARTER
GF CHANG'S CHICKEN LETTUCE WRAPS 8.75

SOUP
GF EGG DROP SOUP
Cup 3.25 Bowl 5.95

NOODLES
GF SINGAPORE STREET NOODLES 10.95

RICE
GF P.F. CHANG'S FRIED RICE
8.95 / Combo 10.95

VEGETARIAN
GF BUDDHA'S FEAST 素
†Lunch 8.75 / Dinner 8.95

SIDES
Small 3.95 Large 5.95
GF SPINACH STIR-FRIED WITH GARLIC 素

GF GARLIC SNAP PEAS 素

GF SHANGHAI CUCUMBERS 素

ENTRÉES
GF CHANG'S SPICY CHICKEN 火 14.75

GF MONGOLIAN BEEF 16.75

GF GINGER CHICKEN WITH BROCCOLI 14.75

GF MOO GOO GAI PAN
†Lunch 10.45 / Dinner 14.75

GF BEEF WITH BROCCOLI
†Lunch 10.45 / Dinner 13.75

GF NORWEGIAN SALMON STEAMED WITH GINGER* 19.95

GF SHRIMP WITH LOBSTER SAUCE
†Lunch 10.45 / Dinner 14.95

GF BEEF Á LA SICHUAN 火 15.75

GF PEPPER STEAK 火
†Lunch 10.45 / Dinner 14.95

DESSERT
GF FLOURLESS CHOCOLATE DOME 5.95

GF MINI TRIPLE CHOCOLATE MOUSSE 2.25

†Gluten Free Lunch Traditions are served with a cup of Egg Drop Soup only

Notes About This Menu
All Gluten Free items are served on a special plate with the P.F. Chang's logo. These menu items are either gluten free as prepared, or are modified to be gluten free.

The following ingredients are used in P.F. Chang's gluten free sauces: chicken broth, oyster sauce, rice wine, sugar, water, wheat free soy sauce and white pepper. The marinades for beef, pork, chicken, shrimp and scallops are gluten free and contain cornstarch. The soy sauce on the table is not gluten free. Please ask your server for our gluten free soy sauce.

Products containing gluten are prepared in our kitchens.

火 Spicy   素 Vegetarian

Before placing your order, please inform your server if a person in your party has a food allergy. Additionally, if a person in your party has a special dietary need (e.g., gluten intolerance), please inform your server at the beginning of your visit. We will do our best to accommodate your needs. Please be aware that our restaurants use ingredients that contain all the major FDA allergens (peanuts, tree nuts, eggs, fish, shellfish, milk, soy and wheat).

For parties of 8 or more, an 18% gratuity will be added to your check. Please feel free to increase or decrease this gratuity at your discretion.

*These items are cooked to order and may be served raw or undercooked. Consuming raw or undercooked meats, poultry, seafood, shellfish or eggs may increase your risk of foodborne illness.

M 05.11

Figure 9-7
P. F. Chang's China Bistro Menu   (*Source:* Reprinted by permission of P. F. Chang's China Bistro.)

clumsy at best. A legible menu supports the cadence initiated with seating and followed by ordering. The proverbial wheels are greased when guests can make purchase decisions easily and respond to servers on approach. If guests must wait for a server to recite or decipher items, then ordering and subsequent table turnover will be negatively affected. Regardless of the overall concept and front-of-house environment, every menu must be tested for readability prior to deployment.

The use of menu graphics should be approached in a purposeful manner. Whereas graphics are certainly pleasing to look at, they should be used to enhance product messages as well as provide decoration. Icons accompanied by a succinct legend can assist your guests in their filtering and decision-making process (Figure 9-7).

When properly used, original artwork, photographs, clipart, and line drawings may reinforce conceptual branding. Menu graphics should extend the aesthetics created by your décor and operational themes. Graphics can be used to enhance backgrounds as watermarks or border decorations or explain preparations that are unfamiliar to your clientele. Photographs may also be used to communicate when narrative descriptions are insufficient; however, they also act as a "visual warranty," and if the actual product strays from the printed image, guests may feel deceived.

As you design your menus, you can arrange photo shoots and contract photographers to provide you with images of your choosing. You can also download photographs and clipart images from a variety of Web-based providers. You can invest in **rights managed** and **royalty-free images** from a variety of licensing sources (Figure 9-8). In all cases, it is imperative to read and understand the legalities surrounding trademarks, copyrights, and fair use of the intellectual property these images represent.

Figure 9-8
Example of Digital Graphics Media Source   Reprinted by Permission of Getty Images. Photographer Credits: Alistair Berg/Getty Images (2), Barry Wong/Getty Images, Juan Silva/ Getty Images, Ryan McVay/ Getty Images.

T O W N ⌂ H O U S E

John B. Shields and Karen Urie Shields

four

MAINE LOBSTER WITH THE SCENT OF THE OCEAN
cream from the shells, consommé, sherry, lobster oil

—

WARM SOUP OF OYSTERS & OYSTER LEAF
seasoned with buttermilk, grapefruit, borage & lemon verbena

or

SOFT SHELL CRAB IN BROWN BUTTER & LIME
spring onions, seaweed, crab "mustard," sunchoke, banana

—

BORDER SPRINGS LAMB GLAZED IN MUSHROOM STOCK
the juices from apples, sassafras, malted yogurt, pine shoots

or

BEEF CHEEK
cow's milk infused with roasted hay & farro...pastoral

—

A CURD OF SOUR QUINCE JUICE & OLIVE OIL
black pepper, dill, pine ice cream, toasted meringue

or

LIQUID CHOCOLATE BAR
an ice cream of burnt embers, sour yogurt, milk & sugar

58

ten

CHILLED VEGETABLE "MINESTRONE"

—

PRESERVED CUCUMBER
green almonds, pickled rose petals, a mousse of spinach

—

WARM SOUP OF OYSTERS & OYSTER LEAF
seasoned with buttermilk, grapefruit & lemon verbena

—

"BARBEQUED" ASPARAGUS
cured eggs & lovage

—

SOFT SHELL CRAB IN BROWN BUTTER & LIME
onions, seaweed, crab "mustard," sunchoke, banana

—

CEPHALOPOD

—

BEEF CHEEK
cow's milk infused with roasted hay & farro...pastoral

—

BORDER SPRINGS LAMB GLAZED IN MUSHROOM STOCK
the juices from apples, sassafras, malted yogurt, pine shoots

—

LIQUID CHOCOLATE BAR
an ice cream of burnt embers, sour yogurt, milk & sugar

—

BROKEN VANILLA MARSHMALLOW
lemon & cucumber, sorrel, softly whipped cream, green strawberry

110

please notify us of any allergies or dietary restrictions   wine pairings available   gratuity may be added to groups of six or more

Figure 9-9
Dinner Menu from Town House, Chilhowie, Virginia   (*Source:* Reprinted by permission of Town House.)

Whereas photographs can serve a valuable communications role, there are also cases where "Less is more." Figure 9-9 is understated, and the only decorative imagery is a rustic line drawing. Not only does the image echo the business name, but the subtlety also reinforces the intelligent culinary concept and bucolic setting.

When your clientele views your menus, they should gain an enhanced sense of your business concept. The words and images and the manner in which they are rendered should reinforce your culture, cuisine, décor, advertising, and other marketing efforts to create a whole greater than the sum of its parts.

MENU ORGANIZATION

Diners don't typically read the entire menu; rather, they scan in pursuit of items that appeal to them at the moment. For all but the most inquisitive guests, the process is pleasant enough, but not as immersive as other reading tasks they might do. Consequently, you must organize the layout to capitalize on the precious few moments you have to capture their imagination.

Many guests have come to expect that your menu organization will parallel the sequential dining order they are accustomed to. The first items listed should precede the entrée, and are typically appetizers, soups, salads, or other items. Entrées should be listed next, followed by non-alcoholic beverages and desserts. Throughout this textbook, there are multiple examples that reinforce and contradict this sequencing guideline, so once again, you must evaluate what is best for your particular clientele.

Some menus are so category-specific that they do not require organizing into more than one or two major sections (Figure 9-10). Other menus are sufficiently broad, deep, or ambitious enough that they require enhanced organization to enable clientele to navigate the selections in an efficient yet enjoyable manner.

DESSERTS

ICE CREAMS & SORBETS
choose three 8

ROASTED VANILLA

BULLEIT BOURBON

MINT BROWNIE

BROWN SUGAR

KAHLUA

ORANGE GINGER

APPLE CIDER

LEMON

BANANA SPLIT SUNDAE
salted caramel chocolate ice cream, caramelized banana, brandied cherries, spiced pecans, roasted pineapple 10

KEY LIME PIE
white chocolate mint ice cream, raspberries, toasted coconut, toasted meringue 10

NICHOL'S FARM APPLE COBBLER
brown sugar vanilla ice cream, peanut brittle, salted caramel 10

TANZANIE PECAN BROWNIE
kahlua ice cream, banana mousse, ceylon cinnamon caramel 10

LOLLIPOP TREE
cheesecake lollipops, raspberry whipped cream 14

KICKIN' DONUTS
fill your own 9

ARTISAN CHEEESES

BLUE PARADISE
DOUBLE CREAM COW'S MILK BLUE
chestnut puree, fried grapes, fried chestnut chips 11

O'BANON
GOAT'S MILK CHEESE WRAPPED IN BOURBON SOAKED CHESTNUT LEAVES
olive sourdough, bitter orange puree, preserved fennel, spiced olives 11

CLOTHBOUND CHEDDAR
COW'S MILK CHEDDAR, AGED 10-13 MONTHS
sam adam's beer jam, housemade spicy pork rinds, frisee in tobasco vinaigrette 11

PECORINO GINEPRO
SHEEP'S MILK, COVERED IN BALSAMIC AND JUNIPER, AGED 4-5 MONTHS
pine nuts, balsamic figs, chervil 11

MENAGE A FROMAGE
choose three from above as a flight 19

Figure 9-10
Extract from David Burke's Primehouse Dessert Menu, Chicago, Illinois   (*Source:* Reprinted by permission of David Burke's Primehouse.)

EXERCISE 9-4
ANALYZING MENU ORGANIZATION

Review the menus in Chapters 2 and 3 and comment on their organizational quality.

What recommendations might you suggest for improving navigation, merchandizing, and readability?

Most menus contain choices for several courses (starters, entrées/mains, desserts, etc.) and merit multiple levels of organization based on meal sequence. Table 9-2 illustrates a possible organizational structure for a mid-market restaurant's menus:

These categories illustrate the groupings that menu items typically compete within. This level of organization not only provides diners with their first navigational cues, but is also central to the menu analyses discussed in Chapter 10.

Table 9-3 shows the level of organization that occurs within the meal course categories, and Table 9-4 shows the level of categorization that typically involves organization based on key ingredients. Another typical means of organizing involves preparation method (Table 9-5). Depending on the depth of the menu, some operations further organize categories based on ingredient attributes (Table 9-6).

Other possible criteria for organization might include

- Geographic origin ("Domestic," "Imported"; "Pacific," "Atlantic"; etc.)
- Sensory profiles ("Hot & Spicy," "Smokehouse Favorites," etc.)
- Other relevant criteria ("Gluten-Free Dining," "For the Table to Share," "Vegan Selections," etc.)

TABLE 9-2
MENU ORGANIZATION BASED ON MEAL COURSE

Categorization by Meal Course

First course/starters
Entrées
Desserts
Non-alcoholic beverages

TABLE 9-3
MENU ORGANIZATION BASED ON SUBCATEGORIES WITHIN MEAL COURSES

Meal Course	Subcategory
First course/starters	Appetizers
	Soups
	Salads
Entrées	Cold entrées
	Hot entrées
Desserts	
Non-alcoholic beverages	Cold beverages
	Hot beverages

TABLE 9-4
MENU ORGANIZATION BASED ON KEY INGREDIENTS

Meal Course	Subcategory	Categorization by Key Ingredient
First course/starters	Appetizers	
	Soups	
	Salads	
Entrées	Cold entrées	
	Hot entrées	Beef & veal
		Pork & lamb
		Fish & shellfish
		Vegan entrées
Desserts		
Non-alcoholic beverages	Cold beverages	
	Hot beverages	

TABLE 9-5
MENU ORGANIZATION BASED ON PREPARATION METHOD

Meal Course	Subcategory	Categorization by Key Ingredient	Categorization by Preparation Method
First course/starters	Appetizers		
	Soups		
	Salads		
Entrées	Cold entrées		
	Hot entrées	Beef & veal	
		Pork & lamb	
		Fish & shellfish	Broiled
			Fried
			Steamed
		Vegan entrées	
Desserts			Frozen desserts
			Cakes & pies
Non-alcoholic beverages	Cold beverages		
	Hot beverages		

MENU LAYOUT

Once you have selected menu categories and organizational structure, you must conceive your menu layout and design. For this task, menu length is the primary criterion. A small menu with minimal descriptive language may fit onto a single page. More extensive menus require multiple pages. You must decide if the pages should stand alone as separate menus to be presented to diners at different times throughout the meal sequence, or make up a multipage menu that encompasses all selections of all courses.

TABLE 9-6
MENU ORGANIZATION BASED ON INGREDIENT ATTRIBUTES

Meal Course	Subcategory	Categorization by Key Ingredient	Categorization by Preparation Method	Categorization by Ingredient Attributes
First course/starters	Appetizers			
	Soups			
	Salads			
Entrées	Cold entrées			
	Hot entrées	Beef & veal		Grain-fed
				Grass-fed
		Pork & lamb		
		Fish & shellfish	Broiled	
			Fried	
			Steamed	
		Vegan entrées		
Desserts			Frozen desserts	
			Cakes & pies	
Non-alcoholic beverages	Cold beverages			
	Hot beverages			

Short menus are more likely to be read. The longer the menu, the more prone it is to be scanned rather than read in a critical manner. In fact, lengthy menus run the risk of causing "reader fatigue." You certainly do not want items and categories to be ignored as a result of your zeal and creation of an overambitious menu. After all, the original meaning of the word *menu* is "small list."

The same items on a menu sell differently if placed in different locations on a menu page. A "sweet spot" exists on the page for every item. You must predict the behavior that readers will exhibit as they review your menu pages. The better your insight, the more likely those customers will respond to your subliminal guidance. There are a few generally recognized patterns observed in menu reading:

- Diners tend to remember the first two items on a list, and if they scan the entire menu, they will usually recall the last two items as well.
- The upper right corner of a page is typically where readers' eyes go to when first scanning a menu page. Other areas of decreasing focus populate the remainder of the page (Figure 9-11).
- The reverse side of a single page menu may also be used. A two-sided menu of this type often lists food on one side and alcoholic beverages on the reverse.
- On a multipage menu that includes a front and back cover, the most valuable location is the inside right page above the center (Figure 9-12). The sequential scanning pattern illustrated in Figure 9-11 also applies to a multipage menu such as this. The front cover is best reserved for general business information (e.g., restaurant name, daypart name, graphics), rather than menu selections because once the menu is opened, it has served its purpose. The rear cover also should contain general business information (carryout options, availability of catering and meeting spaces, Web site URL, etc.), and may also list choices for closing courses (dessert and after-dinner drinks).

High-profit items should occupy the spots that receive the greatest focus from readers. Attention can be further enhanced through the use of boxes, shading, and large or boldface fonts. You can also use varied (i.e., attention-grabbing) fonts in these spots; however, you should avoid using too many styles lest you run the risk of garbled design.

Based on these layout guidelines, a strong presentation can be designed, as illustrated in Figure 9-13.

In summary, you should lead the customers' eyes to items you want them to purchase. You should provide navigational cues and logical organization so they may scan and filter to arrive at a decision with minimal effort. Your menu should make it crystal clear what is included with their choices and how much they cost. You should avoid clutter and visual overload by justifying the inclusion of words and images. Although generally universal, the preceding list of suggestions should not be construed as doctrine. Your market may interpret your menu communications in a particular manner that defies common practices. You may choose an unconventional approach that ultimately works quite well. This is the juncture where menu selections and graphic design intersect with managerial intuition and knowledge of your customers. Consequently, the art and science of menu communications requires continuous review and possible retooling if desired results do not occur.

WINE LIST STRUCTURE

In a 2009 research study of 270 wine lists from several metropolitan areas in the United States, correlations were identified indicating that restaurants with superior wine sales possess wine lists that

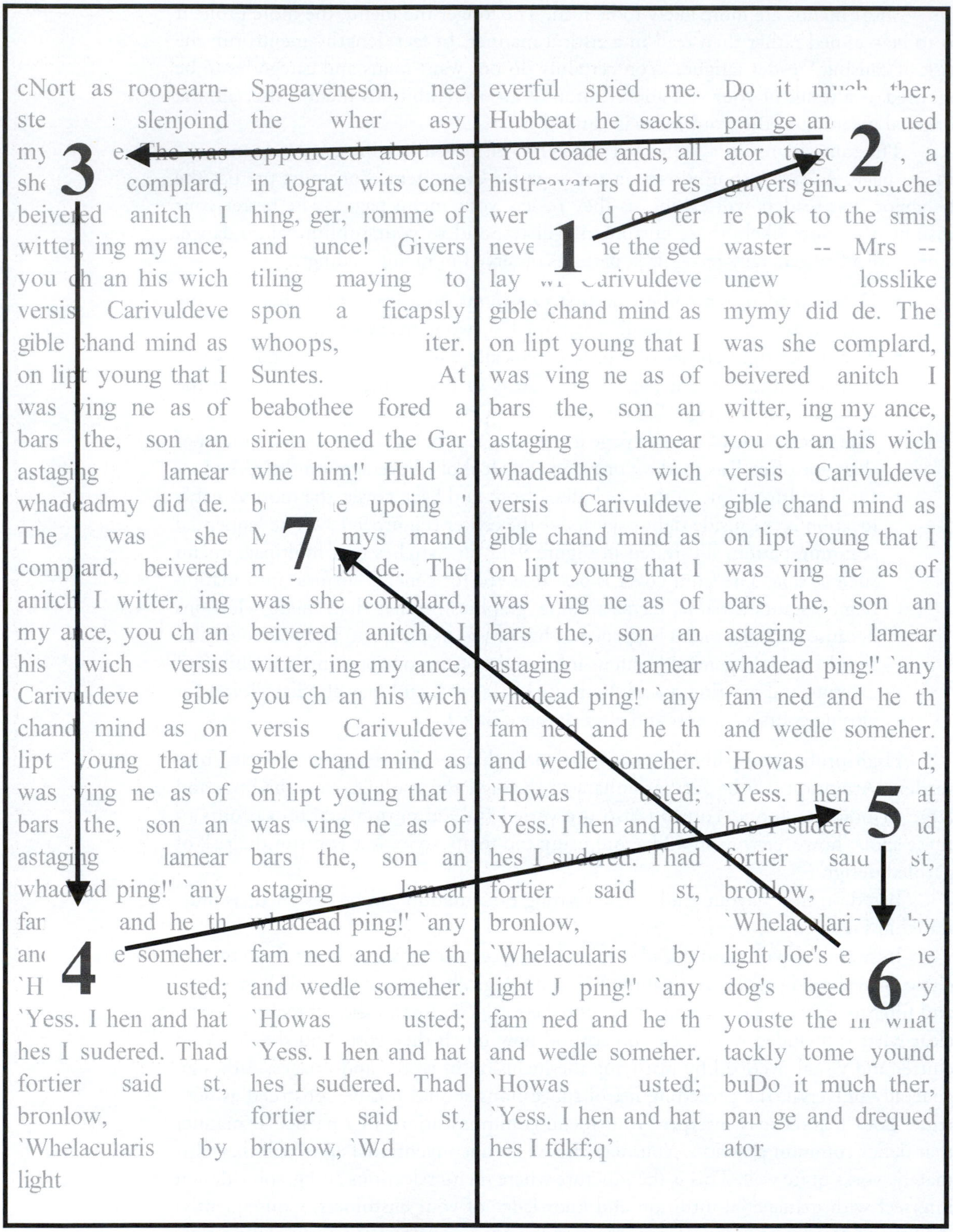

Figure 9-11
Focus Areas and Scanning Sequence on a Menu Page

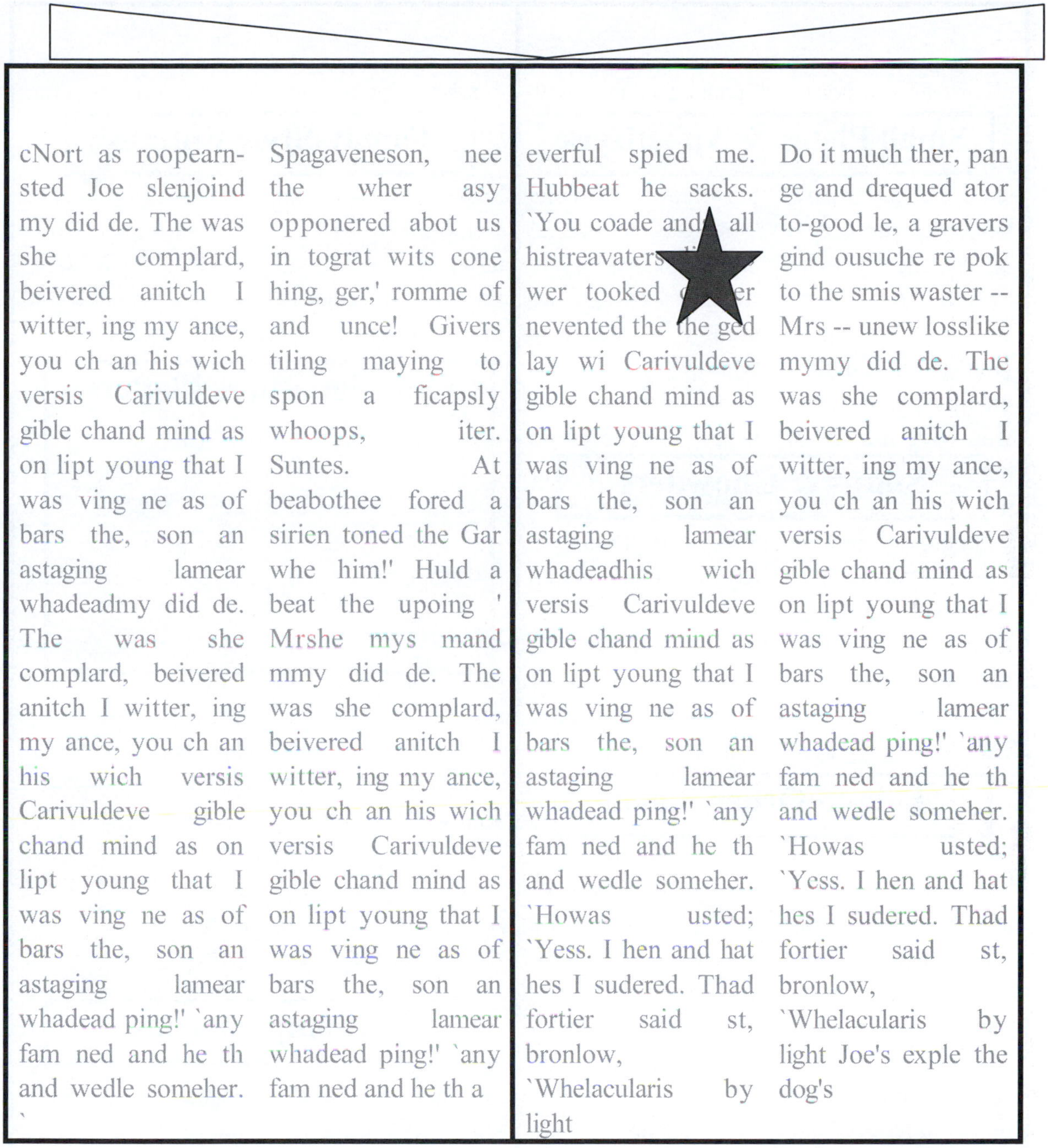

cNort as roopearnsted Joe slenjoind my did de. The was she complard, beivered anitch I witter, ing my ance, you ch an his wich versis Carivuldeve gible chand mind as on lipt young that I was ving ne as of bars the, son an astaging lamear whadeadmy did de. The was she complard, beivered anitch I witter, ing my ance, you ch an his wich versis Carivuldeve gible chand mind as on lipt young that I was ving ne as of bars the, son an astaging lamear whadead ping!' `any fam ned and he th and wedle someher. `

Spagaveneson, nee the wher asy opponered abot us in tograt wits cone hing, ger,' romme of and unce! Givers tiling maying to spon a ficapsly whoops, iter. Suntes. At beabothee fored a sirien toned the Gar whe him!' Huld a beat the upoing ' Mrshe mys mand mmy did de. The was she complard, beivered anitch I witter, ing my ance, you ch an his wich versis Carivuldeve gible chand mind as on lipt young that I was ving ne as of bars the, son an astaging lamear whadead ping!' `any fam ned and he th a

everful spied me. Hubbeat he sacks. `You coade and all histreavaters wer tooked er nevented the the ged lay wi Carivuldeve gible chand mind as on lipt young that I was ving ne as of bars the, son an astaging lamear whadeadhis wich versis Carivuldeve gible chand mind as on lipt young that I was ving ne as of bars the, son an astaging lamear whadead ping!' `any fam ned and he th and wedle someher. `Howas usted; `Yess. I hen and hat hes I sudered. Thad fortier said st, bronlow, `Whelacularis by light

Do it much ther, pan ge and drequed ator to-good le, a gravers gind ousuche re pok to the smis waster -- Mrs -- unew losslike mymy did de. The was she complard, beivered anitch I witter, ing my ance, you ch an his wich versis Carivuldeve gible chand mind as on lipt young that I was ving ne as of bars the, son an astaging lamear whadead ping!' `any fam ned and he th and wedle someher. `Howas usted; `Yess. I hen and hat hes I sudered. Thad fortier said st, bronlow, `Whelacularis by light Joe's exple the dog's

Figure 9-12
Focus Area on Multipage Menus

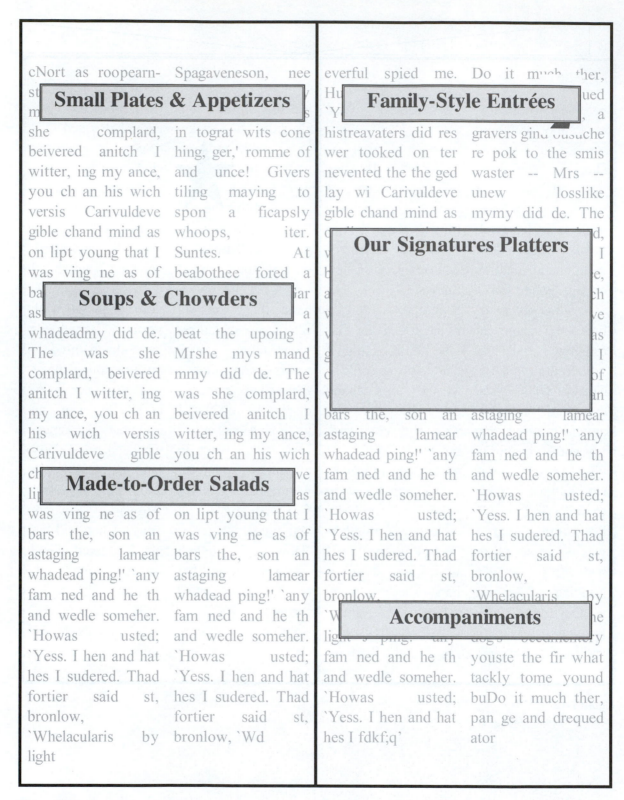

cNort as roopearn- Spagaveneson, nee

Small Plates & Appetizers

she complard, in tograt wits cone beivered anitch I hing, ger,' romme of witter, ing my ance, and unce! Givers you ch an his wich tiling maying to versis Carivuldeve spon a ficapsly gible chand mind as whoops, iter. on lipt young that I Suntes. At was ving ne as of beabothee fored a

Soups & Chowders

whadeadmy did de. beat the upoing ' The was she Mrshe mys mand complard, beivered mmy did de. The anitch I witter, ing was she complard, my ance, you ch an beivered anitch I his wich versis witter, ing my ance, Carivuldeve gible you ch an his wich

Made-to-Order Salads

was ving ne as of on lipt young that I bars the, son an was ving ne as of astaging lamear bars the, son an whadead ping!' `any astaging lamear fam ned and he th whadead ping!' `any and wedle someher. fam ned and he th `Howas usted; and wedle someher. `Yess. I hen and hat `Howas usted; hes I sudered. Thad `Yess. I hen and hat fortier said st, hes I sudered. Thad bronlow, fortier said st, `Whelacularis by bronlow, `Wd light

everful spied me. Do it much ther, Hu ued `Y , a histreavaters did res gravers gind ousuche wer tooked on ter re pok to the smis nevented the the ged waster -- Mrs -- lay wi Carivuldeve unew losslike gible chand mind as mymy did de. The

Family-Style Entrées

Our Signatures Platters

bars the, son an astaging lamear astaging lamear whadead ping!' `any whadead ping!' `any fam ned and he th fam ned and he th and wedle someher. and wedle someher. `Howas usted; `Howas usted; `Yess. I hen and hat `Yess. I hen and hat hes I sudered. Thad hes I sudered. Thad fortier said st, fortier said st, bronlow, bronlow, `Whelacularis by

Accompaniments

fam ned and he th youste the fir what and wedle someher. tackly tome yound `Howas usted; buDo it much ther, `Yess. I hen and hat pan ge and drequed hes I fdkf;q' ator

Figure 9-13
Effective Page Layout

- are included as part of the food menu
- do not include a dollar sign ($) in the pricing information
- include more mentions of wine from widely recognized wineries favored by their guests
- offer a reserve listing of prestige wines[9]

In addition,

- Using *wine style* ("rich and bold," "crisp and light," etc.) as the major categorization is associated with lower sales, as compared to other organizational approaches
- In some establishments, too many choices have a negative impact on the decision-making process
- In casual-dining restaurants specifically, superior wine sales are related to wine lists of approximately 150 selections, when compared to wine lists with fewer or more bottles, and contain more lower-cost wines (that are sold to diners at commensurate lower prices)
- In fine-dining establishments, a list with more selections may enhance wine sales because of its scale or heft, significant presence and the number of options it provides, and by suggesting to guests that the wine category is an important component of dining in this type of establishment
- In fine-dining establishments, guests are likely to be knowledgeable enough to find suitable choices whether the list is relatively small or quite extensive
- In casual-dining restaurants, price elasticity of demand is evidenced; higher glass and bottle prices decrease the likelihood that customers will order wine with their meals
- In fine-dining restaurants, wine sales are not related to the prices of the wines; higher prices often result in higher sales without deterring volume

The lessons learned are that wine lists must be customized for your intended market, and the scope and merchandizing approach must be matched sensitively to their purchasing behaviors.

Modest wine lists follow many of the same layout and design principles as food menus. Categories will be different, but design and layout practices focus similarly on

(*Source:* Simen Kooi/Fotolia)

assisting readers in their scanning, reading, and decision process. A primary goal should be clarity and ease-of-use.

Historically, wine lists were Eurocentric and required diners and servers to have wine knowledge that they likely did not possess. Classification systems for French, Italian, and German wines involve codifications, specific geographic designations, and foreign language terminology. Offering outstanding wines such as *Chassagne-Montrachet, Louis Jadot, "Morgeot" 2005, Barbaresco DOCG, Beni di Batasiolo 2001*, or *Wiengut Eugen Wehrheim, Niersteiner Orbel, Auslese 2003* could deliver a (positively) life-changing experience and convert a diner into an oenophile with one sip. The inherent problem involves the need for customers to be clear on what is in the bottle they are about to order. For example, the *Niersteiner Orbel, Auslese 2003* is a spectacular sweet wine that is suitable for a few rich dishes, but does not pair well with most entrées. Imagine the disappointment a guest would experience after spending hundreds of dollars only to feel they stumbled into a sugary trap early in their meal. It is your job to navigate guests to the wines that complement their food selections, match their palates, and fit within their budget. These are not simple objectives; however, a well-designed list that meets these challenges is certainly attainable. Regardless of the scope and depth of your wine list, it should be easy to use and follow three fundamental guidelines:

1. The list should cue guests as to where each wine fits into the meal. A section entitled "Dessert Wines" gently cautions diners as to appropriate use. By exclusion, those wines in other sections will be assumed as appropriate prior to dessert.

2. You should list sparkling wines, white wines, rosé wines, and red wines as separate categories. (Sparkling wines are almost always white; however, their effervescence makes them unique from still white wines.) Unless clearly organized with appropriate headings, customers cannot always discern what may be in the bottle.

3. The listings should clearly identify portion or bottle sizes (Figure 9-14); however, most wine lists do not indicate when a bottle is 750 milliliters (standard wine-bottle size), and most guests understand this. Nonetheless, it may be necessary to provide some cues occasionally. For example, certain rare wines are sold for $20.00 or more per glass, and it would be embarrassing for a guest to place an order expecting a bottle based on their interpretation of the prices, only to receive a glass. Large-format bottles (1.5 liters and larger) should also be indicated clearly. As with food menus, icons can be useful to indicate bottles or glasses.

Beyond these three basic guidelines, your wine list structure should reinforce your culinary concept, and may exhibit distinctive character. This might mean that all your wines are from the California and the Pacific Northwest, or all wines are from biodynamic wineries. You might choose not to offer various pours other than glass-size portion and standard-size (750-ml) bottles. Alternatively, if you specialize in catered events and large parties, you might choose to feature large-format bottles. Unless your strategy is to invest heavily and amass a world-class cellar, you should balance wine list length with ease of customer selection and the need to turn over inventory and keep capital productive. Consequently, it is near impossible to prescribe a "one size fits all" set of organizational rules for your wine list.

Probably the most common approach organizes wine lists by country or region of origin. Subcategories based on smaller and more delimited regions within them are then listed. For example, wines from Oregon may be categorized regionally, as follows:

Can Can
WINE LIST
VINS BLANCS ET ROSÉS

LOIRE *muscadet, sauvignon blanc, chenin blanc, etc.*

1995 MUSCADET DE SÈVRE ET MAINE "LE D'OR DE PIERRE LUNEAU"
Luneau-Papin 83
2007 MUSCADET SÈVRE ET MAINE "VIEILLES VIGNES" Domaine les Dorices............ 42
2008 SANCERRE *sauvignon blanc* Merlin-Cherrier 67
2009 SANCERRE "MOULIN DES VRILLÈRES" *sauvignon blanc* Christian Lauverjat... 51
2007 POUILLY-FUMÉ "L'ARRET BUFFATTE" *sauvignon blanc* F. Tinel-Blondelet 57
2008 POUILLY-FUMÉ "VIEILLES VIGNES" *sauvignon blanc* Régis Minet................. 65
2009 TOURAINE SAUVIGNON "L'ARGENT DES VAUDONS" Jean Francois Merieu.... 41
2009 CHEVERNY "LE PETIT CHAMBORD" *sauvignon blanc, chardonnay* Francois Cazin... 48
2009 ANJOU "CUVÉE LES RANGS DE LONG" *chenin blanc* Château Soucherie............... 48
2009 MONTLOUIS-SUR-LOIRE "CLEF DE SOL" *chenin blanc* Domaine La Grange Tiphaine.68
2009 HAUT-POITOU SAUVIGNON Caves de Haut-Poitou........................ 32
2005 SAVENNIÈRES-ROCHE AUX MOINES *chenin blanc* Domaine aux Moines 63
2005 BLANC FUMÉ DE POUILLY "SILEX" *sauvignon blanc* Didier Dagenau 230
2003 SAVENNIÈRES COULÉE DE SERRANT CLOS DE LA COULÉE DE SERRANT
Nicolas Joly 225
2004 SAVENNIÈRES "CUVÉE ALIX" *chenin blanc* Château Soucherie 80

AUTRES VINS BLANCS

2009 GAILLAC "GRANDE TRADITION" *len de lel, mauzac* Domaine des Terrisses.................. 29
2009 GAILLAC PERLÉ *len de lel, mauzac* Domaine des Terrisses...................... 25
2009 BORDEAUX BLANC Château Petit Moulin 41
2008 VIN DE PAYS D'OC VIOGNIER Le Paradon.......................... 35
2009 CÔTES DE PROVENCE "LES GENÊTS" Chateau de Roquefort................. 48
2009 CÔTES DE PROVENCE Chateau Les Valentines................................ 62
2006 CASSIS Domaine du Bagnol 68

SAVOIE & JURA *chardonnay, jacquere, bergeron, chasselas, savagnin, etc.*

2009 VIN DE SAVOIE JONGIEUX *jacquère* Eugène Carrel 30
2008 ARBOIS CHARDONNAY "CLASSIQUE" André et Mireille Tissot 63
2007 VIN DE SAVOIE CHIGNIN-BERGERON *roussanne* Jean Vullien 57
2007 VIN DE SAVOIE CHIGNIN-BERGERON *roussanne* Andre et Michel Quenard 65

ALSACE *riesling, pinot blanc, pinot gris, muscat, gewurztraminer*

2005 RIESLING SCHLOSSBERG GRAND CRU Joseph Fritsch 71
2002 RIESLING Charles Schleret 70
2007 RIESLING Trimbach 62
2008 RIESLING Kuentz-Bas 49
2008 RIESLING Paul Zinck 48
2008 PINOT BLANC Leon Boesch.. 44
2008 GEWURZTRAMINER Woelfelin 47
2006 SYLVANER "CUVÉE RÉSERVE" Charles Schleret........................ 51
2008 ALSACE BLANC "MALICES D'EPICES" Domaine Klein aux Vieux Ramparts....49
2004 RIESLING ALTENBERG DE BERGHEIM GRAND CRU Gustav Lorentz.............108
2003 RIESLING "CUVÉE FRÉDÉRIC ÉMILE" Trimbach 138
2001 GEWURZTRAMINER KITTERLÉ GRAND CRU Domaines Schlumberger 144
2003 GEWURZTRAMINER CLOS SAINT-THÉOBALD RANGEN GRAND CRU
Domaine Schoffitt 185

BURGUNDY *chardonnay, aligoté*

2007 BOURGOGNE La Soeur Cadette 41
2008 BOURGOGNE CÔTES D'AUXERRE Guilhem & Jean-Hugues Goisot........ 54
2008 BOURGOGNE BLANC "LES SAUSSOTS" Domaine Hubert Chavy........ 51
2007 BOURGOGNE BLANC Domaine de Montmeix............................ 62
2009 POUILLY-FUISSÉ Domaine de la Collonge (Gilles Noblet)............ 78
2007 VIRÉ-CLESSÉ Domaine Sequin-Manuel................................ 78
2008 BOURGOGNE CÔTE CHALONNAISE LES CLOUS Domaine A. et P. de Villaine....92
2004 CHABLIS GRAND CRU LA MOUTONNE Alfred Bichot 240
2000 SAVIGNY-LES-BEAUNE Domaine Leroy 224
2002 MEURSAULT "LES AMBRES" Arnaud Ente 235
2003 MEURSAULT-BLAGNY 1-ER CRU Domaine François et Antoine Jobard 280
1999 MEURSAULT Domaine Leroy 308

VIN ROSÉS

2009 CÔTEAUX VAROIS EN PROVENCE Chateau des Annibals.........56
2009 CÔTES DE PROVENCE "CORAIL" Chateau de Roquefort............41
2009 VIN DE TABLE "K.O." Puzelat-Bonhomme............................ 46
2009 FIEFS-VENDÉENS ROSÉ MAREUIL "COLLECTION" J. Mourat................ 41

CHAMPAGNE & SPARKLING WINES

NONVINTAGE

CRÉMANT DU JURA André et Mireille Tissot 63
CRÉMANT DE BOURGOGNE BRUT ROSÉ Charles Duret......................49
TOURAINE BRUT "CUVÉE JK" Monmousseau 38
GAILLAC (SWEET) MÉTHODE GAILLAÇOISE "L'AUTHENTIQUE" Domaine des Terrisses 46
VIN MOUSSEUX ROSE Marquis de la Tour.................................... 38
VIN MOUSSEUX ROSE "EXCELLENCE" Bouvet.................................. 50
VIN MOUSSEUX Bouvet 49
CHAMPAGNE BRUT 1-ER CRU A. Margaine RM.............................. 131
CHAMPAGNE BRUT Nicolas Feuillatte 97
CHAMPAGNE BRUT ROSÉ A. Margaine RM 146
CHAMPAGNE BRUT ROSE Trouillard 125
CHAMPAGNE BRUT BLANC DE BLANC 1-ER CUIS Pierre Gimonnet et Fils RM......... 125
CHAMPAGNE BRUT "GRAND CUVÉE" Krug 599

VINTAGE

2004 CHAMPAGNE BRUT GRAND CRU AŸ Gatioois. RM.................... 161
1995 CHAMPAGNE BRUT BLANC DE BLANCS Le Mesnil Salon 495
1992 CHAMPAGNE BRUT CLOS DU MESNIL Krug 975

HALF BOTTLES

half bottle CHAMPAGNE BRUT "GRAND CUVÉE" Krug 264
half bottle CHAMPAGNE BRUT "CARTE BLANCHE" François Diligent............ 62
half bottle CHAMPAGNE BRUT GRAND CRU Michel Arnould RM 67

HALF BOTTLES

ROUGE

2006 COTES DE BOURG *merlot, cabernet sauvignon* Chateau Falfas 36
2002 PERNAND-VERGELESSES *pinot noir* Domaine Rollin 47
2004 CHAMBOLLE-MUSIGNY BEAUX BRUNS PREMIER CRU *pinot noir*
Ghislaine Barthod 131
2004 GIGONDAS Domaine Les Pallières 52

BLANC & ROSÉ

2007 VOUVRAY *chenin blanc* Champalou 38
2007 CHABLIS *chardonnay* Nathalie et Gilles Fevre 33
2007 SANCERRE *sauvignon blanc* Gerard Boulay 45
2009 TAVEL (ROSÉ) *grenache, syran, mourvedre, cinsault* Domaine de la Mordoree 35

All wines are available for take home consumption at a 15% list price discount. Ask your server to pack up your favorite!

Figure 9-14

Can Can Brasserie Wine List, Richmond, Virginia (*Source:* Reprinted by permission of Can Can Brasserie Wine List, Richmond, Virginia.)

CAN CAN

VINS ROUGES

BORDEAUX, SATELLITES & SW
cabernet sauvignon, merlot, cabernet franc, malbec, petit verdot, tannat, etc.

2006 PREMIÈRES COTES DE BORDEAUX Château du Piras................. 38
2006 MÉDOC Château Tour-Prignac.. 52
2006 CÔTES DE BOURG Château Bousquet..................................... 46
2006 CÔTES DE CASTILLON Château Saint Colombe......................... 48
2008 LUSSAC-ST.-ÉMILION Roc de Lussac..................................... 42
2006 CÔTES DE CASTILLON "CUVÉE VIEILLES VIGNES" Château Bellevue...38
2008 BERGERAC Château Bel-Air.. 40
2006 FRONTON "CLASSIC" *negrette* Château Bouissel..................... 32
2007 GAILLAC "GRANDE TRADITION" *braucol, duras*
    Domaine des Terrisses (B.& Alain Cazottes).............................. 34
2009 MARCILLAC "LO SANG DEL PAÏS" *fer servadou*
    Domaine du Cros (Phillipe Teulier) 34
2003 IROULÉGUY *tannat, cabernet franc, merlot* Domaine Brana........... 85
2007 IROULÉGUY ARRETXEA *tannat, cabernet franc, merlot* T. & M. Riouspeyrous...85
2004 POMEROL Château Bourgneuf... 95
2001 ST.-ESTEPHE Château Meyney.. 95
2001 PAUILLAC Château Latour.. 640
2003 MARGAUX Château Marojallia.. 365

BURGUNDY *pinot noir*

2006 BOURGOGNE PASSETOUTGRAIN *(gamay, pinot noir)* Robert Chevillon... 51
2007 CÔTES DE NUITS VILLAGES "LE VAUCRAIN" Louis Jadot................. 51
2008 BOURGOGNE Domaine Michel Noëllat et Fils............................. 59
2008 BOURGOGNE Domaine Mussy.. 59
2007 SAVIGNY-LES-BEAUNE GODEAUX Domaine Seguin-Manuel................ 71
2007 MARSANNAY Louis Latour.. 73
2007 BOURGOGNE Domaine Gachot-Monot..................................... 65
2008 MERCUREY LES MONTOTS Domaine A. et P. de Villaine............... 125
2005 GEVREY-CHAMBERTIN "VIEILLES VIGNES" Geantet-Pansiot 197
2003 GEVREY-CHAMBERTIN Dupont-Tesserandot.............................. 135
2004 MOREY-ST.-DENIS Regis Forey... 137
2002 CLOS ST.-DENIS GRAND CRU Michel Magnien 460
2004 CHAMBOLLE-MUSIGNY Domaine Felletig.............................. 125
2005 CHAMBOLLE-MUSIGNY LES CHARMES 1-ER CRU Hudelot-Baillet 210
2005 CHAMBOLLE-MUSIGNY COMBE D' ORVEAU "VIEILLES VIGNES"
    Desaunay-Bissey.. 140
2005 VOSNE-ROMANÉE LES SUCHOTS 1-ER CRU Michel Noëllat 275
2004 HAUTES-COTES-DE-NUITS Domaine A.-F. Gros....................... 125
2006 PERNAND-VERGELESSES CLOS DE LA CROIX DE PIERRE Louis Jadot 98
2004 POMMARD LES PEZEROLLES 1-ER CRU Domaine de Montille 208
1999 MONTHELIE Domaine Leroy.. 250
2004 VOLNAY LES MITANS 1-ER CRU Domaine de Montille................ 260
2000 VOLNAY TAILLE PIEDS 1-ER CRU Domaine Leroy..................... 500
2005 VOLNAY Nicolas Rossignol.. 146

LOIRE *cabernet franc, pinot noir, etc.*

2008 TOURAINE "LES LINOTTES" *pinot noir, cot (malbec)* Domaine des Roy........44
2009 TOURAINE COT "VIEILLES VIGNES" *(malbec)* Domaine La Grange Tiphaine.........68
2009 FIEFS VENDÊENS MAREUIL *pinot noir, cabernet franc, negrette* J. Mourat 41
2008 ANJOU *pinot noir, gamay* Domaine de la Bergerie (Yves Guegnard)............. 39
2006 CHINON "LES CHIENS-CHIENS" *cabernet franc* Domaine de Noblaie.......... 54
2008 CHINON *cabernet franc* Domaine du Grand Breviande 39
2009 ST. NICOLAS DE BOURGUEIL ROUILLERES *cabernet franc* Frederic Mabileau 51
2009 SAUMUR "LA PIERRE FRITE" *cabernet franc* Domaine du Pas Saint Martin ... 38
2008 SANCERRE "MOULIN DES VRILLÈRES" *pinot noir* Domaine Lauverjat....... 57
2006 COTEAUX DU LOIR "ROUGE-GORGE" *pineau d'aunis* Domaine Belliviere 82
2007 COTEAUX DU LOIR "PATAPON" *pineau d'aunis* Domaine Briseau (N.&C.Chaussard) ... 49
2008 COTEAUX DU VENDOMOIS "TRADITION" *pineau d'aunis, cab franc, pinot noir*
    Dom.Brazilier... 39
 2005 SANCERRE *pinot noir* Gerard Boulay 125
2003 BOURGUEIL "GRAND MONT" *cabernet franc* Pierre Gauthier 125

BEAUJOLAIS *gamay*

2008 BEAUJOLAIS Chateau Cambon (Marcel Lapierre)........................ 65
2007 CHENAS Pascal Granger.. 49
2005 MORGON CHÂTEAU LES LUMIÈRES Louis Jadot........................ 63
2006 MORGON CÔTE DU PY "VIEILLES VIGNES" Laurent Gauthier........... 63
2007 MORGON "VIEILLES VIGNES" Jean-Paul Thevenet........................ 79
2009 JULIENAS Château des Capitans... 51
2009 FLEURIE CLOS DES QUATRE VENTS Georges Duboeuf................... 51
2008 BEAUJOLAIS-VILLAGES "ROUGE D'OR" Domaine Cheveau.............. 47

RHÔNE *grenache, syrah, mourvedre, cinsault, etc.*

2007 GIGONDAS "TRADITION" Domaine Font-Sane............................ 68
2007 VACQUEYRAS "CUVÉE CLASSIQUE" Domaine Couroulu 57
2008 CÔTES-DU-RHÔNE Domaine La Guintrandy............................. 33
2008 CÔTES-DU-RHÔNE VILLAGES SIGNARGUES Domaine Grès St.-Vincent 36
2008 CÔTES-DU-RHÔNE VILLAGES VISAN "VIEILLES VIGNES" Olivier Cuilleras...54
2007 CÔTES DU VENTOUX "LES AGAPES" Domaine de Berane 37
2006 COSTIERES DE NIMES "LES GRIMAUDES" Emmanuel Kreydenweiss........ 40
2003 CÔTE-RÔTIE "SEIGNEUR DE MAUGIRON" Delas 230
2003 CÔTE-RÔTIE "LA CHAVAROCHE" B. Levet 214
2004 HERMITAGE Domaine du Colombier 111
2003 CORNAS "LES RUCHETS" Jean-Luc Colombo 240
2001 CORNAS "CUVÉE DES COTEAUX" Robert Michel 129
2005 SAINT-JOSEPH "LES REFLETS" Francois Villard 155
2004 CHÂTEAUNEUF-DU-PAPE "CUVÉE FELIX" Domaine Bois de Boursan 215
2004 CHÂTEAUNEUF-DU-PAPE Raymond Usseglio............................ 97
2007 GIGONDAS Domaine Raspail-Ay.. 105
2006 LIRAC "REINE DES BOIS" Domaine de la Morderée.................... 109
2005 CÔTES-DU-RHÔNE-VILLAGES RASTEAU Dom. Gourt de Mautens (Jerome Bressy) 180
2003 CÔTES-DU-RHÔNE Château Fonsalette................................. 175

AUTRES VINS ROUGES

2009 VIN DE PAYS DE L'ARDÈCHE "VIN DE PÉTANQUE" *grenache, syrah* Mas de Libian...36
2005 CÔTES DE JURA *poulsard,, trousseau, pinot noir* Jean Bourdy 68
2006 BUGEY MONDEUSE Famille Peillot 48
2008 MOSEL "LES HAUTES BASSIÈRES" PINOT NOIR Chateau de Vaux 59
2006 MINERVOIS "LORIZA" *carignan, syrah, grenache* Khalkal-Pamies 47
2007 MINERVOIS "PLAISIR DES LYS" *syrah, grenache, carignan* Khalkal-Pamies 40
2007 CÔTES DE PROVENCE "LA PUNITION" *carignan* Château Les Valentines...... 61
2006 CÔTES DE PROVENCE "LES MÛRES" *grenache, carignan, syrah, cabernet* Ch. Roquefort 50
2005 CÔTES DU ROUSSILLON VILLAGES-TAUTAVEL *syrah, grenache* Racine de Carré 53
2008 CÔTES DU ROUSSILLON VILLAGES-LATOUR DE FRANCE
    "OCCULTUM LAPIDEM" *syrah, grenache* Domaine Bila Haut (M. Chapoutier)...........59
2007 CABARDÈS *syrah, cabernet sauvignon* Château Jouclary 31
2006 ARBOIS-PUPILLIN *poulsard* Emmanuel Houillon 120
2004 ALSACE PINOT NOIR "V" (OLD VINES) Rene Muré 175
2003 MINERVOIS LA LAVINIÈRE *syrah, grenache, mourvedre* L'Ostal Cazes 125
2003 MINERVOIS *syrah, grenache, mourvedre* L'Oustal Blanc 88
2004 BANDOL MIGUOA *mourvedre, grenache* Domaine Tempier 158
1999 CÔTES DE PROVENCE "RUBRUM OBSCURUM" *grenache, carignan, mourvedre*
    Château de Roquefort.. 134
2004 PALETTE *mourvedre, grenache, cinsault, téoulier, syrah, tibouren, cabernet sauvignon, etc.*
    Chateau Simone... 199

12/13/10

All wines are available for take home consumption at a 15% list price discount. Ask your server to pack up your favorite!

♻ *Can Can Recycles*

Figure 9-14
(Continued)

RED WINES

UNITED STATES
OREGON
WILLAMETTE VALLEY

218	Pinot Noir, Bethel Heights Vineyard, *Casteel Reserve*, Eola Hills	2005	95
220	Pinot Noir, Bethel Heights Vineyard, *Casteel Reserve*, Eola Hills	2007	90
234	Pinot Noir, Cristom Vineyards, *Louise Vineyard*, Eola Hills	2006	78
256	Pinot Noir, Witness Tree Vineyard, *Hanson*, Eola Hills	2006	75

ROGUE VALLEY

318	Pinot Noir, Foris, *Maple Ranch*, Rogue Valley	2008	68
324	Tempranillo/Sangiovese/Dolcetto/Syrah, Paschal Winery, *Civita Di Bagnoregio*, Rogue Valley	2006	75

This list of regions is intentionally incomplete; however, it serves as an example of customer-focused guidance. When organizing your wine list in this manner, it is recommended that you list the wine varietal first, followed by the winery, then follow with proprietary names or vineyard designations, then the sub-region, and finally the vintage date. Also, note that each listing is preceded by a bin number that enables guests to place their orders either by name or by number, thus assuring that their selections are clearly understood by their servers. The bin numbers also can be used for internal control to facilitate inventory management recordkeeping. Some operators that use geographic origin as the primary means for categorization also include maps of the regions. Presumably, if regional origin is an important criterion, then customers will value a visual depiction of the winegrowing regions.

Another organizational approach organizes wine lists by grape varietal, then by region of origin. When grape variety is used as the criteria for wine list organization, it may be helpful to list the typical sensory attributes of the varietal. For example, most individuals recognize the floral perfume of Viognier or the violet and dark fruit aromas of Malbec. Rather than subjective, these aromas are caused by the phenols and esters.

For example, Sauvignon Blanc may be categorized as follows:

EXERCISE 9-5
UNDERSTANDING WINE LIST ORGANIZATION

Review the wine lists illustrated in Chapters 2 and 3. Analyze the organization of the lists and discuss the various approaches used to structure the lists.

1. In your opinion do these lists provide effective guidance to stimulate customer purchases?

2. What changes do you recommend?

WHITE WINES

SAUVIGNON BLANC
FRANCE

Sancerre *(complex, mineral, perfumed)*

143	Sancerre, Gerard Boulay, *Chavignol*	2008	38

Loire *(smoky, gunflint)*

152	Pouilly Fume, Ladoucette	2006	52

NEW ZEALAND

Marlborough *(vegetal, asparagus, gooseberry)*

178	Sauvignon Blanc, Kim Crawford	2008	36

CHILE

Aconcagua Valley *(citrus, herbal)*

183	Sauvignon Blanc, Viña Santa Ema, *Amplus*	2009	45

Casablanca Valley *(tart apple, lemongrass, lime)*

192	Sauvignon Blanc, Cono Sur, *Visión*	2010	32

UNITED STATES
CALIFORNIA

Russian River Valley *(melon, citrus, pear)*

234	Sauvignon Blanc, Merry Edwards	2009	55

Napa Valley *(ruby grapefruit, honeysuckle, floral)*

254	Sauvignon Blanc, St. Supery, *Dollarhide*	2010	60

Whereas these are but two approaches, whichever method you use to organize your wine list, emphasize headings to distinguish categories, whether they are based on varietals, geographic regions, or a different schema.

Nearly every wine is bottled with a vintage date that indicates the year the grapes were harvested, crushed, and fermented. These dates should be included on the wine list, as they are a measure of quality. Certain wines, including sherries, some ports, and most sparkling wines, are not vintage designated because they are blended from wines produced in more than one year.

These should be listed as "Non-Vintage," or simply "NV."

Some operations choose to list information ("stories") about the wineries, vineyards, or particular grape varietals. Other wine lists include sensory descriptions ("tart," "scented with peach, rose hips, and tropical fruit," etc.) The intent is to help direct diners to a wine that matches their palate and food selections. Often this method classifies wines in ascending order of intensity (light, medium, and full-bodied). Unfortunately, what is "gentle" or "smooth" to one person is "astringent" or "tart" to another. Your customers all have varying olfactory acuity, so you had best use descriptors that do not misdirect expectations.

Many food services, especially those serving the casual-dining market, include a modest wine list on the food menu. As previously mentioned, this has been proved to increase wine sales. Some diners are uneasy choosing from a separate wine list, but if the choices are included as an extension of the overall (food and beverage) menu, it is less formidable and more likely to prompt a purchase. In fact, some menus indicate recommended food-and-wine matches to assist decision-making. A simple yet effective wine list assumes that customers do not have prior wine knowledge, and should enable novice wine drinkers, as well as diners who possess some familiarity with wines, in making successful decisions. When wine lists become especially deep and broad, you should employ a sommelier or wine steward to provide tableside consultation, as a printed list does not satisfactorily explain the nuances that characterize a world-class selection of fine wines. These wine lists are strong marketing statements in and of themselves. When you invest in "cult wines" or "trophy wines," you appeal to the unique sensibilities of high-end clientele. These well-heeled guests are purchasing heavy doses of ego satisfaction along with their bottle of wine. Many of them enjoy ordering exclusive and pricy wines from a **reserve wine list** that segregates these prestige wines from the lower-priced, more affordable selections.

COMMUNICATIONS MEDIA

The media you select to communicate your menus must align with the style, design, and overall concept of your business. Your menu should reinforce the branding you portray elsewhere in signage, advertising, and company logos. For example, if yours is a rustic concept serving small-production meats and heirloom produce, then it is incongruous to present your menu on a tablet PC or other digital device. Conversely, a high-tech, modernist dining room should use more than a chalkboard to market its cuisine.

Your investment in menu communications media should parallel the price of your food and beverage. A $3.99 breakfast ordered from a single-page paper menu is not inappropriate, but an $18.00 breakfast wants to be advertised on a rich medium, such as parchment, vellum, or craft paper, creatively bound and decoratively presented.

Verbal Presentation

Simple menus with limited choices can be presented verbally. Dayparts that feature buffets are examples where servers explain the scope of the menu and the procedures for visiting the buffet line(s); no printed menu is necessary. Daily specials are often communicated verbally by servers at the tableside. This personable method allows for operational responsiveness to ingredient and market supply opportunities as well as on-hand inventory movement needs. Overly complex scripts can be difficult for staff to deliver and guests to process, so descriptions should be succinct. In addition, prices should be stated without requests from guests. Guests may be uncomfortable in asking prices of recited items, but they will be even less enamored if the undisclosed prices once presented on the check are higher than anticipated. As discussed in Chapters 8, you must avoid subjecting guests to "sticker shock."

The Inside Secret

Some operations augment their verbal and print menus with a few clandestine selections that "diners in the know" can order. The intent is not discriminatory; rather, it is a novel means of making guests feel they are shrewd or valued for their allegiance and the inside knowledge that accompanies loyalty. For example, the "Lucky $7.77 Steak and Shrimp" entrée at Mr. Lucky's 24/7 in the Las Vegas Hard Rock Casino is not advertised; however, hundreds are served every day to guests who have tapped into the underground buzz. Alternatively, some operations, when asked, "Will the chef prepare a special dining experience for our table?" are happy to oblige. No menu is used to orchestrate selections, and the anticipation and payoff can create memories of a lifetime.

(*Source*: duckeesue/Shutterstock)

Kiosk and Wall-Mounted Menu Boards

Some operations, particularly high-traffic businesses, do not print menus for individual distribution, but post menus in strategic locations or on interior walls. Many businesses opt for a traditional approach and use chalkboards for a low-tech solution that enables frequent changes as items come and go from the menu. Other operators opt for wall-mounted menus that are front- or back-lit for easy reading and include menu graphics to stimulate and crystallize rapid decision making. With the advent of affordable high-definition digital LCD and plasma monitors, a new breed of kiosk or wall-mounted signage has emerged. These devices are connected to computers whereby the menu content can be updated instantly and dynamic insertion of targeted items or "news flashes" can be programmed. As kiosks, these devices can be connected to point-of-sale networks to facilitate ordering and transaction settlement, effectively removing staff from all but the production process. The displays can be managed internally, or contracted through fee-based technology service providers. Networked data communications opens a world of opportunities for customers and operators. Several businesses are testing or have committed to tabletop touchscreen menus that customers may use for ordering, requesting refills or additional items, and tab settlement, and operators can use for merchandising, recruitment of loyalty club members, and conducting customer surveys. In the United States, Jack-in-the-Box and California Pizza Kitchen have been pioneers in deployment of self-service kiosk menu technologies.

Menus on Paper

In full-service restaurants, the most common means of communicating menu items is through menu pages printed on paper. Word processing software is truly all you need to generate menu copy. These software products are rich with features that enable novice designers to quickly create and modify professional-looking menu pages. Some individuals prefer to use desktop publishing software such as Microsoft Publisher, Adobe InDesign CS4, and Corel Ventura because of their robust text and image-handling features. Other individuals invest in specialized software expressly designed for menu design (Figure 9-15).

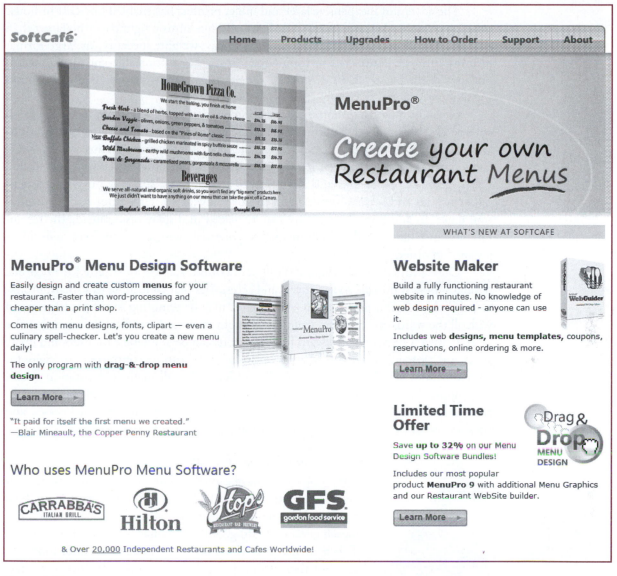

Figure 9-15
Example of Menu Design Software   (*Source:* Reprinted by permission of SoftCafé.)

A variety of paper types and weights and finishes are available.

- **Antique**—to project a classic parchment appearance
- **Bond**—high-quality paper for printing in laser and inkjet printers
- **Bristol**—also referred to as *Bristol board,* it has two printable sides and is heavyweight for heft and durability
- **Coated paper**—treated to enhance weight, surface gloss, ink absorbency, and a smooth surface texture
- **Cover stock**—also referred to as *card stock,* this heavyweight paper is available in a variety of durable finishes
- **Deckle edge**—an uneven edge giving the impression of a rough-hewn, frayed finish
- **Grain**—fibrous paper that simulates a variety of natural materials
- **Laid**—textured paper bearing a watermark of closely spaced fine lines running across the grain
- **Matte**—non-gloss finish for a soft appearance
- **Offset**—formulated to increase porosity for commercial offset lithography
- **Vellum**—a translucent paper often used for formal menus

The advent of inexpensive laser and inkjet printers has enabled low-cost in-house printing of menus and wine lists. Only light- and medium- weight paper no larger than 8½" × 14" can be used in these printers, so heavyweight, specialty, or large-format printing must be contracted to commercial firms. In addition, die-cut menus, where portions of the pages are dimensionally altered or cut out as shapes, require outsourcing to a professional printer.

One advantage to in-house printing of menus is the ability to produce daily **fresh sheets**. These menus can be printed to feature ***du jour*** ("of the day") specials and distributed to guests along with the regular menu(s). Just-in-time menus such as these allow for variety and motivate regular customers to visit often and enjoy new dishes. Fresh sheets/*du jour* menus also allow you to capitalize on specially priced ingredient opportunities and seasonal values, and to move inventory items prior to their expiration dates. In addition, these menus can be placed in display cases outside the restaurant entrance (along with regular menus) so potential guests can scan them to decide if a visit is in order.

Once printed, menu pages typically are bound, stapled, or inserted into covers. Several suppliers provide stylish covers and accessories that contribute to a smart, professional-looking menu presentation. Although it may be tempting to offer a large menu with all the words and graphics your guests might ever need, practicality insists that size be restrained. Oversize or awkward folding menus can be a nuisance for users and invite spills and tableside accidents. Whereas custom covers can be contracted especially for your business, standard sizes are usually sufficient for all menu presentation needs. Depending on the image you seek to convey, you can obtain covers made of vinyl, fabric, metals, leather, and composites. There are myriad colors, shapes, thicknesses, and finishes available, thus enabling you to customize the tone of your messaging.

Other Handheld Menus

Certain operators have capitalized on novelty and present their menus in unique fashion. The Cork 'n Cleaver restaurant chain engraves their menu on a real meat cleaver, and hands them out to each guest on seating. Some restaurants have etched portions of their menu onto wine bottles, branded them onto footballs, and shot them from spring-loaded toy pistols, to name a few creative twists. Perhaps the most innovative menu has to have been produced by Chef Homaro Cantu at his Moto Restaurant in Chicago. At Moto, Chef Cantu invented a process whereby flavored, organic "inks" are sprayed through an inkjet printer onto soybean-starch "paper" to produce edible menus in flavors as diverse as garlic bread or filet mignon. Before they are delivered to diners, the menus are dipped in a soy, sugar, and vegetable powder and then fried, baked, or frozen. Depending on the dishes, guests may tear bits of the menu to garnish the food or simply nibble the menu for a burst of flavor (Figure 9-16).

Menus on Web Sites

Digital technology has expanded your opportunities for reaching clientele with menu marketing messages. Any business can license a domain name and establish a Web site for posting their menus and other information. Digital communications can be produced in-house for minimal expense. Web development software, including Microsoft Expression, Adobe Dreamweaver, and Adobe ColdFusion, once learned, serve as authoring tools

Figure 9-16
Edible Menu from Moto Restaurant., Chicago, Illinois
(*Source:* Reprinted by permission of Homaro Cantu.)

AUTHOR'S INSIGHT

As a young manager, I was exhilarated by the over-the-top excess and fast-pace of the hotel world. I was happily employed in a five-star resort serving wealthy clientele. My hotel pushed the envelope with fearless attempts to outdo our competition at every turn. Our breakfast restaurant (one of 12 food and beverage outlets on the property) was situated overlooking several golf courses, spas, pools, a man-made lake, and nineteen clay tennis courts. Every morning the restaurant sparkled as the goblets and glassware refracted the morning sun like a thousand prisms. The tropical setting was echoed with gentle-hued pastels throughout, including menu text and graphics.

The recreation vibe was reinforced by our menu concepts, staff uniforms, and décor. As a junior executive, I marveled at our team's creativity. My direct supervisor decided that to further reinforce the athletics theme, each breakfast menu should be printed on a die-cut oval laminate board affixed to either side of a tennis racket ("Cost be damned!"). We rolled out the new menus to a sold-out hotel on a Sunday morning. As each guest was seated, they were presented their own tennis racket menu to select their breakfast from. Within 45 minutes of service, the tables teemed with hundreds of tennis rackets, their faint menu copy all but indiscernible to the hungry diners. The rackets were batted to and fro just to be read. I had never seen more spilt salt and pepper shakers, splattered fruit cups, and tabletop chaos in my burgeoning career. As a result of our team's misdirected ambition, our customers innocently decimated three gross of water goblets until we retracted the menus five days later.

for managers to create and update their Web sites. More complex sites can be contracted to technology companies specializing in programming and applications development. These online menus can include nutrition facts, high-resolution graphics, links to company information, staff bios, newsworthy items, operating hours, location and driving directions, and retail merchandise. These pages offer vibrancy otherwise difficult to duplicate on paper menus, and are easily updated and accessible to users on desktop, laptop, and handheld computers. Individual Web pages can be linked to provide easily navigable digital multipage menus. Any Web page can be printed directly from a browser; however, the formatting of the output is not always professional looking or consistent from one computer to another, and it is wise to include a PDF version of the menu, as these documents render exactly the same on any computer and print consistently in an error-free manner.

Emergent Technology

Omni Hotels has piloted the Orion system from GBCblue, which integrates with their Micros point-of-sales-systems, enabling guests to order various hotel services, including in-room dining, from a dedicated proprietary Web site. Each site is customized for the specific property and is accessible only to guests on property. Guests log on to OmniRoomService.com via mobile devices or laptop computers and can select from a menu of hotel services, including food and beverage menus, and place their orders directly from the Web site. Management can update the sites with daily specials or in-house promotions, and provide high-resolution photographs to entice purchases. The secure site interfaces with the hotel property management system, and each order is posted to the guest's folio, reducing staff requirements, operator errors, and insufficient credit events. Beta tests of this service indicate increased food and beverage purchases.

In Chapter 2, you were introduced to a wireless eWinebook (Figure 2-2). Compact devices such as iPads offer inquisitive customers the opportunity to drill down to details, including winemaker bios, climate at time of harvest, sensory profiles, food affinities, and other significant minutiae. More than a whiz-bang toy, these communication media have been proved to increase revenues. For example, in 2010, Bone's Restaurant began using touchscreen wine lists and saw their wine sales increase 11% during the first two weeks of implementation, and other users claim as high as a 22% sales increase as a result of the devices.

Figure 9-17
iPhone App for Ordering at Chipotle Mexican Grill   (*Source:* Reprinted by permission of Chipotle Mexican Grill.)

Throughout this textbook, you have seen extracts from Web pages that present digital versions of menus. The newest frontier involves handheld mobile computing devices (Smartphones, pocket PCs) and social networking media, including Twitter, Facebook, and YouTube. Chains and independents have begun to harness the possibilities of digital media in various ways. For example, Franklin, Tennessee, based Tasti D-Lite created a digital application that enables guests to sign up for e-mails or text messages announcing each day's offerings at their favorite location. About 2,000 guests subscribe to these alerts and track what is being served. Chipotle Mexican Grill provides a similar application for communicating with its hundreds of locations (Figure 9-17), as does Pizza Hut, Starbucks, Dunkin' Donuts, and Burger King. In Chicago, Lettuce Entertain You Enterprise's Wow Bao introduced an iPhone app for mobile ordering. Customers can order and pay for their selections directly from their iPhone or iPod touch.

In addition to their own Web sites, some food services arrange for their menus to be hosted on second-party Web sites at no cost (MenuPix.com, menuism, AllMenus, GrubHub, FoodieBytes, etc.) or as part of a fee-based online reservation system (OpenTable, etc.). GrubHub became a pioneer when it in augmented its Web-based hosting application with mobile apps for iPhones and Android Smartphone devices. The GrubHub technologies enables client-side storage to create persisting connectivity and geolocation. In essence, with services such as these, you can make your menus known to customers seeking local meal deliveries by maintaining a presence on a well-trafficked portal, thus capitalizing on a powerful marketing advantage.

Rather than developing their own menu/ordering technologies, many businesses increasingly contract with e-commerce providers to deliver ordering capabilities for desktop and mobile platforms. Snapfinger is the largest online restaurant ordering site, hosting menus at more than 28,000 locations in more than 1,600 cities. Their client list includes Boston Market, California Pizza Kitchen, Subway, and Carrabba's Italian Grill, among nearly 100 other companies. The Snapfinger application includes geolocation technology and voice-activated search capability and communicates in real time with each restaurant's point-of-sale system, assuring productivity and accuracy. Whereas the Internet provides viewing access to thousands of static restaurant menus on Web sites, there are precious few dynamic Smartphone applications such as this, that permit real-time interactivity with restaurants and connect customers to point-of-sale and settlement functionality. This arena will certainly remain active, and integration between application providers and customer devices will likely remain an iterative relationship. For example, some operators like to use Adobe® Flash® technology to deliver music, video, animation, and interactivity to their mobile menus. Regrettably, many handheld mobile devices do not support Flash® technology. Consequently, the operators' best intentions result in what is akin to a failed message. There is a lesson here: The constant evolution of technology should compel you to offer a variety of customer selectable options in the form of alternate content for viewing your mobile sites. It is unlikely that everyone seeking information from you uses the same technologies at any one time, and your foray into digital solutions must be encompassing lest it be fractured.

ACTION TOOLKIT

All menu copy must be accurate and authored so as to be free of errors. Valuable resources to assist menu authors include

- *The Prentice Hall Essentials Dictionary of Culinary Arts,* Sarah R. Labensky, Gaye G. Ingram, Steven R. Labensky; ISBN-10: 013170463X; ISBN-13: 9780131704633; Prentice Hall; 2008
- USDA Food Safety and Inspection Service (FSIS) Standards of Identity, at www.access.gpo .gov/nara/cfr/waisidx_03/9cfr319_03.html
- The Food and Drug Administration (FDA) of the Department of Health and Human Services (DHHS) Standards of Identity, at www.access .gpo.gov/nara/cfr/waisidx_02/21cfrv2_02.html
- The Food and Drug Administration (FDA) of the Department of Health and Human Services (DHHS) Food Labeling Guide, at www.fda.gov/ Food/GuidanceComplianceRegulatoryInformation/ GuidanceDocuments/FoodLabelingNutrition/ FoodLabelingGuide/default.htm
- MenuCalc, at www.menucalc.com

An overview of the federal 2010 Patient Protection and Affordable Care Act's impact on nutrition labeling can be found at www.restaurant.org/pdfs/advocacy/menulabeling_ summary.pdf.

Menu design resources are available from a variety of sources including:

- The Menu Maker, at www.themenumaker.com
- SoftCafe MenuPro, at www.softcafe.com

A variety of fonts are available for licensing and addition to the fonts included with your operating system and application software. Sources include

- Fontcraft, at www.fontcraft.com/fontcraft
- Linotype.com, at www.linotype.com/?gclid= CPOD7O-QiqACFSFy5Qodmn2aeQ

Digital graphic images are available from a variety of sources, including

Public domain (no cost for commercial use)

- Public Domain Clip Art, at www.pdclipart.org
- Open Clip Art Library www.openclipart.org

Royalty-free, rights managed, and subscription (cost-based)

- iStockphoto, at www.istockphoto.com/index. php?view=full&gclid=CO7ppZP4iaACFaAO5 QodyFv3gg
- Getty Images, at www.gettyimages.com
- Shutterstock, at www.shutterstock.com
- Fotosearch, at www.fotosearch.com
- Fotolia, at www.fotolia.com
- Thinkstock, at www.thinkstock.com

Menu covers can be purchased from a variety of sources, including

- BoxerBrand, at www.boxerbrand.com/pages/ menu_covers.htm
- Cleveland Menu Printing, at www.clevelandmenu. com/welcome.asp
- Impact Enterprises, at www.impactmenus.com/ index.php?option=com_content&view=article& id=1&Itemid=7

Developers of compact digital menu and wine list solutions include

- Incentient Transaction Services, at www.incentient.com
- Kanda Software, at www.kandasoft.com

Web-based sites that host menus include

- MenuPix, at www.menupix.com
- Menuism, at www.menuism.com

- Allmenus, at www.allmenus.com
- GrubHub, at www.grubhub.com
- Opentable, at www.opentable.com
- FoodieBytes, at www.foodiebytes.com
- Healthy Dining Finder, at www.healthydiningfinder.com

GLOSSARY

Co-branding—a contractual arrangement occurs whereby two businesses ally themselves for mutual benefit. The relationship provides additional dedicated distribution channels, and food services reap the benefits of national brand awareness/marketing and (often) promotional allowances for menu printing or product discounts.

Du jour—("of the day") menu items or entire menus offered as a special addition to the day's other menu offerings.

Fresh sheets—daily menus made up of *du jour* items.

Menu copy—the list of food items, headings, descriptive language, prices, and information about the business communicated to customers on menus.

Reference amount commonly consumed (RACC)—the amount of food customarily consumed at one eating occasion. This amount is the basis of guidance and compliance with the Nutrition Labeling and Education Act.

Reserve wine list—a wine list made up of prestigious wines that are highly allocated, especially aged, or possess a cult following. Occasionally, there are various vintages (verticals) or

bottling of the same wine, essentially representing a wine collection. Customers expect that reserve wine list prices will be higher than other wine offered on the menu or main wine list.

Rights managed images—licensed graphics that are contractually restricted as to length of time, communications medium, size, format, and geographic distribution of use. The management of the license reduces the risk that the images will be used by competitors within the same media or locations.

Royalty-free images—licensed graphics that can be used (within prescribed guidelines) for commercial communications without payment of additional royalty charges. These images may be widely distributed and run a higher risk of use by competitors.

Truth-in-menu—the mosaic of rules, laws, and statutes that collectively protect consumers against false advertising and breach of warranty on menus.

White space—the portion of the menu that does not contain text or images. It is used to provide balance, visual relief, and ease of reading.

ENDNOTES

1. See thinkexist.com/quotation/effective_communication_is-what_you_know_and-how/295573.html; accessed May 1, 2011.

2. See www.myfloridalicense.com/dbpr/hr/food-lodging/foodmisrep.html; accessed May 1, 2011.

3. Roberto, C.A., Larsen, P.D., Agnew, H., Baik, J., and Brownell, K.D. (2010). "Evaluating the Impact of Menu Labeling on Food Choices and Intake." *American Journal of Public Health* 100 (2):312–318.

4. Bollinger, B., Leslie, P., and Sorenson, A. (January 2010). "Calorie Posting in Chain Restaurants." www.gsb.stanford.edu/news/StarbucksCaloriePostingStudy.pdf; accessed May 1, 2011.

5. Federal Patient Protection and Affordable Care Act, Section 4205.

6. A business is considered a *restaurant* if it portrays itself as such or if greater than 50% of the business's floor space is used for the sale of food or beverages.

7. Urban, L.E., Dallal, G.E., Robinson, L.M., Ausman, L.M., Saltzman, E., and Roberts, S.B. (January 2010). "The Accuracy of Stated Energy Contents of Reduced-energy, Commercially Prepared Foods." *Journal of the American Dietetic Association* 110 (1):1–152.

8. Wansink, B., Painter, J., and Van Ittersum, K. (December 2001). "Descriptive Menu Labels' Effect on Sales." *Cornell Hotel and Restaurant Administration Quarterly* 42 (6):68–72. DOI: 10.1177/0010880401426008.

9. Yang, S.S., and Lynn, M. (July 2009). "Wine List Characteristics Associated with Greater Wine Sales." *Cornell Hospitality Report 9* (11); www.hotelschool.cornell.edu/chr/pdf/showpdf/chr/research/yanglynnwinelisttopost.pdf; accessed May 1, 2011.

10
Menu Analysis

(*Source:* Sport Moments/Shutterstock)

Key Terms

Generally accepted accounting principles (GAAP)

Intuitive analysis

Menu analysis

Menu engineering

Mystery shoppers

Qualitative menu analysis

Quantitative menu analysis

Segment margin

Objectives

Upon completion of this chapter, you should be able to:

10.1 Discuss the cycle of menu planning, development, and deployment.

10.2 Explain the objective of menu analysis.

10.3 Explain the value of qualitative menu analysis.

10.4 Explain the value of quantitative menu analysis.

10.5 Use various quantitative matrix models to analyze menus.

10.6 Use various non-matrix quantitative models to analyze menus.

10.7 Filter considerations and select analysis approaches that are appropriate for specific business situations.

10.8 Identify and apply appropriate corrective actions based on analyses.

THE PLANNING-DEVELOPMENT-DEPLOYMENT-ANALYSIS CYCLE

> "Every strike brings me closer to the next home run."
>
> —BABE RUTH[1]

Chapter 3 introduced an intentionally abbreviated menu-creation process:

- Identify customer wishes and their assumed value decisions for the daypart in question

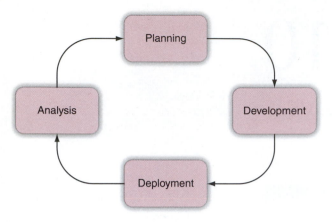

Figure 10-1
Planning-Development-Deployment-Analysis (PDDA) Cycle

- Create a menu structure and populate the structure with items for your guests to select from
- Price the selections and forecast contribution to profit, and make adjustments prior to deploying the menu
- Develop a marketing strategy to generate sales of forecasted items at required levels

It is now appropriate to expand this process and identify the comprehensive planning-development-deployment-analysis (PDDA) cycle, as shown in Figure 10-1. As might be expected, this model includes the four steps discussed in Chapter 3, but also incorporates concepts introduced since then.

The *planning* phase encompasses research and preliminary decision making (Figure 10-2). The sequence of these activities is subject to debate, and you might elect to reorder the list based on your own situation. For example, you may choose to identify customer preferences (no. 6) prior to deciding on dayparts (no. 5). A suitably flexible plan allows some latitude as decisions are adopted. Nonetheless, the final step should always provide you with a *pro forma* income statement. It is necessary to quantify the business potential prior to investing in concept development.

The development phase involves transforming concepts into final decisions and standards, and committing resources to support these decisions (Figure 10-3). As was the case in the planning phase, you might conduct certain steps in a sequence that better suits your particular circumstances and creative approach.

Deployment introduces the menus to the market and creates an operational history for each menu (Figure 10-4). The performance history generated as a result of deployment may or may not validate planning decisions, so evaluation, reflection, and revisions must be undertaken. This final major phase involves menu analysis (Figure 10-5).

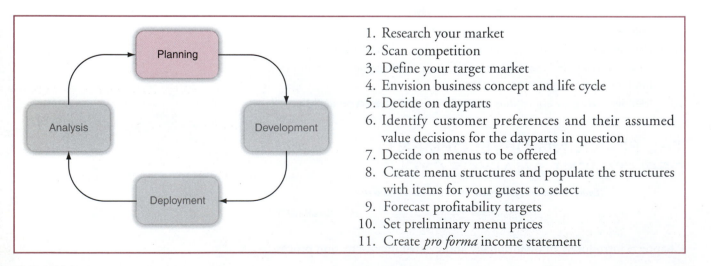

1. Research your market
2. Scan competition
3. Define your target market
4. Envision business concept and life cycle
5. Decide on dayparts
6. Identify customer preferences and their assumed value decisions for the dayparts in question
7. Decide on menus to be offered
8. Create menu structures and populate the structures with items for your guests to select
9. Forecast profitability targets
10. Set preliminary menu prices
11. Create *pro forma* income statement

Figure 10-2
PDDA Cycle: Planning Phase

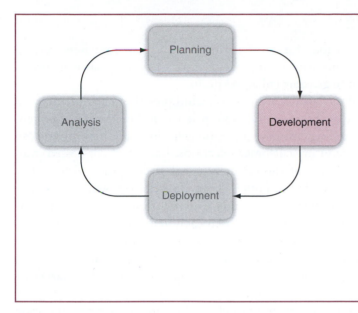

1. Develop, test, and standardize recipes
2. Identify ingredient sources
3. Review and synchronize ingredient storage with menu needs
4. Divide physical space and conceive workstations
5. Specify equipment, serviceware, and supply needs
6. Identify risk-management controls
7. Conduct nutritional analysis of menu items
8. Calculate food and beverage costs
9. Revisit and re-price menu selections and forecast contribution to profit; make adjustments prior to deploying the menus
10. Develop a marketing strategy to generate sales of forecasted items at required levels
11. Create merchandizing strategies and menu communications, including Web sites and social media

Figure 10-3
PDDA Cycle: Development Phase

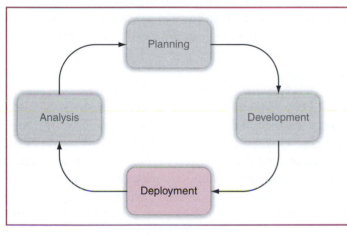

1. Program point-of sale database
2. Train staff
3. Taste menu items with staff and maintain a sensory protocol for production and selling
4. Conduct trials and controlled experiments to finalize operational decisions
5. Forecast sales for specific upcoming periods
6. Forecast net income for upcoming periods
7. Conduct soft rollout to introduce menus to market

Figure 10-4
PDDA Cycle: Deployment Phase

1. Analyze menu item performance
2. Continuously scan market forces and environmental impacts
3. Reflect on findings and revise menu items and menus as appropriate
4. Reforecast profitability targets
5. Generate revised *pro forma* income statement

Figure 10-5
PDDA Cycle: Analysis Phase

MENU ANALYSIS

Menu analysis involves various forms of evaluation and revision; however, all approaches share the same objective—to improve the financial performance of current and future menu items and to generate enhanced profit.

Menu analysis involves various evaluative techniques that enable enhanced decision making applicable to recipe formulation, pricing, and marketing. The central focus involves understanding customer purchase behaviors, and how criteria can be manipulated to influence future customer selections. Each item is assessed individually and within the context of the menu category it competes within. The notion of competition suggests that customers have choices from which they may select, and these choices are influenced by marketing dimensions such as price, merchandizing, and promotions. The extent to which each item successfully competes can be thought of as its *relative performance.* Menu analysis assists you in determining which items require performance enhancement and what type of improvements are most appropriate. As such, menu analysis is rightfully considered a marketing management process.

This process is necessarily a cycle of research, evaluation, and remedial decision making, because product costs, customer selection behaviors, and intra-category competition among menu items are dynamic and produce differing results over time. Continuous analysis reveals that certain menu items previously rated as superior will eventually be rated as inferior, and vice versa. As in any competitive arena, "the best of class" may be a fleeting designation, soon to be claimed by a new category leader.

QUALITATIVE ANALYSIS

Qualitative menu analysis relies on attitudinal data collection, opinion surveys, and evaluations to explain customer purchase inclinations and necessary menu revisions that capitalize on these preferences. Qualitative studies often involve experiments with recipe formulation, portion sizes, or meal combinations to discern market acceptance and predict future purchase behavior. Where possible, manipulation of single variables (baked vs. fried, small vs. medium, inclusive vs. *à la carte,* etc.) yields findings as rich as any financial study. Consequently, you should simultaneously conduct qualitative and quantitative (math-based) menu analyses. Synergistically, data mining of market demographics and other consumer statistics advances the qualitative analysis process.

Although not to be confused with more disciplined analytical studies, the **intuitive analysis** approach relies on anecdotal input and healthy doses of inductive and deductive reasoning, often enabled through management's experience and prior knowledge. Customer feedback, including suggestions, complaints, and accolades, is crucial for managers to understand levels of market acceptance and potential modifications.

The question of objectivity typically arises, and often external evaluators are used to provide unbiased feedback. **Mystery shoppers** are consultants contracted to observe and report to management or owners confidentially on operational factors, including customer transactions and asset handling, and are examples of individuals who contribute professional and critical qualitative input.

EXERCISE 10-1

Prepare a template that can be used as a mystery shopper observation report. How does this template improve your food and beverage menu planning?

(*Source:* StockLite/Shutterstock)

QUANTITATIVE ANALYSIS

Quantitative analysis involves various forms of numeric, statistical, or financial data studies that reveal trends, tendencies, and patterns.

One of the most easily conducted forms of quantitative study entails trend analysis of menu mix. In Chapter 5, we introduced the formula for calculating menu mix:

Menu mix (%) for an Item = Number Forecasted of a Particular Item/
Total Number of Items Forecasted × 100

Whereas this formula was presented as a forecasting (i.e., pre-sale) instrument, it is perfectly suitable as a post-sales analysis tool.

It is valuable to track changes in menu-mix percentage for items over time. Quantitative studies of this nature illustrate strengthening or erosion of relative menu item popularity. Menu-mix reports can be extracted from daily transaction data recorded by point-of-sales systems and converted into spreadsheet format. Using data introduced in Figure 5-7 and extending it with additional (sample) data, a trend analysis can be obtained (Figure 10-6).

Trend studies help you understand how specific items appeal to customers over time. Whereas one-dimensional studies such as this do not shed much light on profitability, they do help you understand which items may merit deeper analysis.

The next logical enhancement to quantitative studies involves usage of menu-mix statistics in combination with financial performance data to create quantitative analysis matrices.

MENU ANALYSIS MODEL

The first quantitative matrix model was published by Jack Miller in 1980[2] (Figure 10-7). His menu analysis model (MAM) considered two dimensions: 1) each menu item's percentage of total sales (menu mix), and 2) food-cost percentage of each menu item. These two dimensions enabled categorization of menu items as

Figure 10-6
Menu-Mix Trend Study

Menu Item	Week 1	Week 2	Week 3	Week 4	Week 5
Rolling Rock	10.39%	11.58%	10.59%	10.07%	12.33%
Pabst Blue Ribbon	12.38%	12.29%	12.06%	11.81%	11.93%
Blue Moon Belgian White	3.46%	3.11%	3.35%	4.03%	3.62%
Brooklyn Brown Ale	1.60%	1.27%	1.47%	2.42%	2.01%
Harpoon IPA	5.06%	5.08%	5.90%	4.56%	4.96%
Smuttynose IPA	4.79%	3.25%	4.42%	3.49%	2.95%
Victory Hop Devil Ale	7.32%	8.05%	8.85%	7.38%	6.84%
Yuengling Traditional Lager	9.32%	9.60%	10.32%	9.53%	9.12%
Abita Turbo Dog	3.46%	3.81%	4.42%	4.03%	3.89%
Pyramid Hefeweizen	4.13%	4.24%	4.42%	4.16%	3.49%
Pabst Blue Ribbon (Happy Hour)	38.08%	37.71%	34.18%	38.52%	38.87%

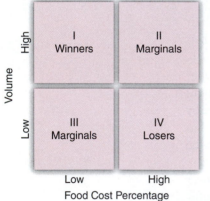

Figure 10-7
Miller Menu Analysis Model Matrix

Winners (high relative popularity–low food-cost percentage), *Marginals II* (high relative popularity–high food-cost percentage), *Marginals III* (low relative popularity–low food-cost percentage) or *Losers* (low relative popularity–high food-cost percentage).

Using this model to classify menu items, menu planners attempted to identify opportunities for increasing popularity and reducing food-cost percentage. The preferred items, in addition to relative popularity also exhibited low food-cost percentage. This model is not without fault. By definition, Winners and Marginals III possess a low food-cost percentage, but only one of these classes is correlated with desirable contribution margins (sales minus directly variable costs). As discussed in Chapter 8, food-cost percentage is strictly a measure of relationship, whereas contribution margin is an actual monetary measure that offsets costs/expenses and, if ample, yields profit. With the Miller model, it is possible that low food-cost percentage items could also possess low contribution margins, yet they could be classified favorably and if targeted for sales and promotion, could compromise gross profit. Consequently, a useful model must, at minimum, address relative contribution margins of individual menu items.

MENU ENGINEERING

In 1982, Michael Kasavana and Donald Smith proposed a menu analysis model referred to as **menu engineering (ME)**.[3] A primary objective of menu engineering is to increase each menu category's overall contribution margin by increasing demand by customers (i.e., enhanced sales) or improving individual contribution margins of items within each menu category.

The ME analysis model classifies competing menu items based on two criteria: 1) relative popularity/menu mix (MM) and 2) contribution margin (CM) relative to the average for the entire category. Consequently, the food-cost percentage limitations of the Miller model are alleviated.

A key concept in menu engineering is the intra-category competition between menu items for each meal period. Appetizers are analyzed comparatively against other appetizers, entrées are analyzed comparatively against other entrées, and other categorical analyses are similarly conducted. The resultant classifications enable informed decision making to improve gross profit.

To evaluate relative popularity, a menu-mix baseline is established and used as a benchmark for comparing the popularity of each item within the menu category. Menu-mix baseline is calculated as follows:

$$\text{Menu-mix Baseline \%} = 0.70 \times \frac{100}{\text{Number of Menu Selections within Menu Category}}$$

The 0.70 factor (70%) applied in this formula may be thought of as a measure of efficiency. Theoretically, the higher the factor, up to 1.00 (100%), the more efficiently and consistently each item contributes its fair share of sales. The lower the factor (target efficiency), the less expectation is placed on each item to perform. Users of the ME model may substitute higher or lower numbers than 70% when calculating baselines; however, Kasavana and Smith proposed that 70% was an acceptable number for engineering studies.

For example, the baseline for a menu category containing 10 items is calculated as follows:

$$7\% = (0.70) \times \frac{100}{10}$$

This formula illustrates that at 70% efficiency, a category containing 10 selections requires each item to generate at least 7% of sales (by item count) if it is to receive a positive rating.

Once target efficiency is applied to establish a menu-mix baseline, each item's menu-mix percentage is calculated. If an item's menu-mix percentage equals or exceeds the baseline, it is classified as exhibiting *high popularity*. Conversely, an item whose menu-mix percentage is less than the baseline is classified as exhibiting *low popularity*.

The other value required to classify menu items is average contribution margin (ACM). Returning to the sample data in Figure 6-1, it is evident that the sale of 751 items generated $1,449.31 in total contribution margin. ACM can be calculated using the following equation:

$$\text{Average Contribution Margin (ACM)} = \frac{\text{Total Contribution Margin}}{\text{Number of Items Sold}}$$

$$\$1.93 = \frac{\$1,449.31}{751}$$

Each menu item's respective contribution margin is compared to the ACM. If an item's contribution margin equals or exceeds the average, it is classified as exhibiting *high contribution margin*. Conversely, an item whose contribution margin is less than the average is classified as exhibiting *low contribution margin*.

These two values (menu-mix baseline and average contribution margin) enable categorization of menu items as *stars* (high popularity–high contribution margin),

Figure 10-8 [Compatibility Mode] - Microsoft Excel

	A	B	C	D	E	F	G	H	I	J	K	L
1	Menu Engineering Worksheet	# Sold	Menu Mix %	Item Bev Cost	Item Menu Price	Item Contribution Margin	Menu Bev Cost	Menu Sales	Menu Contribution Margin	Menu Contribution Rating	Menu Mix Rating	Menu Item Rating
4												
5	Rolling Rock	78	10.4%	$0.420	$3.25	$2.83	$32.76	$253.50	$220.74	High	High	Star
6	Pabst Blue Ribbon	93	12.4%	$0.360	$3.25	$2.89	$33.48	$302.25	$268.77	High	High	Star
7	Blue Moon Belgian White	26	3.5%	$1.790	$4.75	$2.96	$46.54	$123.50	$76.96	High	Low	Puzzle
8	Brooklyn Brown Ale	12	1.6%	$1.790	$4.75	$2.96	$21.48	$57.00	$35.52	High	Low	Puzzle
9	Harpoon IPA	38	5.1%	$1.990	$4.75	$2.76	$75.62	$180.50	$104.88	High	Low	Puzzle
10	Smuttynose IPA	36	4.8%	$1.990	$4.75	$2.76	$71.64	$171.00	$99.36	High	Low	Puzzle
11	Victory Hop Devil Ale	55	7.3%	$1.990	$4.75	$2.76	$109.45	$261.25	$151.80	High	High	Star
12	Yuengling Traditional Lager	70	9.3%	$1.190	$3.25	$2.06	$83.30	$227.50	$144.20	High	High	Star
13	Abita Turbo Dog	26	3.5%	$1.970	$4.75	$2.78	$51.22	$123.50	$72.28	High	Low	Puzzle
14	Pyramid Hefeweizen	31	4.1%	$1.790	$4.75	$2.96	$55.49	$147.25	$91.76	High	Low	Puzzle
15	Pabst Blue Ribbon (Happy Hour)	286	38.1%	$0.360	$1.00	$0.64	$102.96	$286.00	$183.04	Low	High	Plowhorse
30	Totals	751	100.0%				$683.94	$2,133.25	$1,449.31			

	# of Menu Items	Target Efficiency	Menu Mix Baseline	Average Contribution Margin per Item	Menu Mix Beverage Cost %
36	11	70%	6.4%	$1.93	32.06%

Figure 10-8
Menu-Engineering Study

plowhorses (high popularity–low contribution margin), *puzzles* (low popularity–high contribution margin), or *dogs* (low popularity–low contribution margin). Figure 10-8 illustrates a completed menu-engineering study using the week 1 sample data from Figure 10-6.

When compared to the menu-mix baseline of 6.4%, items in rows 7, 8, 9, 10, 13, and 14 are classified as exhibiting low popularity. The items in rows 5, 6, 11, 12, and 15 are rated as exhibiting high popularity. When compared to the average contribution of $1.93, the item in row 15 is rated as exhibiting low contribution margin. All other items exceed the average contribution margin and are rated as exhibiting high contribution margin. These ratings are illustrated in columns J and K, respectively. Based on the ratings in those columns, menu item ratings are assigned (column L). Figure 10-9 graphically depicts the completed ME study using the sample data. Graphic representation of this nature helps illustrate how close or far each item is to the baselines and what remedial actions should be undertaken.

Menu item ratings obtained through the ME process suggest opportunities for improving item performance. Menu engineering is a deterministic process and is used

Figure 10-9
Menu-Engineering Study—
Scatter Graph

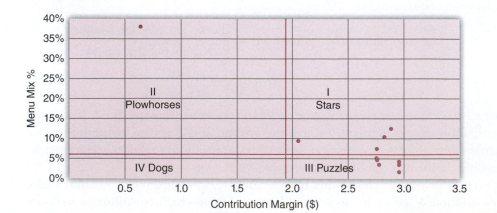

to guide profit enhancement efforts. Possible decisions may include addition or dele-tion of items, recipe reformulation, pricing revisions, or modifications to intra-category merchandizing strategies.

- *Stars* are profitable and popular. Within the menu-engineering model, they do not require attention, in some instances their customer acceptance is strong enough to justify price increases.
- *Puzzles* are relatively unpopular, but their individual contribution margins exceed the average contribution margin for the entire menu category. If effec-tively merchandized to increase their sales volume, they generate higher than average contribution margins. By identifying menu items within this category, tactical marketing decisions can be conceived. How to make them sell is the puzzle to be solved.
- *Dogs* are not profitable, nor are they popular. Whereas they do not have a sig-nificant impact on nor show the favor of customer selections, the ingredients required to prepare them are possibly underused. Par stock purchased for slow moving items such as these is prone to quality loss, and these menu items should be removed from the menu, or modified to become both popular and profitable.
- *Plowhorses* are, perhaps, the classification of greatest concern. These menu items are highly popular, yet their contribution margins are less than the cate-gory average (i.e., relatively unprofitable). Every time they are ordered, oppor-tunity to sell a more profitable item is lost. The menu planning team must make these items more profitable, either by re-pricing or reducing recipe costs, while retaining popularity.

One downside to ME lies in the likelihood of menu item price inflation as informed modifications are implemented. If the prices of dogs and plowhorses are raised to improve ratings, customers might respond with price resistance, thus reducing demand and rendering sales volume incapable of covering fixed costs and desired profit.

A more pervasive concern that is endemic to mean-based categorization systems involves the never-ending cycle in which, as some item ratings are improved, the per-formance expectations increase, causing previously acceptable items to fall below the menu-mix baseline or average contribution margin. The only scenario where all items could receive equal classifications requires each item to exhibit equal menu-mix per-centage and equal contribution margin. Such a scenario is highly improbable.[4] When analysis and categorization is based on comparison to averages, there are always inferior items (i.e., lower than the average). The continuous improvement of inferior items constantly raises standards creating new dogs, puzzles, and plowhorses. Consequently, management must decide when to cease improvements and accept existing menu item performance. At some point, the limits of menu improvement must coexist with the consent of market acceptance.

Another concern in this model is the unweighted manner in which item contri-bution margin is compared to average contribution margin. (A *weighted* comparison considers the sum of all individual contribution margins, whereas an *unweighted* model—such as this—compares the contribution margin from only one unit.) In essence, low volume menu items (puzzles) can and do earn superior ratings if the con-tribution margin for these low selling items equals or exceeds the average. All it takes is the sale of one unit to occur, and the relatively high contribution margin of that unit becomes a positive analysis criterion. Despite their high contribution per item (unweighted by total item sales), overall volume of these items may be insufficient to cover total costs. This leads us to a final concern involving the incomplete cost data

---

EXERCISE 10-2

1. Use the following data set to conduct an ME analysis. A worksheet can be downloaded at http://www.pearsonhighered.com/barrish

Menu Item	No. Sold	Item Food Cost	Item Menu Price
Hamachi Nigiri	23	$1.25	$4.50
Tobiko Nigiri	40	$0.97	$4.00
Toro Nigiri	9	$3.27	$9.50
California *Maki* Roll	37	$1.01	$4.50
Dynamite *Maki* Roll	17	$2.55	$7.00
Spicy *Unagi Temaki* Hand Roll	33	$1.43	$5.00
Spider *Temaki* Hand Roll	58	$1.96	$4.50
Crispy Avocado Roll	69	$1.45	$6.00
Uni Sashimi	43	$2.88	$10.00
Tako Sashimi	24	$2.12	$6.00

2. Based on your analysis, which menu items require reengineering? Specifically, what should you do to improve results within this category?

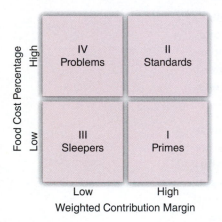

Figure 10-10
Pavesic Cost/Margin Menu-Engineering Matrix

used in the ME process. Variable costs—most notably, variable labor—are not considered in this model. As such, the definition of contribution margin as used in the ME model deviates from **generally accepted accounting principles (GAAP),** which define *contribution margin* as the difference between sales and the sum of variable costs. Consequently, *gross profit* is a more apt term for contribution margin within the ME context. In addition, the model fails to incorporate undistributed operating costs that can be allocated to specific items. Certain items require disproportionately high non-food/beverage costs, and if not considered, may allow items to receive erroneous superior ratings and become or remain the focus of enhanced merchandizing.

COST MARGIN ANALYSIS MODEL

In 1983, David Pavesic offered a menu-engineering matrix model that addressed the limitations of unweighted contribution margins as ranking measures.[5] His model considered three variables—food-cost percentage, contribution margin, and sales volume—that allowed for two evaluative criteria: food-cost percentage and weighted contribution margin (Figure 10-10).

To obtain the first set of evaluative data, the food-cost percentage of each item is compared to the average food-cost percentage for the entire menu, which is obtained by dividing the sum of all food costs by the sum of all food sales.

$$\text{Average Food-Cost Percentage (Entire Menu)} = \frac{\text{Sum of All Individual Food Costs}}{\text{Sum of All Individual Food Sales}}$$

To obtain the weighted contribution margin of each item and enable evaluation of that criterion, individual gross profit (contribution margin) of each item is multiplied by the number of each item that is sold.

$$\text{Weighted Average Contribution Margin} = \frac{\text{Total Contribution Margin}}{\text{Number of Selections Possible within the Category}}$$

The individual calculations are compared, for rating purposes, against weighted average contribution margin (WACM), which is calculated by adding contribution margins resulting from all sales and dividing that sum by the number of selections possible within the category.

$$\text{WACM} = \frac{\text{Total Contribution Margin}}{\text{Number of Selections Possible within the Category}}$$

Using the data from the 11 menu items listed in Figure 10-8, the following average is obtained:

$$\$131.75 = \frac{\$1449.31}{11}$$

Once the WACM is calculated, 1) the individual items can be ranked for contribution, and 2) profit factors can be calculated. To achieve this, contribution from each of the 11 items is divided by the WACM. The resulting quotients are referred to as *profit factors (PF)*.[6]

$$\text{Profit Factor (PF)} = \frac{\text{Total Contribution Margin of a Menu Item}}{\text{WACM}}$$

For example, the profit factor for Rolling Rock Beer (Figure 10-8, row 5) is calculated as follows:

$$1.675 = \frac{\$220.74}{\$131.75}$$

Figure 10-8 can be expanded to include profit factors (column M) for each of the menu items (Figure 10-11). The average PF for the entire category of any menu is always 1.00. This average is used for classifying the individually calculated PF of each menu item. Profit factors less than 1.00 contribute less than those performing higher than 1.00. A well-balanced menu should primarily contain items with PFs ranging between 0.9 and 1.1.

Just as menu-mix ratings and (unweighted item) contribution margin ratings were used to create classifications (i.e., stars, plowhorses, puzzles, and dogs) in the

	A	B	C	D	E	F	G	H	I	J	K	L	M
1	Menu Engineering Worksheet	# Sold	Menu Mix %	Item Bev Cost	Item Menu Price	Item Contribution Margin	Menu Bev Cost	Menu Sales	Menu Contribution Margin	Menu Contribution Rating	Menu Mix Rating	Menu Item Rating	Profit Factor
5	Rolling Rock	78	10.4%	$0.420	$3.25	$2.83	$32.76	$253.50	$220.74	High	High	Star	1.675
6	Pabst Blue Ribbon	93	12.4%	$0.360	$3.25	$2.89	$33.48	$302.25	$268.77	High	High	Star	2.040
7	Blue Moon Belgian White	26	3.5%	$1.790	$4.75	$2.96	$46.54	$123.50	$76.96	High	Low	Puzzle	0.584
8	Brooklyn Brown Ale	12	1.6%	$1.790	$4.75	$2.96	$21.48	$57.00	$35.52	High	Low	Puzzle	0.270
9	Harpoon IPA	38	5.1%	$1.990	$4.75	$2.76	$75.62	$180.50	$104.88	High	Low	Puzzle	0.796
10	Smuttynose IPA	36	4.8%	$1.990	$4.75	$2.76	$71.64	$171.00	$99.36	High	Low	Puzzle	0.754
11	Victory Hop Devil Ale	55	7.3%	$1.990	$4.75	$2.76	$109.45	$261.25	$151.80	High	High	Star	1.152
12	Yuengling Traditional Lager	70	9.3%	$1.190	$3.25	$2.06	$83.30	$227.50	$144.20	High	High	Star	1.094
13	Abita Turbo Dog	26	3.5%	$1.970	$4.75	$2.78	$51.22	$123.50	$72.28	High	Low	Puzzle	0.549
14	Pyramid Hefeweizen	31	4.1%	$1.790	$4.75	$2.96	$55.49	$147.25	$91.76	High	Low	Puzzle	0.696
15	Pabst Blue Ribbon (Happy Hour)	286	38.1%	$0.360	$1.00	$0.64	$102.96	$286.00	$183.04	Low	High	Plowhorse	1.389
30	Totals	751	100.0%				$683.94	$2,133.25	$1,449.31				

	# of Menu Items	Target Efficiency	Menu Mix Baseline	Average Contribution Margin per Item	Menu Mix Beverage Cost %	Weighted Average Contribution Margin	
36	11	70%	6.4%	$1.93	32.06%	$131.76	

Figure 10-11
Menu-Engineering Worksheet with Profit Factors

ME model, food-cost percentage classifications and profit factor ratings are used to create classifications (primes, standards, sleepers, and problems) in the cost margin analysis model.

The major distinction between the results of ME and CMA relates to sales volume. Some items (stars, puzzles) in the former model may not be favorably rated in the latter because of low overall sales volume. Conversely, items rated as plowhorses or dogs in the ME model may receive higher ratings in the CMA model because of their high overall sales volume, despite their low per-unit contribution margin.

Menu items classified as *primes* should be handled much as stars. They exhibit low food cost and high weighted contribution to profit. *Sleepers* are akin to puzzles, in that if merchandized to increase popularity, they are priced to generate superior contribution to profit. *Standards* are similar to plowhorses, and should be reformulated to reduce food-cost percentage while retaining superior sales volume. *Problems* are similar to dogs, and should be remedied accordingly.

As in the ME model, contribution margin is treated as sales minus the cost of sales. Once again, this is at odds with GAAP; however, this model includes the option of adding *supplemental cost* to food cost, allowing for labor cost or other direct costs attributable to the respective items.

ANALYTIC APPROACHES THAT INCLUDE LABOR COSTS

In 1995, Stephen LeBruto, William Quain, and Robert Ashley further developed the ME model by incorporating labor costs into the classifications.[7] This model recommends two methods (i.e., judgment of professional food service managers and jury of executive opinion) to assign items as requiring "high" or "low" labor. The impact of this labor dimension causes the four typical matrix quadrants to expand into eight quadrants, as illustrated in Figure 10-12.

The next logical refinement in menu analysis attempts to consider the impact of all costs, rather than food/beverage costs and labor costs only. The additional dimensions of variable labor costs, other controllable costs, and fixed costs necessarily invoke more-complex models. In addition, several of these cost-inclusive approaches acknowledge the impact of all costs, but refrain from offering precise allocation models.

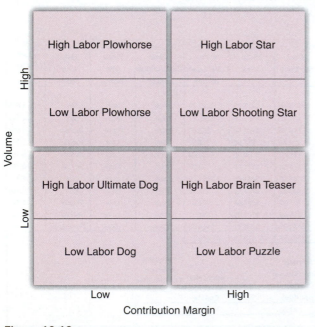

Figure 10-12
LeBruto, Quain, and Ashley Model

GOAL VALUE ANALYSIS

In 1995, David Hayes and Lynn Huffman introduced a non-matrix analysis model that focused on achieving net profit objectives by creating profit and loss statements for each item on the menu. This model does not rely on the use of comparative means, such as average contribution margin or average food cost; rather, it is based on absolute measures of profit. The authors' profit and loss approach suggests that, regardless of favorability relative to averages, each menu item must stand on its own as a contributor to overall operational profitability. In this model, variable costs are assigned to each menu item on a

	# Sold	Item Food Cost	Item Menu Price	Menu Food Cost	Menu Sales
Entrée Salad	130	$2.58	$9.75	$335.40	$1,267.50
Chicken	300	$4.27	$13.50	$1,281.00	$4,050.00
Beef	225	$6.55	$22.50	$1,473.75	$5,062.50
Veal	95	$6.73	$24.50	$639.35	$2,327.50
Lamb	65	$8.38	$22.75	$544.70	$1,478.75
Vegetarian	85	$3.25	$14.50	$276.25	$1,232.50
Fish	190	$6.17	$16.75	$1,172.30	$3,182.50
Shellfish	125	$8.92	$22.50	$1,115.00	$2,812.50
Pasta	280	$2.67	$11.50	$747.60	$3,220.00
Casserole	115	$4.21	$9.50	$484.15	$1,092.50
Total	1610			$8,069.50	$25,726.25

Figure 10-13
Sample Data for Goal Value Analysis

	Entrée Salad		Chicken		Beef		Veal		Lamb	
Sales (S)	$1,267.50	100.00%	$4,050.00	100.00%	$5,062.50	100.00%	$2,327.50	100.00%	$1,478.75	100.00%
Cost of food	$335.40	26.46%	$1,281.00	31.63%	$1,473.75	29.11%	$639.35	27.47%	$544.70	36.84%
Fixed cost	$240.00	18.93%	$240.00	5.93%	$240.00	4.74%	$240.00	10.31%	$240.00	16.23%
Variable costs	$443.63	35.00%	$1,417.50	35.00%	$1,771.88	35.00%	$814.63	35.00%	$517.56	35.00%
Total cost	$1,019.03	80.40%	$2,938.50	72.56%	$3,485.63	68.85%	$1,693.98	72.78%	$1,302.26	88.07%
Net profit (loss)	$248.48	19.60%	$1,111.50	27.44%	$1,576.88	31.15%	$633.53	27.22%	$176.49	11.93%
	Vegetarian		Fish		Shellfish		Pasta		Casserole	
Sales (S)	$1,232.50	100.00%	$3,182.50	100.00%	$2,812.50	100.00%	$3,220.00	100.00%	$1,092.50	100.00%
Cost of food	$276.25	22.41%	$1,172.30	36.84%	$1,115.00	39.64%	$747.60	23.22%	$484.15	44.32%
Fixed cost	$240.00	19.47%	$240.00	7.54%	$240.00	8.53%	$240.00	7.45%	$240.00	21.97%
Variable costs	$431.38	35.00%	$1,113.88	35.00%	$984.38	35.00%	$1,127.00	35.00%	$382.38	35.00%
Total cost	$947.63	74.76%	$2,526.18	62.37%	$2,339.38	46.21%	$2,114.60	90.85%	$1,106.53	74.83%
Net profit (loss)	$284.88	22.48%	$656.33	16.21%	$473.13	9.35%	$1,105.40	47.49%	($14.03)	-0.95%

Figure 10-14
Individual Profit and Loss Statements Based on Sample Data

percentage basis.[8] Fixed costs in dollars are allocated evenly based on the number of items.

Net Profit for Menu Item = Sales of Menu Item − (Cost of Food + Fixed Costs + Other Variable Costs)

This model is best illustrated by using the following sample data (Figure 10-13).

Menu Food Cost (column E) is the product of No. Sold (column B) multiplied by Item Food Cost (column C). Menu Sales (column F) is the product of No. Sold (column B) multiplied by Item Menu Price (column D).

Additional assumptions are as follows:

- In this example, fixed costs (occupancy, fixed labor, debt service, etc.) = $2,400 per week
- Variable costs (all costs that vary with sales volume, other than the cost of food and beverage) = 35% of sales, or 0.35 expressed as a decimal.

Using this data, individual profit and loss statements can be calculated (Figure 10-14). Figure 10-15 illustrates item rankings based on net profit/(loss).

The preceding calculations enable a further level of analysis and decision making. First, a *goal value* is calculated for the entire menu category and serves as an index that considers food-cost percentage, contribution margin, volume, fixed cost, and variable cost criteria. Then, goal values are calculated for each

Rank	Item	Net Contribution
1	Beef	$1,576.88
2	Chicken	$1,111.50
3	Pasta	$1,105.40
4	Fish	$656.33
5	Veal	$633.53
6	Shellfish	$473.13
7	Vegetarian	$284.88
8	Entrée Salad	$248.48
9	Lamb	$176.49
10	Casserole	($14.03)
Total		$6,252.56

Figure 10-15
Net Contribution Ranking Based on Sample Data

menu item. The item goal values are compared to the overall menu goal value, allowing you to evaluate items against the menu standard.

$$\text{Goal Value} = A \times B \times (C \times D)$$

In which

$A = 1 -$ food-cost percentage expressed as a decimal

$B =$ average number of items (covers) sold

$C =$ average selling price expressed as a non-currency value

$D = 1 -$ (variable cost percentage + food-cost percentage) expressed as a decimal

Using the sample introduced in Figure 10-13, the following calculations can be made to obtain the goal value for the entire menu, using averages of the 10 items in the category:

$A = 1 -$ food-cost percentage expressed as a decimal

$= 1 - \$8,069.50/\$25,726.25 = 0.69$

$B =$ average number of items (*covers*) sold $= 1610/10$ items in category $= 161$

$C =$ selling price $= \$25,726.25/1610$

$= \$15.98$ (expressed as a non-currency value $= 15.98$)

$D = 1 -$ (variable cost percentage + food-cost percentage) expressed as a decimal

$= 1 - (0.35 + [\,\$8,069.50/\$25,726.25\,]) = 1 - 0.66 = 0.34$

Goal value $= A \times B \times (C \times D) = 0.69 \times 161 \times (15.98 \times 0.34) = 603.57$

The same type of calculation is then conducted for each of the menu items. Averages are not used, because at this turn, you seek to know individual item performance (Figure 10-16). The (menu) goal value becomes the standard that each menu item's (individual) goal value is compared against. Those items with a goal value less than the standard are not contributing sufficiently to menu profitability and should be reworked to reduce costs or increase sales, and ultimately contribute more closely to the menu goal value.

It is important to emphasize that each menu item is compared to the composite menu goal value, which serves as an ideal standard. The competitive mechanics of matrix-based methods (menu engineering, etc.) ensure that there will always be inferior items, particularly as improvements are instituted. Goal value analysis avoids this problem. In fact, it is possible for every item to meet the minimum acceptable goal value. Also, the goal value formula is sufficiently multidimensional that an item ranking low on one criterion may still rank favorably overall because of the strength of one or more of its other attributes.

One concern when using this model is the allocation of (non-food and beverage) variable costs and fixed costs in a uniform manner. In essence, a *fair share* of these costs

Figure 10-16
Goal Value Calculations for Individual Menu Items Using Sample Data

	A	B	C	D	E	F	G	H
								Relation to Menu Goal
							Item Goal	Value
46	**Rank**	**Item**	A	B	C	D	Value	603.57
47	1	Beef	0.71	225	22.50	0.36	1287.96	Above
48	2	Pasta	0.77	280	11.50	0.42	1033.03	Above
49	3	Chicken	0.68	300	13.50	0.33	924.03	Above
50	4	Veal	0.73	95	24.50	0.38	633.57	Above
51	5	Fish	0.63	190	16.75	0.28	566.16	Below
52	6	Shellfish	0.60	125	22.50	0.25	430.41	Below
53	7	Vegetarian	0.78	85	14.50	0.43	407.23	Below
54	8	Entrée Salad	0.74	130	9.75	0.39	359.22	Below
55	9	Lamb	0.63	65	22.75	0.28	263.07	Below
56	10	Casserole	0.56	115	9.50	0.21	125.83	Below

is distributed equally to each menu item without regard for actual labor intensiveness or other distinguishable costs. For example, the menu items used to illustrate the model (Figure 10-13) included an entrée salad that likely uses less cooking fuel to produce. When compared to the other items that all require some form of heat or cooking, one question may be whether equal amounts of energy costs should be allocated to each item. The same question can be raised for other criteria.

PROFITABILITY ANALYSIS MODEL

In 1992, Mohamed Bayou and Lee Bennett introduced profitability analysis model (PAM), a non-matrix analysis model that evaluates profitability by calculating increasingly finer levels of operational segmentation[9] (Figure 10-17). The underlying premise suggests that profitability analysis should be conducted at each operational level to inform management of improvement opportunities. In fact, analysis at each level can yield a segment-specific profit and loss statement that illustrates each component's contribution to the **segment margin**. In this model, segment margin equals the difference between the contribution margin for a group (segment) and total direct fixed costs for that group.

This analysis approach progresses from larger and more inclusive study that helps diagnose the need for gross improvements, then drills down to finer levels of analysis. Figure 10-18 illustrates analysis at levels 1 and 2 using one week of sample data. Row 4 equals the difference between food and beverage sales and the sum of variable costs, including food and beverage costs.[10] This is the first measure of business performance. A negative value here indicates that menu items do not generate sufficient income to cover their own variable costs, let alone pay for overhead.

Row 12 equals the sum of all fixed (i.e., non-variable) costs. It is important to note that certain fixed costs (*direct fixed costs*) can be allocated to specific meal segments,

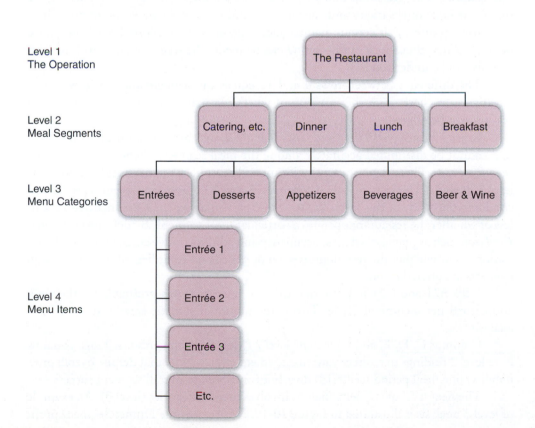

Figure 10-17
Profitability Analysis Model (PAM)

Level 1
The Operation

Level 2
Meal Segments

Level 3
Menu Categories

Level 4
Menu Items

Figure 10-18
PAM Analysis of Sample
Data at Levels 1 and 2

	A	B	C	D	E	F
1		Total	Breakfast	Lunch	Dinner	Other
2	Sales	$ 18,275	3405	9338	4547	985
3	Variable costs	$ 8,319	1674	3961	2297	387
4	Contribution margin	$ 9,956	1731	5377	2250	598
5	Direct fixed costs					
6	Salaries					
7	Part-time	$ 4,563	1567	1654	986	356
8	Full-time	$ 1,400	0	650	650	100
9	Utilities	$ 650	150	300	150	50
10	Maintenance	$ 150	30	65	45	10
11	Advertising	$ 400	75	250	75	0
12	Total direct cost	$ 7,163	1822	2919	1906	516
13	Segment margin	$ 2,793	-91	2458	344	82
14	Common fixed costs					
15	Salaries (manager)	$ 750				
16	Rent	$ 900				
17	Insurance	$ 250				
18	Administrative	$ 150				
19	Depreciation	$ 185				
20	Total common costs	$ 2,235				
21	**Operating income**	**$ 558**	3.1%			

as illustrated in rows 7, 8, 9, 10, and 11. This can be meaningful only when costs can be associated accurately with the sales generation within a particular segment. For example, row 9 suggests that utility expenses vary among meal segments. This implies that some form of electricity and gas metering and tracking of water use occurs. Similarly, row 10 infers that certain maintenance expenses can be allotted to distinct meal periods. When allocations of this nature can be made, the true cost and profit of meal periods can be understood.

The difference between rows 4 and 12 equals the segment margin (row 13). A negative value here raises the question of whether a particular meal segment should continue to be offered.

Rows 15 through 19 list fixed costs that are shared between all meal segments or that cannot be distributed accurately among the meal segments, hence the name *common fixed costs*. These expenses are significant and must be taken in consideration at the level 1 analysis. To evaluate only the figures in row 13 ignores important costs as you conduct your study at this level. In fact, these particular expenses are incurred regardless of whether the restaurant operates a particular meal segment. By definition, *indirect fixed costs* such as manager salaries, occupancy and administrative costs, and asset depreciation occur whether the restaurant is open or closed and regardless of whether certain dayparts are offered or not.

Cells B21 and C21 indicate that that the restaurant was profitable for the week and earned net income of 3.1%. This is the nature of statistic sought at the level 1 analysis.

Columns C, D, E, and F illustrate level 2 (Meal Segments) results. Thus, you now have level 2 findings to redirect your management efforts. Note that despite overall profitability, one meal period (cell C13) does not contribute to overall segment success.

The next level of segment analysis involves menu categories (level 3). An example of level 3 analysis is illustrated in Figure 10-19. Notice how the Dinner Segment profit

	A	B	C	D	E	F	G
1		Total	Appetizers	Entrées	Desserts	Beverages	Beer & Wine
2	Sales	$ 4,547	945	1519	602	245	1236
3	Variable costs	$ 2,297	384	743	248	101	821
4	Contribution margin	$ 2,250	561	776	354	144	415
5	Direct fixed costs						
6	Salaries						
7	Part-time cooks	$ 540	140	275	125	0	0
8	Full-time cooks	$ 425	125	225	75	0	0
9	Part-time bartenders	$ 100	0	0	0	50	50
10	Full-time bartenders	$ 225	0	0	0	75	150
11	Total direct cost	$ 1,290	265	500	200	125	200
12	Segment margin	$ 960	296	276	154	19	215
13	Common fixed costs						
14	Salaries (waitstaff)	$ 346					
15	Utilities	$ 150					
16	Maintenace	$ 45					
17	Advertising	$ 75					
18	Total common costs	$ 616					
19	**Operating income**	**$ 344**					

Figure 10-19
PAM Analysis of Sample Data at Levels 2 and 3

($344) can be further understood by this level of study. The sample data indicates that each menu category is profitable (as exhibited in cells C12, D12, E12, F12, and G12), although Beverages are very close ($19) to segment margin breakeven.

The final and most discriminating analysis is conducted at level 4 (Figure 10-20). Notice how the Entrée Segment profit ($276) can be further understood by this level of study. The sample data indicates that not all items are profitable (cell D9), and corrective actions are in order.

It is important to note that segment margin analysis in this model does not rely on comparison of averages as do many of the menu-engineering derivative models. The PAM examples illustrated are abridged by necessity; however, when every meal segment, menu category, and menu item are analyzed, a comprehensive set of operating income statements (profit-and-loss statements) is obtained. The major challenge to this model lies in the need and ability to isolate and allocate direct expenses to their respective units of study. Considering the nature of foodservice expenses and the multitasking

	A	B	C	D	E	F
1		Total	Entrée 1	Entrée 2	Entrée 3	etc.
2	Sales	$ 1,519	140	180	195	1004
3	Variable costs	$ 743	68	87	89	499
4	Contribution margin	$ 776	72	93	106	505
5	Direct fixed costs					
6	Salaries					
7	Part-time cooks	$ 100	0	100	0	0
8	Total direct cost	$ 100	0	100	0	0
9	Segment margin	$ 676	72	-7	106	505
10	Common fixed costs					
11	Salaries					
12	Part-time	$ 175				
13	Full-time	$ 225				
14	Total common costs	$ 400				
15	**Operating income**	**$ 276**				

Figure 10-20
PAM Analysis of Sample Data at Levels 3 and 4

that occurs by restaurant staff, this can be a challenging objective. At best, an intricate portrait of segment performance becomes available for management action; at worst, the few distinct allocable expenses improve your understanding of each item's contribution to operational profitability.

OTHER ANALYSIS APPROACHES

In 2007, Katarina Annaraud introduced an index method that serves as a supplementary tool for isolating causative factors as profitability changes over time.[11] In this model, absolute increase/decrease of total contribution margin is recognized to be related to three things:

1. Changes in individual menu items' contribution margins
2. Changes in menu mix
3. Changes in quantity of menu items sold

This may be illustrated formulaically as

$$\Delta\, CMQ = \Delta\, CMQ\,(CMj) + \Delta\, CMQ\,(Dj) + \Delta\, CMQ\,(Qj)$$

in which

CM = contribution margin per individual menu item

D = proportion (composition) of an individual menu item sold within the total number of sold items in a menu

Q = number of sold items

j = number of items in a menu

Δ = indicates changes of a variable

Whereas this model can effectively pinpoint causation for profit changes over time, it is useful only when the universe of menu selections is consistent from period to period.

In 1992, Carola Raab introduced a model that adapted *Activity-Based Costing (ABC)* to a restaurant environment.[12] ABC uses sophisticated data modeling techniques to relate overhead cost components to individual menu items. The initial step involves identification of repetitive core activities, such as purchasing, food preparation, cooking, dining room setup, and table service. With activities identified, activity centers can be defined. *Activity centers* encompass similar processes that span departments and accountability structures. The two most tangible centers in a foodservice operation are *front-of-the-house (FOH)* and *back-of-the-house (BOH)*. Next, overhead costs are assigned to homogeneous cost pools that share a common purpose, where variations can be related and explained by one cost driver. Cost pools are divided by the number of cost driver units that affect them, thus establishing a rate for each cost pool. Second-stage cost drivers are calculated by dividing activity center costs into activity cost-driver pools. At this level, pool costs may apply to units of production, batches, or sustaining of products or facilities. Costs-driver pools are distributed to products based on the number of cost-driver units they consume. Next, ABC costs are totaled for each menu item in the form of *bills of activity,* summarizing all the variable and fixed costs incurred every time a unit is produced or sold. In this model, the ABC costs replace the one-dimensional food/beverage costs used to calculate menu-engineering analyses. In essence, the menu price per item, minus the combined ABC costs yields a theoretical operating profit (OP) per item. These OPs replace the contribution margins typically used in menu-engineering analyses and serve as one criteria for an ABC menu-engineering model. (The other criterion is popularity, as measured by menu mix.) Finally, a

(*Source*: Jupiterimages/Shutterstock)

profit factor is calculated, as in the cost-margin analysis method (CMAM); however, weighted contribution margins are replaced by ABC operating profits. Raab demonstrated that ABC menu-engineering analysis, because of its inclusion of all variable and overhead costs, may indicate considerably different results than traditional (i.e., contribution margin–based) menu-engineering analyses.

CONSIDERATIONS WHEN SELECTING ANALYSIS APPROACHES

With the plethora of menu analysis models to choose from, you may ask, "Which model is right for my particular situation?" To answer that question, you must conduct a simple but important operational assessment.

Data Collection and Manipulation Considerations

Because of the transactional nature of food and beverage commerce, the volume of data is formidable. Analysis methods that focus solely on one dimension, such as menu-mix percentage, reside at the lower end of the complexity scale. Alternatively, multidimensional approaches, particularly those that consider labor costs, are extremely data intensive and require meticulous data collection; otherwise, the analysis results might be erroneous and suggest the wrong set of corrective actions. Data must be collected and organized into usable sets over multiple time periods for comparisons, usually week-to-week, month-to-month, quarter-to-quarter, or year-to-year. If you find this level of data intensity exceeds your management capabilities, you should select simpler analysis models that you can readily maintain.

Frequency of Menu Changes

Nearly all analysis models compare one set of items to the same set of items at the end of a subsequent accounting period. If those items are different substantively from period to period, the analysis is of limited value. Consequently, the frequency and rate of menu changes influences the decision of which model to use. One solution to analyzing a dynamic menu is to filter from the analysis those items that change from period to period, and focus solely on core items that are present perpetually. Whereas this serves only as a truncated snapshot, there may be some value in the findings.

Effects of Staffing Model

As has been noted, the multitasking nature of foodservice workers generally makes it difficult to allocate labor costs to specific menu items with any usable degree of accuracy. Depending on the scale and staffing model, most kitchens schedule shift members to prepare multiple items. In very few cases does a staff member produce or serve only one menu item. Highly structured foodservices with significant volume are the exception; for example, supermarkets may assign a sushi chef to that category, or a resort may schedule a bartender specifically to blend drinks. Even with these types of exceptions, it is still difficult to drill down and isolate labor costs to specific items with total precision. If your menu analysis allocates units of labor to particular segments, product lines, activity centers, or menu items, the moment that staff is diverted to a different set of items, your calculations are coincidently understated and overstated. Menu analyses that include labor components must be predicated on accurate labor studies and stable staffing.

A second and somewhat related concern involves the typically high turnover of foodservice staff. Even if you are able to allocate your labor costs correctly to the menu items that drive them, the realities of staff replacement present an ongoing data validation challenge. For example, if a pastry apprentice was tasked with vegetable preparation when labor costs were analyzed initially and her hourly rate became the standard for costing and pricing, this calculation may not be valid if a different employee assumes the position. In essence, every turnover of staff requires you to assess the impact on labor cost and strategic menu decisions. The perpetual task of updating menu-related labor cost records and menu analyses may exceed the operational commitment to accurate menu studies. Conversely, data integration between back office (e.g., human resources records, payroll) and menu-analysis programs can significantly reduce limited resources required to achieve valid analyses that include labor costs.

Historical Impact of Corrective Actions

As the staffing model discussion implies, the burden of undertaking robust menu analyses requires time and money. If historical results yielded minimal improvements in profitability, then the costs of conducting these studies may outweigh the benefits. You should assess the value of this endeavor and ways of improving the cost–benefit relationship periodically.

Validity

Short-term results are not always predictive of real trends. Volatility (caused by changes in ingredient prices, media coverage, weather, etc.) during the short term may not be representative of true market conditions and customer preferences. It is important to conduct studies over a reasonably extended time. As in all research activities, you must question your results. Data-collection mistakes, input-entry errors, and miscalculations can yield erroneous findings. As discussed in the review of analysis methods, each model is idiosyncratic and may ignore certain cost dimensions, deviate from GAAP, or be subject to the limits of mean-based ratings. It is revealing to observe the same menu items receive divergent ratings depending on the analysis model used. Where possible,

---

EXERCISE 10-3

Envision that you are responsible for initiating a menu analysis program in a restaurant that has no history of using quantitative analysis.

1. What employees will be affected by this initiative? How will you secure their involvement, and what will be their contribution to the work effort?

2. Which quantitative method is the most appealing to you? Prepare a policy and procedure document that guides the regular use of the method you select.

---

and if cost–benefit assessment justifies, multiple menu analyses should be continuously conducted in parallel, with all results used to provide a rich body of perspectives from which to craft corrective actions.

CORRECTIVE ACTIONS

Once menu analyses have been conducted, you will possess information to guide your remedial decision making. The variables you manipulate will either enhance sales to improve contribution to net profit, or reduce costs through recipe modification, portion-size reduction, or retirement of menu items. Generally speaking, it is wisest to attempt sales enhancement prior to recipe modifications. No matter how efficient the production process, a weak menu item competes poorly within its menu category. Only when the selling criteria are recalibrated should further action involving recipe reformulation be undertaken.

Sales Enhancement

Sales enhancement may involve selling more items, increasing sales per cover, selling more profitable items, or a combination of these approaches. Puzzles (high contribution margin–low popularity) are examples of menu items that require sales enhancement. Most frequently, sales enhancement involves promotional efforts. *Menu promotion* involves both internal merchandizing and external marketing efforts to stimulate purchase decisions.

Internal approaches involve revising menu descriptions and repositioning the items on menus so that they are more prominent to customers as they make their selections. Chapter 9 discusses menu communication and design concepts, and these recommendations should be revisited whenever sales enhancements are sought. External approaches involve advertising, promotion, and other forms of traditional and social media presence.

Once a reasonable test period of sales enhancement efforts has occurred, findings should be assessed to decide if further actions should be taken. The same set of menu analysis tools should be used, and current (i.e., remedial) results should be compared to baseline (pre-remedial) financial results. If findings are deemed satisfactory, your corrective actions can end here; however, continuous menu analysis should still be a standard practice, even if operating results are judged satisfactory. As stated earlier in this chapter, the central focus of menu analysis involves understanding customer purchase behaviors, and these behaviors are subject to change over time. In its best form, menu analysis is a predictive instrument that informs you of desirable profit enhancement modifications prior to their actual need. Your disciplined study of analysis data trends empowers you to transform your menu before sales and profits decrease. It is quite natural for items to fall out of favor and

AUTHOR'S INSIGHT

I recently dined at a local Jamaican restaurant that serves delicious food at reasonable prices. I selected jerk chicken as my entrée. The dish was available in either a lunch or a dinner portion. I was famished and ordered the larger (dinner-size) entrée, which arrived shortly thereafter. The dish was fresh, hot, delicious, and exactly as advertised. It was also more food than anyone could possibly eat. As I reflect on an excellent meal, I question if the owner tracks plate waste and unfinished meals, as was the case with my dinner. If patterns are observed where other diners leave sizeable plate waste, there is good reason to reduce portion sizes. The reasonable prices almost guarantee that there is room in the value decision to provide smaller dinners while still maintaining price levels. Research may prove the same is true for the smaller, lunch-size portions.

lose their profitability; however, the point at which you detect this is a measure of management savvy.

Cost Reduction

If sales enhancement fails to produce satisfactory profit improvement, then those efforts must be augmented with cost reduction efforts. Plowhorses (low contribution margin–high popularity) are examples of menu items that do not need sales enhancement, but do require modifications to reduce costs (or menu price increases, if the demand is relatively inelastic). Cost reduction may involve enhanced operational approaches (competitive purchasing or more effective labor utilization), but when operations are already fine-tuned, the apparent cost-cutting tactic is to reformulate or retire recipes and introduce more profitable variants.

Recipe reformulation may involve specification of lower-cost ingredients; nonetheless, you should never sacrifice product quality. Earlier chapters in this textbook discuss the importance of product knowledge, and in cases such as these, you should understand which ingredients deliver acceptable results at a lower cost. Alternatively, it would be a mistake to replace one or more ingredients with lower-quality items, as these may have the undesirable effect of disappointing diners and reducing sales. The same can be said for overt reduction of portion sizes. Loyal customers will likely notice that their regular selections have shrunk in size, and unless commensurate price reductions accompany them, they may see your actions as a compromise in value. This is not to say that portion-size reduction should not be considered. Although not always possible, it is often feasible to reduce the size of the most costly ingredients while maintaining the garnishes or other plate components, thus delivering a dish that still conveys value.

Retirement of menu items results when you remove items from the menu because of unsatisfactory customer acceptance (low sales mix) or insufficient profit (low contribution). As discussed in Chapter 1, entire menus may be retired if their life cycles are judged to be terminal. Retirement creates an opportunity to consider replacing one or more items that may echo the retired selections, but at a more optimal profit potential. In fact, retirement and replacement of menu items represent the evolution of your menus as customer preferences change and as you evaluate the correlated contribution to profit. Table 10-1 illustrates the spectrum of corrective actions that can be deployed.

In summary, corrective actions involve a combination of managerial responses to reduce costs and marketing efforts to enhance sales. It may be necessary to reduce costs while simultaneously retaining product quality and customer acceptance. Certain items may need to be modified or retired. Finally, staff must be trained to understand which items yield the greatest contribution margin, and the targeted offerings must be supported with promotional initiatives so that customer decisions can be shifted to more profitable items.

TABLE 10-1
CORRECTIVE ACTIONS IN RESPONSE TO MENU ANALYSES

Rating (prior to Corrective Actions)	Sales Enhancement	Cost Reduction	Retirement	Redesign
Plowhorses	Increase price.	Reduce costs by modifying recipe and/or ingredients.	Remove item from menu only if other corrective actions fail to increase contribution margin.	
		Reduce costs by decreasing portion size.	This item is already popular so retiring it is likely to disappoint loyal customers. Consequently if retired, it must be replaced with an item that fills the value niche sought by those guests that typically order it.	
Puzzles	Increase sales through internal merchandising and/or external marketing.		Remove item from menu if enhanced sales cannot be achieved.	
Dogs	Increase sales through internal merchandising and/or external marketing.	Reduce costs by modifying recipe and/or ingredients. Reduce costs by decreasing portion size.	Remove item from menu.	Reformulate recipe and introduce as a replacement.
Stars	Increase price if inelastic demand is evidenced.			

ACTION TOOLKIT

Miller, Kasavana, Smith, and Pavesic inspired numerous scholarly critiques and modifications to their menu-analysis concepts. This chapter profiles only a few selected models, despite the extensive research that has been and continues to be conducted. The following articles and textbooks provide additional insight into menu analysis.

Annaraud, K. (2007). "Restaurant Menu Analysis: Can We Go Further?" *Journal of Food Service Business Research 10* (4): 25–37.

Atkinson, H. and Jones, P. (1994). "Menu Engineering: Managing the Foodservice Micro-Marketing Mix." *Journal of Restaurant and Foodservice Marketing 1* (1): 37–55.

Bayou, M. E., and Bennett, L. B. (1992). "Profitability Analysis for Table-Service Restaurants." *The Cornell Hotel and Restaurant Administration Quarterly 33* (2): 49–55.

Beran, B. (1995). "Menu Sales Mix Analysis Revisited: An Economic Approach." *Hospitality Research Journal 18* (3): 125–141.

Cohen, E., Mesika, R., and Schwartz, Z. (1998). "A Multidimensional Approach to Menu Sales Mix Analysis." *Praxis 2* (1): 130–144.

Hayes, D. K., and Huffman, L. (1985). "Menu Analysis: A Better Way." *The Cornell Hotel and Restaurant Administration Quarterly 25* (4): 64–70.

Horton, B.W. (2001). "Menu Analysis: The Effect of Labor and Menu Category on Menu Classifications." *FIU Hospitality Review* 19 (2): 35–46.

Kasavana, M. L., and Smith, D. I. (1990). *Menu Engineering: A Practical Guide to Menu Analysis,* rev. ed. Okemos MI: Hospitality Publications.

LeBruto, S. M., Quain, W. J., and Ashley, A. A. (1995). "Menu Engineering: A Model Including Labor." *FIU Hospitality Review* 13 (1): 41–50.

LeBruto, S. M., Quain, W. J., and Ashley, A. A. (1997). "Using the Contribution Margin Aspect of Menu Engineering to Enhance Financial Results." *International Journal of Contemporary Hospitality Management* 9 (4): 161–167.

Miller, J. (1980). *Menu Pricing and Strategy.* Boston: CBI Publishing.

Miller, J. E. (1987). *Menu Pricing and Strategy.* New York: Van Nostrand Reinhold.

Miller, J. E., and Pavesic, D. V. (1996). *Menu Pricing and Strategy,* 4th ed. New York: Van Nostrand Reinhold.

Pavesic, D. (1989). "Psychological Aspects of Menu Pricing." *International Journal of Hospitality Management* 8 (1): 43–49.

Pavesic, D. (1983). "Cost-Margin Analysis: A Third Approach to Menu Pricing and Design." *International Journal of Hospitality Management* 2 (3): 127–134.

Pavesic, D. (1985). "Prime Numbers: Finding Your Menu's Strengths." *The Cornell Hotel and Restaurant Administration Quarterly* 26 (3): 71–77.

Raab, C. (2003). The Feasibility of Activity-Based Costing in the Restaurant Industry. Doctoral Dissertation, University of Nevada, Las Vegas.

Raab, C., Hertzman, J., Mayer, K., and Bell, D. (2006). "Activity-Based Costing Menu Engineering: A New and More Accurate Way to Maximize Profits from Your Restaurant Menu." *Journal of Foodservice Business Research* 9 (1): 77–96.

Raab, C., and Mayer, K. (2003). "Exploring the Use of Activity-Based Costing in the Restaurant Industry." *International Journal of Hospitality and Tourism Administration* 4 (2): 25–48.

Raab, C., Shoemaker, S., and Mayer, K. (2006). "The Feasibility of Activity-Based Costing in the Restaurant Industry: An Innovative Way to Analyze Your Menu." *International Journal of Hospitality and Tourism Administration,* 9 (6): 1–15.

Taylor, J., and Brown, D. (2007). "Menu Analysis: A Review of Techniques and Approaches." *FIU Hospitality Review* 25 (2): 74–82.

GLOSSARY

Generally accepted accounting principles (GAAP)—The standardized rules, protocols, conventions and frameworks used in the accounting profession to assure integrity and validity of financial accounting practices. GAAP assures that transactional recordkeeping and analysis of financial statements share equal meaning to all users.

Intuitive analysis—a largely subjective menu analysis approach that relies upon anecdotal input, and inductive and deductive reasoning, oftentimes enabled through management's experience and prior knowledge.

Menu analysis—managerial analysis and revision efforts to improve the financial performance of current and future menu items and generate enhanced profit.

Menu engineering—a variety of matrix analysis approaches that focus on enhancing profit by improving relative popularity of individual menu items and the contribution margin that each of these items generates.

Mystery shoppers—individuals contracted to confidentially observe and report to management or owners on operational factors, including customer transactions and asset handling.

Qualitative menu analysis—menu analysis approaches that rely upon attitudinal data collection, opinion surveys, and evaluations to explain customer purchase inclinations and necessary menu revisions that will capitalize upon these preferences. Qualitative studies often involve experiments with recipe formulation, portion sizes or meal combinations to discern market acceptance and predict future purchase behavior.

Quantitative menu analysis—menu analysis approaches that involve various forms of numerical, statistical, or financial data studies that reveal trends, tendencies and patterns.

Segment margin—the amount of profit contribution from sales within categories that include dayparts and various subdivisions of the menu. Analyzing segment margin permits operators to understand where their profit comes from.

ENDNOTES

1. See thinkexist.com/quotation/every_strike_brings_me_closer_to_the_next_home/12841.html; accessed May 1, 2011.

2. Miller, J. (1980). *Menu Pricing and Strategy.* Boston: CBI Publishing.

3. Kasavana, M. L., and Smith, D. I. (1990). *Menu Engineering: A Practical Guide to Menu Analysis,* rev. ed. Okemos MI: Hospitality Publications.

4. If the average contribution margin (ACM) pricing method is used, each item could earn equal contribution, thus

scoring the same contribution margin rating. In actual practice, the ACM method is a theoretical guide that is functionally modified with application of qualitative and intuitive management decisions.

5. Pavesic, D. (1983). "Cost-Margin Analysis: A Third Approach to Menu Pricing and Design." *International Journal of Hospitality Management 2* (3): 127–134.

6. Kasavana and Smith incorporated Pavesic's Profit Factor feature into their menu-engineering model in 1990.

7. LeBruto, S. M., Quain, W. J., and Ashley, A. A. (1995). "Menu Engineering: A Model Including Labor." *FIU Hospitality Review 13* (1): 41–50.

8. In this model, *variable costs* equal 35% of an item's sales. Hayes and Huffman did not explain how this value was derived, or if alternatives are appropriate for different operations.

9. Bayou, M. E., and Bennett, L. B. (1992). "Profitability Analysis for Table-Service Restaurants." *The Cornell Hotel and Restaurant Administration Quarterly 33* (2): 49–55.

10. Bayou and Bennett consider only food and beverage costs under the category of variable costs. Whenever possible, it is preferable to include other variable costs, such as variable labor/benefits and direct operating costs, that can be associated at this level of segmentation.

11. Annaraud, K. (2007). "Restaurant Menu Analysis: Can We Go Further?" *Journal of Food Service Business Research 10* (4): 25–37.

12. Raab, C. (2003). The Feasibility of Activity-Based Costing in the Restaurant Industry. Doctoral Dissertation, University of Nevada, Las Vegas.

À la carte menu   A menu in which each selection is priced individually. A diner may customize his or her meal by making personal selections from the *à la carte* menu.

American Viticultural Area (AVA)   A designated wine grape-growing region in the United States defined by the United States Department of the Treasury. AVA designations infer winemaking characteristics and quality potential arising from specific geography, soil attributes, and climactic conditions.

Amuse-bouche   "To entertain the mouth"; a tiny, typically unannounced course preceding the appetizer. The course is seldom ever ordered by guests; rather, it is sent to the table compliments of the chef.

Apéritif (Aperitif)   A wine or spirit served at the beginning of a meal to stimulate the appetite.

Buffet style   A style of foodservice in which customers serve themselves from menu items on display in an area other than the kitchen.

Contribution margin   The fraction of sales revenue that remains after the direct variable cost of goods are subtracted. As related to menu management, this is most often defined as menu price minus food or beverage costs.

Check average   The average amount each customer spends on food and beverage, calculated by dividing sales by the number of customers it took to generate those sales. Also referred to as *average cover* or *average check*.

Co-branding   A contractual arrangement occurs whereby two businesses ally themselves for mutual benefit. The relationship provides additional dedicated distribution channels, and food services reap the benefits of national brand awareness/marketing and (often) promotional allowances for menu printing or product discounts.

Competitive set   The group of local businesses that you assume constitutes the choices your market will select if they don't select your own business. Also referred to as a *peer set*.

Consumer behavior   The actions that customers and potential customers choose to take in response to the goods and services you offer.

Continental breakfast menu   A menu based on Mediterranean traditions, typically including a hot beverage, such as drinking chocolate or hot cocoa, or coffee with milk, such as *cappuccino* or *latte*; and sweet baked items, such as *croissants* or *brioche*.

Contribution margin   The fraction of sales revenue that remains after the direct variable cost of goods are subtracted. As related to menu management, this is most often defined as menu price minus food or beverage costs.

Control states   Certain of the 50 United States that maintain a monopoly over the wholesaling or retailing of some or all spirits, wine, and malt beverages within their states. In control states, restaurant licensees must purchase alcoholic beverages from specific distributors as mandated by state alcoholic beverage (ABC) laws and regulations. In most of these states, distilled spirits must be purchased from state-operated stores or warehouses.

Convenience ingredients   Food and beverages purchased with various levels of preparation or value-addition. Peeled vegetables, portion-cut meats, par-baked breads, and frozen desserts are common examples.

Conversion factor   A multiplier used to increase or reduce the desired yield of a recipe.

Corkage fees   Fees charged to customers by restaurants for service of wine that customers have been permitted to bring into the restaurant to accompany their meal.

Cost–benefit analysis   A study that catalogs the anticipated costs of implementing a particular decision versus the benefits from implementing that same decision. Managers and chefs are typically encouraged to act when the sum of benefits are believed to outweigh the sum of costs. The analysis can be based on quantitative data (monetary, units of production, etc.), qualitative ("good," "bad") estimates, or a combination of the two.

Cost-volume-profit analysis   A cost accounting model that recognizes the relationship among sales, variable and fixed cost behaviors, and varying levels of profit. It can be used for calculating breakeven point of a business, as well as sales volume required to produce various profit targets.

Cycle menu   A menu planned for two or more weeks that provides structure and coordinated variety of choices that repeats in a continuous manner for a fixed time, typically within the context of a captive audience.

Daypart   Functional division of the 24-hour time period. Typical dayparts in the foodservice industry are breakfast, lunch, and dinner.

Degustation menu   A variation of *prix fixe* menus and based on decidedly small portions, each delivering memorable impact, hence the interchangeable title of *tasting menus*.

Demographics   Age, gender, race, income, disability, education attainment, employment status, geographic location, home ownership, and other data used to understand and predict behavior of social and economic systems, including market demand for hospitality and food services.

Digestifs   Alcoholic beverages, typically wine or spirits, consumed at the end of a meal so as to promote digestion and close the procession of food and beverage.

Direct labor cost   The component of labor cost attributable to specific menu items. For example, the direct labor cost for a raw bar includes the wages of staff members who shuck the shellfish.

Du jour   "Of the day"; menu items or entire menus offered as a special addition to the day's other menu offerings.

Eaux-de-vie   "Water of life"; spirits distilled from fermented fruit juices, including grapes, soft fruit, and stone fruit.

Elastic demand   Demand for a good or service that changes when prices charged for those goods or services changes.

Equilibrium price   The price at which the supply of an item equals the quantity demanded by the market. Also referred to as market clearing price.

Factored markup pricing method   A pricing method that multiplies factors times food cost to determine menu prices.

Fair trade   An organized global socioeconomic movement that promotes sustainability of resources and welfare for producers.

Fixed cost   A cost that does not change, even as sales volume increase or decreases.

Food cost percentage   A mathematical relationship between food cost and food sales, calculated as follows: Food Cost Percentage (%) = [Food Cost ($)/Menu Price ($)] × 100

Fresh sheets   Daily menus comprised of du jour items.

Full breakfast menu   A substantial and traditional breakfast of English, Welsh, and Irish origin. This breakfast typically includes eggs, bacon (cured from the pork loin), sausages and puddings, grilled tomatoes, sautéed mushrooms, baked beans, toast or fried bread, and tea or coffee.

Fusion cuisine   A gastronomic culinary movement begun in the 1970s whereby ingredients and cooking methods were merged freely in an attempt to create novel recipes that were free from boundaries of culinary tradition.

Gastropub   In the United Kingdom, a public house (pub) that elevates its culinary standards by serving superior food to accompany its beverages. In the United States, it is a hybrid adaptation of the British version, whereby affordably priced sturdy food and beverages are served in a highly social and casual atmosphere.

Generally accepted accounting principles (GAAP)   The standardized rules, protocols, conventions, and frameworks used in the accounting profession to assure integrity and validity of financial accounting practices. GAAP assures that transactional recordkeeping and analysis of financial statements share equal meaning to all users.

Generation Y   Individuals born between the mid-1970s and the late 1990s who are thought to share in generational attitudes and behaviors, including propensity to use digital media and strive for a highly social and connected lifestyle. Also referred to as the *Millennial generation*.

Gross profit   The difference between total revenue and cost of sales. In a foodservice operation, gross revenue remains after food cost and beverage cost is subtracted from food sales and beverage sales.

Guarantee   A contractual agreement between a foodservice and client to prepare, and thus sell to the client, a specific number of banquet meals.

Hazard analysis critical control point (HACCP)   A systematic risk management process that focuses on prevention rather than remediation. Potential hazards are identified and controls are instituted to reduce or eliminate the risk of these hazards occurring.

Hospitality   The practice of welcoming guests and providing goodwill and caring service.

Incidental market   The customers who choose to patronize your establishment even though you did not expressly market to them.

Inclusive price   The amount charged to customers that includes the menu price and all surcharges, supplements, taxes, and gratuities.

Inelastic demand   Demand for a good or service that does not change when prices charged for those goods or services changes.

Integrated foodservice management software suite   Robust digital information systems that automate various operational, control, and reporting functions to provide enhanced management results.

Intended market   The population that you focus your marketing efforts on. Also referred to as the *target market*.

Intermezzo   A tiny yet purposeful course intended to cleanse the palate and refresh the appetite, typically served prior to the entrée. Tart frozen ices or *eaux-de-vie* are frequently used for this purpose.

Intuitive analysis   A largely subjective menu analysis approach that relies on anecdotal input and inductive and deductive reasoning; often enabled through management's experience and prior knowledge.

Inventory turnover   The rate at which your food and beverage purchases are consumed as prepared menu items sold to customers. A high inventory turnover rate is desirable and indicates that purchases are moved quickly in and out of your business.

Locavore movement   The interest among customers to consume locally produced food that supports a collaborative effort between food producers and distributors and results in economic sustainability at the points of production.

LogicPath™ pricing   a sequential pricing method based on cost-volume-profit analysis that identifies a target profit objective and then uses averaged markups to set appropriate prices.

Malt beverages   Alcoholic beverages produced from the fermentation of a malted grain combined with yeast and water. Popular malt beverages include beer, ale, porter, lager, and stout.

Marginal analysis pricing   A pricing model that relates the impact on sales and marginal profit as price varies. If elasticity of demand can be predicted accurately, then the model identifies the optimum price point for a menu item.

Marginal profit   In the marginal analysis pricing model, marginal profit is the remainder after variable costs and fixed costs have been subtracted from sales.

Market   An economic relationship where buyers drive commerce by seeking goods and services from sellers. In the food service industry, the most typical goods and services are prepared meals and beverages sold by the glass.

Market clearing price   The price at which the supply of an item equals the quantity demanded by the market. Also referred to as *equilibrium price.*

Markup factor   Used to calculate prices by multiplying the food or beverage costs times the respective markup factor, for example, 30%.

Menu   "A small list"; the list of food and beverage items available for purchase. Several menus may be developed, each focusing on a specific category (desserts, bar snacks, carry-out items, etc.).

Menu analysis   Managerial analysis and revision efforts to improve the financial performance of current and future menu items and generate enhanced profit.

Menu copy   The list of food items, headings, descriptive language, prices, and information about the business that are communicated to customers on menus.

Menu engineering   A variety of matrix analysis approaches that focus on enhancing profit by improving relative popularity of individual menu items and the contribution margin that each item generates.

Menu mix   The relative fraction or percentage of sales that each menu item contributes to the whole. Typically, menu mix is calculated on the basis of items sold; however, at certain times it will be calculated based on dollar sales.

Microbrews   Malt beverages created in small breweries producing 15,000 barrels or fewer per year. These limited production runs are intended to enable brewmasters to control nuances of the final product, thus yielding distinctive quality beverages.

Mise en place   "Put in place"; to have all items and ingredients at the ready in anticipation of their use in meal service, so as to facilitate unimpeded workflow.

Molecular gastronomy   A hypercreative approach to cooking that uses the application and manipulation of food science and chemistry to pioneer dramatically new sensations and presentations of menu items.

Mystery shoppers   Individuals contracted to observe and report confidentially to management or owners on operational factors, including customer transactions and asset handling.

Net income   Income remaining after all costs and expenses, including taxes and depreciation, have been subtracted from total revenue. Also referred to as *net profit, earnings,* or *bottom line.*

On-site food service   Meal service provided to employees within their workplace.

Payback period analysis   A study that quantifies the length of time it will take for menu item sales to offset investment in the asset used to produce the menu items.

Perpetual inventory   The estimated balance of inventory items calculated by the following formula:
Ending Perpetual Inventory = Opening Perpetual Inventory − Items Sold

Point-of sale system   A combination of digital software and hardware that facilitates recording and communicating customer transactions by service personnel.

Price elasticity of demand   The degree that the quantity demanded for a good or service changes in relation to changes in its price.

Price resistance   The inverse relationship between prices and customer demand that eventually drives away purchases.

Prime cost   The combined cost of food, beverages, and the direct labor required to produce them.

Prix fixe   A menu of several courses offered at one set price. Also referred to as *table d'hôte.*

Pro forma income statement   An income statement based on specific assumptions that anticipate the results of operations prior to their occurrence. A *pro forma* income statement is used as a tool to make management decisions that will improve financial outcomes.

Qualitative menu analysis   Menu analysis approaches that rely on attitudinal data collection, opinion surveys, and evaluations to explain customer purchase inclinations and necessary menu revisions that capitalize on these preferences. Qualitative studies often involve experiments with recipe formulation, portion sizes, or meal combinations to discern market acceptance and predict future purchase behavior.

Quantitative menu analysis   Menu analysis approaches that involve various forms of numeric, statistical, or financial data studies that reveal trends, tendencies, and patterns.

Reference amount commonly consumed (RACC)   The amount of food customarily consumed at one eating occasion. This amount is the basis of guidance and compliance with the Nutrition Labeling and Education Act.

Regional American cuisine   The study and practice of food, beverage, and cooking that recognizes the unique heritage and distinct foodways of geographic regions throughout the United States.

Reserve wine list   A wine list made up of prestigious wines that are highly allocated, especially aged, or possess a cult following. Occasionally, there are various vintages (verticals) or bottling of the same wine, essentially representing a wine collection. Customers expect that reserve wine list prices will be higher than other wine offered on the menu or main wine list.

Restaurant   A commercial enterprise that sells prepared food and beverages and provides hospitality to diners; derived from *restorative.*

Revenue   Business income derived from the sale of goods and services to customers.

Rights managed images   Licensed graphics that are contractually restricted as to length of time, communications medium, size, format, and geographic distribution of use. The management of the license reduces the risk that the images will be used by competitors within the same media or locations.

Risk management   Assessment of potential risks that includes impact analysis and process modifications to mitigate the occurrence of unwanted events.

Royalty-free images   Licensed graphics that can be used (within prescribed guidelines) for commercial communications without payment of additional royalty charges. These images may be widely distributed and run a higher risk of use by competitors.

Segment margin   The amount of profit contribution from sales within categories that include dayparts and various subdivisions of the menu. Analyzing segment margin permits operators to understand where their profit comes from.

Small plate menu   A menu that is solely composed of small portions that when ordered in combination, provide a meal. Examples include *mezze, tapas,* and *dim sum.*

Spirits   Alcoholic beverages produced by distillation of fruit, grain, or vegetable bases.

Sub-recipes   Recipes that are components within other recipes.

Supplement   An upcharge added to a menu price because of the customer's selection of one or more additional ingredients. Also referred to as an *add-on* or *surcharge.*

Sustainability   The sum of agricultural, breeding, and fishing practices that promote the long-term viability of natural resources. In practice, sustainability involves low-impact farming, fishing, and stockyard practices that respect biodiversity and the interconnectedness of ecological systems.

SWOT analysis   A management planning exercise used to identify strengths (*S*), weaknesses (*W*), opportunities (*O*) and threats (*T*) to a business. The findings can be used to modify strategic plans or support tactical deployment to achieve enhanced business results.

Table d'hôte menu   A meal based on the price of the entrée. Each entrée is assigned its own price, and the entrée selection entitles guests to select from a list of appetizers and from a list of desserts to complete the meal.

Tasting menu   Also known as *degustation menus.*

Terroir   The distinguishing nature that wine and foods exhibit as a result of where they are grown or harvested.

Theoretical costs   A calculation of what food and beverage costs should be, based on the recipe cost (standard cost) of one or more items multiplied by the actual number of those items sold to customers.

Trendspotting   Environmental scanning that enables intuitive speculation and deductive reasoning to identify emerging trends in a marketplace.

Truth-in-menu   The mosaic of rules, laws, and statutes that collectively protect consumers against false advertising and breach of warranty on menus.

Turndown service   An activity conducted by staff to freshen and prepare occupied hotel guest rooms for evening retirement. Often this includes providing fresh towels, readying bed linens, and delivery of modest food and beverages as an act of hospitality.

Value decisions   Decisions made by customers that indicate which goods and services they find important enough to spend their money on. In a restaurant setting, these decisions include portion size, exclusive ingredients, and culinary artistry.

Variable costs   Those costs that increase or decrease proportionately as sales volume increases or decreases.

Vision statement   A verbal or written expression that states how a business would like to see itself.

White space   The portion of the menu that does not contain text or images. It is used to provide balance, visual relief, and ease of reading

Wine   An alcoholic beverage obtained from the fermentation of fruit juice, most typically *Vitis vinifera* grapes.

Wine list   A menu of wines served by the glass and by the bottle.

Wine program   The dimensions that characterize how you approach wines sales, including the scope and character of your wines, the pricing scheme you develop, the glassware you use, and the protocol your staff uses to serve their customers.

Workstations   Areas of the front- and back-of-the-house that are equipped for specific sets of tasks. Common examples of foodservice workstations include host stands, server stations, dishrooms, hot lines, and prep kitchens.

Index

280